Copyright © 2016 by the President and Fellows of Harvard College
All rights reserved
Printed in the United States of America

First printing

Library of Congress Cataloging-in-Publication Data

Names: Ford, Caroline C., 1956–
Title: Natural interests : the contest over environment in modern France /
   Caroline Ford.
Description: Cambridge, Massachusetts ; London, England : Harvard University Press,
   [2016] | Includes bibliographical references and index.
Identifiers: LCCN 2015022765 | ISBN 9780674045903 (hardcover : alk. paper)
Subjects: LCSH: Environmentalism—France—History—19th century. |
   Environmentalism—France—History—20th century. | Environmental protection—
   France—History—19th century. | Environmental protection—France—
   History—20th century. | Environmental policy—France—History—
   19th century. | Environmental policy—France—History—20th century.
Classification: LCC GE199.F8 F67 2016 | DDC 363.700944—dc23
   LC record available at http://lccn.loc.gov/2015022765

NATURAL INTERESTS

THE CONTEST OVER ENVIRONMENT
IN MODERN FRANCE

Caroline Ford

Harvard University Press

Cambridge, Massachusetts
London, England
2016

NATURAL INTERESTS

To Sanjay

Contents

List of Figures and Maps   ix

Introduction   1

1. François-Antoine Rauch's New Harmony of Nature   16
2. Saving the Forests First   43
3. The Torrents of the Nineteenth Century   66
4. Environment and Landscape as Heritage   92
5. The Internationalization of Nature Protection   114
6. Reforestation and the Anxieties of Empire in Colonial Algeria   138
7. The Greening of Paris   164

Conclusion   190

Notes   201
Bibliography   247
Acknowledgments   273
Index   275

Figures and Maps

Figures

1. Frontispiece, François-Antoine Rauch, *Harmonie hydro-végétale et météorologique* 26
2. Frontispiece, *Annales Européennes* 34
3. Frontispiece, "Mexicans contemplate the rich productions of upper Mexico," *Annales Européennes*. 37
4. "The deplorable state of many cantons of France," *Annales Européennes*. 38
5. "Regeneration of the sweet bounties of nature in all of the cantons of France," *Annales Européennes* 38
6. "Grandes inondations de 1840" 83
7. N. de Laly, "Awful disasters caused by terrifying floods". 84
8. E. D. Balthus, "Inondations à Lyon" 85
9. "Rue Saint-André des Arts, January 1910, Paris" 87
10. *Le Zouave* by Georges Diebolt 88
11. Algerian Forest Pavilion at the 1906 Marseille Colonial Exhibition 144
12. *Bulletin of the League for the Reforestation of Algeria* 149
13. The boutique Deyrolle, 46 rue du Bac, Paris 167
14. 32 boulevard Malesherbes, Paris. 169
15. "Plans des parcs et jardins de Paris en 1789 et 1900" 174

16. "Projet d'ensemble des parcs et jardins à établir dans Paris".......... 176
17. "The Louvre of social housing," 8 rue de Prague, Paris.............. 184

Maps

1. Forested Regions of Algeria................................. 140
2. Forested Region III 141

NATURAL INTERESTS

Introduction

IN 1801 Citizen Rougier-Labergerie presented a *mémoire* to the Lycée de l'Yonne on the effects of the destruction of France's forests in which he asked, "Is it not possible, in honoring the fine arts, in cultivating them, in encouraging them, to honor at the same time, to encourage and to make prosper the productions of nature, the original source of all wealth and of social happiness?"[1] The plea in Rougier-Labergerie's question was one reflection of the decisive shift in the way in which government officials, politicians, learned societies, naturalists, and the larger public in Europe began to consider the natural world and how it should be managed at the beginning of the nineteenth century. In his pathbreaking work *Traces on the Rhodian Shore,* the geographer Clarence Glacken argued that the eighteenth century marked the end of an epoch in the history of Europe's relationship to nature more generally. What followed in his view was "of an entirely different order, influenced by the theory of evolution, specialization in the attainment of knowledge, acceleration in the transformation of nature," a growing pessimism, and new understandings about the role of cultural geography, history, and the persistence of customs in affecting and changing the land.[2] This was a period in which nature was in many senses tamed and conquered through technology and science, while it also came to be idealized and to acquire new affective meanings.[3] At the same time, it gave rise to anxieties, which could encompass sentiments of insecurity, unease, or even fear, about alleged climate change and environmental degradation, and these anxieties were based on newly emerging scientific theories, which came to be shaped by broader social and political interests. Indeed, these anxieties governed various initiatives, practices, and policies intended to preserve, conserve, and protect the "natural" world in its various forms in Europe in the nineteenth and twentieth centuries. Rougier-Labergerie's plea and those similar to it challenge a widely held view that concern about the protection of the natural environment emerged late in France (and in southern Europe more generally) and that such sentiment is more associated with the period following World War II.[4] The tardy emergence of a politicized "green movement" in France has been cited as further evidence and has led historians to downplay the existence of a broadly shared environmental consciousness in French society before the war. They have tended to point to its growing significance only much later in the twentieth century, as witnessed, for example, in the creation of a ministry of the environment in 1971.

The tendency to minimize the existence of "environmentalism" or an environmental consciousness prior to the second half of the twentieth century in France has in part been the result of regarding the French context through the lens of a history of ecological thought that is grounded almost exclusively in a scientific literature and in Scandinavian, Anglo-Saxon, and German sources. Ernst Haeckel, of course, coined the term "ecology" in 1866 for his work on the patterns of relations between organisms and their environments. Studies of the emergence of ecology as a "new science" in the nineteenth century have focused on the Swedish naturalist Carl Linnaeus, Germany's Alexander von Humboldt, Alfred Russell Wallace, Karl Möbius, and Eugen Warming, among others, in spite of the work of an important group of naturalists in France associated with the Jardin du Roi and the Museum of Natural History who have been studied in their own right in other contexts.[5]

This book explores the nineteenth and early twentieth centuries as a key, if often neglected, moment in the history and development of an environmental consciousness in France and one that should to be considered beyond the writings of a small circle of savants and naturalists. This was a century during which a number of initiatives were launched in both metropolitan and colonial France, which reflected a new environmental awareness that came to be expressed by government officials, politicians, writers, painters, and, most significantly, by the public or civil society at large. This work examines the social groups that constituted this new public, and how and why these varied historical actors began to argue that the natural world was in need of protection as well as the kinds of measures they proposed. A central question in this book is the extent to which they were guided by "preservationist" or "conservationist" motivations.[6] Preservationism, as it emerged as a movement during the nineteenth century, was engaged in the battle to protect historical monuments, landscapes, and, ultimately, natural sites for aesthetic and historical reasons, while conservationism as a movement had more utilitarian concerns. Sometimes the two movements converged, but more often than not they diverged from one another.

This book explores the history and range of new environmental initiatives from the end of the eighteenth century to the 1930s as well as the emergence of an environmental consciousness that underpinned them. While historians have focused on some of these individual initiatives, because of their broad scope they have often not been linked with one another or examined as a synthetic whole or from the perspective of both metropolitan France and its empire.

The term "environmental consciousness" requires some explanation. It should not be confounded with ecology, a branch of biology concerned with the relationship of organisms to one another and to their physical environment, or with specific scientific theories and hypotheses about the natural world, which have been the subject of a number of studies in France.[7] My use of the term "environmental consciousness" denotes how the environment was apprehended by a broad swath of individuals and social groups in French civil society, and it is the premise of this book that by examining these more inchoate environmental apprehensions, as they came to be expressed in a variety of different venues in the nineteenth and early twentieth centuries, one can in fact understand the various sources of "environmentalism" in France as a body of thought and a set of practices later in the twentieth century. To this extent, this is not a study of ecological ideas or theories espoused per se. It is centrally concerned with pathways between social groups, between metropole and colonies, and between France and other areas and nations of the world in an attempt to situate France within a network of European and non-European environmental ideas, models, and frameworks. Indeed, the question of how ideas about the environment circulated and were apprehended has been neglected by historians of the environment of France, even as historians of science and of the early modern period have put the problem of circulation on a continental and global scale into sharp focus.[8] Ultimately I take up the larger question of how the natural environment became an object of concern in civil society in a way that it had not in preceding centuries and how and why various social actors began to argue that it should be conserved, preserved, and protected for future generations.

This work is placed within a three-pronged historiographical context. Environmental historians and historians of the French environment *avant la lettre* have taken three separate and sometimes interrelated approaches, which can be broadly defined as literary-cultural, material-scientific, and institutional. The first approach is well illustrated by Daniel Mornet's history of environmental perception, *Le sentiment de la nature en France,* published in 1907, which explored the evolution of ideas about nature during the Enlightenment. This tradition has continued well into the twentieth and twenty-first centuries, where it was taken up, for example, in Glacken's 1967 *Traces on the Rhodian Shore.* This work has evolved and found expression in the field of cultural history and in what has been termed sensory history in the seminal work of Alain Corbin, who has contributed greatly to the field's development in his works *Le miasme et le jonquille: L'odorat et l'imaginaire social (XVIII–XIX siècles); Le territoire du vide: L'occident et le désir du rivage; Les cloches de la terre: Paysage sonore et culture sensible dans les campagnes;* and *Le douceur de l'ombre: L'arbre, sources d'émotions, de l'antiquité à nos jours.*[9] While *Le territoire du vide* explored how the sea was transformed from an object of fear into one of pleasure, *The Foul and the Fragrant* charts the growth of an ecological consciousness in Paris, which led to measures taken to sanitize the city in the early nineteenth century. Corbin is above all concerned with how nature and landscape have been perceived through time, and he argues that landscape provides a way of experiencing the environment on an aesthetic and sensory level. As a historian, Corbin is as much concerned with landscape and environment as with sensory perceptions and human emotion.[10] However, Corbin's work has not generally been considered to be a part of the official canon of environmental history as it has been institutionalized within the French academy in recent years, because of the perspective he takes and the sources on which he relies, which include literary descriptions that reveal perceptions of nature.

In contrast to Corbin, some environmental historians remain fervently attached to the notion of an uncontested "material reality." Alfred Crosby, for example, observed that environmental historians of North America "tend to be more interested in dirt than perceptions, per se, of dirt," and some scholars have aggressively espoused the cause of dirt.[11] In this vein, David Blackbourn cajolingly asked, "But what about *real* geographies—if you will pardon that provocative adjective?"[12] He goes on to say, "I am interested, on the one hand, in the material, physical process of transformation, for it seems to me that the time is ripe for the historical pendulum to swing back some way towards the material."[13] Changing perceptions and subjective apprehensions, which are often reflected in written texts, have nonetheless enhanced the growing amount of scientific research undertaken by archeologists or paleobotanists, for example—seeking to understand the material traces of past environments. Blackbourn himself admits that environmental history cannot be "usefully separated from political history or the history of mentalities."[14] Even where texts reveal perceptions that do not square with reality, that disjunction provides a window onto the relationship between past societies and their environments. Indeed, Richard White stressed as early as 1990 the centrality of cultural perceptions in pursuing environmental history, citing the French anthropologist Maurice Godelier, who argued that the "social perception of an environment consists not only of more or less exact representations of the constraints upon the functioning of technical and economic systems, but also of value judgments ... and phantasmic beliefs.... Livestock is not simply meat, milk or leather, and trees are not just wood and fruit."[15] The history of landscape has, then, been studied from material and representational perspectives, that is, in terms of odors, sounds, and tastes, which have been so compellingly examined by Corbin, and this has established landscapes as *lieux de mémoire* (places of memory) that are worthy of investigation and analysis.

The second path pursued by environmental historians of France, the material-scientific, has drawn on a number of disciplines—from geography, anthropology, and archeology to botany, medicine, and zoology—and has been fostered by the Centre national de la recherche scientifique (CNRS) in France and often pursued by research groups. They include the numerous scholars associated with the Programme pluridisciplinaire de la recherche sur l'environnement (PIREN), which was founded in 1984–1985 and associated with the CNRS, as well as the Groupe d'histoire des forêts françaises. One of its key figures, Andrée Corvol, has organized many conferences in France, out of which a number of edited volumes were published. She herself was responsible for the publication of an invaluable three-volume bibliographic work identifying the vast, disparate, and scattered archival and documentary sources that environmental historians must use to write environmental histories of France. *Les sources de l'histoire de l'environnement* has appeared for the eighteenth, nineteenth, and twentieth centuries.[16] Historians of the forest, moreover, have explored the environmental impact of the French Revolution and its decade of turmoil as well as the myths that took shape regarding that impact, and their work has altered long-standing narratives regarding revolutionary change.

Both cultural and more "materialist" approaches to environmental history share a common desire to explore the relationship between humans and nature instead of an autonomous nature per se. French historians took an early interest in the history of rural environments, and French policy makers have focused considerable attention on territorial development and management—*aménagement du territoire*. This might explain the propensity of historians associated with the early *Annales* to study rural society as well as peasant communities and their *milieu,* a term the French often used in place of "environnement." The term "environment" did, however, finally come into common usage in the 1980s, although it might be argued that *environnement* was an old French word dating back to the thirteenth century that reentered the language in the field of human geography in 1921 before gaining common currency in France in the 1970s, when it was in a sense recognized just at the moment when the Ministry of the Environment was created.[17]

The third approach to environmental history has focused on state and institutional structures that regulated and shaped the environment in the early modern and modern periods—institutions that included, for example, France's public works service (Ponts et Chaussées) and the its forest service (Eaux et Forêts), as well as legal courts, whose records have left an invaluable documentary trail of conflict and confrontation. It is here that we find the history of important turning points in regulation of the natural environment in, for example, the 1810 Napoleonic decree regulating manufacturing establishments considered "dangerous, insalubrious, or incommodious," and the beginnings of what would become a policy of *aménagement du territoire.*

In exploring environmental anxieties in France from the early nineteenth century to the interwar period, this book draws on all three of these approaches, but it lays particular stress on how concrete events, such as floods, political upheaval, urbanization, and colonial expansion, shaped those sensibilities. From the late eighteenth century to the interwar period France experienced three revolutions, numerous uprisings, and many changes in political regimes, which included dictatorships, monarchies, and republics. These changes in regime would have a significant effect on how the state managed (or did not manage) natural catastrophes or crises and how each regime viewed its role in this regard more generally. The nineteenth century was also a century in which France constructed an empire, and environmental issues lay at the heart of that project.

"Environmental anxiety" and "environmental nostalgia" came to pervade the way in which the French confronted the natural world in postrevolutionary France, and the two terms need some explanation. The notion of "environmental anxiety" has been defined by one environmental historian of the British Empire as "concerns generated when environments do not conform to European preconceptions about their natural productivity or when colonisation set in motion a series of unintended environmental consequences."[18] This book uses the term more broadly to describe the sentiment engendered by the debate and commentary among scientists, government administrators, and the general public about a perceived environmental degradation and its negative impact on humans from the end of the French Revolution to the 1930s. Environmental nostalgia, by contrast, was expressed in terms of emotional attachments to specific landscapes as *patrimoine* (heritage) and to sites as "natural monuments," which led to a growing awareness of the threat of environmental destruction and a longing for the preservation of both peopled as well as unpeopled landscapes and traditional ways of life. This nostalgia was articulated differently in a metropolitan and colonial context, but it was a key thread linking preservationist policies in both.

The word "nostalgia" is derived from the two Greek words *nostros*, return home, and *algia*, longing, and as such describes a longing for home, which may no longer exist or which never existed. It was coined by the Swiss physician Johannes Hofer in a medical dissertation in 1688, in which he saw it as a "sad mood originating from the desire to return home to one's native land."[19] The concept of nostalgia actually entered nosological theories that circulated in clinical medicine in Paris at the beginning of the nineteenth century and "timidly" became part of the emergent "vocabulary of psychiatry."[20] As Svetlana Boym has argued, nostalgia implies a "sentiment of loss and displacement, but it is also a romance with one's own fantasy."[21] She suggests that it is a "historical emotion" associated with modernity and frequently follows political, social, or economic revolutions.

Studies of ecology and environmentalism have downplayed the role of nostalgia. Works on the emergence of ecological or environmental thought, which has been seen to underpin subsequent environmental protection and conservation, have privileged their scientific/biological and economic origins, even though some scholars have recognized the role of Romanticism and an eighteenth- and early nineteenth-century cult of nature as playing a significant role in its evolution. Nostalgia has sometimes been characterized as "reactionary" and "retrograde," but it nonetheless played a significant role in advancing conservationist and preservationist causes, which were neither necessarily situated on the left or right of the political spectrum in the nineteenth century, and thus was a powerful agent of social change.[22] Historians of Britain and North America as well as scholars in the field of "ecocriticism" have gone further than French or other European historians in exploring nostalgia's spatial dimensions, which will merit careful consideration in this book.[23]

Environmental nostalgia also extended to Europe's colonial possessions, but it was expressed in different ways. There, it often manifested in the form of a longing for an imagined wilderness, for unpeopled landscapes, though its role in shaping conservationist or preservationist policies and practices has been inadequately explored in the burgeoning field of imperial environmental history, pioneered by John M. MacKenzie and William Beinart, among others. Historians of Britain, France, and Germany have nonetheless increasingly turned their attention to the way colonial powers regarded the environmental spaces they colonized, regulated, managed, and commodified.[24] Many of these historians have focused on the conflict among settlers, colonial administrations, and indigenous populations and the connections between practices in different colonies within European empires. One of the dominant narratives of imperial environmental history is declensionist and emphasizes the environmental destruction that ensued from the rapaciousness of colonial states. At the same time, colonial states frequently blamed environmental problems on indigenous practices and on irresponsible indigenous stewardship with respect to the land. Imperial environmental historians have also focused on health anxieties and the ability of Europeans to adapt to foreign climates.[25] Much of this work has been undertaken by historians of the British Empire, but increasingly historians of the French Empire have begun to consider these issues.[26] This book will explore some of these themes, the environmental anxieties that colonial landscapes engendered, and how they differed from those in metropolitan France.

To address the question of the scope and scale of this study, one must inevitably ask why one might focus on France as a national entity when early modern environmental historians have tended to consider the environment from either a global or a local perspective. The nineteenth century witnessed the rise of the nation-state, so it is perhaps not surprising that environmental historians of this period have "de-emphasized the global and transnational" in looking at this period.[27] This book is no exception and is predicated on the idea that changing environmental sensibilities and initiatives were not identical within or across continents and nations, even though individuals or groups were often in dialogue and influenced one another. Environmental consciousness was shaped by history, culture, and differing social and political realities on the ground. It must, however, be acknowledged that national boundaries were porous. Resources were shared, and ideas circulated. For example, the state forest services in Britain, France, and Germany were highly conscious of each other's practices. Gifford Pinchot, the first chief of the national forest service in the United States, attended the French national forestry school in France. John Croumbie Brown (1808–1894), a Scot employed by the Cape Colony government in Africa to advise on the biological impact of colonial settlement, was a keen observer of France, authoring a book on the problem of deforestation.[28] Moreover, the way in which the environment was perceived was increasingly influenced by Europe's encounter with non-European environments and by imperial expansion. For this reason, this book does not limit itself to the boundaries of metropolitan France and considers the way in which non-European environments within France's colonial empire came to affect changing sensibilities, particularly in French North Africa.

It has been argued that the first initiatives taken to protect the environment came from urban elites and that the motivations behind them were primarily aesthetic.[29] In a special issue of the *Revue Forestière Française* devoted to the protection of nature, published in 1955, François du Vignaux, director general of the French forest service, suggested, referring to France, that the movement for the protection of nature, which was originally oriented toward the conservation of picturesque sites and landscapes, "today has larger ambitions and is interested in the safeguard of the ensemble of natural resources" at the disposal of humanity.[30] Environmental historians of France have continued to echo this view, suggesting that among the reasons for an alleged early lack of "larger ambitions" was the fact that France was slow and late to industrialize, and therefore did not confront the environmental devastation that resulted from industrialization as early as Great Britain or the United States.[31]

While urban elites in France called for landscape preservation on aesthetic grounds in the nineteenth century, they were one of several groups that came forward, which in turn led to specific measures to safeguard the natural world. A new environmental consciousness came from five separate but overlapping sources. The first came early on from "technocrats" or experts associated with the French forest service (Eaux et Forêts) and the service for bridges and roads (Ponts et Chaussées), which were charged with managing France's forests, waterways, and rivers during the ancien régime. The second came from "hygienists," specialists in a newly defined field of scientific study, who began to document the environmental consequences of urban growth and industrialization in Paris and other cities in the nineteenth century, and the third came from an urban bourgeoisie with aesthetic concerns and a discourse linking the protection of landscape to the preservation of French national identity in the 1840s. Fourth, it was the scientists and naturalists associated with the Museum of Natural History in Paris who made an argument for the protection of environments in France's colonies, beyond the borders of metropolitan France, and they were joined in some instances by European settlers, as in the case of Algeria.[32] Fifth, calls for environmental reform came from civil society at large, which sometimes experienced catastrophe and witnessed ways in which the environment was changing. This book adopts Yves Luginbühl's consideration of *nature-paysage-environnement* as a complex that was constituted as a hybrid entity shaped by utilitarian, aesthetic, and hygienic perspectives.[33] As the nineteenth century wore on, a broader French public clearly became more vocal in expressing anxieties and concerns about the natural world, which led to specific, concrete initiatives and action that reflected these perspectives.

One of the first institutions to be established for the purpose of monitoring and regulating the urban environment in France was the Conseil de salubrité publique for the department of the Seine, which was set up on 7 July 1802. It was an early response to complaints that poured in from ordinary Parisians and hygienists alike about the effects of rapid urbanization on sanitation and health. Hygienists, in particular, became increasingly disturbed by the possible spread of contagion and the harmful effects of miasmas, which has been so well documented by Alain Corbin.[34] For example, Corbin noted the growing sensitivity of Jean-Noël Hallé, who had been appointed to the first chair in public hygiene in Paris in 1794, to odor and urban blight, and he charts the steps taken to clean up and purify France's capital city in the decades that followed.

Montfaucon, which was once the site of France's royal gallows, was the hygienist's nightmare and summed up the phenomenon of urban blight. The hygienist Alexandre Jean-Baptiste Parent-Duchâtelet noted in 1833 that the area consisted of a cesspool whose reservoirs "cover an area of 32,000 square meters, not to speak of 12 acres given over to dry refuse and horse butchers' yards; some 230 to 244 square meters of human excreta are carted there daily and most of the corpses of 12,000 horses and 25,000 to 30,000 smaller animals are left to rot on the ground."[35] The Belleville town council, and the communes of Pantin and Romainville, which were most affected by prevailing winds, lodged protests, but many other parts of the city were not immune. Parent-Duchâtelet concluded that "Montfaucon must be abolished; it is repugnant to the population of Paris and the surrounding country and public opinion is running strongly against it."[36]

Similarly, manufacturing establishments received their fair share of criticism. The Institut de France demanded that the prefect of police in Paris make an exhaustive inventory of industrial establishments, which resulted in the first formal pathbreaking decree (15 October 1810) regulating manufacturing establishments that were deemed to be "dangerous, insalubrious or incommodious."[37] The model of the Parisian Conseil de salubrité soon spread to the principal cities of France between 1822 and 1830, when it became evident that the field of public hygiene had come into its own.

The emergence of public hygiene as a branch of study was intimately bound up with anxieties about the spread of disease. In 1829 the first number of *Annales d'Hygiène Publique et de Médecine Légale* was published, and while its prospectus acknowledged that France lagged behind

Germany, it argued that the centralized nature of France's institutions would make it better able to combat the environmental consequences of rapid urban growth and industrialization.

The cholera-morbus epidemic that afflicted Paris in 1832, as well as the expansion of industrial manufacture, led to further calls for regulation and to complaints concerning noise, dust, and smoke, which were put at the doorstep of the Conseil de salubrité. The manufacture of chemical products and the widespread use of gas and coal led hygienists associated with the institution to shift their attention from the harmful effects stemming from putrefactions emanating from animal and vegetal waste toward mineral and metallic pollutions. By the middle of the nineteenth century hygienists began to identify the effects of industrial pollution on the population at large. While chemists at the beginning of the century were convinced that emanations from chemical plants "only affected workers who worked in the ateliers," by 1848 they recognized that such emanations could spread much beyond a factory's immediate vicinity.[38]

The appointment of Baron George Haussmann as prefect of the department of the Seine in 1853 was a turning point in the process of coming to terms with the environmental consequences of urban growth and industrial expansion. He embarked on a far-reaching plan to rebuild large parts of Paris from the ground up, turning to architects and engineers to create a new urban environment.[39] In 1860, for example, Montfaucon, the much-reviled cesspool, was wiped off the map of Paris, and the site was transformed into the parc des Buttes-Chaumont.

As the state and municipal officials battled the deleterious results of rapid urbanization and industrialization, the building of France's railway lines during the Restoration and the July Monarchy allowed middle-class Parisians to escape the city and discover the countryside, which created a new appreciation for France's landscapes among painters, writers, and bourgeois day tourists. At the same time, new environmental apprehensions were also to play a role in the construction of France's overseas empire, beginning with the conquest of Algeria in 1830. Richard Grove's trailblazing book on the central importance of European colonial experience for the development of Western environmental attitudes argued that the seeds of modern conservation lie in the seventeenth century, if not earlier, and "developed as an integral part of the European encounter with the tropics and with local classifications and interpretations of the natural world and its symbolism."[40] It was colonial scientists and administrators, like the French colonial administrator Pierre Poivre, who began to have concerns about the effects of deforestation on the island Eden of Mauritius as early as the seventeenth century, fearing that the natural resources available to humanity were not inexhaustible; Poivre proposed measures to reverse the process of deforestation.

This book begins in the late eighteenth century in metropolitan France and ends before the outbreak of World War II in Paris. It also moves between the spaces of the country, where a majority of the French population continued to live, and the city, where policy was largely made. Chapter 1 explores the work of a key figure who has been called the founding father of French ecological thought, François-Antoine Rauch, but it focuses on his role as a popularizer and on his more practical work and initiatives. Born twenty-six years before the French Revolution, he was trained to be an engineer at the Ecole des ponts et chaussées during the turmoil of the revolutionary decade and took a keen interest in the environmental degradation that he witnessed during these years. While he was primarily concerned with the problem of deforestation, he increasingly began to consider the environment as a unified system, and while his focus was first and foremost on France, he gradually began to reflect on France's relationship to the wider world. Rauch and others saw the key challenge facing France as one predicated on what appeared to be widespread deforestation, which accelerated during the French Revolution, and he proposed specific measures to stem the tide of environmental destruction. Chapter 2 takes up the theme of deforestation, which was central to an emerging French environmental consciousness in the first half of the nineteenth century, and it explores debates that ultimately culminated in the creation of a new forest service in 1827 and in comprehensive legislation governing the reforestation of mountainous regions. Chapter 3 examines the environmental anxieties generated by floods that punctuated much of the nineteenth century and that culminated in the great flood of 1910 in Paris. It documents how floods became the subject of extensive public commentary and documentation in, for example, the new medium of photography as well as in lithography and painting, which led to initiatives undertaken by the state to curb them. This chapter explores not only theories that were developed about their causes, but new strategies deployed by the state to prevent them. Dozens of books and pamphlets were published on the subject, which reflected environmental theories about the effect of deforestation on floods and climate change. While the flooding of the Rhône, Loire, and Seine was by no means new, these floods took on mythic proportions in the nineteenth century. Many writers linked deforestation and environmental degradation in denuded mountainous regions with changes in the climate in lowland areas, formulating initiatives designed to restore equilibrium between the two.

As Alain Corbin and Peter H. Hansen have shown, late nineteenth-century nature writing contributed to popularizing mountainous and coastal areas of France by extolling the grandeur of these sites.[41] This new appreciation of nature was further encouraged by the development of tourism among the urban middle classes and led to the passing of a series of laws protecting natural sites and monuments, detailed in Chapter 4. The first legislation passed in France to protect a natural site as an "artistic reserve" by imperial decree was for the forest of Fontainebleau. This legislation was largely the result of initiatives taken by the Barbizon school of painting and those associated with it, including Théodore Rousseau and Jean-François Millet among others. Fontainebleau was conceived of as a "green museum," a haven from the vicissitudes of urban life, but more importantly as a natural *patrimoine,* which was valued principally for its historic associations and links to a pastoral past—a peopled landscape—than as a wild, uninhabited landscape.[42] The protection of Fontainebleau as an artistic reserve was in many ways the crystallization of a new aesthetic appreciation of nature by a largely urban bourgeoisie, while the natural site became a mnemonic device, a monument, and a mirror for the nation itself. I argue that this shaped much of the subsequent legislation regarding the protection of natural nonurban landscapes until after World War II, and that initiatives were based more on aesthetic than on ecological preoccupations. The key legislation was passed in 1906 and 1930 concerning natural sites with historic, artistic, aesthetic, and—in 1930—scientific interest, and drew support from a number of organizations in France, including the Alpine Club, the Touring Club of France, the Society for the Protection of the Landscapes of France, and the Society of the Friends of Trees. New apprehensions concerning landscape emerged in elite, urban circles while at the same time drawing on long-established practical state initiatives regarding conservation—specifically among forest administrators and the corps of engineers associated with Ponts et Chaussées. Political meanings became attached to the value of certain landscapes among commentators and the relationship between peopled landscapes *(paysage culture)* and unpeopled landscapes *(paysage nature).*

While the early initiatives taken to preserve or conserve nature in the form of landscapes, natural resources or sites, and monuments took shape in the context of national debates, by the early twentieth century the preservationist movement became increasingly internationalized. Initiatives that began in a colonial context ultimately led to a series of international agreements regarding the protection of fauna and flora in colonial Africa. Organizations and groups across national boundaries in Europe and other parts of the world increasingly communicated with one another, and this led to the first international congresses devoted to the protection of nature, which were held in France. Indeed, the first international congress devoted to the protection of landscapes took place in Paris in 1909, followed by the first international congress on the protection of nature in 1923, also held in Paris. In the interwar period European colonial powers became increasingly concerned about vanishing species of plants and animals on the African continent, and organized the International Convention Relative to the Preservation of Fauna and Flora in Their Natural State, otherwise known as the 1933 London Convention. France's role in this development and its effect on environmental thought and practice in both colonial and metropolitan France will also be explored. Chapter 5 examines how the preservationist drive in France contributed to the internationalization of the movement, as the growing number of international congresses and conferences devoted to the protection of the natural world in all its forms attests. It was also during these years that the concept of the "national park" and natural reserves became a subject of debate, and the French launched their own versions of both.

Chapter 6 examines nature conservation in France's colonies, which assumed a very different form from that in metropolitan France. Landscape preservationism was linked to broader ideas about ecological conservationism—as the idea emerged in the colonies—which extended to fauna, flora, and larger ecosystems. The chapter explores the nature of these ideas and how they were implemented in French colonial Algeria, where environmental nostalgia of a different kind shaped environmental initiatives. The settler population of North Africa looked to restore a lost landscape that allegedly existed in the region during the Roman Empire, of which they saw themselves inheritors.

Chapter 7 examines how nature beyond the boundaries of the city also came to be "domesticated," tamed, and brought into the urban space of France's capital city in the second half of the nineteenth century. While much attention has understandably been devoted to the Haussmannization of Paris in the 1850s and 1860s, this chapter also examines initiatives undertaken by architects, planners, the municipality, and private property owners to introduce gardens and greenhouses into the city as well as how they were integrated into domestic and commercial architecture. It explores the public's embrace of horticulture, what has been termed a "cult of flowers," and the call for the creation of an extensive array of new parks and "green spaces" where the city's fortifications once stood at the beginning of the twentieth century. Finally, it will look at the phenomenon of the garden city, which emerged during the same period, and how it was implemented in France, particularly in many of Paris's peripheral suburbs.

Between the nineteenth and twentieth centuries there were different and evolving ideas about what kind of nature should be protected and why, whether this applied to *territoire, milieu, espace, environnement,* countryside, landscape—and whether or not to include fauna and flora. In this sense there was no single, unitary "environmental" or protectionist sensibility in France in the nineteenth and early twentieth centuries. Moreover, landscape and environmental protection was not associated with either the French Right or Left in this period. Its political affiliation with the Left would come only in the 1970s, following the period of the *trente glorieuses* (the thirty years of economic expansion following the end of World War II). The movement was taken up and appropriated by different social and political groups prior to World War II. In addition, initiatives taken to protect the environment in France were not always strictly "ecological" in origin. They were guided as much by aesthetic and nationalistic concerns or, in France's colonies, by its own territorial aspirations and desires.

In short, environmental protection did not follow a linear path into the twentieth century in France. It centered almost exclusively on forested land prior to World War II, and it came to imply two different visions of the "natural" world, which were not always distinct from one another. One reflected a "preservationist" conception and the other a "conservationist" view. Preservationism encompassed the protection of the nonutilitarian, aesthetic features of nature or landscape for reasons of history, culture, and national heritage. Conservationism called for the judicious management and use of a resource to ensure the existence of sustainable resources for future generations. The shifting emphases placed on one or the other ultimately came to constitute a bifurcated and dialectical vision of the relationship among landscape, culture, people, nature, and history in France and its colonies in the nineteenth century and the first half of the twentieth. That refracted vision was one in which the preservation and conservation of the historic, cultivated landscapes of metropolitan France came to be inextricably linked to the conservation and preservation of the wild and sometimes allegedly unpeopled landscapes of its empire.

ONE

François-Antoine Rauch's New Harmony of Nature

> For long years I have wandered, and observed Nature in all of its states; not with the science of an enlightened naturalist, but with the heart of a good citizen. Everywhere, I thought I saw it stripped of its force and its original beauty, and the countryside as an inevitable consequence the sad victim of the resultant disorder, through the effect of meteors, the passing of the seasons, and changes in temperature.
>
> —François-Antoine Rauch

On 28 August 1826 François-Antoine Rauch, along with Michel Verd du Verdier de Vauprivas, founded the Société de fructification générale de la terre et des eaux de la France (Society for the General Enrichment of the Land and Waters of France), whose general goal was a complete renewal of France's natural resources. This project, which he believed could be achieved within the space of ten years, would take the form of multiplying France's fauna, most notably its wild game and birds, repopulating its rivers with fish, and reestablishing a more predictable climate. The initiative was the culmination of a life that had been devoted to restoring what he perceived to be a lost harmony in nature. His writings reflect a precocious interest in the interdependence of living things, which underlay investigations into the "economy of nature" and what would become the new science of ecology as it emerged during the course of the nineteenth century. Rauch's name generally does not appear among the seminal figures associated with the science of ecology in the nineteenth century and who came, by and large, from Germany and Anglo-Saxon countries: Alexander von Humboldt, Charles Darwin, Ernst Haeckel, and Aldo Leopold, among others.[1] Nonetheless, Rauch has been dubbed by some the founding father of French ecological thought, and for this reason it is surprising that he has largely been neglected by both environmental historians and historians of science. This might be explained by the fact that Rauch, who was both a former revolutionary and a low-ranking geographer and civil engineer, was primarily a popularizer who shared his thoughts about environmental degradation with the general public while taking on a self-appointed role of advising consuls, emperors, monarchs, and ministers on how to address the environmental devastation he saw around him. By his own admission he was not an "enlightened naturalist" who was formally trained in the sciences. He considered himself an observer of nature "with the heart of a good citizen," and as such his projects, writings, and practical initiatives provide a fascinating window onto the range of environmental anxieties and concerns that were prevalent in France from the end of the eighteenth century into the Bourbon Restoration and the beginning of the July Monarchy.[2]

Rauch published over more than a forty-year period. His first work appeared in 1792, at the height of the French Revolution, and he continued to publish into the Napoleonic period and the Bourbon Restoration. His writings about the natural world came to reveal the emergence of a new and distinct environmental consciousness that was shaped by the experience of the Revolution and reflected the convergence of a number of existing prerevolutionary intellectual currents, including Romanticism, physiocracy, eighteenth-century climate theory, and Rauch's own brand of revolutionary utopianism.

The various components of Rauch's "environmentalism" contributed to an emergent environmental knowledge that came to underpin some significant subsequent environmental regulation and legislation in the first thirty years of the nineteenth century. First, Rauch came to argue for the central role of the French state in regenerating the environment and reestablishing a new harmony in nature, while insisting that forests were at the heart of that project. Second, he focused on the crucial role of forests in regulating climate and, like many of the physiocrats, increasingly placed an emphasis on agricultural improvement. Third, while setting out to engage the French state and its relevant bureaucracies, he sought to reach out to a larger public both in and beyond the borders of France.

※ ※ ※

RAUCH ARRIVED on the public stage relatively young, in 1792, at the beginning of the First Republic, at the age of thirty, with the publication of *Plan nourricier, ou recherches sur les moyens à mettre en usage pour assurer à jamais le pain au peuple français*, after having served as a geographer for the corps of Ponts et Chaussées in several parts of France.[3] He was born in the borderland town of Bitche (Moselle), a commune in Lorraine, in northeastern France, in 1762. The surrounding area was known as pays de Bitche, or Bitscherland in German, and he noted in his first published work that French was not his mother tongue.[4] He was fluent in both German and French, and by his own account he took an early interest in geography, history, and map drawing.[5] He moved to Paris in 1782, at the age of twenty, and entered the Ecole des ponts et chaussées a year later, graduating in 1785. He then served for a year in Liège and in Roussillon as a geographer. After the outbreak of the French Revolution he was assigned to the Pyrénées-Orientales, once again as a geographer rather than an engineer.

Rauch took an early interest in defining the proper role of the state in managing and "regenerating" France's natural resources. *Régénération,* a central part of the revolutionary project, was a political, moral, and social program that was without clearly defined limits and that aimed at nothing less than creating a "new people." Regeneration was not a matter of simple reform and a return to an existing constitution, but rather it was predicated, especially after 1792, on the eradication of the past and the creation of a society on a new basis. This revolutionary conception of regeneration, which was not without its contradictions, as Mona Ozouf has so persuasively argued, flourished in countless pamphlets, brochures, political tracts, and speeches.[6] It is perhaps no accident that degeneration and regeneration became political metaphors in the discourse of the French Revolution, and they were taken up by Rauch early on in his own writings as an engineer in training.[7]

While Rauch was a student at the prestigious Ecole nationale des ponts et chaussées, the governance of the school and the role of the state's engineers became a subject of debate and controversy. Indeed, the minister of the interior, Jean-Marie Roland de la Platière, addressed a circular in October 1792 to the school's students and to the state's corps of engineers. He warned them against being "sterile builders" and encouraged them to undertake tasks designed to improve all aspects of public life. In March 1793 the young Rauch responded with a fifteen-chapter *mémoire*. Regeneration and state intervention were at the core of his "Observations et recherches sur la nécessité d'observer un mode simple et économique dans l'administration générale des travaux publics," and in it he exhorted the corps in the following terms: "O you, happy engineers of the public works, in whose enlightened trust well-disposed and well-meaning Liberty has confided the important and noble task of disseminating all the principles and greatest joys in our lovely country by deftly combining art and nature ... ; be glad that you can bring the fertile brook to the poor man's cabin, open up the vistas and build the hopes of the hardy worker."[8] François-Antoine Rauch also came to the attention of the newly established Committee of Public Safety during the First Republic, accompanying Alexandre Vandermonde (1735–1796) on a mission for the committee and serving as his draftsman. Their report consisted of a study of the fabrication of weapons at Klingenthal in the department of Bas-Rhin between 3 vendémaire and 16 brumaire, year 2 (September–October 1793) and was intended to provide practical intelligence for the nation's defense.[9]

A year earlier Rauch published his *Plan nourricier,* a work intended to solve France's periodic and chronic food shortages, which he boldly submitted to the National Assembly, the king, the government's ministers, and all the departments and districts of the empire in "year 1 of Liberty." He identified himself in his work, which was put out by the Didot publishing house in Paris, as a geographer in the department of Pyrénées-Orientales and a member of the Société économique de Paris. While he conceived of the work before the Revolution, he had briefly abandoned it, only to take it up again in 1790 when he served as a geographer in Roussillon. Many of his proposals were shaped by his experience there, though he argued for their applicability elsewhere in France.

Although there is no evidence that Rauch had any association with the naturalists at the Jardin du Roi, which was refounded in 1793 as the Muséum national d'histoire naturelle, he, like them, was centrally concerned with the problem of the renewal and regeneration of the natural world. As Emma Spary has argued, the Jardin des Plantes, which was attached to the museum, was deeply engaged in the study of generation, degeneration, and regeneration from the beginning of the Comte de Buffon's (1701–1788) intendancy.[10] Its projects were shaped by eighteenth-century discussions of the social significance of climate, which was explored in Jean Le Rond d'Alembert's *Encyclopédie* article "Climat," in which he credited Charles-Louis Secondat, Baron de Montesquieu, as the figure who revived the idea that climate principally shaped social institutions. Like the naturalists of the Jardin des Plantes and the museum, Rauch, an engineer, was persuaded by the idea of the transformative power of nature. The naturalists of the Jardin and the museum pleaded a case for increasing the earth's productivity through a variety of means, and increasingly placed an emphasis on acclimatization, growing exotic fruits and plants from abroad in France, and allowing them to adapt to new conditions. One of the most significant initiatives undertaken by André Thouin (1747–1824), the Jardin du Roi's chief gardener, was the cultivation of breadfruit. Thouin had read John Ellis's descriptions of the breadfruit plant in 1776, and the crop had already come to the attention of French naturalists after Antoine de Bougainville's voyage to Tahiti, where it was a dietary staple.[11] Thouin, ever concerned with the regeneration of nature for the purposes of improving the human condition, saw the breadfruit as the "perfect food for mankind, doing away with the need for other vegetable foodstuffs and balancing the constitution."[12] The breadfruit assumed an iconic status during the French Revolution, with farmers reporting their attempts to acclimatize the exotic plant in metropolitan France.

Rauch made similar arguments about the importation of fruits and plants that were suitable for cultivation in France from around the globe. He drew his readers' attention to breadfruit from the Southern Hemisphere, the date tree from Africa, and trees from Asia in his defense of the general principle of acclimatization, which was simultaneously championed at the Museum of Natural History. He envisioned that the work of the academies and savants in this regard might be organized in new ways, perhaps, in his view, imitating an English model:

> One has the real sense that the learned society in question would be somewhat differently organized from those that exist now, and above all that for some time it would give up special pleadings (however respectable they might be), to focus all its attention in order to increase or simplify the fundamental riches of mankind.... It would be similar to the English learned society, for which the respected M. Saint-Pierre travels the globe with the same aim.[13]

The concern for environmental renewal and regeneration was thus shaped by practical concerns, including a prolonged subsistence crisis during the French Revolution, but it was also part of the initiatives undertaken by the newly created Museum of Natural History. While much attention has been devoted to the museum's overseas missions and to naturalists' overseas voyages more generally during the revolutionary period, less attention has been given to the way in which they intersected with novel initiatives undertaken in the metropole.[14] Indeed, André Thouin was charged by the minister of the interior to dig up the gardens of the Tuileries and Luxembourg in order to replant them with potatoes in year 2 (1794).[15] The newly created Museum of Natural History embarked on similar strategic tasks, which included seizing and confiscating plants from the private gardens of the Parisian aristocracy, many of whom were imprisoned as enemies of the French Revolution, and from nationalized land that came to the state from other sources.[16] Given the matters that occupied Parisians and the revolutionary government in 1794, the initiative is striking and somewhat surprising. The museum's archives have left a voluminous record of Thouin's efforts to collect this vegetation, which was inventoried and added to the museum's collection in years 2 and 3 of the Republic. For example, at 10 a.m. on 12 March 1794 Thouin went to the Hôtel Kinski in the rue St. Dominique in Paris "to divide up and put aside rare trees, bushes and plants," which were both "exotic" and native to France, from the hôtel's garden, in conformity with a decree passed by the National Convention to this effect and with the authorization of the minister of the interior. A total of 289 plants were carefully inventoried and transported to the museum the following day on Thouin's orders.[17] While Princess Kinski was never imprisoned, and died peacefully at home in 1794, many of the properties targeted by the state belonged to émigrés and those condemned by the revolutionary tribunals. On 13 August 1794 Thouin collected plants from the greenhouse and gardens of the "condamné Boutin," who lived in the rue de Clichy in northern Paris.[18] Eight days later he inventoried a collection of seeds, onions, botanical catalogues, and manuscripts, as well as actual plants from the Cape of Good Hope, which had been collected by a condemned prisoner, Dumas Labrousse, at the abbaye de Port-Royal, which had been turned into the prison of Port-Libre in rue de la Bourbe in 1793.[19]

The Revolution's environmental initiatives were many, and Rauch was very aware of them and thought about them in terms of the subsistence crisis. He and others perceived the pragmatic need to regenerate nature and to harness it for human needs. He openly acknowledged the influence of the agronomist Antoine Parmentier (1737–1813), who proselytized in favor of the consumption of potatoes.[20] Parmentier had allegedly lent Rauch several works while he was preparing his *Plan nourricier*. Rauch tapped into a well-established and ongoing eighteenth-century discussion regarding the improvement of the milling process for grain, and principally the substitution of the *moulin rustique* by the *moulin économique,* as advocated by Parmentier, because of the latter's efficiency and superior yield.[21] Further, he pressed for the establishment of a system of public granaries that would provide grain at a fixed price and one below the market, as well as a new method of distribution.

Rauch ended his *Plan nourricier* with a concern of a different order, and he included a letter that he had written to the president of the National Assembly regarding the sale of France's national forests. He observed that the assembly's discussion centered on the needs of the French navy, but that the rapid deforestation that had occurred in France had not been fully addressed. He argued that "bread, wine, and wood formed the first three needs of the people" and that for this reason the sale of the nation's forests would have negative consequences. He stressed "the intimate relationship between forests and the animal world" *(l'économie animale)* and their visible influence on the "harmony of the elements" and the "leaves, fruits that they produce, the plants to which they give birth, the clouds that they attract," as well as the "rivers that they feed, the pasture land that they protect."[22] He called for further study of the question and offered his own services for this purpose on behalf of the French nation.[23] Rauch, however, made no claim to scientific knowledge or to research and insisted that he was a "popular organ," disseminating the work of others.[24]

Rauch's *Plan nourricier*, with its references to Parmentier, Jean-Jacques Rousseau, and the Comte de Buffon, represented an amalgam of physiocratic and Romantic ideas that circulated in France at the end of the eighteenth century. The philosophy of physiocracy, with its stress on agriculture and agricultural associations, was inspired by earlier English literature on economic topics,[25] but these ideas were harnessed by Rauch for the purpose of providing practical solutions to the nation's periodic food shortages, and he repeatedly invoked this problem to offer his own service to the state.

Rauch as an author is rarely absent from his text. In the book's final pages he refers to his own difficult youth, one that might be characterized as unhappy, and he argued that this actually made him a more acute and sensitive observer. While Rauch's plan resembled the innumerable *mémoires* and treatises on agricultural improvement, the milling process, and possible solutions to the problem of periodic grain shortages, his work represented a new departure in a number of different respects. First, it was couched in a revolutionary language that put the state and its servants—and more particularly engineers in the Ponts et Chaussées—at the center of new initiatives designed to organize the agricultural sphere and the natural world. Second, it contained the germ of an idea that was to become central to his future writing and projects: the crucial role that he believed forests played in equilibrating and harmonizing the natural world. Third, he defined the regeneration of nature not in terms of an act of negating the past, as much of the discourse on regeneration did, but rather in terms restoring nature's lost harmony. Regeneration did not, as Stanislaus de Clermont-Tonnère and other revolutionaries suggested, mean the abandonment of the past; for Rauch it signified a nostalgic return to a better past.

Rauch, who continually emphasized his humble social origins and who actively embraced the French Revolution and its projects, was transferred from southern France in 1794 to Dieuze in the newly formed department of Moselle to take up the post of *ingénieur ordinaire*. In many respects with his new posting he returned to his roots, after stints in southern and central France, and he was probably in part selected for his linguistic skills. He was responsible for overseeing public works projects in the districts of Dieuze, Château-Salins, and Sarrebourg, though he would make Dieuze his home.

After Rauch had served for three years, the chief engineer in the department wrote to the minister of the interior, accusing Rauch of professional negligence and asking that he be removed from his post.[26] According to an internal report on the case dated 21 October 1800 (29 vendémaire, year 9), the relationship between the chief engineer and Rauch had become tense. It suggested that Rauch believed that the superior quality of his ideas and projects was not sufficiently valorized and that a "dangerous rivalry" had developed between the chief engineer and himself, necessitating swift action. The report recommended that a post be found for Rauch somewhere else in the vicinity, and Paris adopted this recommendation.[27] In year 7 of the Republic (1799), Paris ordered Rauch to transfer from Dieuze to Verdun in the department of Meuse, but that order met with his resistance.

The actual circumstances surrounding what would become a vituperative debacle over Rauch's move cannot be fully resolved on the basis of the lengthy correspondence surrounding his appointment found in the archives of the Ministry of Public Works. For his part, Rauch objected vociferously to his proposed ouster, claiming that he was a "victim" of "intrigue" at the hands of the duplicitous chief engineer. According to Rauch, the transfer to the Meuse originated in the desire of the chief engineer in the department of Moselle, a man whom he characterized as "profoundly nasty," to replace him without cause in order to appoint his son-in-law in Rauch's place.[28] He therefore protested when he received the order by arguing that the son-in-law could not adequately replace him, as he spoke no German and was in fragile health. Rauch added that he had, in addition, bought an ecclesiastical property in the vicinity, more specifically, a convent that had been nationalized and that had come on the market soon after he arrived in the region. He pleaded that in these circumstances it would be very difficult for him to move his large family and that, in addition, the property required his personal attention. To leave, according to Rauch, would lead to his financial ruin.[29]

Rauch's pleas ultimately went unanswered, and his resistance to the order of transfer led to his unceremonious dismissal from the state's employ on 28 nivôse, year 7 of the Republic (17 January 1799). However, Rauch's predictions about the chief engineer's son-in-law, who replaced him, were on the mark, for he passed away four months later. Rauch immediately demanded that his case be reviewed. For him, the injustice that had been done to him could "naturally be repaired" if the state reassigned him to his former district, which he "should never have lost" because he was the only engineer in the department who had successfully undertaken projects involving navigation, marsh drainage, and irrigation. In addition, he emphasized that he was also the only engineer in the department who could speak German, which was "indispensable in the district of Dieuze," where the population was half German-speaking.[30] His request again fell on deaf ears, and during a three-year, four-month period in which he was in public disgrace for his refusal to accept a new post Rauch wrote a bevy of letters to a slew of ministers, while embarking on an ambitious project whose seeds had been planted eight or ten years before when he published his *Plan nourricier*. On 12 December 1800 he wrote to then minister of the interior Jean-Antoine Chaptal regarding his research on a work entitled *Harmonie hydro-végétale*, which he wished to present to the newly appointed first consul (Napoleon) when, as he hoped, he would be reappointed as an engineer, needing "three or four months of calm" to complete the project.[31] The work in question, *Harmonie hydro-végétale et météorologique: ou recherches sur les moyens de recréer avec nos forêts la force des températures et la regularité des saisons par des plantations raisonnées,* was published two years later, and the introduction as well as an internal governmental report on his case suggest that it may have played a role in Rauch's successful rehabilitation and ultimate reappointment to the state's corps of engineers. The minister of the interior's report on Rauch suggested "equity" would have it that his three fallow years should not be counted against him because he had been treated unjustly when his reappointment was denied. The minister saw that he was making amends by publishing his *Harmonie hydro-végétale,* which the minister judged to be "useful."[32] Rauch dedicated the work to Napoleon Bonaparte, and the final lines of his introduction, which ends in ellipsis, noted that he had completed the work far from the lights of the capital, sullied by "an unjust disgrace," and tormented by the "bitter, difficult and painful" situation in which he found himself. He saw the *Harmonie hydro-végétale* as "only a meager beginning," but one which he would pursue and develop for the benefit of the nation.[33] He looked toward a time when France would be restored to its natural harmony: "We will then see 'la belle France' take on the colors and charms of another Eden, and Nature raise itself to that great majesty which had elevated in such a religious manner the souls of the first men."[34]

Rauch emerged, then, from a three-year period of disgrace and exile with an ambitious new project that transcended his *Plan nourricier*. His two-volume *Harmonie hydro-végétale* is first and foremost a call for the regeneration of nature amid the "ruins of the most astonishing revolution that has yet marked the annales of peoples":[35] "France, today the most illustrious region of the universe, proud of the force and nobility of its first magistrate, is called, by its geographical position and its physical structure to become also the most fortunate part of the earth; all climates, all useful vegetation in the world, can become the domain of the *patrie* of the French."[36] He made reference in his introduction to the letter he had written to the president of the National Assembly regarding the sale of France's national forests in 1792, and which he included in his *Plan nourricier,* thus taking up the theme of deforestation and reforestation, which was only vaguely alluded to in the *Plan nourricier,* and which would come to stand at the center of his work. Indeed, the frontispiece of volume 1 represents a physician showing Napoleon mountains "crowned with cedars, pines, larch trees, evergreens, intermingled with [other] forest trees," and depicting an image of France as it could be in the future (Figure 1).

When it came to Napoleon Bonaparte, Rauch's unabashed flattery was on full display. Addressing him as "Citizen First Consul," he asserted that Rome was only "great and illustrious under its consulates" and acknowledged Napoleon's beneficent role in the regeneration of France and in triumphing over the many "enemies of our liberty and of our grandeur." Further, Nature now called him to the "immortal triumph over its elements, and to the conquest of happiness for even the most distant [future] generations."[37] However, while the arts, sciences, and commerce were being revived, nature, in his view, "this mother" who nourishes all human beings, was in decline after thousands of centuries of "disfigurements" and "insult."[38]

Rauch's *Harmonie hydro-végétale* is based on three fundamental premises. First, there was an original preexisting harmony in nature and an interdependent relationship between mountains, forests, meteors, temperatures, seasons, and water resources as well as animal life, and the work had as its overall goal a description of the means to recreate this harmonious environment through reforestation.[39] Second, the state was to play a central role in restoring the "colors and the charms of another Eden."[40] Third, Rauch contended that "forested countries possess the richest sources of social prosperity."[41]

The work set out to delineate the basis of nature's harmony while highlighting the pivotal role that forests played in sustaining it. He posited that as soon as humanity began to destroy them, changes in temperature as well as in the fertility of the soil and the diminution of animal life could be observed. In order to illustrate his point he highlighted the devastation that resulted in the ancient civilizations of Asia and Africa, including Ninevah, Babylon, and Chaldea, as a result of deforestation, and he emphasized the threat that deforestation posed for France in the present and future. According to Rauch, deforestation was a particular problem for France due to its geographical position and its exposure to westerly winds from the Atlantic, and he argued in chapters 3 and 4 of volume 1 for the planting of trees in mountainous regions to shield the arable valleys below. Rauch outlined several different initiatives that might be undertaken by the state, all of which involved reforestation.

La France régénérée, vous demande à recréer
cette belle nature sur toute sa surface.

FIGURE 1. Frontispiece, François-Antoine Rauch's two-volume *Harmonie hydro-végétale et météorologique*. Paris: Levrault, 1802.

While Rauch conceived of nature as an interdependent system in need of a new equilibrium, he also saw it as a "living monument," which may in part explain the final chapter of the first volume of *Harmonie hydro-végétale*, which appears to have little to do with those preceding it, with their emphasis on reforestation and discussions of tree types. Chapter 8, "Sur le caractère et la grandeur des monuments religieux," begins by characterizing the "magestic spectacle of the universe," which was that of nature as an "uninterrupted series of august monuments" that are offered

HARMONIE
HYDRO-VÉGÉTALE
ET
MÉTÉOROLOGIQUE,
OU
RECHERCHES

Sur les moyens de recréer avec nos forêts la force des températures et la régularité des saisons, par des plantations raisonnées.

Cet ouvrage, médité pour le bonheur des campagnes, embrasse les corrélations existantes entre les montagnes, les forêts et les météores; les températures et les saisons; la régénération des sources, la repopulation des ruisseaux et des fleuves; l'assainement et la culture des marais; la fructification des grandes routes et des voies pastorales; avec quelques vues morales sur les honneurs à rendre dans nos cérémonies funéraires à la nature humaine.

DÉDIÉ

AU PREMIER CONSUL
DE LA RÉPUBLIQUE FRANÇAISE.

Par F. A. RAUCH, ingénieur des ponts et chaussées.

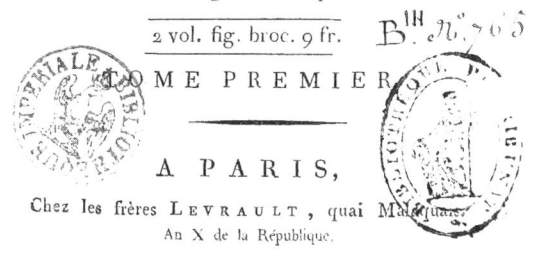

2 vol. fig. broc. 9 fr.

TOME PREMIER

A PARIS,

Chez les frères LEVRAULT, quai Malaquais.
An X de la République.

---

for "religious contemplation." They included stars, mountains, seas, valleys, lakes, rivers, clouds and winds, the cedar tree, and even the humble mosses, which were "as much noble monuments of our planet" as the most illustrious recognized monuments.[42]

For much of the revolutionary decade there had been intense discussion surrounding monuments and commemoration, which laid the groundwork, most notably, for the creation of a new museum of national monuments to protect France's historical past from vandalism, and for the great festivals of the French Revolution.[43] For Rauch, the protection of historical monuments constituted a preservation of France's heritage or *patrimoine* for future generations. The notion of *patrimoine* is derived from the Latin word *patrimonium,* and Emile Littré's *Dictionnaire de la langue française* of 1859 defines it as "an object of heritage transmitted through law from mothers and fathers to their children." It is thus conceived of in material and juridical terms and linked to ancestral inheritance. As it came to be articulated over time, only those monuments or objects that transmitted a shared, and increasingly national, tradition and recalled a common past—and which were privileged or venerated as a result—would be considered as such.[44]

Rauch must have been among the first in France to suggest the idea that nature should be considered as a series of living monuments that recalled a past and that could be related to heroic, religious, and funerary human monuments that existed for posterity. For Rauch, every object in the world had "its language, its sentiment and its character," and monuments of art, for him, were often those of a "time and of a people," so that "when the hand of time comes to efface the characteristic traits in them, the sentiment that they must have produced and transmitted disappears in the ruins, and the charm ceases."[45] However, in uniting "the living monuments of nature" to those of art, which are always more somber, when they stand alone, "the picture completes itself; it seizes the language of all people, of all countries, and of all times."[46] Rauch thus evoked the idea of a perennial universal natural monument that spoke to all of humanity, and one which was endowed with mnemonic power. This view of nature served as a transition to the second volume of *Harmonie hydro-végétale,* whose frontispiece was captioned "Elisée, solemnité des tombeaux."

The idea of nature as a living monument may in part be derived from prevailing discussions of historical monuments, but it may also be associated with Rauch's own training as an engineer in the Ecole nationale des ponts et chaussées at the end of the eighteenth century. Engineers trained by the école were still considered *ingénieurs-artistes,* engaged in "hydraulic architecture," and whose projects were intimately associated with the construction of classical gardens. According to Antoine Picon, Jacques Boyceau's 1636 *Traité de jardinage* "evokes the program of study which could establish a future engineer."[47] The teaching of architecture was central to the curriculum and became much less important as the nineteenth century progressed.[48] Hydraulic architecture, drawing, and garden design were squarely a part of the engineer's training, as were the drawing of geographical maps, figures, ornaments, and landscapes, which were an integral part of the école's program. This kind of training would encourage Rauch and his fellow engineers to consider nature in relation to man-made structures, which was at the heart of the work they were to undertake in building bridges, carving out canals, and constructing levees and dikes. This may be one reason that Rauch might be seen as a founding advocate of landscape preservation, providing an early articulation of an argument in favor of protecting the monuments of the natural world.

While the first volume of *Harmonie hydro-végétale* was centrally concerned with deforestation, reforestation, and climatology, the second volume focused on the regeneration of rivers, lakes, and ponds, marsh drainage, and nature in urban spaces, ending with a call to establish a hydro-vegetal and meteorological observatory at the Ministry of the Interior and in all prefectures and subprefectures of France. These observatories would in turn monitor and provide detailed information about the natural environment. They would document the elevation and length of mountains and their degree of forestation or deforestation; the length of rivers; riparian habitats; the extent of marshes; wind and rain patterns; and the implications of all of these findings for public health. He, in addition, would charge the *conseils généraux* of each of France's newly created departments to submit a yearly report on their physical and moral state. Significantly, Rauch would institute national festivals devoted to tree planting and to the celebration of valleys, lakes, and rivers in order to involve the public at large in the endeavor. The planting of "liberty trees" was, of course, a ceremonial practice that is intimately associated with the French Revolution, and one whose symbolic power was articulated in numerous speeches and written tracts.[49]

In one of the most curious passages of the text, Rauch suggests that France's ambassadors abroad be charged with an additional mission, that of negotiating an exchange of trees and vegetation that France or other countries might lack or need: "Thus the American, the European, the Asiatic and the African, when they are brought to see the hospitable land of the French," would be brimming with joy at the sight of a tree from their own land there.[50] For Rauch the moment had arrived for "la France agricole" or the great system of "économie sociale" to become "an exact science," while allowing the government itself to "decree, follow and direct" the creation of a "powerful, fertile, inexhaustible nature."[51] He invited France's citizens to send him their observations, which he in turn would send directly to the government, noting that letters could be addressed to the publisher C. Levrault in his name. What is particularly interesting about Rauch's project is his explicit call to the French public to become involved in the business of collecting information and expressing its concerns for the larger purpose of regenerating the natural world. Moreover, he voiced his call to action in terms of future generations: "Finally, the present and the future are there to judge us before posterity. If we let all the kingdoms of nature be extinguished with us, we will see [future] generations which must succeed us, curse and shed tears of despair on our tombs."[52]

※ ※ ※

RAUCH WAS ULTIMATELY reinstated as *ingénieur ordinaire* in the service of Ponts et Chaussées in the department of Bas-Rhin on 28 floréal, year 10 (8 May 1802), following his protracted campaign of letter writing. His reinstatement coincided with the publication of *Harmonie hydro-végétale*. He remained in the service of the French state for another four years, at which point he retired (at the age of forty-four) after twelve years of service, while spending three years (euphemistically) "sans activité," or in disgrace. After 1806 Rauch disappeared from the public record for some time, only reemerging three years after the fall of Napoleon and the restoration of the Bourbon monarchy in 1815 with the publication of his two-volume *Régénération de la nature végétale, ou recherches sur les moyens de recréer, dans tous les climats, les anciennes températures et l'ordre primitif des saisons, par des plantations raisonnées*.[53] The title indicates that he again put *régénération* at the center of his new work and that he nostalgically called for the return to an original nature as his self-proclaimed goal. Identifying himself as a "retired engineer," he noted that his work represented a second edition of his previously published *Harmonie hydro-végétale*, but announced that *Régénération de la nature végétale* came with changes and additions. The frontispieces to volumes one and two were no longer included, even though Rauch notes that an engraving should precede each chapter. He acknowledged that the costs were prohibitive, leaving him with the option of a simple description of what the engraving might have been. It must, however, be said that the frontispiece to the first volume of *Harmonie hydro-végétale*, depicting Napoleon, would not have been well received in the early years of the Bourbon Restoration.

Rauch built on his earlier two works, but he once again changed his emphasis and direction. In *Régénération* Rauch's ambitions had become global, and his tone was no longer nationalistic. In his introduction he asserted that the aim of the work was the same as it had been fourteen years earlier, in 1802. He wished to chart the path toward establishing a new harmony in nature in order to restore the earth to its ancient glory. The key source of the environmental devastation that had affected the four continents of the world was, according to Rauch, deforestation, which had resulted in changes in the climate and seasons, violent storms, and other environmental irregularities. While *Harmonie hydro-végétale* was a call to action for France as a nation and was directed to its first consul, Napoleon

Bonaparte, *Régénération de la nature* was clearly intended for a larger international audience, as his observations, in his view, should claim the attention of "all governments, of all peoples."[54] He did not see his work as one of science but rather as one of simple observation, and he believed that the moment at which he wrote was a particularly propitious one for European governments:

> Such are the views I offer my country, and I will dare to say all lands, because they are related to all countries, to all climates. This is not at all a work of science, but the simple result of physical observations, so palpably obvious, of an order so natural and at the same time so important, that, in spite of their general nature and the breadth of their connections, each state could regard them as being their own, and as being able immediately to contribute to its prosperity.[55]

He suggested that after a long period of "political tempests," referring, no doubt to the Napoleonic Wars, which had "shaken and thrown all of Europe into torment," a "peaceful spirit" had come to the continent and with it the "general need to repair the calamities" caused by "a war of destruction." He called for international cooperation:

> The close union, still without precedent in the annals of the world, of all the sovereigns of Europe; a phenomenon that is no less true, no less worthy of being remarked upon, the magnanimous intention where—in the eyes of all observers—these same princes, together as well as separately, are to occupy themselves in the application of principles which can render all peoples happier: everything converges to give birth to the most admirable hopes.[56]

After praising Napoleon's martial spirit in 1802, Rauch appears to have become a pacifist, and directly addressed the problem of the environmental impact of war. He took up this theme in chapter five of the first volume, which concerns forests and their utility, and spoke to the destructiveness of war and the appalling devastation that ensues from it. Indeed, he even suggests that the sovereigns of Europe would soon meet and agree to an end to permanent armies, which result in war.[57]

Deforestation and its effects are again at the center of *Régénération de la nature*, as they were in *Harmonie hydro-végétale*. He explored the primitive state of forests and their influence on moisture, climate, unpredictable floods, and storms before surveying the effects of deforestation in Asia, Africa, America, and Europe. He returned to contemporary France, providing extensive excerpts from printed governmental reports concerning the effects of deforestation and the sale of forested land during the French Revolution in fifty-five of the nation's departments, while arguing that this picture is one that might be applied to most countries in Europe. Rauch ultimately concluded his work, which departed significantly from *Harmonie hydro-végétale*, by commenting on recent weather patterns in France (1817), with a call for specific measures regarding reforestation as well as the restocking of rivers with fish. Moreover, in contrast to his explicit call to his readers to send their observations in *Harmonie hydro-végétale*, he ends instead with the hope that the government would act through its administrators and engineers. Rauch credited himself for a number of measures that had already been undertaken in France in the first decade of the nineteenth century, and reprinted letters that he received in response to *Harmonie hydro-végétale*, including those from a number of foreign ambassadors to France and the prefect of Haut-Rhin. It was clear that the intended audience of the revised work was no longer only the French state and the French people, but the states and governments of Europe.[58]

Rauch placed an emphasis on the regeneration of the natural world in Europe as a whole in a prospectus announcing the publication of a new monthly periodical that was to appear in May 1819, entitled *Annales Européennes de Physique Végétale et d'Economie Publique*. The prospectus indicated that it would be the product of a "society of authors" known for their work on physics, natural history, and "public economy." The prospectus's opening lines reflected the spirit of the newly hoped-for pan-European cooperation following the Napoleonic Wars, which was also reflected in Rauch's introduction to *Régénération de la nature*:

> A unique era in history, that of the union of all the monarchs of Europe, who put forward the precious guarantee of a durable peace, because it is the desire as well as the need of all governments; this serene era, when sentiments of goodwill are at last going to succeed sinister political dreams, seems to invite all European nations to put down the arms of enmity, and forge among themselves an alliance for the exchange of all terrestrial goods by which Providence has enriched the diverse regions of the earth.[59]

The *Annales Européennes* would set out to study humankind's current environment, comparing it with what it had been formerly and what it could be in the future. It would examine climates and their effect on vegetal and animal life as well as the means to increase the productivity of European soil. The cleanliness of the air and water, which were so important to public hygiene, would also be the object of observation and study in order to find the means to enrich European waters. However, the purview of the periodical was meant to be more encompassing and of interest to "all classes of society, particularly administrators, religious leaders, justices of the peace, and property owners," and the prospectus called on prefects, subprefects, and amateur subscribers to the periodical to send observations which they might consider useful for publication.[60] The price of the subscription was thirty francs a year, or sixteen francs for six months, to be paid to Rauch, "ancien officier de génie" and director, at 41 Place Saint-Germain-l'Auxerrois in Paris, or to the Parisian publisher A. M. Didot.

It would not be until three years later, in 1821, however, that the first volume of the *Annales Européennes* actually appeared, at which point both its publisher and Rauch's address in Paris had changed.[61] The volume's frontispiece depicted four female figures representing the world's four continents in a forest of trees from all four corners of the globe (Figure 2). The figure representing Europe sat on an oak tree in the midst of a cow, a horse, a goat, and a ram, surrounded by chickens, while receiving offerings from standing figures representing Asia, America, and Africa, which included an elephant, a banana tree, a Tibetan goat, fish, a llama, breadfruit, a dromedary, a palm tree, and a zebra. While the illustration suggests that the observations in the *Annales* would be drawn from all parts of the world, its central focus was clearly on Europe.

It soon became evident from the journal's choice of subjects and presentation that Rauch, as director, probably wrote and produced each issue himself, even though every installment makes reference to a "society of authors." The first volume's opening lines, concerning the peace and concord among European nations and the goals of the *Annales*, were taken almost verbatim from both *Régénération de la Nature* and the prospectus.[62] They attributed the degradation of nature to the "hand of man," which nonetheless gave "hope of being able to repair the visible wrongs through the same power."[63] This was followed by an ode to the immensity of nature, where both Buffon and Bernardin de Saint-Pierre figure prominently, and a discussion of the state of forests in ancient times. The subsequent numbers took up the themes contained in chapters of both *Harmonie hydro-végétale* and *Régénération de la nature* concerning the process of deforestation on the various continents of the world and its consequences, and the *Annales* reprinted governmental statistics regarding deforestation in the 1790s from various departments in France. While the theme of deforestation remained a central preoccupation in the *Annales* during its seven years of existence, the publication was also deeply concerned with acclimatization, central to the program of the Museum of Natural History in the eighteenth century and to the Société zoologique d'acclimatation, which was founded several decades later by Geoffroy Saint-Hilaire in 1854.[64] The *Annales* included reports on the introduction of Tibetan goats into France and other articles regarding animal life.

In the second volume of the *Annales* Rauch took stock of the subjects explored in the six previous issues. He restated that the periodical was

FIGURE 2. Frontispiece, Rauch's *Annales Européennes*, volume 1. Paris: Eberhardt, 1821.

principally concerned with "the state in which our planet must, at the moment of its birth, have left the hands of the celestial Architect of the Universe."[65] Its "special aim" was to embrace the "immense cause of nature," and he noted that a single governmental ministry had taken out 3,300 francs in subscriptions and that other subscribers consisted of learned societies, administrators, and enlightened laymen as well as foreigners subscribing from abroad.[66] The periodical was founded with investments from forty-eight contributors, and he encouraged his readership to invest in the enterprise even further.

Initially, the *Annales Européennes* and its mission appeared to be well received on the part of the government and the general public. On 8 June 1822 the governmental newspaper *Le Moniteur* described its project as "eminently national" and at the same time European in its scope. It succeeded in analyzing the causes of the ills that "reign in the whole system of nature, and which proceed solely from the hand of man." The *Annales*, in the estimation of *Le Moniteur*, provided a "simple and easy" means to reestablish, successively, not only a happier world in terms air quality, but also to increase the natural sources of water and the land's fertility.[67] *Le Moniteur* announced that the government was sending a circular consisting of five questions about the environment to the country's prefects and that it would in turn send the responses it received to the Royal Academy of Sciences and to the *Annales Européennes*.

The government's circular was prefaced with the observation that for the past several years France had witnessed a cooling in overall temperatures, sudden variations in the seasons, and an increasing number of extraordinary floods and storms, which were attributed to deforestation. In order to study the problem of deforestation in greater depth, the state asked the prefects of France's eighty-three departments to name the forests that existed in each department thirty years ago and describe their location, height, and surface area as well as the types of trees. It also asked them to provide information about who owned the forests and which of them still existed; to evaluate in this context whether floods and storms had become more frequent; and to assess whether winds had become more violent than they were in times past when France was more forested.[68]

In reprinting five departmental responses to the circular—from Mayenne, Marne, Ardèche, Dordogne, and Haut-Rhin—*Annales Européennes*—or rather Rauch, as its principal author—arrived at some preliminary conclusions: Much of the surface of France had become deforested, and floods had become more frequent and more costly. It appeared that the variations in temperature between seasons had become more extreme, and agriculture less productive, in spite of various agricultural improvements.[69] The departmental responses were published regularly in the pages of the *Annales Européennes* every year, and each passing report attested to the devastating effects of deforestation.

There was a two-year hiatus between the publication of volume 3 in 1822 and volume 4 in 1824, which Rauch explained was due to the decision to include more lithographs. However, in one of the last issues of volume 3, the editors acknowledged delays and assured a regularity of publication in the future. Rauch more or less admitted that he was in financial straits and suggested that the only means out of the *Annales*' dilemma was financial support from the French state.[70] By 1824 Rauch found a new publisher for *Annales Européennes,* C. J. Trouvé, and the orientation of the periodical changed once again, as Rauch assumed direct and sole responsibility for its content. No longer was the *Annales* published under the auspices of a "society of authors," but by Rauch himself, director, *ancien officier de génie,* member of the geographical society, and so on. The frontispiece pictured two Mexicans contemplating the botanical riches of upper Mexico, and the volume included lithographs devoted to vegetation and scenes in distant parts of the world (Figure 3).

One lithograph, based on Captain Landolphe's *Voyage du capitaine Landolphe,* represented a forest in Africa filled with parrots and a rain forest in Brazil.[71] Indeed, in 1824 *Annales Européennes* devoted considerable attention to a series of reports on voyages of discovery, including those of Captains Parry, Franklin, and Duperrey, but Rauch slowly began to resurrect a theme that was pervasive in his earliest writing, which concerned how to increase agricultural productivity. This concern led to the proposed founding on 24 November 1824 of the Société de fructification générale, a major focus of the periodical and its subsequent lithographs. One lithograph, captioned "The Deplorable State of Many Cantons of France," depicted a mountain and a valley with a river running through it, which were devoid of any vegetation. While scrawny cows grazed on one side of the river, two men stood with empty fishing nets on the other, as a young woman gazed at one with a distressed and imploring look on her face (Figure 4). This was followed by "Regeneration of the Sweet Bounties of Nature in All of the Cantons of France," which depicted a similar landscape, but in this lithograph it is covered with vegetation of all kinds; a healthy flock of sheep graze, and birds fly overhead. Two men fish in the river, and the net of one is filled with fish (Figure 5).

The general aim of the Société de fructification générale was to "regenerate" all vegetal life, increase the animal and aquatic population, and create a more predictable climate in France in the space of ten years:

FIGURE 3. Frontispiece, "Mexicans contemplate the rich productions of upper Mexico," *Annales Européennes*, volume 4. Paris: C. J. Trouvé, 1824.

FIGURE 4. "The deplorable state of many cantons of France," depicting a distressed environment. "Etat déplorable de beaucoup de cantons de la France," *Annales Européennes*, volume 5. Paris: C. J. Trouvé, 1824.

FIGURE 5. "Regeneration of the sweet bounties of nature in all of the cantons of France," showing a healthy environment. "Régénération des doux biens de la nature, dans tous les cantons de la France," *Annales Européennes*, volume 5. Paris: C. J. Trouvé, 1824.

We live in one of the greatest eras to have ever left their mark on human societies: let us seek to celebrate it, not by imitating the silent and sterile greatness of ancient monuments, but by covering our native land with living monuments, which are chosen amongst the loveliest and most useful marvels of the vegetal kingdom, which having been handed over to Nature, have survived over the centuries, and which by ceaselessly spreading their treasures and their good effects on earth console the poor, seduce the rich, and guarantee the most deserved benedictions for posterity.[72]

Rauch once again took up the distinction he made in *Harmonie hydro-végétale* between man-made monuments and natural monuments, but this time he emphasized that the former were old (and dead), whereas the latter were living and looked toward the future. He saw their preservation as an effort undertaken by the Société de fructification générale and by the state, and enumerated the benefits of the enterprise in terms of climate. At the same time, *Annales Européennes* continued to publish departmental reports that had been written in response to the Ministry of the Interior's 1821 circular concerning deforestation, including a report dated May 1821 from Hervé de Tocqueville, father of Alexis de Tocqueville, who was prefect of Moselle, where Rauch had been assigned as an engineer. Having a familiarity with the department, and more especially with Bitche, where he was born, Rauch noted that if one considered the question of deforestation from a sixty-year as opposed to thirty-year perspective, one would have to acknowledge the considerable amount of trees felled for building projects in Holland.[73]

By 1825 the journal became the mouthpiece of the Société de fructification générale, and its title changed to *Annales Européennes, ou Journal Spécial de la Société de Fructification Générale*. Its purpose was to put before its readers the accomplishments of the society, whose goal was to increase the wealth and productivity of the land that comprised the French nation. To this extent both the European and the international dimension appear to have disappeared from sight, and the society was national in its scope once again.[74] The lithographs and frontispieces had long since disappeared from the pages of the journal, which devoted itself to disparate articles on a variety of topics.

※ ※ ※

ANNALES EUROPÉENNES had obviously been struggling financially for years. The last volume appeared in 1827, three years before the July Revolution, which swept the Restoration away, and François-Antoine Rauch's enterprise abruptly came to a halt. He did not, however, himself disappear entirely, making endless requests for money and to be awarded the Legion of Honor. In 1827 he wrote his first letter concerning the award, which was followed by letters sent between 1828 and the early 1830s, citing an alleged friendship with Bernardin Saint-Pierre and asserting that at sixty-nine he was well advanced in age and should be recognized. Rauch again wrote to the government in 1831 to ask that he be awarded the Legion of Honor for his services as an engineer and as author of *Harmonie hydro-végétal* and *Régénération de la nature,* director of the *Annales Européennes,* and founder of a company that was formed for the purpose of draining wetlands.[75] A year later he wrote to the administration of Ponts et Chaussées repeating his request for the Legion of Honor, noting that King Henri IV had ennobled those who had provided services with regard to the draining of swamps.[76] He received a polite reply a week later which informed him that given the number of engineers worthy of this honor who had not received it, the granting of his request would be difficult.[77]

Rauch had kept up a steady correspondence with the administration of Ponts et Chaussées and various ministers of the interior since his early troubles in Dieuze. He asked to be accorded the pension of a chief engineer—even though he never reached that rank and had left the service many years before—due to his infirmities and his family responsibilities, for which he claimed his meager pension of 1,250 francs did not suffice. He pointed out that most of his classmates had reached a higher rank and that most had been decorated, and that his only son, who had been in the Garde du corps du Roi, had died at the age of twenty, suggesting that the cause of his death could in part be attributed to Rauch's circumstances. These observations, which were clearly made to move the letter's recipient, appeared to have had little effect. The correspondence ground to a halt in 1832, five years before his personnel file was officially closed and his death noted on 24 February 1837.

François-Antoine Rauch's career as an engineer for the French state—three years of which was spent in disgrace—was short-lived. Rauch, author of *Plan nourricier* and *Régénération hydro-végétale,* director of the Société de fructification générale de la terre and founder of a company that drained wetlands, and principal editor of *Annales Européennes,* was nonetheless a man of grand schemes and plans which did not, in the end, amount to a great deal in immediate terms. His purchase of a nationalized religious property during the French Revolution nearly ruined him, and his attempt to produce sugar from beetroot for the domestic market foundered. He appeared to have moved frequently in the last years of his life, which were spent in Paris, and he died at the age of seventy-five in straitened circumstances, if not in outright poverty. While his life appeared to be a tale of setbacks, woe, and failure, which he further dramatized in his voluminous correspondence with the French state, he nonetheless came to express some key features of an emergent environmental consciousness as it came to take shape in the nineteenth century. First, he argued that the "hand of man" was entirely responsible for environmental degradation and that the French state had a crucial role to play in combatting it. Second, he argued that reforestation was the principal means of reestablishing nature's harmony. The far-reaching liberalization of legislation governing forests during the French Revolution, which resulted in wide-scale deforestation, encouraged Rauch, among others, to reconsider the wisdom of such endeavors and led to an almost century-long debate in France about the role of forests in assuring a natural harmony in nature. But Rauch also introduced some key new elements into the environmental discourse of the period. While addressing the interests of France as a nation, particularly in his early *Harmonie hydro-végétale,* which placed food supply at the top of his concerns, he gradually began to argue that the environment should be considered from a transcontinental, if not a global, perspective in his 1818 *Régénération de la nature* and *Annales Européennes,* invoking international cooperation, which became a hallmark of twentieth-century environmentalism. Moreover, he reflected on the environmental effects of European expansion around the globe. In the second number of *Annales Européennes* he penned an essay on deforestation in Asia, Africa, the Americas, and Europe, arguing that Europeans did not explore the globe to admire the magnificent beauty that was present in other continents, but to enrich themselves. "These blind Europeans," according to him, "did not know how to live" naturally, as the natives did, "without destroying anything."[78]

The environmental consciousness that Rauch's writings reveal represented an amalgam of different intellectual and scientific strands of thought and emerged out of earlier concerns about climate and deforestation, as Richard Grove and Clarence Glacken have cogently argued.[79] Rauch's "green language" was not strictly a reaction to the deleterious social and economic consequences of capitalism or industrialization, which Raymond Williams, among others, argues was at the heart of an emerging western European environmentalism. It emerged from physiocratic and medical theories that saw a clear link between hygiene, health, climate, and the natural world more generally and the human condition. Just as importantly—and this aspect of Rauch's thought has been largely neglected—it grew out of France's encounter with the non-European world, and it emerged from the emotional wells of Romanticism, which were fed by desiccation theories.[80] Some historians argue that linking medical theories to concerns about the environment is problematic.[81] Emma Spary, for example, sees these concerns among naturalists as a "Hippocratic project" and emphasizes the purely medical origins and implications of debates about climate, diet, and social institutions. However, as the utopian, physiocratic, Romantic, and pragmatic origins of Rauch's schemes suggest, his conception of a new harmony of nature could not be contained within a narrowly defined Hippocratic project with his insistence on the vast web of delicate interconnections between humans and the natural world. Whatever his setbacks, Rauch's writing revealed ambient anxieties about the state and fate of nature, as evidenced in deforestation, flooding, and imperial expansion, which were all major themes in his work, while foreshadowing the international initiatives to halt the march of environmental degradation in the twentieth century. These themes, and the idea of nature as a living monument that was in need of protection, gradually gained currency, becoming subjects of public debate, discussion, and action as the century wore on.

TWO

Saving the Forests First

Nature, with secret ties, attaches the destiny of mortals to that of forests.
—Alexandre Moreau de Jonnès

Jean-François Rauch's understanding of the environment as a harmonious system of interconnected parts hinged on the central role played by forests in maintaining the balance on which such a system relied. While not necessarily articulating their ideas in the terms that Rauch put forward, commentators in France had long recognized the importance of forests. During the seventeenth century, colonial administrators such as Pierre Poivre, posted in far-flung tropical Edens acquired during French colonial expansion, sounded a clarion call about some of the irreversible effects of deforestation, reflecting the slow emergence of a new "global environmental consciousness" in the context of European overseas expansion.[1] In metropolitan France during the same period, Jean-Baptiste Colbert, among others, was particularly worried about the potential scarcity of maritime timber and was the chief architect of an ordinance that first codified forest law in France, bringing existing laws, custom, and regulations in conformity with one another. The French Forest Ordinance of 1669 ultimately became a "landmark in the history of European forestry" and provided a blueprint for the future.[2] While the principal provisions of the ordinance applied to royal forests, they also addressed ecclesiastical possessions, civil corporations, communities, and individuals with specific legal rights. When the ordinance was issued, Louis XIV articulated its intent as one that transcended the immediate moment, invoking future generations in saying that "it is not enough to have re-established order and discipline, if we do not by good and wise regulations see to it that the fruit of this shall be secured to posterity."[3] The ordinance regulated the pasturing of animals and the cutting of wood and placed restrictions on kilns, furnaces, and charcoal making. It represented a significant landmark in terms of establishing a delicate balance between the rights of use, forest conservation, and the potential contributions of forests to the development of industry and manufacture.

The Forest Ordinance of 1669 remained in place and determined forest law for more than 120 years, but was gradually eroded by the exigencies of continuous warfare at the end of Louis XIV's reign and the rising demand for wood throughout the course of the eighteenth century.[4] As Keiko Matteson has argued, the "century spanning the enactment of the 1669 Ordinance and the eve of the Revolution marks a formative period in the development of French environmental discourse and conservationist policy."[5] A decade before the outbreak of the French Revolution, the Comte de Buffon worried about the effects of deforestation in France and argued in favor of forest conservation.[6] When Arthur Young made his famous trip to France on the eve of the French Revolution, he admired the great expanses of forested land but at the same time marveled at how expensive and difficult it was to acquire wood. By the outbreak of the French Revolution, the extent to which France was affected by deforestation came to be widely recognized. According to reports made to the Constituent Assembly in 1790, there were 6,698,000 hectares of forested land, 925,000 of which belonged to the crown and 949,000 to the Catholic Church. Another 1,024,000 hectares were in communal forests, and 3,800,000 belonged to individuals.[7]

The French Revolution was a turning point in terms of how forests were (or were not) managed and maintained, and marked the emergence of widely shared fears concerning the rate of deforestation, which accelerated rapidly during the revolutionary decade. By the first half of the nineteenth century, forests occupied a new place in the French social imagination as a *territoire spéciale,* with a new juridical status.[8] The debates concerning forests during the French Revolution shaped that status and the emergence of the new environmental consciousness that Rauch and others came to express. This chapter explores how the Revolution dismantled Colbert's forest administration and examines the debate over the extent of deforestation during the revolutionary and immediate postrevolutionary periods. Several key figures framed these debates in the first half of the nineteenth century: Jean-Baptiste Rougier de La Bergerie (1762–1836), Alexandre Moreau de

Jonnès (1778–1870), and Antoine-César Becquerel (1788–1878). The chapter also explores the initiatives undertaken by the French state to combat deforestation from the Napoleonic period to the end of the nineteenth century, with a particular focus on measures that were put in place in the Alpine regions of France during the Second Empire.

※ ※ ※

ALMOST IMMEDIATELY after the French Revolution began, the French forest service sounded an alarm about the increasing number of forest offenses that were committed by the people all over France.[9] Louis XVI himself was so concerned that on 15 August 1789 he ordered thirty Swiss guards to protect the forest of Saint-Germain-en-Laye near Paris, and on 3 November 1789 he issued a proclamation, in case there was any doubt, to affirm that the 1669 ordinance was to be respected.[10] Ad hoc legislation began to be passed to protect full-grown timber forests *(futaie)*, such as that of 26 March 1790, which outlawed *défrichements* or the clearance of any national lands, including state and ecclesiastical property. Attempts to strengthen this legislation in April were, however, unsuccessful. Nonetheless, reports came in to Paris about the inability of forest officials to control incursions into forested land by the inhabitants of surrounding areas, which sometimes resulted in fatal skirmishes. In many cases these incursions constituted attacks on the seigneurial system and the "right of triage" instituted by the 1669 ordinance.[11] The severity of the winter of 1789–1790 also pushed the people into forests in search of game, fallen wood, and other vegetation. Indeed, the disorder engendered by the winds of revolutionary change ultimately led to the call for the end of Colbert's 1669 ordinance and the passage of new legislation, which would determine how forests would be managed, used, and exploited in the future. While the law that was passed for this purpose on 29 September 1791 was not to last long, it did wipe out Colbert's ordinance and had far-reaching consequences both in terms of the process of deforestation and for providing a framework on which the debate about forestation and deforestation came to be articulated throughout the nineteenth century.

The 29 September 1791 law announced the creation of a new forest administration, and this was initially greeted with relief. It rejected proposals that included the selling off of national forests entirely and putting them in the hands of the private sector and instead supported the formation of a Conservation générale des forêts, which would be divided into districts and subdistricts. However, the law did not determine the more specific technical aspects of future forest management, and in March 1792 the Legislative

Assembly suspended the appointment of *conservateurs* and inspectors, restoring former officers from the Eaux et Forêts.

The law made a fundamental distinction between *bois soumis* and *bois insoumis*—forests that were subject to the legislation and those that were not. In the first category were those belonging to the crown, those that were part of the national domain, which would include land confiscated from émigrés, and communal forests, all of which would come under the forest administration. Article 6 of the decree stipulated that "woods belonging to individuals will cease to be subject" to the forest administration, and "each proprietor will be at liberty to administer and dispose of them" in the future as he sees fit.[12] The sale of nationalized land, which included forests, the need for timber in the context of a prolonged period of war, and a spirit of liberalism came to shape the content of the September law, and its most controversial article by far was article 6. While the term *défrichement* or clearing (of forested land) was not used, the article in effect gave individual property owners license to clear forests at will, an act that was forbidden under the 1669 forest ordinance. Article 6 thus opened the door for large-scale clearance, which came to be decried on all sides almost as soon as the law was put into effect.[13] After the law was passed, proprietors began to clear, fell, and break up their forested property in order to get as much profit as they could, and this was particularly true of ecclesiastical property that was sold as nationalized land to the highest bidder.

The pace and extent of deforestation during the French Revolution have been hotly debated ever since, and as early as 1791 questions were raised about the wisdom of selling forests to individual proprietors who would not be subject to any real restrictions. However, the sale of forests as national lands and the deforestation that ensued continued unabated. The extent of deforestation and the ravages wrought by unchecked incursions into forested areas were determined by the local distribution of forests, the property regimes under which they were held, and the needs of local communities, as well as by the effectiveness of local forest officials. Different regions were affected in varying ways. Peasants also took advantage of the chaotic situation, according to Jules Michelet, who in writing about the Pyrenees claimed that they would "cut down two pines to make a pair of clogs."[14] The figures for the Midi were considerable in terms of the ravages wrought during the revolutionary decade, but no region of France was spared. From the departments of the Eure-et-Loire to the Côtes-du-Nord, from the Meurthe to the Jura, in Corrèze, as in the Nord, the deforestation was rife.[15] Whether the French Revolution and its legislation were the primary cause of deforestation in the many regions of France is a thorny issue, as Peter McPhee's study of Corbières in southern France during this crucial period attests.[16] Indeed, Denis Woronoff suggests that the Revolution accelerated a process that had already begun some years earlier, and he points to the effects of the royal edict of 1762 governing *défrichements,* which encouraged deforestation, as well physiocratic ideas, which favored agricultural development to the detriment of forests.[17]

At the end of the Terror many wished to revisit the question of the nation's forests and create a new forest administration that would deal with issues of management in the wake of the devastation they saw around them. After fits and starts, the deputies of the Five Hundred formed a commission of eight members in 1798 to write a new forest code. The commission's report recommended the return of the forest administration to the Ministry of the Interior's jurisdiction and that the state exert greater control over woodland auctions. Events on the ground, however, undermined the commission's proposals. Before they could be voted on, Napoleon and his co-conspirators overthrew the Directory on 18 Brumaire 1799.

※ ※ ※

IT WAS DURING the revolutionary decade that Jean-Baptiste Rougier de la Bergerie came of age and articulated, like Rauch, his diagnosis of the environmental ills afflicting France. Born in the same year as Rauch (1762) in what became the department of Indre, he argued that deforestation was central to understanding the environmental degradation that both he and Rauch observed. While Rauch's social origins were humble, and he rose only modestly through the ranks of Ponts et Chaussées, Rougier de la Bergerie became seigneur de Bléneau as a result of a fortuitous marriage to Cécile Haudry, the niece of a farmer-general (tax collector). He began his professional career as a lawyer in Paris before the Revolution, but early on took an avid interest in agricultural questions and presented his *Recherches sur les abus qui s'opposent aux progrès de l'agriculture* to Louis XVI in 1780, at the age of eighteen.[18] He was employed by his wife's uncle in 1785 and became a member of the Académie royale d'agriculture, replacing Buffon, in 1788. In 1790 he was president of the district of Saint-Fargeau, and was elected deputy a year later, joining the Comité d'agriculture. Rougier de la Bergerie thus came by his interest in the environment and the natural world through his engagement with agricultural questions. To this extent one might trace some of the roots of his thinking to physiocracy, and during the Revolution he also concerned himself with finance, the problem of émigrés, and social issues. After initially supporting the revolutionary legislation pertaining to forests, believing that private interests could manage forests better than the state, he changed his mind. He intervened frequently on the question of the alienation and administration of France's national forests, actively advocating for their conservation. He openly acknowledged the error of his ways after the Revolution, saying that "the revolution gave us the greatest benefits, liberty; it inspired a universal enthusiasm that made the epoch most memorable in the annals of all nations, but let us have the courage to admit, for we are in need of strong truths; it also developed to a great extent egoism and selfish motives, so contrary and fatal to the public good."[19] As early as 1795 he was having doubts and declared, "Would that the Convention soon take effective measures against the *devastation of woods and forests,* where, for a long time, there has also been *vandalism!*"[20] In short, referring to the "criminal lack of foresight" of the former government, the ignorance of landowners, and the constant search for arable land, he decried the disappearance of woodlands in France.[21] Rougier de la Bergerie's use of the word "vandalism" is telling in that during the Revolution it principally became associated with the destruction of France's religious and historical monuments, which prompted Abbé Grégoire to write three reports for the National Convention on the subject, including "Report on the Destruction Brought about by Vandalism, and the Means to Quell It."[22] The growing opposition to revolutionary "vandalism" and a new value placed on the concept of a cultural heritage or *patrimoine* ultimately led to the foundation of the Musée national des monuments français in 1795. While Rougier de la Bergerie, unlike Rauch, never referred to nature as a "living monument," his reference to vandalism reveals the germ of the concept in his own thinking, which foreshadowed legislation concerning "natural monuments" during the nineteenth century. It also indicated the possibility of extending the idea of heritage to the natural world.

While Rougier de la Bergerie was briefly a member of the Jacobin Club at the start of the Revolution, in 1791, there are no traces of him in the club's debates. He left Paris to tend to his estate in 1792, thereby escaping the worst excesses of the Terror, and he was helped in this by Lazare Carnot. In 1797 he founded *Annales de l'Agriculture Française* in which he published his reflections on the problem of deforestation during the French Revolution, *Mémoire et observations sur les abus des défrichement et la destruction des bois et forêts,* identifying himself as a member of the Institut national, the Lycée of the Yonne, and the agricultural societies of Paris and the departments of the Orne, Marne, and Doubs.[23]

Rougier de la Bergerie became prefect of the department of Yonne, a post he occupied for thirteen years. During that time he continued to be interested in agricultural questions and corresponded with the Académie des sciences. In 1815 he took up the post of prefect of the department of Nièvre, which he eventually ceded to his son. During the course of the revolutionary decade and the Napoleonic period he camouflaged the particle in his family name, shying away from any aristocratic associations. When his *Mémoire* first appeared in Auxerre in 1800, he published under the name Citizen Rougier-Labergerie, and only gradually reclaimed the particle in his name after he became a member of the Legion of Honor in 1804 and a baron of the empire in 1810.[24]

Like Rauch, Rougier de la Bergerie framed his work on deforestation in grandiose terms and pleaded for the protection of the environment from human intervention: "Are we finally at the moment when it will be possible to stop the devastating hand of man, [which is] everywhere degrading the soil of the uplands by disastrous and ill-considered clearings and destroying at the same time trees, wood, and forests which nature had made grow in profusion, and which made France the most fertile, salubrious, and happy country in the world?"[25] He acknowledged that France had emerged from centuries of barbarism, civil war, and various calamities caused by superstition, as well as from a period of considerable destructiveness with respect to its forests, which was brought on by what he considered to be the ill-considered policies of past governments, even though he himself had supported liberalization at the beginning of the French Revolution. He then concluded that reason had to be "the only guide for our laws and for the future."[26]

Rougier de la Bergerie echoed the civic indignation that came to be voiced as a result of the sale of forests during the French Revolution and pointed out that nowhere was the problem of deforestation more acute than in mountainous regions and in the Midi. Like many others, he held the myriad governments that came and went during the revolutionary decade responsible for the failure to set up any viable form of forest administration and to prevent deforestation. While he thought that the French monarchy should have been blamed as well, Rougier de la Bergerie was convinced that the French Revolution marked a crucial turning point in the unbridled exploitation of the nation's forests for several reasons. First, in their revolutionary zeal, the French populace conflated the end of feudalism with the right to dispose of individual property in whatever way an owner saw fit. Second, a law passed in 1793 authorized the dividing up of communal property, especially in the Midi. Third, under the provisions of the law of 22 August 1791, forested land belonging to an individual was no longer regulated by the forest administration.[27]

Rougier de la Bergerie compared France's management of its forests with that of Britain and Holland, where forests were in short supply, and he saw in the Midi a possible harbinger of the future for France as a whole in surveying the devastation in the Basses-Alpes, Bouches-du-Rhône, Isère, Gard, Lozère, Aude, Ardèche, Ariège, Pyrénées-Orientales, Basses-Pyrénées,

Hautes-Pyrénées, and Haute-Garonne. Even in heavily forested departments such as Haut-Rhin and the Vosges, the effects of deforestation were, according to him, keenly felt. The culprit everywhere was the agricultural practice of *écobouage,* which involved the burning of vegetation and topsoil to prepare the ground for fertilization and cultivation, and which he considered to be the bane of France. He cited the following proverb: "If écobouage enriches the father, it ruins the son."[28] Rougier de la Bergerie paid particular attention to his own department, Yonne, and saw deforestation to be the consequence of both agricultural development and urbanization.

Rougier de la Bergerie ultimately considered the French Revolution to be a double-edged sword. It gave birth to positive forces that contributed to the public good, while at the same time encouraging egoism and a self-interested spirit of calculation, which were contrary to the public good: "It is thus that for the past ten years, quite apart from the needs created by war, we have seen enormous landed riches either destroyed or falling into the possession of a few individuals, which Nature and the social order had created and preserved only for the good of all men."[29] For him everyone should regard the act of conservation and restoration as a "religious and sacred duty."[30] He made a case for environmental conservation in the name of progress and development, arguing that the fate of big cities and the state "essentially depends on the conservation of cultivated land, on their rivers, on their forests, on the sustenance and even progress of agriculture."[31] In essence, he made an appeal to the state, whose charge included encouraging the progress of industry and commerce as well as maintaining an equilibrium in the relationship between cities and the countryside. In short, he regarded the conservation of forests as an essential duty. In his view, the governments of a republic had to watch over its patrimony, "repair disasters, and work for the happiness of future generations."[32] For him, "the landscape" was a "vast theatre on which every state offers scenes of happiness, of misery or of abjection," and these scenes were directly influenced by how it managed the land.[33]

In many respects Rougier de la Bergerie's *Mémoire* prepared the way for his "Projet d'organisation forestière," which he prefaced with the preamble of Colbert's 1669 ordinance. His project, which consisted of thirty-three articles, proposed provisionally banning all forest clearance and revoking the dispositions of the 1791 law which exempted privately owned forests from policing by the forest administration. He proposed a rigorous ban on the sale of the nation's forests; measures to encourage the planting of trees and the lowering of taxes on forested land. He advocated the creation of the position of *conservateur général* for six years, who would have the rank and salary of a minister, working with the first consul, and whose residence would always be close to the helm of power. In addition, he envisioned the simultaneous naming of thirty-two *conservateurs,* each of whom would be responsible for administering a forest division, and a retinue of sixty-four traveling general inspectors.[34] In short, he called for the creation of a new forest service.

Following the publication of a 465-page work on the history of French agriculture in 1815, Citizen Rougier-Labergerie published a more generalized work on the forests of France under the name Baron Rougier de la Bergerie in 1817, identifying himself as a former member of the Royal Society of Agriculture in Paris and a former prefect. *Les forêts de la France, leurs rapports avec les climats, la température et l'ordre des saisons; avec la prospérité de l'agriculture et de l'industrie* was more ambitious in scope when placed alongside his *Mémoire* of 1800.[35] While he still regarded the French Revolution as a turning point, he no longer saw it as a double-edged sword, at once destructive and liberating. Although the Revolution created a new reservoir of property owners, it unleashed some devastating effects with respect to France's forests. Rougier de la Bergerie presented an overview of forest legislation, choosing the seventeenth century as his point of departure. He set out to prove, first, that for more than a century the forests and rivers of France lacked an equilibrium that was necessary for maintaining climatic equilibrium and stable temperatures. Second, he advanced the thesis that forest clearance had become so extreme that there was no longer a moment to lose for coordinating legislation that would correct what had already occurred and prevent further degradation. Third, he set out to show that *forêts du domaine* were in imminent danger of becoming private property, and that this land constituted what could be protected for future generations by a "special magistrature."[36]

In considering France's forest administration since 1800, Rougier de la Bergerie noted that as first consul, Napoleon allowed his ministers of finance and of the interior to ignore the problem of deforestation and the reports of prefects concerning the environmental effects of the French Revolution.[37] According to him, for Napoleon's ministers forests were considered only as financial resources and were used as such. Indeed, he even went so far as to say, "How Albion must have been delighted by this new depletion."[38] He painted a very pessimistic view of whatever there was of a forest administration, while presenting clear testimony from prefects and observers throughout France regarding the effects of deforestation. Rougier de la Bergerie revitalized the old warning about the effect of vegetation on climate and temperature, a subject that was dear to Buffon, Franklin, Priestley, and other eighteenth-century writers, while suggesting measures to be taken to halt the process of deforestation.

Rougier de la Bergerie's exhortations fell on deaf ears, but after the failure of various revolutionary governments to create a new and viable forest administration during the French Revolution, Napoleon ironically, given Rougier de la Bergerie's criticism of him, did so in one fell swoop only two months after he assumed power. He did so for pragmatic reasons. As Kieko Matteson has argued, the Revolution had thus come full circle in terms of forest policy. After "having initially championed the decentralization of forest oversight, concerned legislators now sought to reinstate the 1669 Ordinance, or at least its powerful controls."[39] For Napoleon, this reflected his broader aim of strengthening and centralizing the organs of the state as well as assuring a steady supply of timber. The new woodland administration was established by decree on 16 nivôse, year 9 (6 January 1801) and consisted of five superintendents, thirty *conservateurs,* three hundred subinspectors, and eighty-five hundred guards, who were under the supervision of the Ministry of Finance. In addition, for military and strategic reasons, the Consulate and the Empire sought to limit clearing in privately owned woods in the law of 9 floréal, year 11 (29 April 1803), which imposed a twenty-five-year moratorium on unauthorized clearing.[40]

※ ※ ※

THE NAPOLEONIC DECREE and legislation did not fully satisfy critics, commentators, and advocates, who continued to decry the extent to which France was losing its forests. Many came forward in the immediate post-Napoleonic period to present new proposals for environmental reform and to comment on the state of France's forests. One such commentator was the adventurer and statistician Alexandre Moreau de Jonnès. A rather colorful character on the eighteenth- and nineteenth-century French political stage, he enrolled in the National Guard on the side of the Revolution at the age of thirteen and a half. He spent some years in the Antilles before returning to France to compile statistics for the French state and wrote on a number of different topics.[41] He was, however, particularly interested in demography, climate, and the Antilles, as a result of the years that he spent there.[42]

Moreau de Jonnès shared Rougier de la Bergerie's concerns about deforestation and in 1825 wrote a more generalized tract in response to a question posed by the Royal Academy of Brussels: What are the changes that substantial deforestation can effect? He won the gold medal for the *mémoire,* and argued that deforestation had a major effect on air quality, the direction and power of winds, and rainfall.[43] He went further than Rougier de la Bergerie in suggesting that the "torrent of revolutions" had caused the "last vestiges of the old forests of Europe to disappear, almost entirely."[44]

He contended that in France approximately one-twelfth of the territory was once covered by forests. Forests, according to him, affected temperature, the quantity and quality of rainfall, humidity, the source and state of rivers, the quality of the air, the soil, and the social state of peoples. He subscribed to the view that deforestation led to rising temperatures and that these atmospheric changes were greater in temperate zones than in tropical zones.[45] While he saw the devastation of forests to be most pervasive in Mediterranean Europe, he regarded the problem as one that affected the European continent as a whole.

Like Rauch, Moreau de Jonnès believed that forests played the triple role of "conserving, increasing and developing the soil's fertility."[46] Like Rauch, he also did not limit his analysis to France, but undertook a survey of the forests of the world. He argued that their destruction in mountainous and coastal areas would lead to environmental devastation and that the "shortage of wood is an irreparable calamity": "Woodland has exerted since the earth's infancy a powerful influence on the human species, its mores, its customs, its habitation, and its labor."[47] For Moreau de Jonnès, "the more countries are covered with forests, the closer they are to the primitive state of the globe," and the more they are deforested, the more they resemble the world's last days, giving the examples of the deserts of Africa and the steps of Upper Asia.[48]

Moreau de Jonnès's ideas bore some resemblance to those advanced by correspondents and associates of the Museum of Natural History during the French Revolution and of the Académie des sciences.[49] The great eighteenth-century naturalist Buffon had reflected on climate change and was optimistic about humanity's power to control the climate and temperatures. He offered proof in the fact that Paris was at the same latitude as Quebec, and yet Paris was warmer because it had fewer trees and a larger population.[50] Buffon did not advocate an unmitigated protection of forested areas, because he believed that it was important to increase the earth's temperature in some places, as human life could not exist without heat. At the same time, he thought that forests conserved moisture for human cultivation and husbandry. Buffon wished to create balances in nature, and while he advocated deforestation in the New World, he maintained that forests should be conserved in the Old.[51] In short, he believed that "large areas inimical to man had to be cleared to make the earth habitable, but once societies were established on them, the forests were resources which had to be treated with care and foresight."[52] Even in the eighteenth century the French monarchy, under the influence of these ideas, began to set up tree nurseries throughout France and in its colonies and embarked on significant projects of large-scale tree planting.[53]

The Royal Academy in Brussels considered Moreau de Jonnès's findings to be significant, and it commissioned a synoptic report on them. C. F. de Nieuport commended the *mémoire* but ended his analysis with a discussion of the utilitarian and strategic implications of the phenomenon of deforestation in Europe. He pointed to Moreau de Jonnès's signaling the "disadvantages that already weigh on our continent, and those that threaten in the not too distant future, if the improvidence of governments continue not to prevent them."[54] He then referred to Moreau de Jonnès's contention that in the space of a century Europe's navies and industries consumed more forested land than France possessed, and that already a shortage was felt from the Manche to the Adriatic and from Guadalquivir to the Rhine. He asked whether naval powers in the Old World would disappear and the "new continents" might come to dominate them in the future.[55]

M. Bosson, a pharmacist from Mantes-sur-Seine in the department of Seine-et-Oise, was the silver medalist in the Royal Academy of Brussels's essay prize competition, and his reflection on the issue was published alongside that of Moreau de Jonnès in the same year. The fact that he was a pharmacist in provincial France revealed the extent to which the debate concerning deforestation had gradually trickled down and out from the capital and involved a broader public.[56] It also showed the extent to which Rauch's writings had reached a larger reading public, as Bosson's *mémoire* made specific references to Rauch's earlier work. In 17 pages, as opposed to Moreau de Jonnès's 196, he described how the continent of Europe had slowly lost its "immense and thick forests" with the coming of humankind and why it was of "high importance" to watch over the conservation of the "great plantations," known as wood and forests.[57] Like Moreau de Jonnès, he argued that the existence of forests, or their absence, could change the temperature of a large territory. Drawing on Rauch's *Annales Européennes,* he concluded that deforestation resulted in the great variations observed in the atmosphere, the irregularity of the seasons, and damaging winds, especially those from the north, and that it had disastrous effects in terms of flooding and the disappearance of springs and rivers.[58] Those charged with the *analyse synoptique,* who were not named, ended with a warning to governments to the effect that it was almost impossible to reverse the damage wrought by deforestation once it was well under way.

※ ※ ※

DEMANDS FOR governmental intervention were evident in the analyses of Rougier de la Bergerie, Moreau de Jonnès, and the pharmacist Bosson. Rougier de la Bergerie and Moreau de Jonnès, in particular, saw a moment of opportunity for embarking on a new course in the founding of a new regime, the Bourbon Restoration, after the fall of Napoleon in 1815. During the French Consulate the decree passed on 15 nivôse, year 11 had created a new forest administration, but in incorporating some of the forest reforms of 1791 and proposals advanced between 1796 and 1799, its ten articles did not clearly address the issue of reforestation or the need to regulate private landowners.

After the fall of Napoleon and the establishment of the Bourbon Restoration, Louis XVIII reorganized the forest administration with a royal ordinance on 22 January 1817, but there were still calls for the implementation of a new forest code and a reorganized system of management, which finally came to fruition in the late 1820s, three years after the creation of the Ecole nationale forestière (Ecole de Nancy) in 1824, which was established to train a new generation of forest officials. The French were guided by German practices and techniques in this regard, and Jacques-Joseph Baudrillart, a forest administrator, was largely responsible for drawing attention to the German model. He published two translations of German forestry manuals, in 1805 and 1808, respectively.[59] When the school opened its doors in January 1825, its director, an Alsatian, Bernard Lorentz, made certain that the curriculum was solidly based on German practices and ideas.[60]

On 29 December 1826 Jean-Baptiste de Martignac told the Chamber of Deputies, "Today we find ourselves between the incoherent remains of an old legislation, the Ordinance of 1669, whose foundation has been overturned, and the beginnings of a new legislation, which was left in rough outline and was never completed," referring to it as a "fragmented legislation."[61] The new code, which was passed by the Chamber of Deputies and the Chamber of Peers on 21 May 1827 and promulgated by the king on 31 July, limited the restrictions that the 1669 ordinance placed on individual property owners. A proposed ban on the clearance of privately owned forests for cultivation resulted in long and passionate debates. In spite of the experience of the French Revolution, the chambers adopted provisions that banned clearance only temporarily, as nothing was "more respectable than the right of property."[62] Indeed, Martignac hoped that liberty to dispose of forested land would be restored except in mountainous areas.

The new code provided for a forest administration that would consist of *conservateurs, inspecteurs,* and *sous-inspecteurs* as well as *gardes généraux* and *gardes généraux adjoints* who were drawn from a corps of foresters trained at the Ecole de Nancy and placed first under the jurisdiction of the Ministry of Finance and then, in 1877, under the Ministry of Agriculture and Commerce. The number of agents fluctuated during the course of the nineteenth century. Their number increased, for example, from 701 in 1846 to 786 in 1875, only to fall to 774 in 1905.[63] They were first and foremost in charge of state forests; however, they also had authority over communal and even privately owned forests, but within the proscribed limits of the forest code.

German forestry had a significant impact on the development of silvicultural systems in France in the nineteenth century. German states had already begun to found schools of silviculture in the eighteenth century, and a whole generation of French foresters became acquainted with them subsequently with the invasion of central Europe and the occupation of the left bank of the Rhine during the French Revolution and Napoleonic periods. Moreover, some of the early leadership of the forest administration hailed from Alsace, including Bernard Lorentz and his son-in-law Adolphe Parade, and long before the founding of the Ecole de Nancy many had lobbied for its creation.[64]

This new corps of foresters gradually established ties with other governmental agents, scientists, and property owners, and they began to wield influence, as did an emerging "forest lobby," with the establishment of *Les Annales Forestières et Métallurgiques* in 1842. From 1844, *conférences forestières,* which were attended by forestry agents, engineers, scientists, and property owners, began to be held on a regular basis, and their debates found their way into *Annales Forestières,* which was absorbed into a new publication, *Revue des Eaux et Forêts,* in 1862.

The reorganization of forest administration in France and the esprit de corps that it created gave rise to a new set of practices, a "new contract between Man and Nature," which was predicated on centralized state control.[65] Indeed, the Napoleonic Civil Code as well as the forest code began to reshape French society's relationship to this natural resource. The value placed on private property since the promulgation of the Civil Code raised the issue of how natural spaces could or should be protected and conserved for the public interest, and how their protection by the state could be reconciled with private interests. The forest administration became the principal spokesman for the fight against "egoism" and "individualism" and the sanctity of private individual property, which were safeguarded by the Civil Code. Its goal was to educate the public about the importance of forest conservation, as the introduction to the first issue of *Annales Forestières* attested: "It is to spread and popularize ideas about the forest, until now generally ignored by the public and ignored with indifference; it is in some way to call for the country itself to educate itself in new ways, but belatedly, and whose necessity is all the more pressing as it is less valued."[66]

The primary purpose of the new administration was *aménagement* (forest management or development) for specific purposes, which might include the procurement of firewood or timber, or soil and tree protection through silviculture, the art and science of cultivating trees. In short, the forest administration existed to grow and manage forests. In spite of the implementation of the new code, however, and perhaps because of its shortcomings, Rougier de la Bergerie's barely veiled 1817 plea to address these issues remained unanswered, and he reiterated them after the July Revolution of 1830 and the establishment of the July Monarchy.[67]

Rougier de la Bergerie's 1831 *Mémoire* was even more pessimistic than that of 1817, and he reminded his audience that for the past forty years he had presented various *mémoires* and studies regarding the role of forests and their importance for society to legislatures, the government, and science academies in France and abroad. However, for him the "indifference of statesmen, legislatures, and *savants en physique* to matters of public necessity, reveals a very unfortunate state of affairs which the whole of society must deplore."[68] He sarcastically observed that these very same men boasted that they acted in the name of the public interest and the sacred fire of liberty, but with regard to the question of France's *eaux et forêts* the country's very existence was under threat. In his view, statesmen and learned men in the eighteenth century were infinitely more engaged in observing and studying nature in terms of the needs of society—activities which, in his view, were absent among similar figures in the early nineteenth century.[69]

The event that galvanized Rougier de la Bergerie into writing his new *mémoire* was the debate in the Chamber of Deputies about the possibility of selling off 300,000 hectares of forested land that belonged to the state in order to raise revenue quickly. Faced with such initiatives and the often ineffective efforts of the new forest service, a legislative proposal was put forward in the Chamber of Peers on 30 January 1843 regarding reforestation in mountainous areas, a concern that came to the fore as a national preoccupation for the first time.[70] However, opposition from numerous mayors in France, whose communes would necessarily assume some of the expense, put a brake on the legislation, and the Chamber of Deputies never issued a report on the subject. While Rougier de la Bergerie's dream of forest reform was never fully realized in his lifetime, he was instrumental in keeping alive the debate about deforestation, and the subject was taken up by Antoine-César Becquerel only a few years later, as well as by François Arago (1786–1853), who contributed significantly to the new science of meteorology.

※ ※ ※

ANTOINE-CÉSAR BECQUEREL was thirty years younger than Rougier de la Bergerie, and he came of age after the Revolution. Born in Châtillon-Coligny in 1788, he became a respected scientist who founded a veritable scientific dynasty.[71] A graduate of the Ecole polytechnique, he became known for his work in applied physics, but took an early amateur interest in the relationship between forests and climate change, publishing two works on the subject in the 1850s and 1860s. His engagement came from his work in his role as chair of applied physics at the Museum of Natural History, where he served for forty years (1838–1878). From 1848 he was charged by the Conseil général of the Loiret with giving an annual report on the *regénération* of the Sologne. By 1853 he was a member of the Academy of Sciences and the Institut de France, as well as a professor at the museum and a member of the Royal Society of London and the Berlin Academy, and he published his first work on the effect of forests on climate: *Des climats et de l'influence qu'exercent les sols boisés et non boisés*.[72] Becquerel ambitiously surveyed forested and deforested parts of the globe and cited the differing views of Arago and Joseph Louis Gay-Lussac on the subject in 1836, when a commission was established to consider article 219 of the 1827 forest code. During the debate the two scientists held opposite views on the effects of deforestation in France. Arago claimed that the removal of the curtain of trees along the coastline of Normandy and Brittany would lead to warmer winters from temperate winds emanating from the sea, while their removal in eastern France would have the opposite effect, resulting in colder temperatures. Gay-Lussac, in contrast, argued that there was no positive proof that forests had a real impact on climate. In his own study on the subject some years later, Becquerel drew on his earlier work on the Sologne, and he ostensibly attempted to set aside any prejudice.

In the first part of the study he explored the different conditions affecting temperature and climate around the world before turning his attention to France and Algeria. Part two focused on a historical survey of the evolution of world's forests, beginning with Hindustan, which he alleged was the cradle of civilization, before comparing the relationship between climates in the past and the present and discussing the nature of the influence of deforestation on climate. He used, in particular, Alfred Maury's *L'histoire des grandes forêts de la Gaule et de l'ancienne France* as a basis for his survey, before examining the causes of deforestation.[73] Becquerel attributed deforestation globally to four main causes: war; the progress of civilization; land use practices, including grazing and industries that use wood; and legislation that was insufficient in terms of preventing abuses.[74] For France, he cited the 29 September 1791 law, which remained in force until 1803, pointing out that during that time 50,000 hectares of forested land were cleared for cultivation, which averaged 4,545 per year. While the 1827 forest code reinstated many elements that were part of the 1669 ordinance, individual property owners could still, in his view, exploit forested land as they wished, as long as they did not clear it for cultivation, which had nonetheless led to the transformation of France's forested landscapes.[75]

Becquerel argued that the effects of deforestation had been significant, resulting in lower water levels in lakes and ponds and diminution in rainfall. At the same time, he suggested, as did those who became increasingly concerned with flooding, that deforestation contributed to the increase in the number of torrents and flash floods in mountainous areas, citing two recent works on the subject by Alexandre Surell, an engineer working for the Ponts et Chaussées, and by a mining engineer.[76]

Becquerel finally tackled the question of the effect of deforestation on climate change, which, as he posited, could be assessed by observing barometrical and temperature variations as well as humidity and the direction and force of wind and rainfall during different seasons of the year. He concluded that forests had a cooling effect with respect to climate and that they served to prevent environmental degradation in mountainous regions and to improve air quality, guarding against "dangerous miasmas."[77] In invoking the danger of miasma, Becquerel drew on the ideas of an earlier generation of public hygienists in France, including the first holder of a chair in public hygiene, who was appointed at the height of the French Revolution, in 1794.[78] Their work gave rise to a host of decrees and legislation aimed at curbing pollution and improving air quality as well as preventing disease and contagion put in place from the French Revolution onward. The Conseil de salubrité du département de la Seine was created on 7 July 1802, and the Institut de France proposed a list of dangerous and insalubrious work sites.[79]

Anxieties and concerns about air quality and its link to disease, especially after the great cholera epidemics of 1832, fed into the new science of climatology, as the work of Becquerel and his son attests. Joseph-Jean-Nicolas Fuster (1801–1876), a physician born in Perpignan who became a professor of medicine and the physician in chief at the Hôtel-Dieu in Montpellier, explored the impact of climate on disease in his 1840 *Des maladies de la France dans leurs rapports avec les saisons, ou histoire médicale et météorologique de la France,* and five years later undertook a study without his own empirical data, but drawing on those of others (something Becquerel would have shied away from) in writing *Des changements dans le climat: Histoire des révolutions météorologiques.*[80] He affirmed that the climate in France had changed considerably since ancient times, and devoted the fourth part of the work to its causes, which included war, conquest, and population increase.

The effect of deforestation on humidity and changes in temperature had, of course, been a scientific preoccupation since the eighteenth century, as the work of the Comte de Buffon attests, and it was one shared by foresters and scholars, who studied the French case closely. What changed in the nineteenth century was the extent to which the French public became engaged in the debate and reforestation turned into a public obsession. Even the Scotsman John Croumbie Brown, who was an honorary vice president of the African Institute in Paris, studied the French case closely, publishing *Reboisement in France; or, Records of the Replanting of the Alps, the Cevennes, and the Pyrenees with Trees, Herbage and Bush, with a View to Arresting and Preventing the Destructive Consequences and Effects of Torrents* in 1876 and *Forests and Moisture: or Effects of Forests on the Humidity of Climate* in 1877. Drawing on the work of a wide array of French scholars, engineers, and foresters, he argued that it was "incontrovertible" that the destruction of forests "has occasioned the drying up of springs, and that the replanting of woods has been followed by their reappearance."[81] The views expressed by the forest administration echoed many of these assessments. This was reflected in the introduction to the first issue of *Revue des Eaux et Forêts* in 1862: "It is not only as productive agents that one must see forests. If one wants to have the exact measure of their importance and the role they have on the play of our economic forces, it is necessary to see how they exert a happy influence on climate and water systems."[82]

The need for state intervention was increasingly voiced by forest officials. Jules Clavé, a forest official who also wrote for the *Revue des Deux Mondes*, argued in 1862 that only the state was "capable of conserving the *patrimoine forestier.*"[83] It was these kinds of assessments and conclusions that gave rise to a project undertaken by the state under Napoleon III to reforest the mountainous regions of France in the 1860s. This project was embodied in the laws of 28 July 1860 and 9 June 1864, which provided for the reforestation of mountainous areas in the Alps, the Pyrenees, and the center of the country over a period of ten years. While Brown attributed these initiatives to a period of political stability after the tumultuous years following the French Revolution—two coups d'état and two revolutions—the formation and coming of age of a new forestry service, pressure exerted by engineers in the face of floods, and new studies of the problem of deforestation also played important roles in the successful passage of the legislation.

The 28 July 1860 law was the first significant step taken by the French state to reforest large areas of France, and it was the brainchild of Eugène

Chevandier de Valdrôme, a liberal engineer who helped to draw up how the law would function and be financed in fourteen articles. The law applied to communal property, private property, and public entities and provided for voluntary and mandatory replanting, for expropriation in some cases, and for subsidies. "Public utility" was invoked as a justifying principle, though it was vaguely defined, and private property owners' forested land was subject to expropriation "by reason of public utility" in cases in which they did not reforest it themselves. If private owners' land was expropriated, they would receive an indemnity, but they could regain their property if they reimbursed the state for the indemnity as well as for costs.[84] The needs of pastoral populations were more or less ignored by the new law.

The law of 28 July 1860 was ambitious in calling into question the rights of property owners who wished to resist a law passed in the name of the public or collective interest, but it was ill received by pastoral groups and peasants. The potential for resistance had already been evident when the forest code was passed in 1827, when there was an almost immediate increase in forest crimes and violations, and a full-scale revolt erupted in the Ariège that lasted for three years. The so-called War of the Demoiselles, which began in 1829 and ended in 1832, constituted a collective attempt to reclaim the forests from both forest guards and private property owners. Disguising themselves as women, the demoiselles attacked the guards and charcoal makers with relative impunity until the revolt was finally brought under control.[85]

In 1829, the year the War of the Demoiselles began, Frédéric Le Play, the conservative and paternalist author of *Les ouvriers européennes* (1855) and *La réforme sociale en France* (1864), began to study the effect of different kinds of environments on social organization. For him, forests had an important role to play in the lives of the individuals and communities that inhabited them. While he deplored the process of deforestation, on which many others had commented, he paid close attention to the relationship between local populations and the forests in which they lived and worked. He supported efforts undertaken by the state to stem the tide of deforestation, but he believed that the project could not fully succeed unless it was accompanied by a "policy of restoring the wise practices and sentiments that our ruling classes worked hard to destroy for two centuries."[86] Part of this project could be achieved only by fostering the human communities that the forest contained rather than banishing them: "Where human stock is fatally uprooted in each generation, how will vegetal stock be saved?"[87] Le Play specifically valorized a peopled landscape shaped by tradition and history. In this sense he did not separate the need to reforest in mountainous regions from the fate of pastoral populations, as many in the forest administration appeared to do.

Le Play's influence began to make itself felt among some forest officials and social observers, however. They included the Comte de Gasparin, minister of the interior during the July Monarchy and a member of the Academy of Sciences; Charles Dupin, minister of the navy and also a member of the Academy of Sciences; Comte Albert de Saint-Léger, *conseiller général* of the Nièvre and cofounder (with Dupin) of the Société forestière; and Jacques-Alexandre Bixio, a cofounder of the *Revue des Deux Mondes* and *La maison rustique du XIXe siècle*. He also had his followers among lesser-known figures who participated in discussions concerning deforestation.

One of Le Play's most ardent disciples was Charles de Ribbe (1827–1899), another social conservative, a lawyer who was born in Aix-en-Provence. He observed the effects of deforestation in southern France firsthand. He met Le Play in 1857 and published his first work on the problem of "torrents" in the Basses-Alpes in the same year.[88] While he supported the law of 28 July 1860, he believed that it could be implemented in a way that would respect human settlements to a greater extent. In his view, their gradual disappearance could lead to a greater number of forest fires, which increasingly ravaged the region.[89]

Some of de Ribbe's observations were echoed by those living in other parts of France. Zéphirin Jouyne, a lawyer from the town of Digne in the French Alps, had published his *Reboisement des montagnes* eight years before.[90] His early interest in agriculture, which is reflected in his *Vues sur l'agriculture des Basses-Alpes et des départements méridionaux*, led him to turn his attention to the issues of deforestation and reforestation.[91] Citing Rauch's *Régénération de la nature végétale*, he declared that in the past twenty-five years "reforestation had become a vital question" and that many in France had become convinced that it was the means by which the nation would be turned into a "terrestrial paradise."[92] However, being a member of the Société centrale d'agriculture des Basses-Alpes, he was aware of the possible difficulties of passing legislation, which was proposed several years earlier, in 1847, as such legislation could threaten the livelihood of those who depended on pasturage. He proceeded to cast doubt on the scientific premises of Rauch and others, making an argument for a more carefully considered program for reforestation that would take into account local populations, even though a myriad of initiatives had been proposed and undertaken to reforest and replant vegetation in the Isère, the High Alps, the Low Alps, the Drôme, Gard, Hérault, Aude, and the high Pyrenees, which Brown and others saw as preventing floods and maintaining moisture in the atmosphere.[93]

Given this skepticism and resistance, how effective was the 28 July 1860 reforestation law? There was evident and widespread hostility to the law from Alpine communes, and François Combes, who had been chief of Alpine restoration in Savoie, wrote that nineteenth-century reforestation projects were "born of a misunderstanding"—notably about planting at higher elevations and the capacity of forests to absorb water.[94] Foresters did not embark on the study of the effects of altitude on vegetation until the first quarter of the twentieth century in spite of the existence of works on the subject in the nineteenth century, including Alexander von Humboldt's *Essai sur la géographie des plantes* of 1807.

By the beginning of the Third Republic, a governmental report was commissioned to assess the law's efficacy and to determine whether it should be renewed. Eugène Tallon, a center-right deputy of Puy-de-Dôme, who presented the report, emphasized the beneficial effects of the legislation, but he criticized the arbitrary and authoritarian way it was implemented. He remarked that this had resulted in resistance and complaints that were in many cases well founded because the legislation had in some cases led to widespread expropriation, insufficient indemnities, and misery among pastoral groups.[95] While Tallon supported the law's renewal, he called for its modification, which included suppressing obligatory reforestation on communal and privately owned land and raising the amount of monetary indemnities provided. Forest officials remained divided among *étatistes*, who supported the legislation passed in 1860 and 1864, followers of Le Play, and, on the other end of the spectrum, those who supported a more liberal law. A revised and more liberal law was finally adopted in 1882 in spite of the violent protests of Louis Tassy, a revered member of the forest service, and Gabriel Demontzey, who was one of the principal architects of the project of reforestation in the Basses-Alpes during the 1860s.[96] Reforestation as a project was ultimately rebranded as "restoration," which implied returning a tract of land to an anterior state. Restauration des Terrains en Montagne, or RTM was thus born and by 1890 absorbed nearly one-quarter of the forest service's annual budget.[97]

While reforestation measures undertaken in the 1860s and 1880s were primarily designed to prevent floods and regulate the climate, the state's mission assumed a very different and particular form in the Landes of Gascony. There, the purpose of reforestation, or simply forestation, was to arrest sand drift and preserve the coastline.[98] These initiatives began as early as the French Revolution when Nicholas-Théodore Brémontier published a *mémoire* on the formation of sand dunes and on steps the state needed to take to arrest the erosion of the coastline; it was originally commissioned by Jacques Necker before the outbreak of the French Revolution.[99] Brémontier's pivotal study was followed by a host of others that continued to be published well into the Third Republic.[100]

The lack of trees in the sand wastes of France began to be perceived as presenting very specific environmental problems, even if these denuded areas were not the result of human intervention. The British writer Charles Richard Weld left a striking description of the drifting sand and sand dunes in the Landes of Gascony during the nineteenth century. The Landes comprised 600 hectares (1,482,600 acres) of what he described as "endless sand" and "interminable wastes"; the area's population lived lives that were "short, feverish and sickly" as a result of bad water and the existence of malaria.[101] The Landes was the subject of a chapter in Arthur Mangin's 1866 *Le désert et le monde sauvage*, in which he provided one of the most detailed early descriptions of what came to be referred to as "the Dunes" or sand hills which formed the "extreme line of the Brittany coast for nearly two hundred miles, from the Adour to the Garonne."[102] These dunes constantly shifted, as there was nothing to hold the sand in place, and measures were finally taken to plant pine trees to hold the soil at the beginning of the French Revolution, in 1789, under the direction of Jacques Necker. This was followed, twelve years later, by a decree on 13 messidor, year 9 (2 July 1801), that provided for the planting of trees along the coast of Gascony under the stewardship of Brémontier and the prefect of the newly created department of Gironde. The legislation governing the plantations of the Landes was extended to all maritime regions by a decree on 14 December 1814, after Napoleon's abdication and exile to Elba. Article 1 stipulated that "in the maritime departments there shall be taken measures for the sowing, the plantation, and the culture of vegetables known to be the most suitable for the fixation of the Dunes."[103] In essence, the decree provided a future framework for plantations under the supervision of prefectures and engineers from the Ponts et Chaussées. This work was interrupted for obvious reasons by the Hundred Days, the defeat of Napoleon at Waterloo, and the transition to the new Bourbon Restoration. Two years into the new regime, on 5 February 1817, an ordinance was issued for the fixation of the Dunes in Gironde and the Landes, which would be undertaken by the director general of the Ponts et Chaussées and the Ministry of the Interior at a cost of not more than 90,000 francs for the two departments. In 1862 the work was transferred to the control of the minister of finance and overseen by the forest administration before it was finally completed.

The concerns about deforestation and its effect on the environment were voiced then with increasing stridency during the course of the nineteenth century, and they reflected a broad range of concerns. The forest administration that was established by Colbert and dismantled during the French Revolution had long articulated its mission in terms of the need to conserve forests as natural resources for productive purposes. When a new forest code was established in 1827, forest officials expressed their defense of France's forests in similar terms. However, as the century wore on, deforestation was invoked to explain a variety of environmental ills, which included climate change, disease, flooding, and eroding coastlines. In addition, the social sphere of those calling for the conservation and replanting of France's forests expanded to include not only forest officials associated with the forest administration and engineers from the Ponts et Chaussées but a wider public. By midcentury a debate was under way concerning which forested landscapes should be protected from clearing and development—mountains and plains—and if a public interest outweighed the claims of private property, as enshrined in the Civil Code. Moreover, Le Play and his followers raised the question of whether the protection of a forested landscape or reforestation projects would take the local inhabitants into account. Were these forested areas to be peopled or unpeopled? In what instances should they be protected, and how? And how was deforestation related to a series of floods that appeared to be occurring with greater frequency as the century wore on? They constituted a new set of questions that would be asked and answered in varying ways from the 1840s to the coming of World War I.

As the work of Rougier de la Bergerie, Moreau de Jonnès, and Becquerel, among others, indicates, the link between forests and water systems became increasingly clear during the course of the nineteenth century, and engineers associated with the Ponts et Chaussées were particularly aware of this link, as Rauch's early writings suggest. By 1898 Jules Méline, the minister of agriculture, decreed that the state's forest administration would officially perform its functions within the Eaux et Forêts. He justified this reorganization in the following terms: "Waters and forests are two terms united by a relationship of cause and effect, two words which, joined together, seemed in former times to form but one. Forever have we instinctively felt that a close link of reciprocal dependence existed [between waters and forests], and that independently of material products furnished [by them], forests rendered services of the highest order by regulating atmospheric waters and regularizing the flow of springs, streams and rivers."[104]

THREE

The Torrents of the Nineteenth Century

> Why, how is it that in our day, in the heart of the nineteenth century, when the sciences and the arts have made immense progress, how is it that floods are so frequent and so widespread?
> —Charles Chauvelot

Alphonse de Lamartine, the poet-deputy who actively participated in the Revolution of 1848, penned a poem following the devastating floods that afflicted France in 1840:

> On the foaming banks of rivers
> Which roll out waves and cries,
> The old, children, widows
> Cry about the wreckage of their homes;
>   the tops of trees are refuge
> Over which man fights with the birds
> And the mournful voice of the deluge
> Is slowly extinguished by the water.[1]

After a torrential rainfall that resulted in extensive damage in the Rhône valley and cost the lives of several hundred people, Lamartine's poem was set to music by the popular composer Daniel Auber and performed in Paris for the benefit of the flood's victims.[2] Between 1740 and 1910 France witnessed a long series of floods. They occurred with such frequency and ferocity that scientists, governmental officials, and commentators of all kinds sought to analyze their underlying causes, to document their stages, to control them, to prevent their recurrence, to mitigate their damage, and to provide new warning systems for the future. During this 170-year period the four major rivers of France—the Seine, Rhône, Loire, and Garonne—overflowed their banks, engulfing countless towns and villages. In some places they also destroyed rich agricultural land. This repeated occurrence contributed to considerable soul-searching, particularly in a period in which the French, and Europeans more generally, prided themselves on their scientific advancements and on the power of technology to master nature. One commentator wrote with some concern in 1856, a year during which France experienced one of its worst floods in modern memory, that such disasters generally occurred every 100 years. For this reason he asked how it was that they now appeared to be occurring every ten years in the "heart of the nineteenth century," making a reference to the prevalent contemporary confidence in technological and scientific advances for harnessing the power of the natural world.[3]

Natural disasters such as earthquakes, hurricanes, floods, and tidal waves are physical phenomena with human, political, economic, social, cultural, and psychological consequences. The French term for them in the nineteenth and twentieth centuries was *calamité publique,* which constituted a kind of "natural cataclysm," as a French dictionary defined them, which could include cyclones, tornadoes, storms, floods, landslides, avalanches, and explosions. By their very nature they presupposed the absence of the direct hand of humans, though there was an increasing awareness that human alteration of the physical environment could create the conditions for such disasters. They became the subject of growing concern during the course of the nineteenth century. Indeed, the nineteenth century witnessed an outpouring of books and pamphlets on floods, the most voluminous of which was Maurice Champion's six-volume documentation of the history of flooding as a recurring natural phenomenon in France from the earliest historical records to the great flood of 1856.[4] While this work presented a valuable narrative account of flooding as a hydrometeorological event over time, it is largely devoid of an analytical framework, and there has been no general comprehensive history of floods in France since then.[5]

Floods and natural disasters can be studied in a variety of different ways. They can be explored in terms understanding changes in climate and the natural environment through historical clues gleaned from the often fragmentary human and physical evidence left behind in their wake. They can also be examined for what they illuminate about facets of the strains and tensions they evoke in human societies, which are not always apparent either to contemporary observers or to historians. They can reveal popular and elite belief systems as those societies sought out the alleged perpetrators or forces that contributed to these natural disasters. They frequently provoked a search for explanations and solutions, as survivors came to terms with the human tragedies wrought by the destruction natural disasters left in their path. They were an occasion to question reigning ideologies, the legitimacy of dominant groups, and often, as Charles Walker has argued in his study of the eighteenth-century earthquakes that wracked Peru in 1746, 1783, and 1797, a "dialectic between the return to traditional beliefs and forms of domination and the search for new meanings and structures" that emerged.[6] In his study of the history of the floods that afflicted Grenoble in the nineteenth century, Denis Coeur suggested that their occurrence can be viewed in terms of how political forces came to terms with them through the formulation of public works policy. This chapter explores the floods that ravaged France in the nineteenth century and the changing responses to them on the part of both the state and civil society, with particular attention to the great floods of 1840, 1846, 1856, and 1910. While floods and natural disasters were by no means new in France, the way in which the state and civil society approached and understood them reflected significant changes in terms of how they came to be managed and controlled over time, while contributing to environmental reforms and to new kinds of environmental knowledge by the beginning of twentieth century.[7]

In some instances the evolving responses to floods reflected the way in which flooding and natural catastrophes in general became a larger prism through which to regard the social and political tensions in postrevolutionary France. They also indicate a growing awareness of environmental threats and prompted lively debate from the 1840s onward. As people moved away from earlier religious understandings, flooding increasingly came to be seen through the lens of the emerging science of climatology and became implicated in discussions about the need to establish an equilibrium between the state and civil society in political terms and between mountain and plain in physical terms by preserving forested areas of France. This had far-reaching implications for traditional forms of land use, property relations, and state interventionism long before what might be considered the strictly ecological initiatives of the second half of the twentieth century. The great flood of 1856 marked a turning point in terms of how floods were understood, controlled, and "mediatized" for a general public that increasingly argued for governmental intervention.

※ ※ ※

HOW DID RESPONSES to natural disasters more generally and to floods more specifically change during the nineteenth century? Natural disasters in the eighteenth century included two small earthquakes in London in February and March 1750, the great earthquake of Lisbon in 1755, earthquakes in southern Italy, avalanches in Switzerland, and volcanic eruptions in Iceland, which generated an enormous amount of speculation about the physical, moral, and religious causes of earthquakes. Europeans generally responded to these calamities in the eighteenth century by employing a religious discourse. The English writer Daniel Defoe found evidence of the divine presence in them, believing that God not only used them as a warning but created them for the purposes of edification and punishment. Continental Europeans responded on an emotional level as well, in fear, horror, and dread. The explanations most frequently invoked were providential in nature, despite a growing skepticism about resorting to the supernatural realm to explain natural disasters. Lisbon's earthquake was important in challenging complacent attitudes toward the earth as a habitable planet after both the earthquake and the tsunami that followed. One answer to the questions these events raised was that they constituted a lesson or a warning, and in some cases punishment. The Lisbon earthquake, which occurred at 9:30 a.m. on 1 November 1755, was probably one of the most costly natural catastrophes, at least since the eruption of Vesuvius in A.D. 79, and one about which there was a huge amount of comment in Europe. It elicited a response from the French philosopher Voltaire in his *Poème sur le désastre de Lisbonne* and *Candide,* among other commentaries. Voltaire saw it as an object lesson and an occasion to highlight the false optimism of seventeenth-century science and the philosophy of Leibnitz. Voltaire's broadsides pushed aside ideas of the harmony of nature, optimism, and meliorism, as well as the idea of celestial design for understanding the natural world, and this was followed by extended debates about the relationship between nature and humankind.

Alongside the relatively rare occurrence of earthquakes, Europe was regularly plagued with floods, which frequently became natural catastrophes. They came to generate strong reactions in northern Europe, where deluges appeared to portend an apocalyptic end to a sinful world, a wiping clean of the slate, or a form of retribution. Some, for example, have called Holland a "flood society," where, as Simon Schama has argued, the drama of the celestial world was allegedly played out and the distinctive traits of Dutch national identity were forged.[8] One of the great fears and collective anxieties that shaped Holland's self-identity was flooding, which was reflected in the construction of an elaborate system of dikes. It is in this culture that the so-called drowning cell or water house—a cellar filled with water in which shirkers were forced to pump water continuously to prevent themselves from drowning—was put in place as part of the Dutch penal system. This form of discipline had a particular resonance in a society marked by a constant fear of submersion.

France shared in the fear of flooding. With its four great rivers, France had also been prey to the phenomenon of flooding for as far back as records could be found. Maurice Champion's six-volume history of floods in France attested to the fact. He wrote that "in the presence of losses and indescribable disasters that floods have caused for so many centuries, it would be an immense service rendered to the country to break free of this terrible calamity."[9] Floods posed great risk during the Little Ice Age in Europe, a period from approximately 1350 to 1860, when colder regions and higher altitudes experienced an abundance of snow.[10] More temperate regions often witnessed excessive rainfall. The Mediterranean saw periods of prolonged drought, punctuated by periods of rare and catastrophic rainfall.[11] The European continent experienced much colder winters than either previously or subsequently. Some of the worst flooding of the Seine during the seventeenth and eighteenth centuries occurred in 1651, 1658, 1733, 1740, 1751, 1764, 1785, and 1799. On 28 May 1733 the levees of the Loire broke between the towns of Roanne and Orléans, and the water rose to levels that were twenty feet above normal.[12] Following the 1651 flood, the pont de la Tournelle was established (1654) as the place at which the Seine was to be regularly monitored and measured. During the 1740 flood, the water measured 7.05 meters, whereas in 1658 the water rose to 8.80 meters.[13]

Floods affected much of western Europe in the winter of 1740. While the banks of the Seine and the Rhône were swollen, some towns in Holland were completely submerged.[14] In Paris, where flooding lasted for six weeks, the population crossed the city in boats, and the older parts of the city of Grenoble were completely inundated. Flooding affected the same areas of Paris again in 1784 and, as in 1740, affected all parts of France, ruining the pavements of one-fourth of the city of Caen, for example, and incurring damages worth 15,000 to 20,000 livres. As the flood of 1740 was considerable, it captured the public imagination. The hydrologist Philippe Buache (1700–1773), who was also geographer to the king of France, was given the task of doing a study of the 1740 Paris flood by the Academy of Sciences in 1741; it was published as "Observations sur l'étendue et la hauteur de l'inondation du mois de décembre" in the same year.[15] This was followed by a second study undertaken by the hydrologist Antoine Déparcieux (1703–1768) for the academy in 1764.[16] As Shelby McCloy has argued, "floods in eighteenth-century France were so common that there were few years that did not see a flood great or small in some part of the country."[17]

The nineteenth century began with one of the worst floods experienced by Paris in a long time, in 1802, shortly after Napoleon I had assumed power. François-Jean Bralle (1750–1831), a hydrologic engineer for the city of Paris who was responsible for establishing fifteen fountains that brought clean water to the city following Napoleon's decree of 2 May 1806—including the fontaine de Mars and the fontaine du Fellah—undertook a study of the flood, which was in many ways as serious as that of 1740, measuring 7.90 meters.[18] The 1802 flood was followed by major floods in 1836, 1840, 1846, 1851, 1852, and 1856. The state spent a total of 84,118,619 francs on reparations and damages, and numerous measures were taken to protect French cities from flooding between 1836 and 1865. The flood of October 1840, which affected southern France, and that of 1846, when the rains of October led to massive flooding in the departments of the Nièvre, Allier, and Loire-et-Cher, were particularly costly in terms of the loss of human life.

The flood of 1840 hit the valley of the Rhône very badly, according to Champion, who asserted that for the populations bordering the Rhône and the Saône, "the overflowing waters everywhere created appalling ravages" and that "the memory of this great public catastrophe is still present in popular remembrance."[19] The city that was perhaps most affected by the flood was Lyon, where the streets of the Brotteaux district were turned into violent torrents, and the upper stretches of the river between Geneva and Lyon reached a height that was far greater than anyone had seen before.[20] Further south, the city of Avignon was equally affected, prompting the Chamber of Deputies to vote a law authorizing an indemnity of 5 million francs.

The great flood of 1846 affected the Loire, Rhône, Garonne, and Saône, though the inhabitants along the Loire and the Rhône suffered the most damage.[21] It occurred less than seven months after the solemn inauguration of the Orléans railway at Tours on 26 March 1846, submerging the tracks when the levees broke, becoming one of the worst floods to affect the Loire valley in the first half of the nineteenth century.[22] It constituted, according to Champion, a "veritable cataclysm."[23] From the seventeenth of October onward, there was incessant rain. Many of the houses in Andrézieux disappeared in the cataclysm, and the rail lines between it and Saint-Etienne were washed away. Writing about Roanne, *Le Moniteur* noted on 27 October that "we are witnessing the most terrible catastrophe that one could see, the flood! The Loire returned to its former course, burst the levée, invaded the canal; it is a horrible disaster."[24] There were a considerable number of deaths from the calamity, which began on 17 October. While the government provided financial aid, Louis Philippe gave 100,000 francs, the city of Paris 50,000, Baron de Rothschild 20,000, and Louis Napoleon 500, and theaters in Paris raised money for flood victims. Indeed, one of the city's most popular actresses, Mademoiselle Rachel, contributed to the effort with great fanfare.[25]

✻ ✻ ✻

WHILE THE 1846 flood generated considerable discussion, the 1856 flood affected all major river basins in the southern half of France. Indeed, it was the largest flood to affect France in the nineteenth and twentieth centuries, covering almost two-thirds of the total surface of the country. Whereas the great flood of 1846 spread to thirty-three departments, the ravages of the flood of 1856 could be documented in fifty of France's eighty-four departments, and the Loire reached a record high of 7.50 meters, in contrast to 7.10 meters in 1846. The lives of 26,000 people living in the Loire valley were severely disrupted.[26] Moreover, the flood occurred at a particularly inopportune moment. The Crimean War had just ended, and while it was an ostensible victory, that victory came at an enormous human and financial cost. In addition, the winter of 1855 had been particularly harsh. The previous year's wheat harvest was meager, and the French state did not have recourse to Russia's vast wheat reserves as a temporary stopgap.

A curious aspect of the 1856 flood was that it did not begin in the winter, like many floods in the nineteenth century, but rather in late May, after two unusually long periods of heavy rain—the first from 15 to 22 May and the second from 28 to 30 May.[27] On 16 May Lyon and its valley were flooded by the rise of the Saône. Three days later the cities of Avignon, Beaucaire, and Arles in Provence were affected. By the thirtieth the water levels in Tarascon were 1.10 meters above where they were at their highest point during the flood of 1840. It appeared worse than the great flood of 1840, which occurred in November, because the harvest had already passed, while in 1856 the season had not begun. It was estimated that 46,000 hectares of planted fields between Toulouse and Bordeaux were submerged and their harvest destroyed. The plain, consisting of 100,000 hectares, 60,000 of which were planted fields, was under water, and the entire harvest lost. A telegram from the Camargue predicted that a very large proportion of the region's livestock had been drowned, and most of the land between Tarascon and the sea was submerged.[28]

Immediate estimates of damage to the natural and built environment were enormous. In mid-July the departmental services of Ponts et Chaussées estimated the damage to infrastructure (waterways, roads, and bridges) to be approximately 26 million francs, with the Loire suffering the worst damage.[29] Damage to individual property (buildings, crops, and movable goods) was more difficult to assess. On the basis of incomplete departmental documentation, Denis Coeur estimates damages of between 55 million and 70 million francs in the Loire valley, between 42 million and 55 million francs in the Rhône valley, and between 8 million and 10 million francs in the Garonne. For the entire area of the territory afflicted by the flood, damages reached a total of 100 million to 130 million francs. The departments most badly affected were Indre-et-Loire, Loiret, Bouches-du-Rhône, Rhône, Lot-et-Garonne, and Tarn-et-Garonne.[30]

News of the flooding of the Rhône reached Napoleon III on 30 May, on the eve of festivities surrounding the baptism of his new son. The emperor, however, immediately left Paris on 1 June to survey the devastation, arriving first in the town of Dijon and moving on to Lyon, Valence, Avignon, and Arles before returning to Paris on 5 June. On 6 June he left again for the Loire valley, where he stopped in Tours, Orléans, and Angers before returning to Saint-Cloud on 11 June.[31] Napoleon III's "compassionate voyage" to the Rhône and Loire river valleys was clearly more than an emperor's attempt to comfort flood victims. In many respects it was a publicity stunt to showcase his benevolence and to legitimize the newly established Second Empire in the immediate aftermath of the Crimean War and the birth the prince imperial, his son and heir, on 6 March.[32] Napoleon had his own propagandists. Charles Robin, author of *Histoire de la révolution de 1848* and *Histoire de l'exposition universelle,* published a pamphlet that documented Napoleon's journey. He wrote that the emperor was "the first to run toward danger" and that France was "electrified by his great devotion."[33]

Before embarking on his journey south, Napoleon III made certain that the Corps législatif had voted to release 2 million francs in aid. It also earmarked another 10 million francs for public works. On 2 June 1856 the emperor issued an imperial decree that granted 300,000 francs in aid, and most cities affected received varying amounts, including 10,000 francs for Vienne and 25,000 francs for the department of Isère; also, a fund of 27,000 francs was put aside for the restoration of artworks that had been damaged by water during the floods. In addition, a number of private subscriptions were created for flood victims, including one initiated by the empress, and the Conseil municipal of Paris provided 100,000 francs.[34]

The 1856 flood was the first French flood to be the focus of sustained media attention. It brought to the fore the first photojournalist to document a flood, in the figure of Edouard Baldus (1813–1889), as well as scores of newspaper journalists who captured the damage it did in both image and word. *L'Illustration,* in particular, provided the country with a daily commentary from the end of May onward, and smaller regional newspapers, such as the *Courrier de Bayonne* and the *Courrier de Gironde,* assigned their own journalists to the event. The media was enlisted to publicize Napoleon as a benevolent leader. Much of the emperor's involvement in the management of the flood was carefully orchestrated, and the floods, more than ever before, became the objects of national as opposed to local attention.[35] Significantly, the emperor himself began actively to call for a systematic study of the causes of floods as well as long-term measures that might be taken to prevent them.

On 19 July 1856 Napoleon III wrote from Plombières to the minister of agriculture, commerce, and public works on flood prevention, and his missive was published in the *Moniteur Universel* on 21 July. Using the metaphor of the way in which rain falls on the roof of a house and collects in its gutters, he wrote that it was incontestable that floods were a result of precipitation in mountainous terrains, as the plain or valley acted as a sponge when there was water falling. He argued that a barrier against the flow of water was required in the form of a dike and requested that the entire management of rivers be placed under a single individual in order that actions might be prompt in moments of crisis. He also requested that those engineers who had the most experience with the management of rivers be dispatched to flood sites. For him, what happened during the flood of 1846 served as a lesson: the two governmental chambers drew up illuminating reports but no system of management was adopted, and the measures taken were partial and only made the effects of the last calamity even more disastrous.

A week later the minister of agriculture, public works, and commerce wrote a circular to all prefects in France regarding a program of study for the management of rivers and floods.[36] He transmitted the program, which was prepared by the *conseil général* of Ponts et Chaussées. It asked for general information from the prefects on their department's rivers—their length, incline, and principal tributaries and their influence on flooding—which was to be submitted at the end of September. While he recognized that some of this information had been provided, at least partially, in special reports, the task now was to coordinate and present it in a more comprehensive way. In addition, the minister required the prefects to give an account of the 1856 flood and to compare it with past floods in order to formulate a plan to protect centers of population from flooding in the future. The program consisted of a general questionnaire concerning departmental rivers and their tributaries and twenty-six specific questions on the 1856 flood.

Responses to the 1856 flood marked a fundamental departure for the French state in a number of significant respects. The telegraph allowed information to be sent and received very quickly, and a now extensive system of railways allowed for more rapid responses on the part of the state. Indeed, it facilitated the emperor's trips to cities that were inundated by the flood. This was the first time that the state attempted to document a flood in any kind of systematic way by employing a photographer and by gathering very precise information on its causes, nature, and course from all of its sites with the view of formulating a comprehensive policy regarding flood and water management. Not only did the state seek information from Ponts et Chaussées and departmental administration, but it was striking that Napoleon III actively encouraged the French public to formulate their own responses and provide their own solutions to the 1856 crisis. Finally, the state and the public alike began to consider floods in a broader historical perspective by asking how floods in the present compared with those in the past. To this extent the phenomenon of flooding began to acquire a historical dimension that transcended the immediate crisis, which presupposed the possibility of long-term environmental intervention. The management of floods during the Second Empire was an extension of Napoleon III's *dirigisme* (state-directed economic policy). In February 1857 he delivered a speech before his "troops," senators and deputies in the Corps législatif, in which he described the task of government in the following terms: "Enlighten and direct, there is our duty." In his vow to control flooding in France, he ironically compared the task to one of political repression: "Everything makes me hope that science will manage to tame nature. It is a point of honor for me that in France rivers, like revolution, return to their beds and remain unable to leave them."[37]

The departmental responses to the minister's circular of July 1856 were comprehensive, but what was most remarkable was the absence of information about past floods in them. The report of the chief engineer in the valley of the Oise noted the "absence of historical documents" but added that the flood that had left the greatest mark on local memory was that of 1784.[38] What became increasingly clear was that the damage associated with flooding in France increased considerably from the Old Regime to the postrevolutionary period. During the Second Empire, the administration of Ponts et Chaussées undertook a study of state expenditures from 1814 and 1865, documenting the principal floods of the period, which included those of 1836, 1840, 1846, 1851, 1852, and 1856. It showed expenditures totaling 84,118,619 francs, divided between reparations for damages incurred and monies spent specifically to protect cities. Funds spent between 1848 and 1866 were far higher than between 1836 and 1847.[39] The most costly flood was that of 1856, which was by far the most expensive of the nineteenth century and which was deemed by the report to be the "most powerful" flood that France had ever seen.[40]

The most common explanation for what appeared to be the growing frequency of floods, especially the three great floods of 1840, 1846, and 1856, was deforestation.[41] Indeed, since the end of the eighteenth century, the two principal works that shaped analyses of the relationship between deforestation and "torrents" most were Jean-Antoine Fabre's *Essai sur la théorie des torrens et des rivières* (Paris, 1797) and Alexandre Charles Surell's *Etude sur les torrents des Hautes-Alpes* (Paris, 1841). Both authors were engineers for Ponts et Chaussées in the mountainous departments of the Var and Hautes-Alpes, respectively, and both wrote their treatises from firsthand observation of the disastrous consequences of regular floods emanating from mountains on the plains below.[42] Writing thirty-four years before Surell, Fabre observed that some of the best lands, situated at streambeds, had become more vulnerable and subject to flooding with the accumulation of rainwater and its runoff from mountain slopes due to deforestation, and he warned about the irreversibility of this process.[43] For him the principal cause of torrents was the clearing of trees, as their branches and leaves served as barriers and filters for rainfall. Without trees, neither light nor heavy rain could be absorbed as rapidly as it began to accumulate. Clearing led to the loosening of the soil on mountainsides. The challenge, for Fabre, was to find the means to control the speed with which water was absorbed as well as its volume and runoff, and this could be achieved by the planting of trees on mountainsides on a massive scale.

Clarence Glacken has argued that Fabre's influential work "begins a new chapter in Western natural science and engineering," and it was one that led to the publication of large numbers of works on the relationship between deforestation, the environment, and flooding as a natural disaster.[44] One of the most important was by a fellow engineer, Alexandre Surell, who, like François-Antoine Rauch, was born in the town of Bitche in Lorraine. Surell began his own study of the issue in 1838 as a twenty-five-year-old engineer assigned to the Alpine region (Hautes-Alpes). After the publication of *Etude sur les torrents des Hautes-Alpes* in 1841, it received an award from the Academy of Sciences in Paris in 1842 and became an instant and influential classic. Indeed, the better-known American conservationist George P. Marsh relied on it heavily in a work that was far more widely read internationally, *The Earth as Modified by Human Action*. Commenting on the lack of vegetation in many Alpine regions of France that he visited, he wrote, "I have never seen its equal even in the Kabyle villages of the province of Constantine; for there you can travel on horseback, and you find grass in the spring, whereas in more than fifty communes in the Alps, there is nothing."[45]

While Surell applauded Fabre as a pioneer who identified an important subject of study, Surell nonetheless criticized his predecessor for not being exacting enough in his observations and for basing his assessments entirely on the Var region: "He reasons too much and is not bothered about citing the facts supporting his deductions. It becomes from that point difficult to untangle that which comes from observation and that which comes from the author in his book, that is to say the part that is certain and the part that is doubtful, and one finishes also by being distrustful about the whole thing."[46] Fabre's work, which was almost presented as a set of aphorisms, posed another problem for the young engineer. He thought that Fabre's conclusions required more hard evidence. This is something he set out to address. His *Etude sur les torrents des Hautes-Alpes* first examined the effects of deforestation, which Fabre had also identified.[47] He described the damage caused by mountain torrents in dramatic language, comparing the rushing streams to a leprosy gnawing away at the mountains and disgorging themselves in the plains below.[48] He warned that the devastation that had occurred in France's forests since the eighteenth century had been disastrous because upland forested areas sustained both agricultural and climatic balance for lowland areas. He was not opposed to the removal of trees and even suggested that this might be done without ill effect in lowland areas.[49] For Surell, however, "in order for mountains to be habitable, mountains must be forested, and the total annihilation of their forests would ineluctably lead to population flight."[50]

Considering the French departments of Hautes-Alpes, Basses-Alpes, Isère, and Drôme, Surell set out to explain why mountain torrents were so formidable and suggested means to combat them. While somewhat skeptical of Fabre, he relied on an earlier work by a former prefect of the Basses-Alpes in the early 1830s, Pierre-Henri Dugied.[51] Musing on why there appeared to be so many more torrents than in the past, Surell argued that the phenomenon could be directly related to deforestation and that it was no accident because forests exercise a real influence on the production of torrents. However, for him it was important to note that it was human actions that played the greatest role in creating this new environmental danger: "It is easy now to understand all the misfortune that man has created in imprudently removing forests from the mountain. He has disturbed the conditions of the established order through a long succession of centuries."[52] He attributed deforestation primarily to grazing, liberal French revolutionary forest legislation, an insufficient number of forest guards, and the inertia of governments. While new dams might be built, the larger task was to prevent the emergence of new torrents, and the key step was that of restoring Alpine vegetation: "It is no longer even a *system of defense* that one must seek"; for him, it was a double "*system of preservation and of extinction*" (emphasis in the original).[53] He called for a new initiative in the area of public works and thought that the state should identify land to be preserved for the public interest. He ended his work with the following question:

> Is it not, moreover, the duty of each state to find out about all of the resources of its territory, and to develop each region according to its natural conditions, without neglecting any? Isn't it also the task given to man to enrich the soil of the planet; and since he derives glory from being its king, in being so would he up-end it, like an evil conqueror, only to leave behind him, everywhere he has brought his civilization, ruins and gloomy deserts?[54]

In short, Surell argued that the state had a "moral duty" to intervene to repair the damage done to the environment and invoked its role as the environment's steward.

The work of Surell, Fabre, and other early nineteenth-century commentators who linked deforestation with the scourge of floods generated a vigorous debate between Surell's numerous supporters and his rarer detractors which would continue for a century. Surell's study was subsequently republished in 1870–1872, with revisions by the author, along with a second volume by Ernest Cézanne (1830–1876), who was also an engineer for Ponts et Chaussées and second president of the Club alpin français, and it was reprinted again as recently as 2002.[55]

About a decade after Surell published his trailblazing work, François Vallès, a fellow engineer and follower of the utopian socialist Charles Fourier, entered the fray of the debate as chief engineer of the department of the Aisne. He was responsible for coordinating a response to the minister's circular concerning the 1856 flood and for suggesting measures to prevent flooding in the future. In his 1857 correspondence, he attached several reports and notes, including "Observations sur les mesures à prendre contre les inondations," and mentioned an essay competition launched by the Académie impériale de Bordeaux regarding how floods might be prevented, while voicing his intention to submit a study based on his twenty-five-year experience as an engineer.[56]

Vallès submitted his study to the academy in Bordeaux under the title *Etudes sur les inondations, leurs causes et leurs effets, les moyens à mettre en oeuvre pour combattre leurs inconvénients et profiter de leurs avantages*, in which he argued against the orthodoxy that deforestation had contributed to a steady increase in the number of floods in France and to their severity.[57] He countered that the belief that deforestation created floods and increased their frequency was a received wisdom that had no basis in scientific reality and that the effects of floods depended on local conditions, including distance from the sea, the nature of the soil and its permeability, and the height of trees.[58] The popular belief about deforestation, in Vallès's view, underpinned the drive to restore forests. He relied in part on the earlier testimony of François Arago, director of the Paris Observatory, who testified on the effect of deforestation on temperature and rainfall before a parliamentary commission set up to study the question of whether to modify France's forest code. To the west of France deforestation could lead to a rise in temperatures, as the removal of trees would allow for the arrival of temperate winds from the sea, while deforestation in the flat plains of the east could lead to colder temperatures to the east. Moreover, Vallès showcased the findings of the renowned hydrologist Eugène Belgrand, who argued that water levels during the flooding of the Seine had become lower than they were in the past. For this reason, Vallès rejected reforestation as a remedial solution to the problem of flooding and focused on more traditional public works programs, which included dikes, dams, reservoirs, and canals. The editor of the volume concluded in the preface to *Etudes sur les inondations* that Vallès's study showed that the situation was less gloomy than was generally believed in terms of the apparent disorders caused by floods.

Vallès's study met with stiff resistance and consternation. One forest administrator, A. F. d'Héricourt, saw it as an attack on the forest service and objected to the study's ironic tone in the *Annales Forestières*. Vallès denied this characterization of his intent, citing a 14 November 1857 letter that he wrote to d'Héricourt in which he argued that not only did he reject reforestation as a solution to the problem of flooding, but he thought that it would make the problem worse.[59] Vallès was not only scorned by forest officials; he was dismissed by those within his own ranks. Attached to his 26 March 1857 letter in the archives of the Ponts et Chaussées is a set of anonymous notes entitled "Observations sur l'ouvrage de M. Vallès," which rejected many of his findings.[60] However, Vallès's work gained such notoriety outside of France that it was translated into English by Charles J. Allen, captain of the United States Corps of Engineers, and published in 1873. In the letter he sent to the chief of engineers, A. A. Humphreys, which served as a preface to the volume, Allen wrote that Vallès's conclusions were "directly opposed to the general ideas regarding the influence of forests upon rain etc." and that they "might be of interest to someone whose duties trench on similar ground."[61]

Vallès did find some support in the historian Maurice Champion, who sought to compile a factual historical record of France's floods in his multivolume *Les inondations en France*. Champion argued early on that the idea that the curse of flooding was a new phenomenon in France and that deforestation was the cause was far from being ratified by historical evidence.[62] He suggested that floods only appeared to be more severe, because in past centuries France's population was far smaller, and therefore fewer people were affected.[63] He contended that there were as many floods in former times, when both mountains and plains were covered with impenetrable forests, as there were at the time he wrote his book.[64] This opposing view of the impact of deforestation on flooding persisted into the twentieth century. On the centenary of the publication of Surell's *Etude sur les torrents,* the geographer Paul Veyret argued in the pages of the *Revue de Géographie Alpine* that Surell had propagated the common myth that deforestation was responsible for the increase in the number of floods and that this myth was not founded in any scientific reality. Veyret noted that in the first part of his book Surell observed that deforestation was a secondary cause of flooding in certain mountainous regions that were completely barren of trees, as in the Vosges or the Massif Central, where flooding had not occurred, so geography and other factors played a greater role. However, in the second part of the book he attributed the existence of torrents in the Alps almost entirely to deforestation. Veyret accounts for this discrepancy by suggesting that the first part of the study was written for Surell's fellow engineers soon after he arrived in the Alps, while the second half was written with the encouragement of the prefect of the Hautes-Alpes, who was fully committed to the narrative concerning deforestation.[65]

The contested views of Vallès, Champion, and later Veyret remained in the minority. A perusal of the documentation on the subject in the archives of Ponts et Chaussées and a review of the considerable nineteenth-century commentary on floods in France show that deforestation was held responsible for the alleged increased in the number and severity of floods in the one-hundred-year period following the Revolution. Indeed, Surell's early call for reforestation was ultimately heeded several years after the great flood of 1856, as the legislation passed in 1860 and 1864 regarding reforestation would show. When the second edition of his *Etude sur les torrents des Hautes-Alpes* was issued in 1870–1872, Surell, who had gone on to become the director of the Chemins de fer du Midi, wrote in the introduction that much of what he proposed and discussed in 1841 had been translated into laws, credits, and public works programs, so that the "deplorable situation" he had evoked then would "no longer exist in several years" if the forest administration continued their actions.[66]

Engineers and forest officials played a significant role in trying to come to terms with environmental damage ostensibly caused by the destructive hand of humans and raised the public's consciousness in this regard, even though Paul Allard has suggested that measures taken by the state were intended to protect populations and natural resources rather than nature in and of itself.[67] These measures, however, left their traces on the landscape. They began with the law of 16 September 1807 regarding drainage and reclamation schemes in France's wetlands, which was followed by a spate of similar legislation in 1854, 1856, and 1860. The measures taken to prevent flooding following the flood of 1856 emanated from both the legislature and the administrations of Ponts et Chaussées and Eaux et Forêts. The law of 28 July 1860 provided for the reforestation of mountainous areas. This was followed by the law of 8 June 1864 that aimed to restore mountainous vegetation. Taken together, this legislation, the Restauration des terrains de montagne (RTM), along with the law of 4 April 1882, which allowed for the acquisition of endangered areas by the state, created the means by which the state could undertake a vast program of environmental management.[68]

※ ※ ※

IT WAS NOT ONLY engineers and forest officials who commented on the phenomenon of flooding in the years following the great flood of 1856. Analyses and commentaries from the general public were sent to the emperor. M. Joubert, an eighty-five-year-old man who had once worked as a civilian for the military, wrote to Napoleon III from Tours on 27 September 1866, 25 January 1867, and 30 October 1867 regarding proposed solutions to the problems of flooding and strengthening the levees on the Loire. Saying that he recognized that many members of the Ponts et Chaussées, especially the "most idle" of them, would want to discredit him, he persisted in putting forward his own humble suggestions: "I see that your majesty desires the truth when it comes to important matters that concern France and after the order you have given . . . relative to floods, the contents of the letter that I had the honor of writing to you in October 1866 . . . are the only [ones] susceptible to giving the satisfactory and certain result."[69]

Several boxes in the F/14 series of the Archives nationales contain a number of such letters from various parts of France, which were inspired by Napoleon III's 21 July 1856 circular that encouraged public debate on flooding.[70] On 10 December 1866, for example, the prefect of the Haute-Loire forwarded the deliberations of the Société d'agriculture de Guy from September, which urged the emperor to take steps to deal with the flooding. That debate continued, moreover, as the century wore on and revealed the extent of public engagement and criticism. For example, in 1866 Léopold Graffin published a pamphlet in which he declared that he had been a victim of the flooding of the Loire three times in the previous twenty years, and put the blame for the floods squarely on the shoulders of the engineers of the Ponts et Chaussées: "Wasted budgets are the ruins on the road to the future; the work of our engineers in the riverbed of the Loire in the first half of the nineteenth century is there to prove it." He went on to affirm that one should not ask sovereigns for thaumaturgic power or expect "the magic wand which pushes back the waves of the Red Sea," but that one should expect more intelligent management.[71] In 1875 a private citizen from Cahors in southern France, A. Bonabry, published a short essay on floods and how to prevent them, which he submitted to the ministers of justice, public works, agriculture, and finance and the prefect of the department of the Seine.[72] He then entered into a five-year correspondence with various public officials, which he documented in a second publication, entitled *Polémique entre l'administration des ponts et chaussées et l'auteur du mémoire: Inondations, causes principales et préservatifs,* which accused the engineers in Ponts et Chaussées of both dismissing his proposals and actually causing floods: "Will we be so blind as to entrust them with the nation's resources again . . . ?"[73] He specifically criticized the construction of dams and reforestation projects as failures, arguing that deforestation was a necessity.[74]

While the state increasingly moved to rectify the alleged environmental devastation caused by man-made flooding during the course of the nineteenth century, as Bonabry's response suggests, popular responses to floods began to change.[75] In the eighteenth century the general public responded to floods more often than not with a kind of fatalism, and more particularly among those who viewed their occurrence as divine acts. Frequently the Church capitalized on these disastrous events by showcasing the courageous acts of clergymen.[76] This continued into the nineteenth century, but providential explanations for floods gradually gave way to other forms of explanation. Moreover, an undeveloped press and poor communication made early modern floods into local affairs. As the century wore on, floods came to be publicized in prints, lithographs, and finally photography as well as in newspaper articles, personal memoirs, treatises, novels, and most especially in poetry and in the theater. The pictorial and literary documentation of floods and their victims gave the periodic floods of the nineteenth century a pathos and emotional charge they did not possess before and transformed these natural phenomena into national events.

One of the early images of nineteenth-century floods came in the form of single-page block prints that were hawked by *colporteurs* (traveling salesmen) and produced by the printer Jean-Charles Pellerin in the town of Epinal. Indeed, floods became a stock-in-trade subject of Imagerie Epinal in the nineteenth century. The 1840 flood was immortalized in an 1841 print depicting a rural landscape containing submerged houses, boats rescuing victims in a swollen river, and women and children clinging to trees (Figure 6). "The Disastrous Inundations of 1866" is set in an urban environment where rescue was highlighted. Another, "Awful Disasters Caused

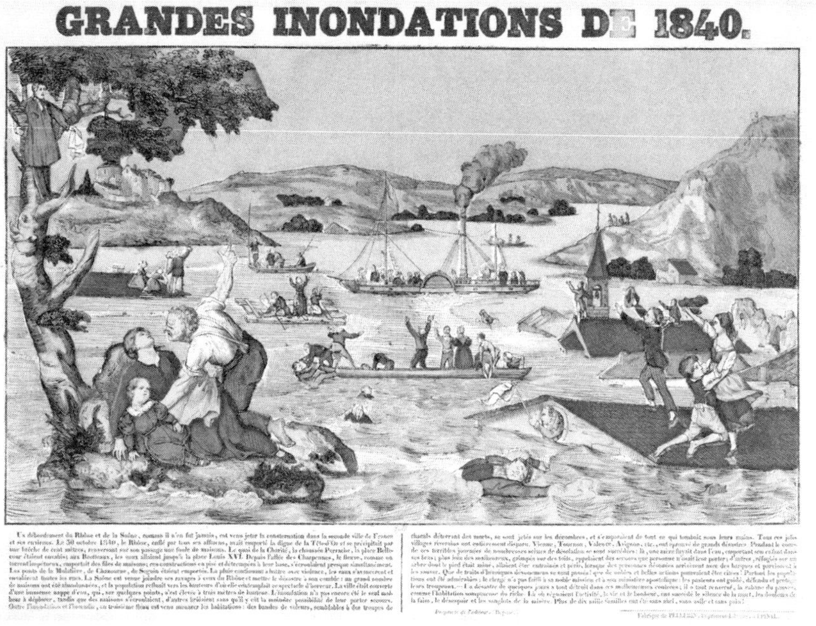

GRANDES INONDATIONS DE 1840.

FIGURE 6. Flood images were widely disseminated in the nineteenth century. "Grandes inondations de 1840." Epinal, 1841.

by Terrifying Floods," depicts a priest in a boat rescuing the victims of the flood in the departments of Aude and Hérault (Figure 7).

Several paintings showcased Napoleon III's benevolence during the great flood of 1856. Napoleon himself commissioned the young academic painter William Bouguereau (1825–1905) to paint a scene depicting the former's act of comforting the flood victims of Tarascon; it now hangs in the city's Hôtel de Ville. Bouguereau's rendition of Napoleon as "father of the people" was complemented by three other paintings: Jean-Raymond Lazèrgues's (1817–1887) *Distribution of Aid to the Flood Victims of Lyon*, which was displayed at the 1857 Salon in Paris; Hippolyte Beauvais's (1826–1857) *The Emperor Visiting the Flood Victims in Angers*; and Eugène Devéria's (1805–1865) *The Flood*, which bore witness to the panic caused by the flood in Avignon. *Almanach de Napoleon*, edited by Alexandre Houssiaux and illustrated by Charlet and Raffet, disseminated other images of Napoleon III's role in the 1856 flood, but increasingly photography bore witness to flooding from the 1850s onward.

In an unusual and unprecedented step, the government of Louis Napoleon hired the Prussian-born photographer Edouard Baldus to document the ravages left in the wake of the flood; this was the first time that photography

FIGURE 7. "Awful disasters caused by terrifying floods." N. de Laly, "Désastres épouvantables causés par les effrayantes inondations." Paris, 1840.

was used by the state to document a natural disaster in France.[77] Baldus first came to Paris in 1838 to study painting and quickly abandoned it in favor of photography. He was employed, along with other photographers, to do a photographic inventory of historic monuments in France after 1851 and became a kind of official photographer of the Second Empire. He was also commissioned by the Baron de Rothschild, chairman of the Société du chemin de fer du Nord, to do a photo album for Queen Victoria, and his work documenting the 1856 flood in many ways marked the apogee of his career and paved the way for his path to French citizenship.

In documenting the flood, the state paid for Baldus's travel expenses, forty francs for each negative, and ten francs for two prints of each image.[78] He arrived in the Rhône valley in early June and visited Lyon, Avignon, and Tarascon. He produced twenty-five negatives of the flood as it was receding in the eight days during which he toured the region. In contrast to the paintings that were produced following the flood, all of Baldus's negatives captured scenes and landscapes that were devoid of human beings and their suffering, but which nonetheless depicted the flood's extraordinary destructiveness. Standing on the terrace of Avignon's cathedral, he took a six-part panorama of the flooded Rhône valley that is almost lyrical in its tranquility. In contrast, his photograph of a ruined house in the Brotteaux district of Lyon attested to the flood's terrible fury (Figure 8). Ernest Lacan, who helped to found France's first journal devoted to photography in 1851, spoke to the immediacy of this form of documentary photography and noted both the aesthetic and documentary quality of these photographs in stressing their "exactitude," which was "unfortunately too eloquent." But he observed that they were nonetheless beautiful "in their sadness."[79]

While floods became the subject of the new medium of photography, they also inspired personal memoirs, poetry, drama, and melodrama from the 1840s onward. In 1840, for example, a doctor, P.-C. Ordinaire, wrote a personal account of his experiences.[80] A victim of the flood himself, he did not intend to produce a literary work, but wished to give an accurate picture of what occurred and to place those occurrences within a historical context.

FIGURE 8. Prussian-born photographer E. D. Balthus documented the destruction caused by the 1856 flood. "Inondations à Lyon." Paris, 1856. Courtesy Bibliothèque Nationale de France/Ecole Nationale des Ponts et Chaussées.

Most importantly, he provided his own prescriptions regarding how to prevent floods in the future.

The prolific vaudeville writer Auguste Jouhaud produced *Les inondés de Lyon,* a melodrama in three acts, at the Théâtre Saint Marcel in Paris on 29 November 1840 after the flooding of the Rhône in that year. It centered on the young Adèle, the daughter of one of the richest manufacturers in Lyon, who had promised her hand in marriage to a supposedly rich ne'er-do-well in search of a dowry to pay off his debts, while Albert, an artisan in the manufacturer's workshop, is scorned by Lambert, the manufacturer, because he is a worker. The flood serves as a catalyst that unmasks Jolivet, saves Adèle from marriage, and serves to unite her with Albert. *Les inondés de Lyon* was followed by Eugène Cranney's *L'inondation de Lyon* and Anicet-Bourgeois and Francis Cornu's *Marie, ou l'inondation,* first presented at the theater of the Porte Saint-Martin in Paris on 23 December 1846, among other plays. This time the play takes place in the countryside, but, like *Les inondés de Lyon,* it centers on the themes of heroism, strength in the face of adversity, rescue, and survival.[81]

Floods became the subject of poetry as well. Perhaps the most famous of such nineteenth-century flood poets was Alphonse de Lamartine, who would go on to become an elected deputy during the Revolution of 1848. After the flood of 1840 he penned a long poem that was published alongside those of the female poets Madame Desbordes, Clara Mollard, and others.[82] Six years later, in 1846, another poet evoked the French Revolution, comparing it to the flood of 1789:

> If from 1789 the revolution
> Began its torments with flooding
> If the overflowing of the river must be a presage,
> Or the first signal of a most terrible storm;
> If to punish us, this sad event
> Is the sky in wrath a warning,
> What evils to dread! What a future to fear!
> Will we dare to complain to the eternal,
> When faith, morals in decrepitude
> Will have ceded their place to perversity . . .[83]

Finally, the great naturalist writer Emile Zola wrote a novella inspired by the flooding of the Garonne in 1875 entitled, quite simply, *L'inondation.*

※ ※ ※

ALTHOUGH FLOODS BECAME the focus of media coverage, painting, photography, poetry, novels, and intense public debate, and although the state increasingly undertook a number of initiatives to either prevent them or minimize their effects, floods continued to afflict France, as the subsequent floods of 1866 and 1875 attest. While the great flood of 1856 left a lasting mark on the nineteenth century for three of the four great rivers of France, it was the flooding of the Seine in 1910 that left an indelible mark on the twentieth century. It would become the subject of innumerable books and articles both at the time and subsequently.[84]

The 1910 Paris flood was caused by unusually heavy rains for several weeks immediately following the New Year. It hit the 2.8 million inhabitants badly, putting entire parts of the city underwater and creating damage that is still visible today on a number bridges connecting the right and left banks of the river (Figure 9). The side of the Alexandre III Bridge, near the Invalides, bears a mark indicating that flood's highest level as well as a plaque commemorating the event.[85] While the pont de la Tournelle had been officially designated as the bridge at which the Seine's water levels were measured from 1654 onward, it was a statue at the pont d'Alma, *Le Zouave* (executed by Georges Diebolt in 1858 to commemorate the victory of the British and the French over the Russians in the battle of Alma in the Crimean War), that served as the popular measure for flood levels from the nineteenth century onward (Figure 10).[86] Water levels reached their highest

FIGURE 9. The 1910 Paris flood was caused by unusually heavy rains. "Rue Saint-André des Arts, January 1910, Paris." Courtesy Bibliothèque Nationale de France/Agence Rol. Agence Photographique.

FIGURE 10. Georges Diebolt's statue *Le Zouave* (1858) at Pont d'Alma served as the popular measure for flood levels in Paris. Photograph copyright © Caroline Ford.

points a week after the flood invaded the city through tunnels, sewers, and the metro. Standing at 6.82 meters on January 28, it would take weeks before it subsided entirely, and the damages were enormous. It destroyed many parts of the city's economy. While there were no deaths, one report put the unemployed at about 50,000 workers, and the overall assessment did not include the city's physical destruction.[87]

The prime minister, Aristide Briand (1862–1932), almost immediately turned to Alfred Picard (1844–1913), a former minister of the navy, member of the Academy of Sciences, and commissioner general of the 1900 Exposition universelle, to head a commission charged with the task of making sense of the flood and charting a course for the city's future. His commission rapidly produced a voluminous report that outlined reasons for the failure of the city's infrastructure and suggested preventive measures for the future. He immediately brought in measuring equipment, established telephone communication between the city's various *mairies* (town halls), raised the river parapets, got rid of certain locks and barriers, and began reconstructing some of the city's bridges. These measures were suspended during World War I.[88] Like Eugène Belgrand, Picard did not favor the construction of dams or reservoirs, but, ironically, this was the solution that was privileged fifteen years later, when another commission was formed following the 6 January 1924 flood in Paris. Under the presidency of the *inspecteur général* of Ponts et Chaussées, two subcommissions were created to study the feasibility of reservoirs and for a *soutien d'étiage* (low water replenishment).[89] The commission completed its work on 28 June 1925 and leaned toward solutions adopted abroad, notably in the United States, where in the valleys of the Miami and the Mississippi reservoirs were constructed. The commission recommended the construction of four reservoirs and voted to finance studies of secondary dams, an approach that Paris pursued in the second half of the twentieth century.[90] Henri Chabal (1868–1935), an industrialist and engineer who undertook important hydraulic public works projects in France and its colonies, as well as in Germany, England, Spain, Italy, and Russia, published *Projet de régularisation du débit de la Seine* in 1920, in which he proposed creating twenty-three reservoirs that would have hydroelectric capacity. He believed that if this had been done earlier the 1910 flood would not have occurred.[91] Three reservoirs were ultimately created in the Morvan and one in the Marne by 1938, and the Conseil général de la Seine allocated 150 million francs in addition to protect France from further flooding. There was, however, considerable resistance to these measures from local communities that were affected by the projects. When the first reservoir, Pannecière, was created a few kilometers north of Château-Chinon in the Morvan villages, cemeteries, forests, and some arable land were submerged.[92]

What the history of nineteenth-century floods indicates is that from the 1850s onward governments slowly began to implement measures both to prevent floods and to manage them more effectively when they happened. In many respects the great flood of 1856 marked a turning point in terms of policies, practices, and public perceptions of floods and their environmental causes. The state began to use dredging and levees as preventive measures and altered the course of rivers through the construction of canals, heading off treacherous bends. France's first levees were constructed along the Loire in 1707, and later they could also be found on the Allier and the Cher and along parts of the Rhône. Perhaps one of the most significant governmental initiatives in the area of flood management had already been launched in the eighteenth century with the establishment of the Ecole des ponts et chaussées (School of Bridges and Roads) under the aegis of the famous engineer Jean-Rodolphe Perronet four years after the 1740 flood. The school trained road, bridge, and harbor engineers and was the first of its kind in the world. This technical corps was ultimately responsible for studying river flows and the periodic floods that occurred from the mid-eighteenth century onward. At the insistence of these engineers, the government undertook a series of studies, following Philippe Buache's 1741 study. Another was authored by his pupil Antoine Déparcieux in 1764.[93] As Paul Allard has argued, the engineers from the administration of Ponts et Chaussées as well as the forest officials from the administration of Eaux et Foréts were at the heart of new nineteenth-century measures taken to control floods.[94] But just as importantly, the public at large began to show a new awareness of the phenomenon, participating in ongoing debates while offering their own solutions to what appeared to be a growing problem, particularly at midcentury. Indeed, during the nineteenth century floods appeared to occupy a place in the national consciousness that they had not occupied before, and their memory continued to pervade literary output well into the twentieth century. In particular, the Paris flood of 1910 continued to be featured as a backdrop for a number of memoirs and novels in the twentieth century. It was the centerpiece of *Le testament français*, a novel/memoir by the Franco-Russian novelist Andreï Makine, which won both the Prix Médicis and the Prix Goncourt in 1995.[95] A year later, in 1996, the American novelist Sarah Smith's *The Knowledge of Water* appeared and, once again, the flood became one of the principal forces shaping the protagonists' lives. In short, the periodic floods that marked the French landscape continued to shape a national environmental consciousness as France entered the twenty-first century.[96]

What the debates and controversy surrounding floods during the course of the nineteenth century reveal was the extent to which the general public, which certainly felt their effects, became engaged in trying to understand their causes and finding measures to control and prevent them from happening in the future. Between 1733 and 1882 Paris alone experienced thirty-one floods of an ordinary severity (six meters), five with heights above six meters, and two extraordinary floods of above seven meters.[97] The engineers of the Ponts et Chaussées had been concerned about flooding since the eighteenth century and were called in by the state in times of crisis, but it was only after 1840 that flooding occupied a place in the public consciousness in France as a whole. This occurred as communication and transportation improved, and as both experts and lay observers began to speculate on the immensity of the problem. After 1856 there was no turning back.

FOUR

Environment and Landscape as Heritage

> Man of the nineteenth century entered nature like an executioner.
> —EDMOND MENCHIKOF

ENGINEERS and forest officials associated with the Ponts et Chaussées and the Eaux et Forêts spearheaded measures that were taken to control floods and combat deforestation, which they saw as inextricably linked. These initiatives, and the fact that they were documented and publicized in the press, resulted in the French public's engagement in a broader debate about the natural environment, which appeared to be at risk. But initiatives to control and protect the natural world came from other quarters as well, and they reflected concerns that had less to do with anxieties about climate change, floods, and deforestation than with the preservation of nature as heritage or *patrimoine*. This can most clearly be seen in the beginnings and development of France's early laws governing the protection "natural monuments," sites, and landscapes in metropolitan and colonial France, which harked back to François-Antoine Rauch's early discussion of natural monuments.[1] These initiatives came from artists, poets, and novelists as well as from the urban middle classes in Paris and other cities in France, where the concern was not for the conservation of natural resources or the protection of nature per se but for safeguarding the aesthetic and historic aspects of the natural world. This impulse was reflected in the initiatives undertaken by the Barbizon school of landscape painters, who, beginning in the 1840s, launched a campaign to protect the forest of Fontainebleau, and in the founding of a variety of associations later in the century that were devoted to particular causes. They included, principally, the Alpine Club, the Touring Club of France, and the Society for the Protection of the Landscapes of France. The pressure these associations put on the government ultimately led to concrete legislation that was passed in various stages between the 1860s and the 1930s, providing a blueprint for landscape protection in metropolitan France well into the twentieth century. However, what was first articulated in a discourse that was at once patriotic and aesthetic, while focusing on metropolitan France, gradually became international in its focus and was extended to France's colonies from the first decade of the twentieth century to World War II.

※ ※ ※

IN FRANCE, heritage or *patrimoine,* was defined in material and juridical terms and linked to ancestral inheritance from the French Revolution onward.[2] As it came to be articulated over time, only those monuments or objects that transmitted a shared tradition and recalled a common past—and which were privileged or venerated as a result—would be considered as such. As Dominique Poulot and the authors associated with Pierre Nora's seven-volume *Les lieux de mémoire* have suggested, the French conception of *patrimoine* has been a work in progress since the French Revolution.[3] France's earliest defense of its *patrimoine* had long been associated with Abbé Grégoire's call to protect the nation's prerevolutionary monuments and religious objects from vandalism during the French Revolution, a call that laid the groundwork for the creation of France's Musée national des monuments français in 1795. This museum confined itself early on to the project of historical conservation within the borders of metropolitan France. During the July Monarchy, in 1830 to be more precise, François Guizot established the post of inspector of historical monuments. Then, the year 1834 saw the creation of the Comité des arts, which was soon replaced by the Commission des monuments français. Under the direction of Ludovic Vitet and Prosper Merimée, the commission established a set of administrative procedures as well as links to learned societies and local archeological commissions.[4]

The French brought this notion of *patrimoine,* which centered on venerated objects and historical monuments, to Algeria in the 1840s when architects, including Amable Ravoisié and Charles Texier, prepared inventories of various archeological sites. Legislation governing the preservation of historical monuments and the protection of a national *patrimoine* was passed slowly during the course of the nineteenth century in metropolitan France. In May 1840 the liberal Catholic Charles de Montalembert argued before the Chamber of Peers that the government should classify historical monuments as having a *utilité public* and that they should be subject to expropriation by the state. A ministerial circular of 14 August 1876 called for the publication of a general inventory of "richesses d'art de la France." This circular prompted the creation of a departmental commission in Algiers charged with doing an inventory there. It was at this moment that the Académie de l'instruction publique et des beaux-arts urged the Ministry of Public Instruction and Fine Arts to apply heritage legislation to Algeria that would protect the colony's ancient ruins. The ministry immediately pleaded a lack of financial resources, even though the Chamber of Deputies began to discuss the passage of a law regarding the conservation of historical monuments in France, with special provisions for Algeria and France's protectorates, in June 1886.

These initiatives were helped by the founding of a number of private associations. One of the most important was the Société des amis des monuments parisiens, which was established in the late 1870s. Charles Normand, son of the architect Alfred Normand, was its principal spokesman, and, significantly, the society elected Albert Lenoir, son of Alexandre Lenoir, who had founded the Revolution's Museum of French National Monuments, as its first president. The society couched its project in the language of patriotism. In preserving the heritage of the past, its members wished to "work for the benefit of France, by trying to protect the buildings and artworks that create the charm and the reputation of her capital. Is it not through them that a constant education is provided imbuing peoples with the love of the forebears?"[5] Soon after the founding of the Parisian society and an analogue in Rouen, a nationwide Comité des arts et monuments was created, along with a periodical, *L'Ami des Monuments*. The publication represented a new departure in that it sought to inform the public and the state about endangered objects, buildings, and natural landscapes in France.[6]

On 30 March 1887 the Chamber passed a law relative to the conservation of monuments and art objects that had historical and artistic interest. Article 16 of the legislation made the law applicable to Algeria and to France's protectorates. Although many years later André Malraux, France's first minister of culture, attempted to broaden the definition of *patrimoine* soon after France's Ministry of Culture was created in 1960, understandings of the term were intimately bound up with historical and architectural "monuments," and this association was eventually extended to "natural monuments" on French soil.[7]

While preservationist societies were being founded in Paris and other urban centers in France, a small coterie of artists and a Parisian bourgeoisie were behind the first attempts to extend the notion of *patrimoine* to natural sites in a more comprehensive way. They began to frequent the pathways of the royal forest of Fontainebleau as temporary residents and as day visitors once train lines were extended from Paris to the capital's environs after 1840, and the historic forest came to occupy an iconic place in the French bourgeois imagination by midcentury.

Fontainebleau was transformed from a place for hunting and harvesting wood into an object of inspiration, a spectacle, a place for spiritual renewal, a natural haven from industrial life, a refuge from political turmoil, and a natural national icon. It also became a landscape of nostalgia, reflecting a new relationship between town and country as well as between the French landscape and the national past. However, ironically, the early impulse behind the protection of so-called natural landscapes in France was born in a forest that was one of the least wild, having long been a royal forest.

For the Parisian bourgeoisie, which had experienced political turmoil several times between 1789 and 1848, the forest took on new meanings. In their growing concern about social and political unrest, pollution and disease, they looked to Fontainebleau as a particular kind of space for rejuvenation, a refuge from social strife and the vicissitudes of urban politics. Moreover, the peasantry of the French countryside, which had long been associated with disorder and violence, gradually came to be nostalgically romanticized as the embodiment of order and social stability. Indeed, it was this selfsame peasantry that routed the Parisian working class during the June Days of 1848 under the command of General Cavaignac. When the novelist Gustave Flaubert's antihero, Frédéric Moreau, and his mistress flee Paris in the midst of the Revolution of 1848, they go to Fontainebleau. In *L'éducation sentimentale* they find in the royal forest a "spectacle of nature":

> The different trees afforded a fascinating spectacle. The beeches, with their smooth white bark, mingled their foliage; ashes gently curved their grey-green boughs; in the hornbeam coppices there bristled holly bushes that seemed to be made of bronze; then came a line of slender birches, bent in elegiac attitudes; and the pines, as symmetrical as organ pipes, seemed to sing as they swayed continuously to and fro. Huge gnarled oaks rose convulsively out of the ground, embraced one another, and solidly established on their torso-like trunks, threw out their bare arms in desperate appeals and furious threats, like a group of Titans struck motionless in their anger.[8]

Soon the "solemnity of the forest" took hold of them both, and "abandoning themselves to the gentle rocking of the springs, they lay sunk in calm intoxication."[9]

※ ※ ※

THE MASSIF DE FONTAINEBLEAU is about sixty kilometers southwest of Paris and lies between the plains of Bière to the north, the valley of the Seine, the Gâtinais to the south, and the plateau of Beauce to the west. It occupies 25,000 hectares, while the forest of Fontainebleau's surface area was approximately 16,917 hectares in 1830. Its vegetation is varied and very poor in places, which accounts for a heavy concentration of pine trees, which were introduced in the eighteenth century as part of reforestation project. About 44 percent of the forest still consists of oak trees, and the landscape is punctuated by scenic gorges and rock formations.

The forest was originally a royal game preserve attached to the château of Fontainebleau, which was built by François I during the Renaissance. While hunting was the exclusive right of the king and the nobility, residents of Barbizon had the right to graze animals and to gather fallen wood. Once a royal forest that was out of bounds for the casual visitor, Fontainebleau and its historic landscapes were "discovered" by a middle-class urban public with the development of local tourism from the 1830s and 1840s onward. The advent of the July Monarchy in 1830 marked a "rupture in the way of perceiving the landscape."[10] The extension of train lines from Paris to Fontainebleau, which would make it easily accessible to Parisians in search of "wild nature," was facilitated by the municipal council of Fontainebleau's deliberations on 8 August 1844, when a proposal to place a train stop several hundred meters from the town was approved.[11]

As Nicholas Green has argued, the discovery of Fontainebleau was intimately bound up with both rapid urbanization and industrialization in and around Paris and with the anxieties they produced among city planners, hygienists, and the general public.[12] From the 1840s onward trips out of Paris to the capital's immediate environs increased in number, as did the number of *maisons de campagne* (country houses or secondary residences), creating new patterns of leisure, recreation, and local tourism for the middle classes, who tried to imitate the manners of the aristocracy on a more modest scale.[13]

As the extension of train lines made Fontainebleau more accessible, the limited number of hotels and inns expanded in the area surrounding it. Tourists from Paris came to Fontainebleau in droves after 1840, when the railway arrived at Corbeil. The mayor estimated that the number of visitors increased from 25,000 in the late 1830s to 70,000 in 1842 and then to 140,000 in 1844 and 319,448 by 1865.[14] The census of 1836 counted fourteen Bellifontains who declared themselves to be innkeepers, and by 1841 the number of inns had increased to seventeen, employing forty-two persons, before declining slightly in 1846.[15] The *hôtel particulier* gradually transformed itself into the more specialized *hôtel des voyageurs,* the grandest of them being the Grand Hôtel de France et d'Angleterre. Indeed, houses *(hôtels)* associated with some of the oldest aristocratic families of France—

de Ségur, de Beaufort, de Rohan, and de la Rochefoucault—provided the structures and building materials for the new accommodation.

The forest of Fontainebleau had its popularizers, who contributed to a new kind of travel writing that was intended for commercial, popular consumption. The writers did not attempt to introduce strange peoples and unfamiliar lands while presenting personal impressions of far-off places, but rather they attempted to provide practical advice and a hands-on guide to local places. Early examples of the guidebook, which served to introduce the reader to the history of sites and monuments, could be published in expensive periodicals ranging from *La France pittoresque* to *Le magasin pittoresque*. Some of the earliest local guides to Fontainebleau included Charles Rémard's *Le guide du voyageur à Fontainebleau* (1820) and Etienne Jamin's *Quatre promenades* (1837), published before the guidebook became a commercial industry under the direction of Adolphe Joanne in France and Karl Baedeker in Germany.[16]

The most influential writer of local guidebooks for Fontainebleau was Claude-François Denecourt, who became a kind of forest impresario. Born in 1788 in humble circumstances in the Haute-Saône, a border region of France, he pursued a military career, fighting in the Napoleonic Wars and serving as a porter-caretaker at Versailles during the Restoration. He supported the Revolution and the Empire before embracing the Restoration, with which he soon became disillusioned. Soon after the beginning of the July Monarchy he was expelled from the army for his political views and embarked on a new career, setting himself up as a wholesale wine and cognac merchant in the town of Fontainebleau, where he came to make a profitable living.

Denecourt's real vocation became that of a "lover of the forest of Fontainebleau" and its cicerone or guide.[17] The forest became a haven and a refuge to which the *sylvain,* or man of the forest, increasingly retreated. He came to meet other denizens of the forest, among them the carpenter-poet Alexis Durand, who shared Denecourt's passion for mapping and surveying. Durand introduced him to Etienne Jamin, a clerk at the château, who wrote his own local guide. While they initially collaborated, their collaboration turned into rivalry when the success of Denecourt's guides incited Jamin's envy.

Following the lead of Jamin and Rémard, Denecourt published his first guide to Fontainebleau in 1839. It was such a success that the Guides Richard commissioned him to write in its collection, wishing to have him as one of its contributors.[18] These guides were followed by the publication of smaller brochures between 1842 and 1853 that reproduced excerpted passages from the larger guides, and a by a series of *indicateurs,* which provided readers with guided walks through the park and forest. Between 1830 and 1848, eleven editions of *L'indicateur* were printed and sold for 2.5 francs. *L'indicateur historique et descriptif de Fontainebleau, itinéraire de la forêt et des environs* was in its eighteenth edition and updated by a collaborator one year after Denecourt's death in 1876.[19] These guides were touted by the local press, especially *L'Abeille de Fontainebleau,* but they were decried by others as lacking in any literary value.

Denecourt ultimately went beyond writing local guides, which were based on meticulous note taking on the forest's paths, topography, and vegetation; he began to leave markings along Fontainebleau's paths in blue paint in places where he feared visitors might get lost, and in so doing contributed to the concept of a "trail." The inspector general of the forest, Achille Marrier de Bois d'Hyver, who was a highly protective and proprietary official, was very suspicious of Denecourt's eccentric activities but could find nothing in them that constituted an infringement of forest laws. Bois d'Hyver ultimately authorized him to chart new paths in the forest, and Denecourt forged relationships with local business interests, hoteliers, and café owners.[20]

Denecourt's activities ultimately became a lucrative source of income. In 1840 he began to edit albums of lithographs and prints, and he became involved in the production of new kinds of souvenirs, which included *genévrines* or "juniperines," small wood charms, and lithographs bound in jackets of wood.[21] Denecourt was at one and the same time a radical republican and a small-scale capitalist who had, in the words of Théophile Gautier, "the physiognomy of a wood-god: his waistcoat is brown, his trousers nutty colored, his hands tanned by the air, reveal[ing] muscles that bulge like veins of oak, [and] his tumbled hair resembles undergrowth; his pallor has a greenish nuance and his cheeks have red veined filaments resembling leaves as Autumn approaches; his feet dig into the ground like roots; his hat silhouettes a crown of leaves, and the vegetal aspect is soon apparent to the attentive eye."[22]

The central goal of these guidebooks was to draw the reader's attention to landscapes and sites that were *pittoresque,* as many of their titles suggest. The picturesque, a term that entered the French language at the beginning of the eighteenth century from Italian, initially referred to that which was worthy of being painted, which included both historical monuments and natural sites, rock formations, hills, ravines, rivers, and old-growth trees exhibiting striking characteristics. The picturesque was also a means of classifying landscapes in aesthetic terms, and it is no accident that the nineteenth century was the heyday of landscape painting and a period when French landscape painting came into its own. Aesthetic appreciation of the picturesque that was brought to bear on French landscape painting was reflected in its evolution. By 1867 one critic, writing about the work of these painters, argued that "through landscape, art becomes national . . . it takes possession of France, of the ground, of the air, of the sky, of the French landscape. This land that has borne us, the air that we breathe, this harmonious and sweet whole that constitutes the face of the mother country, we carry it in our soul."[23]

Denecourt came to plead both in his guidebooks and in letters to Napoleon III for the protection of Fontainebleau as a treasured landscape. He wrote two letters to the emperor in defense of Fontainebleau. One was an actual petition calling for the protection of part of the forest that might be defined as *artistique* and *pittoresque* in the form of "artistic reserves." The other was a more general entreaty, which called on the emperor to consider the forest of Fontainebleau as a "precious museum": "Grace for that which remains of the most valuable beauties of forests! Grace in the name of artists, in the name of poets, in the name of all intelligent men and women who appreciate the sentiment of beauty, the sentiment of conservation of the most beautiful things that France possesses!"[24] He argued that parts of the forest of Fontainebleau should not be considered land to be exploited but rather as comprising "galleries of the most precious museum of sites and of landscapes that France possesses and whose conservation should with reason be assimilated into that of historical monuments" worthy of being protected.[25] Denecourt identified specific sites as worthy of protection and provided criteria for their classification. They included sites that had particularly impressive perspectives, sites that were favored by painters, and particular tree and rock formations. He saw in the forest of Fontainebleau a "national museum" and one of the most beloved and frequented places in Europe, calling it "this unique forest among all forests and at the same time one of the most [beautiful] jewels in the crown."[26] For Denecourt the forest was not simply a natural monument but also a cultural monument, and the forest's paths could be compared to the corridors between galleries in a museum.

The forest of Fontainebleau's embrace by Denecourt or by Frédéric in Flaubert's *Sentimental Education* was one that was shared by a whole generation of bourgeois artists, writers, and tourists who left the capital for the countryside surrounding Paris in the mid-nineteenth century. What they encountered was a highly charged "spectacle," as Flaubert called it, a landscape that resembled organ pipes singing in the wind, muscular titans, and bushes made of bronze. It was an enchanted landscape that induced intoxication, sensuality, and a deep connection with history and the nation's past.

The celebration of Fountainebleau was at the center of the work of both Romantic and realist writers during the nineteenth century, and forty-two writers and poets contributed to a volume that was assembled by Fernand Desnoyers in tribute to Denecourt and Fontainebleau in 1855.[27] They included Théodore de Banville, Victor Hugo, Alphonse de Lamartine, Théophile Gautier, and Jules Janin, among others. The volume's introduction declared that "everyone today knows Fontainebleau. Above all for Parisians, the Lyon railway has made it into a suburb."[28] While most of the contributions celebrated the beauty of the forest in some form, there was one notable exception. Charles Baudelaire contributed to the volume, but his poems remained focused on the urban environment, and he felt compelled to write to Desnoyers to rail against the "new religion" of nature:

> You ask me for verses for your little volume, verses about *Nature,* do you not? About trees, tall oaks, greenery, insects,—the sun, no doubt? But you know well that I am incapable of being moved by plants, and that my soul rebels against this singular new Religion, which will always have, it seems to me, for any *spiritual* being something shocking [about it]. I will never believe that *the spirit of the Gods lives in plants,* and even if it lives in them, I would care little, and consider mine to be much more highly prized than that of sanctified vegetables.[29]

Baudelaire was nonetheless forced to acknowledge the degree to which Fontainebleau, forests, and the cult of nature more generally had captured the imagination of his fellow poets from the early nineteenth century onward. Etienne Pivert de Sénancour's 1804 *Obermann,* which was in part set in a forest, came to the attention of a broad French public when it was reissued 1833, the year the novelist Georges Sand came to Fontainebleau for the first time. Jules Michelet spent time in Fontainebleau with his wife in 1869 as he finished a draft of *L'insecte,* while Flaubert was to complete his master work, *L'education sentimentale,* there in 1869.

The evocative nature of the forest captured in Flaubert's prose was one that was also borne out in a series of paintings undertaken by Théodore Rousseau, Diaz de la Pena, Jean-François Millet, and others associated with a group of painters who established themselves in Barbizon, a village on the edge of the forest of Fontainebleau during the same period. These painters did much to celebrate and popularize the French landscape in their paintings of the rocks, oak trees, sandy dunes, and clearings in the forest. Some of the forest's most notable landmarks—Bas Bréau, Ecouettes, the gorges of Apremont and Franchard, Bellecroix, the plain of Maclenin, Reine Blanche—became the focus of their attention. While they were excluded from the salons of the Académie des beaux-arts during the July Monarchy, their work was purchased by the bourgeoisie of Paris. The industrialist Paul Casimir-Périer, the brother of the deputy Auguste Casimir-Périer, who made a fortune from his investments in railways, decided to invest some of his profits in the work of Rousseau, Dupré, and Diaz.[30] After 1848 the academy and salons began to recognize the work of the Barbizon school painters, and in 1852 Théodore Rousseau was awarded the Légion d'honneur. Three years later the painters exhibited their work at the Universal Exposition.

Artists had already come to the forest of Fontainebleau in the eighteenth century, but it was only in the 1830s that a particular group of artists began to spend extended periods of time there. Rousseau first stayed in Chailly in 1833–1834 and came to Barbizon on a regular basis from 1837 to 1840, staying at Père Ganne's inn as well as in a woodcutter's cabin. Diaz and his family did the same in 1835. Rousseau began renting a house in Barbizon in 1847, and he was joined by Millet, who fled the dirt, poverty, and diseases of Paris. The artists became close, and other painters visited in subsequent years, including the famous caricaturist Honoré Daumier and Antoine-Louis Barye. The painters of Barbizon, who were labeled "naturalists," lived out their bohemian existence far from Paris and depicted not only the natural beauty of the forest but also sectors of a rural economy that was disintegrating under the pressure of tourism and agricultural modernization. They included grazing and wood gathering, which were parts of a disappearing rural world.

In the 1840s Barbizon had a population of about 200, which consisted of landowners, shepherds, and small shopkeepers, as well as some forest guards, and the village had one street. It was surrounded by open fields where wheat, barley, oats, and potatoes were grown. More than Rousseau, it was Millet who captured the rhythms and landscape of Barbizon and its fields, which provided the backdrop for some of his most famous subjects: *The Angelus, The Gleaners,* and *Man with a Hoe.*[31]

A growing ecological awareness affected these painters' art, which was expressed in their concern about how the forest was being managed and cared for. In his analysis of Théodore Rousseau's landscapes, the art historian Greg Thomas has stressed their ecological characteristics, arguing that "calling a mode of representation ecological" is "complicated by the fact that ecology has two distinct sides to it," the scientific and the political; he stresses that this is further complicated by the "ambiguous relationship that existed between both early ecological science and romanticism and between early environmental politics and capitalism."[32]

One of the earliest articles to address the environmental integrity of the forest of Fontainebleau was published in *L'Artiste* in 1839. Signed by A.S.,

"La forêt de Fontainebleau: Dévastations" (The forest of Fontainebleau: Destructions), the article, ironically, criticized, in particular, foresters associated with the forest service (Eaux et Forêts), who had done so much to preserve the integrity of wooded areas since the seventeenth century, for the utilitarian way in which they managed the forest and for making it into a resource for profit. For the author and the artists associated with Fontainebleau, the forest should be preserved as an aesthetic refuge, a mnemonic device recalling a rich historic past, bearing out Madame de Staël's view that "the most beautiful landscapes in the world, if they evoke no memory, if they bear no trace to any notable event, are uninteresting compared to historic landscapes."[33] The article suggested in no uncertain terms that artists and poets were the true guardians of the forest: "For them, a forest is a needed sacred oasis in the midst of impious invasions of a destructive and improvident civilization . . . a magnificent studio where grandiose inspirations reveal themselves . . . a majestic temple where the most beautiful harmonies of nature unite in a worthy manner to praise the Creator."[34] The author then went on to make the claim that "as all artists attest, the forest of Fontainebleau is Europe's most beautiful; it is the only one in France where one can see some vestiges of the virgin forest, crossed in addition by convenient and picturesque roads."[35] He attributed the slow destruction of the forest, which he characterized as vandalism, to three initiatives undertaken by the forest service: the draining of swamps, the cutting of old oak and beech trees, and the planting of pine trees, "this sad exotic vegetation."[36] A number of artists documented these initiatives in their work. Jules Dupré, in particular, executed a series of paintings whose central subjects were felled trees, including *Felled Trees, 1840s*, and Rousseau painted *Clearing of Trees in the Isle of Croissy* in 1847. A.S. saw the situation unfolding in Fontainebleau as one that was about "conserving for France, and even for Europe, a natural monument, without equal."[37]

While the author of the article in *L'Artiste* remained anonymous, it has been argued that Théodore Rousseau was responsible for its publication.[38] Indeed, Rousseau made the protection of the forest of Fontainebleau into a mission, which was reflected in his art. Born in 1812, Rousseau developed a form of landscape painting that set him apart from the academic painters of the period. In paintings that included *Edge of the Forest, The Priest,* and *The Footbridge,* Rousseau idealized "the rural world as a unified whole," a world in which rural people and the landscape interacted with one another.[39] His art was, like that of many of the other Romantic Barbizon school painters, "intensely nostalgic," as a desire to conserve is bound up with an understanding of the threat of a world passing away.[40]

Making a distinction between the "historic" trees of Fontainebleau, which included oaks and beeches, and "newcomers" (pines), Rousseau argued for the preservation of only certain kinds of forested landscape. He established a hierarchy of trees that was based on their history and age rather than on "nature." Oaks were the most valuable, and the incursion of pines to be lamented. They were allegedly introduced into the forest by Marie-Antoinette's doctor, Louis Guillaume Lemonnier, who brought seedlings from the Baltic, but the high point of the plantings came under the stewardship of Marrier de Bois d'Hyver, who transformed many aspects the forest between 1830 and 1847. By 1888 old-growth trees covered only about half of the forest, and empty spaces had to all intents and purposes disappeared as the result of the planting of pines.[41]

Forests and plant life were not valued in and of themselves but rather as an expression of the past, of history. For the artists, pines were an aesthetic monstrosity, representing a foreign invasive species, and the painters would gather in a local inn close to Fontainebleau to combat the forest service's plantations as early as the 1830s. As the artist Emile Michel wrote in 1909:

> Relations with the forest administration were not very courteous. Following the plantation of resinous trees, its agents were held as enemies, deserving the most unflattering epithets. The landscape painters had declared war on them and to oppose the replanting that they judged unaesthetic, it was agreed that one would be admitted to the evening meal only under the express condition of bringing back to the inn at least a pair of young pines pulled up in the plantations: *pine to dine,* according to the adopted formula.[42]

The forest administration retaliated. Around 1852 the forest guards caught François-Henri Nazon engaging in the practice, and he barely escaped imprisonment. John Croumbie Brown, however, who wrote extensively on forest practices in France and in Europe during this period, noted that 98 percent of the soil in Fontainebleau was sand, and asserted that the area would be a "drifting desert" without trees, which included pines.[43]

By 1852 Rousseau was sufficiently exercised about what he saw happening in the forest of Fontainebleau that he penned his own petition, probably with his friend Alfred Sensier, to the new emperor, Napoleon III. He claimed that artists had been "deeply saddened" for the past thirty years by the deeds of the forest administration and that the forest was the "only living souvenir that remains from the heroic times of the Fatherland from Charlemagne to Napoleon." He lamented the "systematic felling, clear-cuts, and unintelligent plantations," about which artists had complained many times during the July Monarchy without having been heeded: "Under your government, Monseigneur, this system continues; the forest administration indiscriminately cuts down trees whose great age, fame, and artistic beauty should make them respected, and in other areas of the forest they sow in profusion unaccountable quantities of Northern Pines that are wiping out this forest's old Gaul character and will soon give us the severe and sad look of Russian forests."[44] Although Rousseau held the forest administration chiefly responsible for the destruction of the forest of Fontainebleau, he also laid blame at the feet of Denecourt, who did so much to popularize it and capitalize on it: "A resident of Fontainebleau, a maniacal old man named Mr. Denecourt, smitten in the wrong way with the beauties of the forest, is going off seeking aid from all quarters and using it to lay out useless trails, to build ridiculous platforms, to make [walls] of grass, to cover with paint, numbers, and inscriptions the forest's most beautiful trees, which he is despoiling and dishonoring."[45] What Rousseau came to propose was that the parts of the forest that artists admired and incorporated into their paintings be placed beyond the reach of the forest administration, and he identified the following sites: Bas-Bréau, the oldest part of the forest; the Apremont Gorges; the plateau of Belle Croix; and the Gorge of the Wolves. In short, he concluded that "if we recognize that the monuments of men, old churches and old palaces, must be respectfully preserved, would it not be just as reasonable to command that the most sublime monuments of nature have like them a tranquil end?"[46]

The foresters, in turn, pilloried the artists and responded by arguing that they foresaw the "ruin" of Fontainebleau. Without judicious cutting and replanting, the trees would choke one another and die. One forest official wrote in the *Revue des Eaux et Forêts* of 1877 that "there is no forest without a forester, any more than there is a garden without a gardener. The virgin forest is nothing other than a poetic fiction."[47] The artists, Denecourt, and his tourists had other critics as well. Arthur Mangin wrote:

> Despite its enormous trees, its rudely broken surface, its stags and roebucks, reserved for imperial sport; despite its adders and problematical vipers, it is now little better than a rendezvous for amateur artists and listless idlers. Its well-kept avenues resound with rapid wheels, and you can scarcely stir a step without finding the associations of the place interrupted by the stalls of vendors of cakes, or the apparatus of itinerant gamblers.[48]

The artists were deeply critical of the foresters, who themselves claimed to be agents of responsible conservation, but they did not criticize or remark on the presence of the peasants who gathered wood, grazed their sheep, or attacked forest guards. These were the very peasants who fought pitched battles with the state over communal rights, which was crystallized in the so-called War of the Demoiselles in 1829. Foresters had railed against peasants and the devastation that they wrought since the French Revolution. The peasants, however, figure very prominently in the paintings of Diaz, Rousseau, and especially Millet, where they are portrayed heroically. Indeed, the peasants, with whom the French state had waged several century-long battles for control over forests, became an integral part of the landscape, which represented a way of life. The domesticated landscapes, which included peasants, constituted landscapes of nostalgia, where local peasant practices appeared to pose no threat. Indeed, the painters came to idealize the waning pastoral tradition. In one painting, one has a snapshot of practices in the forest that would be in clear violation of the law. Arthur Melville's *Faggot Gatherers* depicts a woman brandishing a metal hatchet that she obviously intends to use. The law only allowed for the gathering of fallen wood by women, and any form of cutting was strictly forbidden. The human presence in the forest did not appear to be decried by the painters as long as that presence reflected an older rural economy.

Ironically, three different constituencies, notably artists, foresters, and tour guides, who were all ostensibly devoted to the preservation of the forest of Fontainebleau, fought pitched battles with one another, and none won these battles completely. Rousseau had a sympathetic ear in the Duc de Morny, an art collector and half-brother of Napoleon III. Morny had helped to orchestrate Napoleon III's coup d'état and served as a minister of the interior under the new regime. Rousseau submitted his petition to him and was given a dinner invitation in response. He articulated his argument for the preservation of Fontainebleau in patriotic language and in terms of the innate rights of the natural world. A year later a report was prepared on the future management of the forest, and the report's plan was then instituted by imperial decree eight years later, in 1861. It provided for the protection of twelve areas of the forest, which would not be managed by the forest administration and which would be at the disposition of the artists. Eight of these areas had been mentioned by Rousseau. In all, 1,097 hectares (6.56 percent of the entire forest) were set aside as a *réserve artistique*.[49] The emperor's decree of 13 August 1861 divided the forest into three sections, with 13,724 hectares subject to a new system of clear-cutting, 1,618 managed under the old system of spot-cutting, and 1,631 hectares that were not to be managed. The hectares devoted to the *partie artistique* had been increased from an earlier recommendation to 1,097 hectares. Moreover, the so-called Moscow pines were to be banished from the Apremont Gorges and Bas-Bréau, which were so highly prized by Rousseau and other artists. The old oak groves were preserved and off limits to further cutting. The battle over vegetation and landscape appeared to have been won, and Bois d'Hyver's scheme to systematically sow pines, which grew rapidly, at the expense of oak trees between 1830 and 1848, when he was an *inspecteur* of the forest, was reversed.[50] The oak tree regained its status as a kind of national tree of France, while the decree, in effect, constituted France's first governmental measure to protect a specific natural landscape. It would have far-reaching consequences for determining which landscapes would be protected in metropolitan France in the future and how landscapes would come to be protected subsequently by the state.[51]

In a broad sense, both foresters and artists expressed the desire to protect and safeguard the natural world. However, foresters conceived of landscape protection in terms of conservation. They wished to manage and use the forest as a natural resource judiciously. The artists focused on preservation, which is "posited on the principle of non-utilitarianism," demanding "the prevention of any active interference whatsoever."[52] The conservationist approach was well established in France, but the idea of setting aside significant segments of state forests from any form of management and considering those forests as heritage and history soon took hold. As David Lowenthal has suggested, preservation ultimately became a "principal mode of appreciating the past."[53] France, of course, was not the only country in Europe or North America that began to turn its attention to forest and landscape conservation in the nineteenth century. Natural resources were seen as a "barometer of the health of American society." What was to be conserved in the United States, however, was the "wild country," which, in the words of William Cronon, "became a place not just of religious redemption but of national renewal, the quintessential location for experiencing what it meant to be an American."[54]

※ ※ ※

THE VALORIZATION of the forest of Fontainebleau as an aesthetic and historic landscape paved the way for more general later legislation governing the protection of natural sites and monuments. The battle waged among artists, foresters and tourists, however, pointed to tensions and disputes about how the forest should be protected and for whom. The growing hordes of tourists also gave rise to new pursuits, which included outdoor sports from the 1870s onward. The forest soon became a locale for cycling and rock climbing, which were encouraged by the founding of a number of voluntary associations that came to embrace the cause of landscape and nature protection. They included the Club alpin français (1875) and the Touring Club de France (1890). These associations and the Société pour la protection des paysages de France (SPPF, Society for the Protection of the Landscapes of France), founded in 1901, began to spearhead more comprehensive legislation governing the protection of natural sites. While some of these associations were oriented toward particular kinds of causes, all shared a common concern about preserving the beauty of the natural environment. All of these associations, which were established during or after 1870, recruited members from among the middle class, including the liberal professions, civil servants, men of letters, and increasingly from what the politician Léon Gambetta called the *nouvelles couches sociales,* a rising petite bourgeoisie, which included primary school teachers, the "black hussars of the Republic."

The French Alpine Club, which was initially founded by a group of French alpinists and officially created on 2 April 1874 with the motto "For country, for the mountain," is a case in point. Its membership, which ranged from 5,500 to 7,500, was largely made up of civil servants and the liberal professions, and it was, like the other associations founded in this period, almost overwhelmingly male. Only 1.6 percent of its members were women in 1875, and only 3.8 percent of new members from 1876 to 1883 were women. Georges Sand was one of the Alpine Club's few female members, but she was a founding member, perhaps attesting to her early enthusiasm for mountainous landscapes following stays in Cauterets in 1825 and her journey to Chamonix in 1836.[55] Other adherents to the organization included the architect Eugène Viollet-le-Duc; Onésime and Elisée Reclus; Adolphe Joanne, an author of some of the most popular guidebooks of the period; the publisher Georges Hachette; and Alexandre Surell, the Ponts et Chausées engineer. They began to call for the protection of mountainous terrain as both scientific and cultural heritage.

The 1890s saw the foundation of new organizations, including the Société des amis des arbres (the Society of the Friends of Trees), which was established in Nice and transferred to Paris in 1894, while in 1898 some of the members of the club created an offshoot, the Société des peintres de montagne (the Society of Mountain Painters).[56] These diverse and interlinked organizations were dedicated to the preservation of forests and mountainous regions, but their motivations differed from those of the foresters and engineers. They regarded the forests of the Alps from an aesthetic and touristic perspective.

The Touring Club de France, which was founded on 26 January 1890 in Neuilly-sur-Seine, had as its explicit purpose the promotion of tourism in all of its forms. However, it was also devoted to the protection of everything that a voyager might consider picturesque or aesthetic. The SPPF was founded some years later, on 1 March 1901, and its aim was more generalized in that it envisioned the protection of the diverse regions of France and the safeguarding of their beauty from the ravages of industrialization and public advertising: "First article.—The Society for the Protection of the Landscapes of France has the general goal of spreading and developing the notion that all natural beauty, as a whole or in part, can be the object of public utility . . . necessary to the honor and wealth of the country."[57] The SPPF was involved in a number of early initiatives to protect specific sites, which included the Gimel cascade and the valley of the Granges. While it claimed to be a proponent of the railway, its members declared themselves to be against the effects of industrialization and the advocates of legislation designed to sanction those who would destroy France's natural environment.[58]

In 1901 Henri Cazalis, a doctor and a poet who published on a wide variety of subjects under the pseudonym Jean Lahor, issued a kind of manifesto for the SPPF. Its epigraph was a quote from Edmond Menchikof: "Man of the nineteenth century entered nature like an executioner." He declared that not only historical monuments should be protected. For him it was also necessary to protect and save "our mountains, our valleys, our forests, our torrents," which were also "sublime" and imperiled "monuments" of nature. This mission, according to Cazalis, should be done in the name of saving France's *patrimoine,* or heritage.[59] But he defended his project in aesthetic terms too, and cited the efforts of the Barbizon school painters and the creation of Yellowstone Park in 1872.[60] For Cazalis, the culprits responsible for the destruction of natural landscapes were industrialists and merchants, and he drew particular attention to new commercial practices, which included advertising posters. He also targeted tourists and railways. In his view, industry should not destroy the landscapes of France, and if industry and individuals have rights, "nature and beauty also have theirs."[61] Cazalis, however, went beyond the confines of France in declaring the necessity of "international measures," which, he argued, needed to be studied and pursued, and he cited initiatives taken by the czar to protect Russia's steppes.[62]

In some respects the SPPF was an outgrowth of an earlier, more generalized organization, the Société pour la protection de l'esthétique de la France, and a specific event triggered its founding: a court case that was successfully won for the protection and surveillance of the sources of the river Lizon in the Doubs.[63] The goals of the SPPF were close to those of its sister organization, the Bund Heimatschutz, founded in Germany a few years later, in 1904, and it was intimately associated with France's regionalist movement, absorbing much of the membership of that movement's organizations. Jean Charles-Brun, the president of the Fédération régionaliste française, was also a founding member of the SPPF, and the goal of his organization was to preserve the regional traditions and cultures of France, which were threatened by the centralized power of the French state. André Thierry was an honorary president of the SPPF and the president of the Society for National Ethnography, founded in 1895, whose aim was to foster local culture and traditional ways of life. For this reason the politics of the SPPF was often characterized as conservative. However, its members included Radical Socialists, like Charles Beauquier (1833–1916), moderates, and monarchists, whose common ground was their aesthetic concerns and a kind of patriotic regionalism. *Paysage* did not simply represent landscape but also embraced the concept of *pays* and a regional past. The French equivalent of Heimat became the *petite patrie*.[64] While the membership of all of these associations was drawn largely from the middle classes and associated with artistic, intellectual, and governmental circles, these circles frequently overlapped. Abel Ballif, president of the Touring Club de France, was also a member of the SPPF's governing board. The Nobel laureate René Sully Prudhomme was the SPPF's most prominent member.

The earliest justifications for a more general legislation governing the protection of natural sites and monuments in France following the creation of the *séries artistiques* at Fontainebleau were aesthetic and nationalistic. They were also predicated on a particular conception of landscape or *paysage*. This concept was closely linked to the idea of *pays* or the *petite patrie*, which was defined not only by the physical characteristics of a landscape but by the human culture that shaped these landscapes, in the form of local heritage, and, as noted, it bore some relationship to the German concept of Heimat.[65] The Heimatsbewegung assumed its own form in France, and the *pays* was valorized alongside all of the material things connected to nature, which included buildings, folk art, and traditional dress and ways of life. The members of the SPPF very often opposed advertising, new construction of any kind, and the expansion of railways and industry because they believed that these developments destroyed the integrity of natural sites.

Those responsible for legislation governing the protection of natural sites and monuments were politicians and members of voluntary associations, whereas the initiatives taken to protect forests and to control floods tended to come from Eaux et Forêts and the administration of Ponts et Chaussées, even though the public at large was engaged in discussions surrounding these questions. A brief consideration of some of the key figures associated with the landscape protection movement also reveals the overlapping circles in which they moved.

Charles Beauquier, a Radical Socialist deputy of Doubs and president of the SPPF, is often viewed as the main standard-bearer for legislation governing the protection of natural sites and monuments. He called for the creation of commissions composed of artists, members of the Alpine and Touring clubs, and members of the *conseil général* in different localities and of the municipal councils in all of the departments of France. The commissions would be charged with classifying sites to be protected by the state. Beauquier came to his own views about landscape protection early on. At the age of thirty-three he published *Philosophie de la musique* in which he likened instrumental music to landscape painting.[66] He was a member of the League for the Protection of Birds and one of the co-founders in 1901 of the SPPF serving as its president from 1901 to 1915. He declared in the Chamber of Deputies on 4 March 1902 that public opinion had been mobilized in favor of landscape protection and that it was not possible to suppose that "in a country like France, which pretends to march at the head of civilization, one allows natural beauty to be degraded and suppressed."[67]

Three separate pieces of legislation were drawn up in 1901 and 1902. The first, of 28 March 1901, was put before parliament by Beauquier. The proposed legislation called for drawing up an inventory of sites of natural beauty in each department in France by a commission to be named by the *conseil général* and the *conseil municipal* of each department's main administrative center as well as by artists, art amateurs, members of the Alpine Club and the Touring Club, and persons to be named by the government. The sites classified by the commission would then be evaluated by inspectors from the Ministry of Fine Arts and provision made for the payment of indemnities to property owners.

The second legislative proposal was signed by several other deputies and left the initiative to the department or commune, which would present its requests for classification to the Ministry of Fine Arts. A commission consisting of the prefect as president, the department's chief engineer, two *conseilleurs généraux,* and five members chosen by the prefect from the region's artistic and literary notables would be convened only in case of a dispute.

The third proposal came from the president of the Touring Club of France, Abel Ballif, and called for the application of articles 1 through 6, 12, and 13 of the law of 30 March 1887, governing historic monuments, to sites of artistic, geological, and historic interest. He proposed the formation of a commission that was far more diverse in terms of its membership and called on communes to assume much of the financial responsibility for the law.[68]

At the heart of these initiatives was a concern about probable cases of resistance on the part of property owners and the cost of protecting natural sites and monuments. Some proposals allowed for the principle of expropriation and drew on the authority of the state. While the proposals went through a number of modifications, the Chamber of Deputies voted for passage of the law on 2 February 1905. It then went to the Senate, where on 6 March 1906 Maurice Faure, who was a member of the Radical Party and a senator from the Drôme, presented a report on the law that suggested minor modifications. He pleaded for the passage of the law in a language of patriotism:

> Patriotism, gentlemen, is not only a moral entity, an abstract conception, a geographical and historical conception. It is in some way the material and visible representation of the country itself, with particular physical characters and its diverse elements, with its mountains, its forests, its plains, its rivers, its shores with the multiple and varied aspects of its soil, such as they were formed and transmitted by the long succession of centuries.[69]

The Senate ultimately passed the law proposed by Beauquier with an amendment for its application in Algeria and other colonies on 27 March 1906, and the law was finally ratified by the Chamber of Deputies on 10 April 1906 and promulgated on 21 April 1906. The so-called Beauquier Law consisted of six articles. The first instituted a commission for natural sites and monuments in each department, over which the prefect presided and which was composed of the department's chief engineer for Ponts et Chaussées, the *chef de service* for Eaux et Forêts, elected members of the *conseil général*, five members chosen from among the artistic, scientific, and literary notability, and representatives of the Touring Club, the Alpine Club, and the SPPF. Articles 2 through 6 of the law set out the task of the commission in terms of identifying sites for protection and the rights of the state and property owners in matters of classification.

Drawing on the work of John Ruskin and Hippolyte Taine, Fernand Cros-Mayrevieille, who would come to play an important role in SPPF and in the movement for the protection of nature more generally, defended a thesis at the Faculty of Law at the University of Paris on the protection of historical and natural monuments a year after the Beauquier Law was passed. He followed Faure's logic and argued that monuments and beautiful sites "develop national pride, elevate ideas."[70] Defining what made natural monuments distinct from historical monuments, he took up the articulation of the concept by Raoul de Clermont, an agronomist and lawyer, who also became a member of the SPPF: "A group of elements resulting from nature, like rocks, trees, sudden and accidental changes in the appearance of terrain and other transformations which, separately or together, form an impressive aspect, a landscape worthy of being conserved. A landscape is a part of nature presenting an aesthetic character through the disposition of its contours, forms and colors. A site is a part of a landscape whose aspect is particularly interesting."[71]

The devastation engendered by World War I and lacunae in the law led some to push for the rewriting of the Beauquier Law.[72] The move came from several directions, but at the center of the debate was a conflict between respect for private property as well as the free disposal of it and the safeguarding of the nation's *patrimoine,* which was articulated in aesthetic terms.[73] Pragmatic arguments in favor of new legislation were also put forward by the Touring Club de France and the Office national du tourisme. The latter, which kept statistics on foreign tourists, estimated that in 1930 France welcomed 850,000 from England, 200,000 from North America, 400,000 from South America, and 600,000 from other parts of the world. These figures did not include internal tourism, and it was estimated that 500,000 in France earned their living from tourism.[74] While the economic importance of tourism was continually emphasized, other considerations came into play:

> It must be admitted finally that the role of tourism is not exclusively economic. It also has—and here is its most novel aspect—an intellectual impact. Travel not only shapes the young, but also a public of any age. It develops its culture, its curiosity and desire to understand. Thus conceived, tourism comes to perfect, most fortunately, general education. With the museum and the monument, the site becomes a complement of the school.[75]

Indeed, the pedagogical role played by the museum of nature and the economic stimulus provided by the development of tourism began to shape renewed debates about the passage of more expansive legislation concerning the protection of natural sites and monuments.[76] Pierre Leroux de la Roche wrote in 1932 that many arguments could be made for protecting France's natural sites and landscapes, but the most decisive was one of an "economic order": "It's worthwhile in effect to emphasize the important place of tourism in the national economy, for it is in ensuring the safeguard of our aesthetic capital through the rational protection of our sites and landscapes that we give tourism its *raison d'être.*"[77] He stressed that tourism was an activity pursued not only by elites but also by the masses and that World War I had "exerted a decisive influence on its evolution."[78]

Such sentiment inspired the 2 May 1930 law that reorganized the institutions charged with the protection of natural sites and monuments for their artistic, historical, scientific, legendary, and picturesque significance, replacing the Beauquier Law of 21 April 1906. Along with the law of 31 December 1913 pertaining to the protection of natural monuments, the 1930 law expanded the 1906 law to include sites and monuments with a zoological, botanical, geological, and mineralogical significance, indicating that the law had now moved beyond primarily aesthetic considerations. In this way the law marked a change with respect to which kinds of landscapes were considered worthy of protection and how landscape preservation was justified. Why did this shift occur? Part of the answer lies in the gradual "internationalization" of the movement to protect natural landscapes and nature more generally.

The SPPF, the Touring Club, and other associations that were founded at the turn of the century were both aware of and in contact with their counterparts in Europe and North America. Raoul de Clermont documented international organizations and initiatives in commenting on the founding of Heimatschutz in Germany in 1904, which was prompted by concerns about the Rhine River, and on the Ligue suisse pour la protection de la beauté, which was founded by Marguerite Burnat-Provins. This had been preceded by Theodore Roosevelt's presidential decree to designate Pelican Island as a U.S. federal reserve in 1903.[79] Indeed, as early as 1901 the first steps toward the internationalization of nature protection were taken, and France took the lead in 1909, 1923, and 1931 by sponsoring international conferences devoted to the protection of the natural world. These meetings brought together a variety of European and non European nations, but what was clearly discernible with time was that international agreements that were forged came to be increasingly directed to the non-European continents of the world.

FIVE

The Internationalization of Nature Protection

> In fact, Nature, like all living beings, can be loved in multiple ways; some want to leave her to be entirely free, others want to hold her more or less close.
>
> —P. Lemoine

WHILE THERE WAS significant debate in France about the need to protect landscapes and monuments from the 1840s onward, these discussions were not aired on an international stage until the early twentieth century, when a series of international conferences regarding the protection of landscapes, fauna, flora, and nature more generally were organized. One of the first was the Convention for the Preservation of Wild Animals, Birds, and Fish in Africa, otherwise known as the London Convention, which was held in London in 1900. Its purpose was to reach an international agreement on the protection of the fauna of Africa. It was followed two years later by another in Paris, the International Convention for the Protection of Birds Useful to Agriculture, which resulted in an agreement signed by representatives from Germany, Austria-Hungary, Belgium, Spain, France, Greece, Luxembourg, Monaco, Portugal, Sweden, and Switzerland. However, it was ratified only by Belgium, France, Hungary, Sweden, and later, the Netherlands.[1] The history of these congresses and many of those that followed illustrates the very different perspectives that European delegations offered on the problem of preservation, conservation, and the protection of nature more generally on the European continent and across the world. This chapter explores the internationalization of nature and landscape protection from the early twentieth century to the 1930s and the role that French officials, administrators, and lay representatives played in shaping the ongoing debate about how to safeguard the natural world. Ultimately, initiatives that emerged from the internationalization of the movement resulted in the creation of national parks and reserves both within Europe and in Europe's colonial empires. They established a model for international cooperation, and they laid the basis for thinking about conservation and landscape preservation in the years following World War II.

※ ※ ※

THE CREATION OF voluntary associations and the staging of international congresses devoted to the protection of fauna, flora and landscapes were part of a larger preservationist movement. As Astrid Swenson has argued, a preoccupation with heritage became an international phenomenon in the years between 1870 and 1914, when a modern preservationist movement was established. The concept of "heritage," which was born during the French Revolution and the Napoleonic Wars and the destruction that followed, became a subject for a European-wide debate concerning the protection of national heritage more generally for future generations. "Heritage," moreover, came to include monuments, popular traditions, culture, and, ultimately, nature. The term was appropriated by diverse social groups in England, Germany, Belgium, France, and Italy, where they began to pressure the state to pass a wave of protectionist legislation.[2]

Preservationism was popularized by international conferences that were organized through initiatives undertaken by a varied set of organizations and societies, which ranged from the Bund Heimatschutz to the Touring Club of France, the Society for the Protection of the Landscapes of France (SPPF), and the League for the Protection of Birds. Initially they were devoted to specific causes, but they all pursued both preservationist and conservationist goals in Europe, North America, and colonial Africa.

As noted, one of the earliest international conferences was convened in London in 1900, by the European colonial powers holding territories in sub-Saharan Africa. The travel writer and big game hunter Hermann von Wissmann was the primary champion of the London Conference, which was three years in the making and devoted to the protection of the fauna of Africa. All of the principal European powers were represented—Great Britain, France, Portugal, Spain, Belgium, Germany, and Italy. The purpose of the convention was to create uniform game regulations and licensing systems, to identify animals to be protected, and to establish closed seasons for hunting. While depriving indigenous populations of the use of traditional hunting techniques, the convention did not ban European weaponry.

The conference's overall aim was to consider measures that might be taken to conserve game, and it looked to the establishment of game reserves, which were defined as sufficiently large tracts of land having all the qualifications with regard to food, water, and salt to provide animals within them "necessary quiet during the breeding time."[3] Game reserves, like forest reserves, were to serve a productive function through conservation, thus assuring a steady supply of game for hunting. To this extent they were clearly in the tradition of the European royal game estate.

The participants signed the 1900 London Convention at the end of the conference with the understanding that it would be valid for fifteen years. However, the French declared that they would not ratify it unless Abyssinia and Liberia agreed, even though those countries had not been invited to the conference. The Belgians refused to sign it unless the French did, and Portugal held out as well. The result was that the convention never came into full effect and was put out of mind with the coming of World War I.[4] Various colonial governments did, however, begin to rewrite their game laws and discuss the establishment of protected areas in the form of reserves and parks.

The London Convention was followed by an international congress of a very different kind. At France's initiative an international congress was convened to generate a dialogue between nations on the issue of landscape protection. The 1909 International Congress for the Protection of Landscapes was held in Paris between 17 and 20 October in the offices of the Musée social and under the auspices of the SPPF, which had been founded eight years earlier.[5] Its aim and scope were entirely different from that of the London Convention. The other sponsoring organizations included the Saint Hubert Club, the Fédération régionaliste, and the Touring Club of France. The Saint Hubert Club of France had been founded seven years earlier. Comprising hunters, its mission was to protect France's wild game. By 1904 it boasted a membership of 7,650, which expanded to 37,567 by 1910.

French government officials, including the president of the Republic, appeared prominently on the masthead of the congress's program. Participating countries included Germany, Britain, Austria, and Belgium. The principal organizers were deeply involved in the newly formed SPPF, and they included Raoul de Clermont and Fernand Cros-Mayrevieille, lawyers at the Cour d'appel in Paris, as well as Louis de Nussac, who was the chief editor for the *Bulletin de la Société pour la Protection des Paysages de France*. One of the key inspirations for the congress was Charles Beauquier, deputy of Doubs, president of the SPPF as well as the principal architect of the Beauquier Law of 1906. Members of honor included the president of the French Republic, Armand Fallières, and Frédéric Mistral of the Fédération régionaliste as well as the presidents of the Touring Club of France and the Saint Hubert Club.

The four-day congress was divided into five sections, which were devoted to (1) landscape protection and legislation, (2) forests, (3) rural landscapes, (4) urban landscapes, and (5) landscapes considered from a scientific and artistic perspective, and their connection to hygiene, sport, and to the protection of fauna and flora. The sections indicated the myriad ways in which "landscape" had come to be defined; in addition to forests and rural landscapes—which were at the center of long-standing concerns about the preservation of nature—were urban landscapes and those that might be considered from the perspective of science, art, and hygiene.

The congress appeared, in many respects, to be a self-congratulatory affair. Dr. Conwentz, a conservator of natural monuments in Prussia, commended his French counterparts for organizing it: "It is France that has the credit, in convoking this congress, to open the path toward an international *entente cordiale* in this domain at once social, aesthetic and scientific."[6] Many of the presentations focused on summarizing the 1906 Beauquier Law and on cataloguing the sites that had been classified in the previous three years. The list of the sites in France was extensive and included three in Brittany, one in Corsica, and one in eastern France. Those selected, such as the Rocher de Croah'zec in Finistère or La Roche Bernard in Morbihan, indicated a preference for unusually shaped natural landmarks, but some historic castles and ruins were not left out. Urban sites were notably absent from the list and reflected the fact that rural landscapes had been privileged as sites early on, even though there was discussion of proposing the Champs-Elysées, the Tuileries garden, and the Ile de la Cité in Paris.[7]

The 1909 congress illustrated the degree to which the early organizational and legislative initiatives of the associations devoted to landscape protection, tourism, and mountain climbing came together to foster further measures to protect landscapes and sites that were frequented by a growing urban public. Just as the forest of Fontainebleau—which was first appreciated and valorized by painters and which then became a "spectacle of nature" for middle-class consumption—was designated a protected site, so were some of the better-known natural landmarks in rural France. The congress also revealed the extent to which these protectionist associations were in communication with their counterparts across national borders, and at the congress's conclusion its participants resolved to meet every two years and discussed Germany and Italy as possible venues for future meetings.

During the same year the 1909 congress on landscape protection was held, Theodore Roosevelt convened forty-five nations to a world conference in The Hague to consider the best means to conserve the world's sources of energy. This was followed by an international congress on zoology in Graz, Austria, in 1910 and a conference on the protection of nature in Bern, Switzerland, on 17 November 1913. Paul Sarasin, of the Swiss League for the Protection of Nature, argued for an international conservation body and approached a number of countries around the world (including Argentina, Japan, and the United States) about creating such an association. This led to the signing of an Act of Foundation of a Consultative Commission for the International Protection of Nature in Bern, which was constituted by fourteen countries in 1914, but the agreement came apart because of World War I and because the Swiss government did not support Sarasin's proposal to approach the League of Nations about it after the war.[8]

Congresses of the International Literary and Artistic Association, with which many of those associated with the First International Congress for the Protection of Landscapes in 1909 were connected, also continued to be held in 1910, 1911, and 1913. However, as international tensions increased in the years that immediately followed and with the outbreak of World War I in 1914, a second congress for the protection of landscapes was not convened in either Germany or Italy, while Germany soon became the number one enemy of France.

The war led to considerable environmental devastation in northern France, which essentially became the war's western front and was crisscrossed by an elaborate system of trenches. French artilleryman Henry Malherbe described them as "mangled earth" and noted the degree to which new forms of technological warfare transformed the environment beyond all recognition, with battlefields "covered with innumerable scars, swollen and artificial mounds and heaps," and with "broken trees lying on the blackened and shell-pitted earth," which was "impregnated with the smell of chemicals."[9] The destruction of Louvain and Reims led to a public outcry about the violation of international conventions and to an international protest campaign.[10]

The Treaty of Versailles revealed the extent of France's hostility toward its former enemy, Germany, and its harsh terms, which were demanded by France, shaped the postwar political climate. France spent much of the 1920s engaged in reconstruction of the country's infrastructure. Although enmities and mistrust persisted, initiatives were taken to foster peace in a new international order, as evidenced in the creation of the League of Nations in 1919 and the signing of the Locarno Pact of 1925, promoting Franco-German reconciliation, and found their expression in the domain of environmental protection. Indeed, the "Spirit of Locarno" came to be extended to the natural world.

Two years before the signing of the Locarno Pact, the First International Congress for the Protection of Nature, which was defined in terms of fauna, flora, and natural monuments, was held in Paris between 31 May and 2 June 1923.[11] The French societies responsible for its organization were similar to those that participated in the 1909 International Congress for the Protection of Landscapes. They included the Société d'acclimatation, the French League for the Protection of Birds, and the SPPF. In contrast to the 1909 congress, the Museum of Natural History in Paris and its president, Louis Mangin (1852–1937), who was the museum's director from 1920 to 1931, played a central role in the planning and organization of the 1923 congress.[12] Mangin also served as its president, and the congress was held at the museum. William T. Hornaday of the Wildlife Protection Fund in New York and France's Ministry of Agriculture were explicitly thanked for their financial support by the congress's organizers, and ministers of agriculture, colonies, education, and the interior served as honorary presidents. The countries participating included Belgium, Canada, Spain, the United States, the United Kingdom, the Netherlands, Hungary, Italy, Japan, Luxembourg, Poland, Romania, Russia, Switzerland, the new states of Czechoslovakia and Yugoslavia, and France. Germany, which had played such a key role in the 1909 international congress, was conspicuously absent, attesting to the strained relationship between France and its enemy.

Albert Chappellier, secretary of the French League for the Protection of Birds, Louis de Nussac, general secretary of the SPPF, and Raoul de Clermont met to constitute an organizing committee on 27 November 1922 in the offices of the Société d'acclimatation in Paris, with Louis Mangin presiding. They established how the congress would be organized, and the 1909 conference served as a model. Like the 1909 conference, the congress was divided into five sections, devoted to fauna; flora; soil and underground; sites and landscapes; and the general protection of nature. In many ways it was to be a continuation of earlier discussions concerning the creation of national parks and the extension of protectionist legislation, such as the 1906 Beauquier Law.[13] There was some difference of opinion among the French participants about the value of parks in relation to artistic reserves. Emile Sinturel, an inspector at the department of Eaux et Forêts, argued that only a limited number of parks should be created and only then in poorer regions with little agricultural value.[14] Charles Valois, in contrast, saw them as "museums of nature," which should be set up in the same way that the earlier artistic series in Fontainebleau were organized. He also recommended the introduction of flora and fauna into such parks, thus implicitly arguing against national parks being left to the hand of nature.[15]

Marcel Plaisant, a deputy from the department of Cher, announced that he had proposed a law in the Chamber of Deputies that would extend the Beauquier Law for the protection of sites of picturesque and artistic merit to include natural monuments of scientific, historic, and legendary interest.[16] The proposed extension was significant in that it reflected a shift toward scientific groups and associations, such as the Société d'acclimatation and those associated with the Museum of Natural History—organizations that became increasingly vocal in the post–World War I period.

While the voices of the artistic and touristic community were certainly present at the congress, as reflected in Paul Descombes's and Emile Sinturel's discussion of the "séries artistiques" in France's forests and the extension of such measures to additional forests, a great deal of attention was devoted to the creation of national parks and reserves in France's colonial empire—a demand that had been absent from the 1909 congress. Auguste Chevalier (1873–1956), director of colonial agronomy at the Museum of Natural History, explicitly demanded measures for the protection of sites in France's colonies.[17] He called on colonial governors to draw up a list of natural sites that they deemed "remarkable" and to take specific steps to protect them. Citing measures taken by other nations to create national parks and reserves, he argued that it was imperative for France to establish them in its empire.[18]

In the 1920s and 1930s there was a growing concern for the protection of colonial fauna and flora, which was reflected in the creation of the Comité national permanent pour la protection de la faune colonial and the founding of the Office international de documentation et coordination pour la protection de la nature. Indeed, at the very start of the conference Louis Mangin noted that among its different sections, the program of the section devoted to fauna was the fullest because "Fauna is still much more directly threatened in [its] existence than Flora or Sites."[19] The interventions of the representatives of the Museum of Natural History revealed the extent to which colonial France figured significantly in discussions at the 1923 congress in a way that it had not in 1909. Louis Mangin ended the congress by arguing that the French (and Europeans more generally) were responsible for the environmental devastation to be found in their colonial possessions, requiring both attention and action: "In Corsica, in North Africa, in the colonies, the damage is even more serious," and "it is in Senegal, in Guinea, in Dahomey, in Sudan that a magnificent fauna is in danger of extermination."[20] Moreover, Mangin contended that "colonial flora" were also "less managed" than that of Europe.[21]

Mangin's concluding speech at the congress was noteworthy in that it reflected a shift in terms of how initiatives taken to protect nature were articulated. While the aesthetic motivation was not absent, Mangin downplayed it and emphasized conservation for future posterity: "But we do not intervene only for aesthetic satisfaction, we also want to denounce and keep in check, even from a simple practical point of view, the disastrous destruction of incalculable riches whose prudent exploitation should be assured for all time."[22]

※ ※ ※

FOLLOWING THE CONGRESS, specific initiatives were undertaken in France to protect the natural environment. In 1924 a law modifying certain aspects of an 1844 law that regulated hunting was passed, and through actions taken by the Société nationale d'acclimatation, a botanical and zoological reserve consisting of 15,000 hectares was established in the Camargue. In many respects this activity culminated in the 2 May 1930 law governing the protection of natural sites and monuments. After 1923 most of the national parks that France established until World War II were created in its colonies. A 30 December 1924 decree mandated the creation of a national park in French Antarctic territories, while an 18 January 1925 decree initiated measures to regulate hunting in Cochin China. Shortly thereafter the minister of colonial affairs sent a letter to Abel Gruvel at the Museum of Natural History inviting him to suggest measures to restrict hunting in France's colonies and guidelines for the creation of national parks. Accordingly, the Commission for the Protection of Colonial Fauna was established for this purpose; it was headed by Gruvel and would become a permanent organization staffed with others associated with the Museum of Natural History. Its recommendations were incorporated in a circular that the minister addressed to the governors of Indochina, Madagascar, French West Africa, French Equatorial Africa, Togo, and Cameroon, which invited them to initiate measures to control hunting. The commission established contacts with similar organizations in Belgium, the Netherlands, Britain, and the United States. While the French committee was particularly concerned with animal species, the protection of flora and forests was not neglected. The committee was especially vigilant and intervened in debates concerning the protection of African elephants as well as bans on the hunting of the white rhinoceros and the export of tusks.

The internationalization of the preservation movement continued apace, and a second conference devoted to the protection of nature was convened in Paris in 1931, coinciding with the International Colonial Exhibition, which opened in Paris in May. Delegates from foreign governments included those from Belgium, Spain, the United Kingdom, the Netherlands, Latvia, Norway, Poland, Romania, Switzerland, and Czechoslovakia. Germany, Belgium, Spain, the United States, the Netherlands, Italy, Poland, Romania, and Czechoslovakia sent representatives from protectionist societies and organizations that included the Save the Redwoods League, the American

Museum of Natural History, the Royal Society for the Promotion of Nature Reserves, and the Society for the Preservation of the Wild Fauna of the Empire.[23] France's ministries of foreign affairs, agriculture, colonies, education, and tourism were also represented, and sponsoring organizations in France included the French Alpine Club, Ecole nationale des eaux et forêts, Laboratoire forestier de Toulouse, League for the Protection of Birds, Société nationale d'acclimatation de France, the SPPF, and the French Botanical Society.

When the organizational efforts for the International Colonial Exposition were launched, the Commission for the Protection of Colonial Fauna and Flora began its own organizing efforts, which were supported by the Société nationale d'acclimatation de France, the SPPF, and the League for the Protection of Birds. An organizing committee, which first met on 11 July 1930, drew representatives from each of these associations. It included Edouard Bourdelle from the Museum of Natural History; Clément Bressou, a veterinarian and general secretary of the Société nationale d'acclimatation; M. Carougeau, an inspector of veterinary services; Raoul de Clermont, director of the SPPF; Abel Gruvel, professor at the Museum of Natural History; Louis Mangin; Georges Petit, an assistant at the museum; and Charles Valois, secretary of the Conseil de la Société d'acclimatation. The Second International Congress for the Protection of Nature, which was to meet at the Museum of Natural History in Paris from 30 June to 4 July 1931, was thus born and placed under the patronage of the Commissariat général of the International Colonial Exposition.

Given the origins of the congress, it is not surprising that the French section should include a former minister of colonies, Albert Lebrun, who was appointed president, and that among its vice presidents were Mangin and Gruvel, general secretary of the Committee for the Protection of Colonial Fauna and Flora. The congress itself, like the first congress eight years earlier, was divided into five sections. There were delegates from nine foreign governments (Belgium, Spain, Great Britain, the Netherlands, Latvia, Norway, Poland, Romania, Switzerland, and Czechoslovakia) and representatives from many more organizations and societies.

The solemn opening session of the congress took place in the Cuvier amphitheater of the Museum of Natural History on 1 July 1931. Albert Lebrun, a former minister of colonies, was one of the first to take the podium and directly address the problem of environmental degradation in Europe's colonies, while laying the blame at the feet of both the colonized and the colonizer: "Through atavism and through laziness, the native cuts down and burns thousands of hectares of forests," while European farmers also destroyed native forests, resulting in the modification of climates and droughts that force local populations to choose between dying of hunger or emigrating.[24] He noted that in certain French colonies land had decreased from being 92 percent to 10 percent forested. He painted a picture of shrinking forests, unbridled hunting that resulted in the decimation of 40,000 elephants, male and female, annually, and the virtual extinction of the white rhinoceros, whose tusks commanded exorbitant prices in China.[25] Indeed, the proceedings of the congress noted that it was in France's colonial empire that environmental devastation was the most pronounced.[26]

Paul Reynaud, the minister of colonies, echoed Lebrun's observations, emphasizing the "white man's burden," which reflected a widespread European colonial discourse that claimed that indigenous populations were incapable of being proper stewards of the land, leaving it to Europeans to step in: "But then, gentlemen, must one not think that we have our part in the responsibility for this, if we have not been able to discipline the native and combat his destructive activity through scientific methods?"[27] He emphasized that an international group of nations had to "work together to avoid the destruction of forests and compensate, to prevent the massive decimation, all the more cruel as it is useless, of their animals, almost legendary in being part of the heritage of our imagination, which we must leave to our successors."[28] However, discussion of the international regulation of the import and export of both fauna and flora would prove just how difficult international cooperation would be. Dr. P. G. Van Tienhoven, president of the Society for the Conservation of Natural Monuments in the Netherlands and of the Dutch Committee for the International Protection of Nature, proposed that governments should agree to ban the importation of any animal or plant life from a region where their export has been banned.[29] M. Leplae, the director general of Belgium's Ministry of Colonial Affairs, quickly intervened by pointing out that in the Belgian Congo the ivory trade was considerable and lucrative, and for this reason it would be difficult to regulate it. Lord Onslow, president of the British Society for the Preservation of the Fauna of Empire, proposed having an international convention similar to that of 1900 on the regulation of big game hunting in Africa to decide such issues. A set of resolutions were agreed upon, ranging from animal trade to curbing the number of tourists traveling to sensitive areas.

Lord Onslow persuaded the British government to sponsor a new convention a few years later. The Foreign Office and the Colonial Office, however, agreed that it should be confined to addressing problems in Africa. A preparatory commission was established in 1932 under the Economic Advisory Council, and Lord Onslow served as its chair.[30] Its second draft report then served as a basis for what would become the Convention

Relative to the Preservation of Fauna and Flora in Their Natural State, otherwise known as the London Convention of 1933, whose primary purpose was one of promoting the "concentration of fauna in specially constituted sanctuaries."[31] The commission envisioned that each European colonial power should establish national parks similar to Kruger National Park in South Africa in their African territories. It also discussed the creation of smaller reserves. There were government representatives from Great Britain, France, Belgium, Italy, Portugal, Spain, Egypt, Anglo-Egyptian Sudan, and South Africa, with observers from India, the Netherlands, and the United States. They accepted Onslow's draft convention as a basis of discussion. The convention that was signed obligated signatory governments to commit to the possibility of establishing national parks, where visitors would be allowed but governed by restrictions, as well as strict nature reserves, where all human presence would be banned, which was a French proposal. It also had appendixes listing species that would be completely protected from hunting or capture, which included seventeen mammals, three birds, and one plant.[32]

The congress differed from the two prior international conferences devoted to the protection of nature and from the 1909 congress on the preservation of landscapes, which had been held in Paris, because its aim, like that of the London conference of 1900, was far more specific. The 1933 convention was formally enacted on 17 January 1936, and a meeting to review the progress of its implementation was held in May 1938. Ultimately signed by the Union of South Africa, Belgium, Britain, Egypt, France, Italy, Portugal, and Anglo-Egyptian Sudan, the convention laid stress on the main goals of the 1900 London Convention but placed most of its emphasis on the creation of parks and reserves rather than on game laws and regulations. All but France and Spain ratified the agreement in 1935. It was then superseded by the African Convention on the Conservation of Nature and Natural Resources in 1968. After France took the lead in 1909, 1923, and 1931 in organizing international congresses for the protection of nature, its failure to ratify the agreement was striking. The country was caught in the grip of the protracted struggle between French pro- and antifascist forces and experienced an attempted coup d'état in 1934, so the government's attention was perhaps directed elsewhere. While French naturalists associated with the Museum of Natural History were deeply engaged in the debate concerning the establishment of parks and reserves, much of the impetus behind the conventions of 1900 and 1933 came from big game hunters, who were few in number in France and its colonies. As Marc Coic has argued, the London Convention of 1900 and that of 1933 were in effect "international *hunting* treaties" rather than "conservation treaties": "these hunters were often far more concerned with the protection of specific hunting grounds and prized prey than with the safeguarding of entire habitats, ecosystems, or bioregions."[33]

The international congresses and conferences and France's participation in them changed gradually in terms of their focus, their composition, and their intent. While the 1909 International Congress for the Protection of Landscapes focused most of its attention on the protection of landscapes and natural sites for aesthetic and historical purposes in metropolitan France, the First International Congress for the Protection of Nature expanded the range of subjects to be addressed to include fauna and flora and surveyed the problems of environmental degradation beyond Europe's boundaries. The explicit focus on colonial territories on the part of French participants was largely shaped by the participation of the scientists and researchers at the Museum of Natural History, and more particularly its director, Louis Mangin. Moreover, this was not surprising, as France's colonial empire was at its height in the interwar period.

France, then, took the lead in the internationalization of a movement to protect the natural environment, and the impetus behind these initiatives came from a number of different sources and constituencies, which included foresters, painters and poets, a new middle-class public, and naturalists associated with the Museum of Natural History. What was striking was the way in which aesthetic considerations comfortably existed alongside practical and scientific considerations, which came to be expressed in a variety of calls to both preserve and conserve the natural world as living monuments, as *patrimoine* in the form of landscapes, and as national parks and natural reserves. By the early 1930s it became clear, however, that the French had come to articulate their own conception of the natural park and the natural reserve, which departed from the model espoused by most of the delegates at the 1933 London conference.

※ ※ ※

ON 20 JANUARY 1933, P. Lemoine told the audience at a meeting of the French Society of Biogeography that on several occasions international and national congresses had called for the protection of nature and ultimately convinced governments and public opinion that measures had to be taken to prevent the destruction of animal life and existing natural landscapes. The most effective of these measures, in his view, was the creation of natural reserves or national parks, which existed "in most countries of the world and in their colonies." However, he noted that their "constitution and organization" had been improvised at best and reflected differing goals. Some, *réserves de conservation,* kept any form of human intervention at a minimum and were left "in a state of nature."[34] Others, *réserves de réintroduction,* were those where biologists were permitted to reintroduce plant or animal life that had once flourished and had since disappeared. Still others, *réserves d'acclimatement,* had a value in terms of tourism, and their organization allowed for the introduction of fauna and flora that would be of interest to the general public. These reserves, according to Lemoine, were those that had been created in French colonial Algeria or as forest reserves, zoological parks, botanical gardens, and arboreta in metropolitan France.[35]

It is no accident that the diversity of these forms of landscape protection was discussed at length at the London Convention of 1933. Moreover, the majority of colonial parks and reserves established on the African continent by the British, French, and Belgians were created in the interwar period. These included thirteen national parks in French Algeria, ten natural reserves in Madagascar, Albert National Park in the Belgian Congo, and Kruger National Park in South Africa. Some of these initiatives came out of a desire to protect vanishing wildlife on the continent and satisfied sportsmen and tourists alike. However, the parks that were established by the European colonial powers differed greatly in form, intent, and organization even as they shared common concerns and interests, as the calling of the 1933 international conference clearly demonstrated.

The French delegation made it clear that they considered the national park, a vast territory accessed by roads and favoring tourism, to be an "American conception," as evidenced in the first national park created in the world—Yellowstone—in 1872. The definition of "national park" adopted by the conference was the following:

> The expression "national park" designates an area (a) placed under public control, whose limits will not be altered and in which no part can be transferred except by a competent legislative authority; (b) set aside for the propagation, protection and conservation of wild animal and vegetal life, and for the conservation of objects of aesthetic, geological, pre-historical, historical, archeological and other scientific interest for the service of public recreation; (c) in which hunting, animal slaughter or the capture of fauna and the destruction or collection of flora are forbidden except ... under the direction or the control of park authorities.[36]

The French delegation charged Georges Petit (1891–1973), a laboratory vice director at the National Museum of Natural History in Paris, to present an alternative "French notion" regarding the protection of nature, which was embodied in the *réserve naturelle intégrale,* which was to be found in its purest form on the island of Madagascar, off the coast of Africa in the Indian Ocean.[37] The French established the models of the national park and the *réserve naturelle intégrale* in both metropolitan France and its overseas colonies from 1913 to World War II, but there was a particularly sharp debate regarding the question of the form and purpose of these protected sites in France's African colonies, where France's first extended network of national parks and natural reserves was established. How did the French first conceive of national parks and reserves, and to what extent did those established in metropolitan and colonial France resemble the original American model? Were the parks and reserves established in metropolitan France, North and West Africa, and Madagascar different from one another? To what extent did they differ from British and other colonial counterparts in Africa?

As we have seen, France's first governmental initiative to protect a natural landscape was that of Fontainebleau when it was set aside as a *réserve artistique* in 1861. France's first national park was established in the French Alps by a decree issued by the Ministry of Agriculture on 31 December 1913, less than one year before the outbreak of World War I—relatively late by international standards—for the purpose of restoring land that had been devastated by the overgrazing of sheep and goats. La Bérarde, which subsequently assumed the name parc du Pelvoux, was formed through the French state's acquisition of 4,248 hectares from the commune of Saint-Christophe-en-Oisans in the department of the Isère in 1914, in addition to 5,798 hectares from Pelvoux and 3,368 hectares from Guillaume-Peyrouse and Clémence-d'Ambel in the Hautes-Alpes in 1923 and 1924.[38]

There was a clear divide between those who conceived of landscape protection in terms of conservation (for the purpose of managing natural resources) and those who conceived of it as preservation of a landscape in and of itself for historical or aesthetic reasons in metropolitan France. Those who followed in the tradition of the foresters conceived of landscape protection in the form of parks as a means of effecting reforestation, conserving natural resources, and preventing natural disasters such as floods.[39] Those who followed in the footsteps of the Barbizon school painters were associated with myriad nature associations, the most influential of which were the Touring Club and the SPPF, who embraced a more preservationist, aesthetic vision of landscape protection. It was the latter that was embodied in Beauquier Law and later in a second law, passed on 2 May 1930, that strengthened it by adding landscapes having zoological, botanical, and geological interest to a potential list of protected sites.

Preference for the "biological" natural reserve held the greatest sway in the interwar period among naturalists and scientists, however, who were major proponents of landscape protection in France's colonies, and they included representatives from the Museum of Natural History in Paris and the Société d'acclimatation. A series of such reserves were established early in metropolitan France. These included the Zoological and Botanical Reserve of Camargue, a vast tract of marshy wetlands in southern France; the Reserve of the Seven Isles on the Breton archipelago around Perros-Guirec in the department of Côtes-du-Nord; the Natural Reserve of Néouvieille in the Pyrenees Mountains; and Le Lauzanier in the lower Alps, bordering Italy.[40]

As most of Pelvoux's land was inaccessible as a result of being above an altitude at which most trees and other forms of vegetation could grow, it satisfied neither the scientific community nor the Touring Club of France. Initially administered by a Touring Club committee and the Eaux et Forêts, Pelvoux increasingly became a tourist attraction; with the opening of new paths and roads, and with the construction of cabins and hotels, the scientists considered the experience of Pelvoux to be a failure.[41] Scientists and naturalists began to favor reserves in metropolitan France, which could be distinguished from national parks for their scientific purpose. From 1906 to 1930, 459 of these reserves were established on metropolitan soil.

The first truly successful national parks were established in France's colonies, however, and this paradox can be explained by the barriers to consolidating large tracts of land in metropolitan France for public use. The metropole was already more or less densely populated, and laws governing individual property were almost sacrosanct. Although Algeria was also densely populated along its coastline, tropical Africa and Madagascar, where large tracts of land had been expropriated by the colonial administration, were much less so. Moreover, the local populations in these colonies were not citizens, and the colonial administration could deny their traditional grazing rights as well as expropriating their land, often without compensation.

In the post–World War I period initiatives directed to the protection of landscapes were extended to France's colonial possessions in Africa, where the tension between conservationism and preservationism was also evident. Indeed, as a participant at the Second International Congress for the Protection of Nature noted, all eyes were turned to France's colonial empire.[42] The series of parks and reserves that were set up in each of France's colonies differed in terms of whether they were located in a settler colony, as in the case of Algeria, with real or imagined long-standing historical ties to the metropole, or in a newly acquired territory, such as Madagascar. These differing colonial arrangements determined how the French considered the land they occupied, and they governed policies of landscape protection. The issues raised by the colonial context were emphasized, for example, by A. Joubert, an official for the department of Eaux et Forêts in Montpellier, who contended that in countries with "young civilizations," such as the

United States, it was a relatively simple enterprise to isolate vast areas of "primitive nature" that had not been touched by humans. According to him, the task became more difficult in countries that had long been inhabited and that had been subject to humanity's destructive influences. The landscapes of metropolitan France and North Africa, which were regions of "old civilizations," as Joubert defined them, presented the French, in particular, with a challenge.[43] Indeed, one official in the Algerian forest service argued that not in Algeria or perhaps in any part of North Africa would one find a region whose "integral conservation" would inspire enthusiasm, even though it had a collection of interesting sites: "Nothing comparable here to a Yellowstone Park."[44] He further noted that Algeria, for example, was so overpopulated that there was no area where virgin natural territory remained untouched. Animal life, including bears and the stags of the Barbary Coast, had largely disappeared, and the last Algerian lion was killed in 1893 close to the town of Batna. Only wild boar and gazelles appeared to be unaffected. The establishment of protected landscapes therefore had to take into account two aspects of a common question: First, should one seek to establish a system through which to protect landscapes in such a way as to ban the destructive actions of humans while encouraging existing forms of animal life? Second, how could one find means of encouraging forms of nature that had been profoundly altered and return them to their original state?

Those who drove the debate over these questions and who played a growing role in discussions concerning the protection of landscapes and nature in France's colonies were the scientists and naturalists associated with the Museum of Natural History in Paris. Michael Osborne, among other historians, has stressed the important role of science in the colonizing process in the nineteenth century.[45] Early in the 1860s the Société zoologique d'acclimatation, which was established in 1854 at the Museum of Natural History aided the French state in its quest for colonial expansion. Since the eighteenth century the Jardin du Roi, which would become a national Museum of Natural History, had collected specimens in the form of plants and animals throughout the globe for scientific study, but from the late eighteenth century, the naturalists at the museum began to reflect on how the fauna and flora of Brazil, Mexico, or China might be acclimated and productively used in France. In many respects the Société zoologique d'acclimatation was a culmination of these earlier scientific forays, and its first president, Geoffroy Saint-Hilaire (1805–1861), embarked on a series of travels throughout France in the 1840s to aid the cause. After his death the museum and the society experienced several rifts, but by the 1890s both took an active interest in France's growing colonial empire.[46] While in the

1850s and 1860s members of the Société zoologique d'acclimatation, in particular, served as uncritical scientific consultants for the French state in colonial affairs, the society began to recognize that the acclimatization of exotic organisms and the unregulated use of natural resources could lead to environmental degradation.[47] In 1893 the Museum of Natural History, in collaboration with the Ministry of the Colonies, established a special training course for naturalists undertaking missions in tropical regions. Indeed, colonial missions became an integral part of the normal activities pursued by the museum's different laboratories.[48]

By World War I naturalists associated with the museum were at the center of discussions concerning the creation of national parks and reserves. For Joubert, the national park, according to its original "Anglo-Saxon formula," was above all a "touristic conception," sometimes with the aim of protecting wild game, whereas the "biological" natural reserve necessarily restricted access and was smaller in size.[49] Their common aim, in his view, should be to assure the maintenance, and often the reintroduction, of a landscape's original fauna and flora to the greatest extent possible.

It was the model of the national park, however, as opposed to the natural reserve, that won out in the jewel in France's colonial crown, Algeria, after considerable debate. In a meeting of the Natural History Society of North Africa on 3 February 1912, M. R. Maire, professor of botany at the University of Algiers, proposed that the society adopt a resolution regarding land in certain forested regions of Algeria to be turned into reserves and natural parks. The resolution was justified in terms of the existence of regions that had a particular scientific, artistic, and touristic interest, as in metropolitan France, but he called for the creation of protected areas in order to restore fauna and flora to their original "integral natural conditions."[50] In its resolution, the society noted that landscape protection was "particularly desirable" in forested regions where the zoological and botanical vestiges of earlier climates were still very numerous.[51] It therefore concluded that reserves should be established in these areas and that all forms of grazing and agricultural and commercial activity should be banned, including the removal of dead wood. Maire transmitted a letter on behalf of the society in this regard to Charles Lutaud, governor general of Algeria, and proposed the creation of twenty reserves that would cover 45,000 hectares. Soon afterward the president of the Société d'horticulture d'Alger, L. Trabut, made a similar proposal, arguing for the creation of a national park analogous to those established in other countries. The propositions of the Natural History Society of North Africa were seconded by a number of scientific, silvicultural, and touristic organizations in metropolitan France.

Lutaud responded by saying, "Excellent idea," and instructed the director of the Algerian forest service to formulate a proposal.

At the beginning of 1913 the North African Station for Forest Research proposed the creation of twenty reserves, comprising a surface area of approximately 45,000 hectares, in the three departments of Algeria—Alger, Constantine, and Oran—and it noted that in eight of them the government would have to ban further cultivation and provide monetary indemnities for indigenous Algerians who cultivated the land in the area.[52] The station, however, proposed the creation of only one national park, the state-owned forest of Téniet-el-Haâd in the department of Alger, which it considered to be best suited for this designation because of its easy access, high altitude, and cool and dry climate. In addition, it noted that the forest presented no problems in terms of the displacement of an indigenous population because no rights of cultivation or grazing existed in these areas. The forest was filled with very old cypress groves as well as cork trees that already attracted numerous visitors.

This proposal languished for five years until a tourist commission instituted by the Algerian colonial administration, which included the head of the North African Station for Forest Research as a member, officially adopted it. In the meantime the administration had come to see the "scientific" basis of the proposal to be subordinate to tourism, which shaped the decree signed by the governor general on 17 February 1921. It laid the groundwork for the creation of not one but thirteen national parks in Algeria. Acknowledging the necessity of "assuring the protection of the natural beauty of the colony, developing tourism and encouraging the creation of vacation centers," the first article of the decree stipulated that forests or parts of forests which could become centers of scientific/botanical study, tourism, or recreation could be designated national parks.[53] According to article 4, all plant and animal life within the confines of the park would be protected. All cultivation and livestock grazing were banned, and concessions of ninety-nine years would be granted to encourage the building of hotels.

France's first national parks on the African continent were thus created in Algeria. They covered an area of 27,600 hectares and included Les Cèdres (Téniet-el-Haâd) (1923), which had originally been proposed as a park by the Station de recherches forestières de l'Afrique du Nord; Dar-el-Oued Taza (1923 and 1927); L'Ouarsenis and Djebel Gouraya (1924); L'Akafadou, Chrea, Le Djurdjura, and Les Planteurs (1925); Saint-Ferdinand (1928); Aïn-N'sour (1929); and Le Babor, La Mahouna, and Bugeaud-L'Edough (1931). However, the colonial administration established only six of the twenty reserves proposed by the station in 1913. The Natural History

Society of North Africa, which originated the initiative, was sorely disappointed, and for one official in the department of Eaux et Forêts this outcome demonstrated the "fundamental antinomy" between the conception of the scientific reserve and the national park, even though the six reserves were established within the boundaries of these parks. While a national park was an area with an aesthetic interest to be preserved and exhibited because "a beauty that belongs to all must be accessible to all," in his view a scientific reserve did not necessarily have an aesthetic character and should be kept as much as possible in an original state of nature and subject to scientific observation.[54] It was for this reason that the French delegation, which was largely composed of scientists associated with the Museum of Natural History, demanded that the distinction be made in the final text of the London Convention of 1933.

The distinction that was made between a national park and a scientific reserve governed policies and practices regarding the protection of natural landscapes in French colonies throughout Africa. Tunisia, which was a protectorate without a large settler population, in contrast to Algeria, had one forest "park"—Aïn-Draham, which was created just after World War I—and no *réserves naturelles,* which L. Lavauden, professor at the Institut national agronomique, attributed in part to resistance among the indigenous Muslim population, drawing on a store of Islamophobic assumptions: "On the one hand the Muslims, even enlightened ones, remain closed to the idea that it could be useful to respect, to protect the fragments of the old fauna and flora that have been able to survive in their country. It may even be that their mistrustful orthodoxy sees in initiatives of this order the survival or resurrection of an idolatry, in this cult of nature [that] is abominable to the faithful Muslim."[55] However, Lavauden also found the French authorities in the colony to be largely indifferent to parks and reserves. He argued that Tunisia was not without areas that could be designated as natural reserves, such as the island of Djebel Ischkeul and the forest of Gommiers, which was one of the last refuges of the North African elephant, mentioned by Pliny, which had long since disappeared elsewhere. He lamented, as did a number of other commentators, that the "destruction" was ostensibly and largely the work of the Arab population, even if they were not the only agents of environmental degradation.[56] Similarly, despite a decree promulgated on 11 September 1934 by the Moroccan government providing for the creation of reserves and parks, most were game reserves, and there was a tension there, as elsewhere, between the national park and natural reserve.[57]

The colonial administration's apparent preference for the model of the national park as opposed to the *réserve naturelle intégrale* in Algeria, in contrast to its other African colonies, can in part be explained by Algeria's larger investment in tourism, particularly in the years preceding France's centenary of Algeria in 1930, which was celebrated in both Algeria and France, and the International Colonial Exhibition, which was held in Paris in 1931. It might also be explained by the presence of a considerable European settler population, which did not exist elsewhere in France's empire.

One of the striking aspects of the governmental decree regarding the establishment of national parks and natural reserves in Algeria—in contrast to other parts of colonial Africa, where the preservation of big game was often initially at the center of proposals to create reserves—was that it exclusively targeted forested landscapes.[58] Article 1 of the Algerian governor general's decree stipulated that only "forests or parts of forests" would be considered in determining the areas to be designated national parks or natural reserves.[59] Once designated, the removal of dead wood, setting fires, and the grazing of animals would be prohibited. Policing of the parks and the establishment of roads would be undertaken by the Algerian water and forest service, which would determine fines for park violations. Indeed, many of the most ardent defenders of landscape protection in the form of parks or reserves in North Africa were officials in the forest service, which explains in part why forested landscapes as opposed to other kinds of landscapes were privileged for protection in the context of the Maghreb.

The national parks and natural reserves in North Africa were relatively modest in size due to the density of the population and the complex nature of its agricultural and pastoral practices. Moreover, some settlers resisted their creation, fearing that the parks and reserves might ultimately threaten their own agricultural or commercial enterprises. However, the French state and the Touring Club of France were largely successful in launching most of the proposals they put forward.

These proposals were linked to larger anxieties that characterized this unique European settler society, which was concerned about environmental degradation and deforestation, to which problems of climate and rainfall were often be traced. The myth of the granary of Rome was also invoked in ways that made landscape protection in the form of reforestation, national parks, and reserves into landscape reclamation projects with a particular historical resonance.[60] The forested and coastal locations selected for all of France's national parks in Algeria are significant in this regard. Algeria, as part of "la plus grande France," France's only colony to be administratively divided into three departments, was viewed as an extension of the metropole whose Mediterranean landscape it had come to reclaim. For this reason, the principle of preservation as much as conservation tended to guide measures to protect the natural landscape.

While the model of the national park as a protected landscape was adopted in North Africa, French West Africa and Madagascar took a different route. The favored type of landscape conservation in French West Africa was the forest reserve, and the initiative came from the forest service and representatives from the Museum of Natural History in Paris. Louis Mangin, its director, lamented the situation in Afrique-Occidentale Française (French West Africa): "It is above all in French West Africa"—in Senegal, Dahomey, Sudan—that "a magnificent fauna is in danger of extermination" due to the disappearance of its natural habitat and hunting.[61] Thirty-four such forests, some of which welcomed tourism, were created in the Ivory Coast between 1926 and 1932, and seven in Senegal between 1932 and 1934.[62]

In French Equatorial Africa, which included parts of the Congo and Gabon Oubangui-Chari (Chad), the park of Bamingui-Bangoran, occupying 1 million hectares, included a *réserve intégrale* of 150,000 hectares. Similarly, in French Congo the national park of Odzala (450,000 hectares) was established, which included the *réserve intégrale* of Ofoué (150,000 hectares), indicating that the two protectionist models could exist side by side.

In Madagascar three naturalists from the Museum of Natural History took a particular interest in the problem of deforestation on the island: Roger Heim (1900–1972), Henri Humbert (1887–1967), and Henri Perrier de la Bâthie (1873–1958). All three decried its effects on fauna, soil erosion, and the climate and supported the creation of natural reserves. The model of the *reserve naturelle intégrale* was most successful in Madagascar, where the governor general created ten reserves by decree in 1927 and placed them under the stewardship of the Museum of Natural History in Paris. Following the London Convention of 1933, the Museum and the colonial administration created an eleventh reserve of 71,200 hectares in the province of Tuléar. All rights of cultivation and grazing were strictly forbidden, and the area was out of bounds for the general public. Georges Petit, who headed the French delegation at the London Convention of 1933, described the aim of the reserves as one that worked toward "conservation of the last vestiges of flora in their natural state" and the conservation of the "last representatives of the great island's indigenous fauna." He argued, moreover, that it was the only enterprise "of this type conceived in a French possession."[63]

The idea of creating such reserves was launched in 1925 when the Commission for the Protection of Colonial Fauna, set up by the minister of colonies, charged Petit, about to go to Madagascar on a scientific mission for the Museum of Natural History, with studying the merits of national parks or natural reserves while he was there. After speaking with the governor general about the urgency of creating such reserves, he made a presentation to the Malagasy Academy, which in turn named a commission to study how this might be achieved. The report was published in the colony's *Bulletin Economique* in 1927, which recommended, in contrast to France's other African colonies, that the reserves be administered by the Museum of Natural History and the Société d'acclimatation rather than by the forest service. A decree of 1927 provided for the creation of the reserves, and this was followed by the foundation of two national parks in the massif d'Ambre and in Isalo, 800 kilometers northwest of Tuléar.[64]

With the exception of Algeria, the model of landscape protection that was preferred in all of France's African colonies—Madagascar, Tunisia, Morocco, and French West Africa—was the *réserve naturelle intégrale* or the forest reserve whose purpose was not one of reclamation but of restoration.[65] It was one that was concerned with the protection of fauna and flora and that sought to restore landscapes to their original natural state. P. de Peyrimhoff had already stressed the "fundamental antinomy" that separated the scientific reserve from the national park. A national park, in his view, focused on the spectacular and the aesthetic and implied a human presence that would consume, appreciate, and possibly defile it. A scientific reserve was, for him, "a region where the natural production, independent of any aesthetic character, is still intact or almost preserved and permits, in this state, diverse disciplines to study them in privileged conditions."[66] It therefore precluded the intervention of humans or any domesticated plants or animals, remaining in a state of nature. These different conceptions of landscape protection illustrate the competing impulses that guided conservation and preservation in France and its colonies in the twentieth century.

In many respects it was in France's colonies that scientists, colonial administrators, foresters, and protectionist societies had the opportunity to experiment with different forms of landscape preservation and conservation and to later use this knowledge for the creation of a series of new parks and reserves in metropolitan France after the passage of the law on national parks in 1960. Indeed, that law incorporated three models with which the French had already experimented in their colonies in terms of the protection of nature. The first included zones of national parks and protected natural "monuments." The second provided for the creation of game parks and reserves, which had been common in French West Africa, and the third consisted of *réserves intégrales,* which had first been established in Madagascar. In addition, in 1933 the Society of Biogeography and the Société national d'acclimatation, under the direction of the Museum of Natural History, undertook a study of natural reserves and national parks throughout the world. Its classification and evaluation of these reserves and parks led to the conclusion that the former should be the French model and the favored form of landscape protection.

The guiding forces behind French initiatives came from different directions: from the French experience in international congresses; from scientists, many of whom were associated with the Museum of Natural History in Paris as well as with colonial administrations; from forest officials who advocated the creation of forest reserves; from diverse informal groups dedicated to the protection of nature, including the Alpine Club and the SPPF in metropolitan France; and from the tourist industry, the government, and the public at large. The irony surrounding French initiatives behind creating national parks from 1913 to the 1930s was that a majority of these parks were created outside of metropolitan France, in French colonial Africa.[67] Throughout the nineteenth century, forest officials, in particular, blamed the peasantry for environmental degradation and deforestation in the metropole. This pattern was repeated in France's colonies, but the denigration of the *indigène* became even more pronounced in the colonial context. At the First International Congress for the Protection of Nature in 1923, for example, Louis Mangin had noted that in Corsica, in North Africa, and in French colonial possessions more generally the damage to the environment was much greater, and he attributed this to the indigenous population, adding that the environment was better managed in Europe.[68] In cases in which the French acknowledged their contribution to environmental degradation, it was less in terms of their own actions than in terms of their not policing the indigenous population sufficiently, as Paul Reynaud's intervention at the 1923 congress suggested.[69]

In addition to parks and natural reserves, the French created other kinds of environmental spaces that occupied a specific place in the colonial imagination. These spaces were *stations thermales* and *stations climatiques* (hydrotherapeutic and climatic resorts), which became in some sense landscapes that were reserved for Europeans, excluding indigenous populations as much as possible. They were established to cure colonial ills and to remove a European population from the climatic rigors of a non-European climate temporarily. They included Antsirabe in Madagascar, Cialos on the island of Réunion, off the coast of Africa in the Indian Ocean, and Kourbous in Tunisia. They constituted familiar sites of leisure, sociability, and medicine and were chosen because they replicated as closely as possible the environments that European settlers and colonial administrators had left behind in Europe.[70]

In a broad sense landscape protection in the form of national parks or reserves was conceived of in metropolitan France in terms of preservation.

This had much to do with the early history of landscape protection in France and the aesthetic and nationalist impulse that underpinned it. With the exception of Algeria, France's colonized landscapes, lacking in those associations, were considered differently. While the aesthetic impulse behind landscape protection was never absent, and forested landscapes were always privileged, as in metropolitan France, "scientific" interests had an important place. This might in part be attributed to the fact that governmental administrators associated with the forest service and scientists associated with the Museum of Natural History in Paris led the charge, as opposed to big game hunters in the case of Britain. The initiatives of forest administrators were tempered by one organization that did cross the Mediterranean and that was encouraged by the French government: the Touring Club of France. What became clear, however, was that despite the differences between colonial and national conceptions of national parks and reserves before World War II, the process by which landscape protection came to be implemented was profoundly shaped by Europe's colonial encounter, the internationalization of the movement to protect nature in all its forms, and the differing national perspectives on these questions in the decades following World War I.[71]

SIX

Reforestation and the Anxieties of Empire in Colonial Algeria

> Since the beginning of time, on the dry earth of this limitless land scraped to the bone, a few men had been ceaselessly trudging, possessing nothing but serving no one, poverty-stricken but free lords of a strange kingdom.
>
> —ALBERT CAMUS

FRANCE'S COLONIAL ENCOUNTER became central to the way in which the French state developed ideas and policies that came to affect the environment in both metropolitan France and the colonies that it came to possess, as the proceedings of the international congresses devoted to nature protection that were held between 1909 and World War II demonstrated.[1] This chapter focuses on an important dimension of the French colonial encounter by exploring the multiple ideological underpinnings of reforestation drives in colonial Algeria from the 1860s to World War II. While the British were, of course, also concerned with forested landscapes during the same period in colonial India, this chapter seeks to understand what made the French Algerian case distinct and to shed light on how different forms of colonial domination determined differing relationships to land and landscape.[2] To this extent, it considers how a particular form of environmental consciousness, as it emerged in French Algeria, might be compared to other colonial contexts and to that of metropolitan France. Forest conservation was disputed among colonial administrators, naturalists, military authorities, and foresters and among French and European (Italian, Maltese, and Spanish) settlers themselves, which speaks to the difficulty involved in seeing a single, unified "colonial project" with respect to landscape conservation in the French Empire.[3] Despite differing views among French settlers and colonial administrators, an imperial conception of the North African past, a settler insistence that Algeria be reclaimed as a Europeanized "Mediterranean" landscape, and France's competition with other colonial powers in Africa gave rise to conservation policies that were justified in unique ways in the Maghreb. This environmental consciousness was as much shaped by the form that colonialism assumed in Algeria—settler colonialism—and French conceptions of their role in the Maghreb's history as by any "ecological" concern.[4] Just as importantly, however, French attitudes and policies toward the environment reflected broader colonial anxieties about climate, race, and the fate of European "civilization" itself, which were at the heart of an evolving environmental awareness among the French in their empire by World War II.

※ ※ ※

TO ASSESS THE ISSUE of deforestation and reforestation in French colonial Algeria, one must begin with a consideration of the nature and distribution of Algerian forests toward the end of the nineteenth century before exploring French anxieties surrounding deforestation and the arguments for reforestation, as well as initiatives for environmental reform, such as measures taken by the state to create a forest code that was specific to Algeria in 1903.[5]

By the second quarter of the nineteenth century, Algeria, which was divided into three administrative departments, had as its boundaries the Sahara Desert to the south, Tunisia to the east, Morocco to the west, and the Mediterranean to the north. Its territory could be divided into four main topographical areas—the Tell Atlas, the Hauts-Plateaux or high plains, the Sahara Atlas, and the Sahara—and six types of forested regions, which included the Algerian-Tunisian region; the cork-producing region of Kabylia, which juts into a part of the north of Tunisia; the high plains of Constantine and the Aurès; the Ouarsenienne region; the Oran-Moroccan region, which included part of Morocco; and the Saharan Atlas (Map 1).[6]

A variety of types of property and land tenure existed when the French invaded Algeria, which included private property *(melk)*, collective, communal property *(arch)*, and property controlled by the Ottoman government, as well as unused land. These forms of land tenure as well as traditional land management practices in forested and agricultural areas were poorly understood and little respected by the French. One of the most widely used practices in both agricultural and forested areas was *keçir*, a technique that consisted of clearing land for planting by setting controlled fires in a cycle of every four years, which would allow for the planting and harvesting of crops as well as fertilization from the ashes that were produced. In the intervening four years the forest was left for the grazing of animals (Map 2).[7]

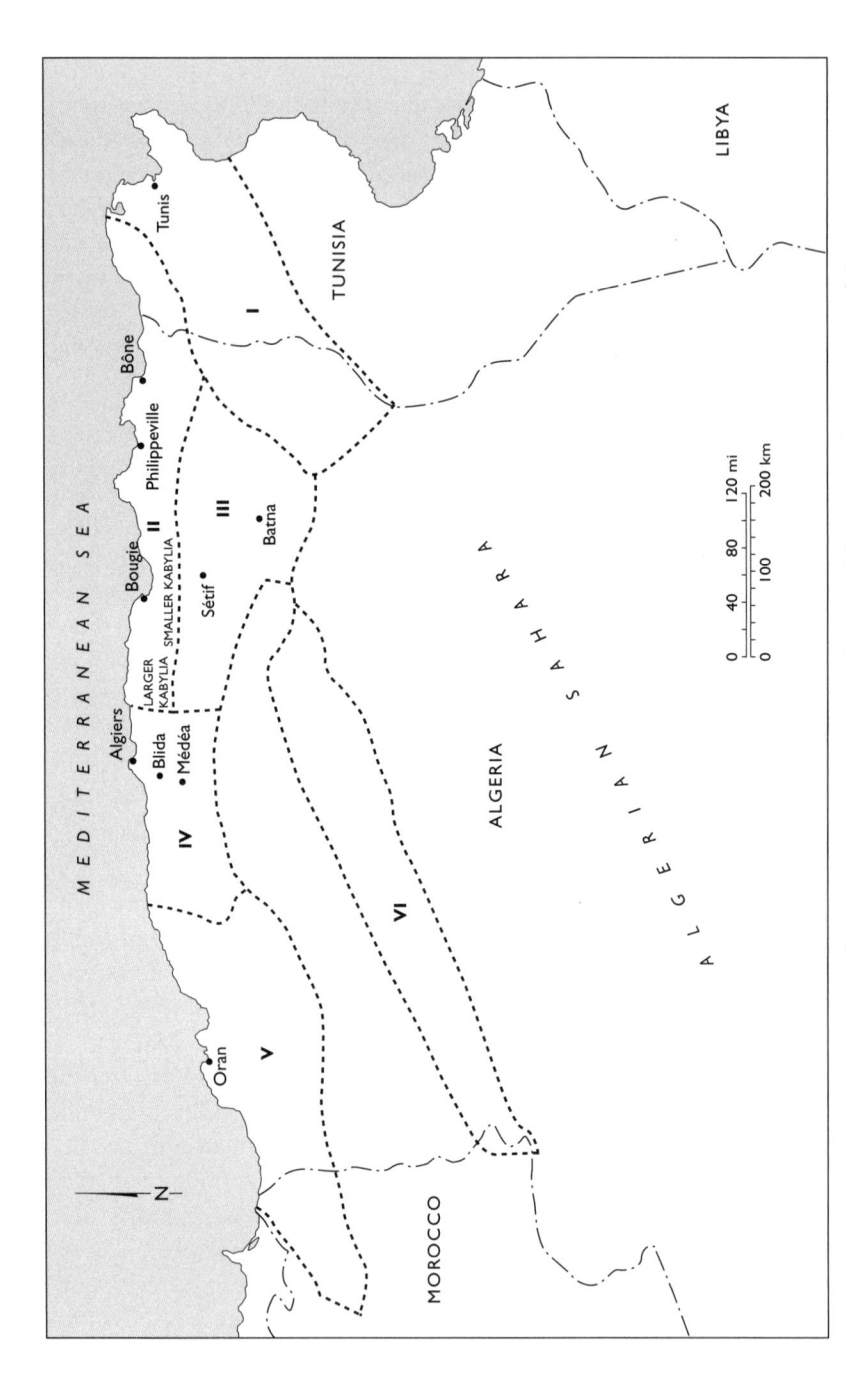

MAP 1. Forested Regions of Algeria. Map drawn by Bill Nelson. Reprinted from *American Historical Review* 113, no. 2: 341–362.

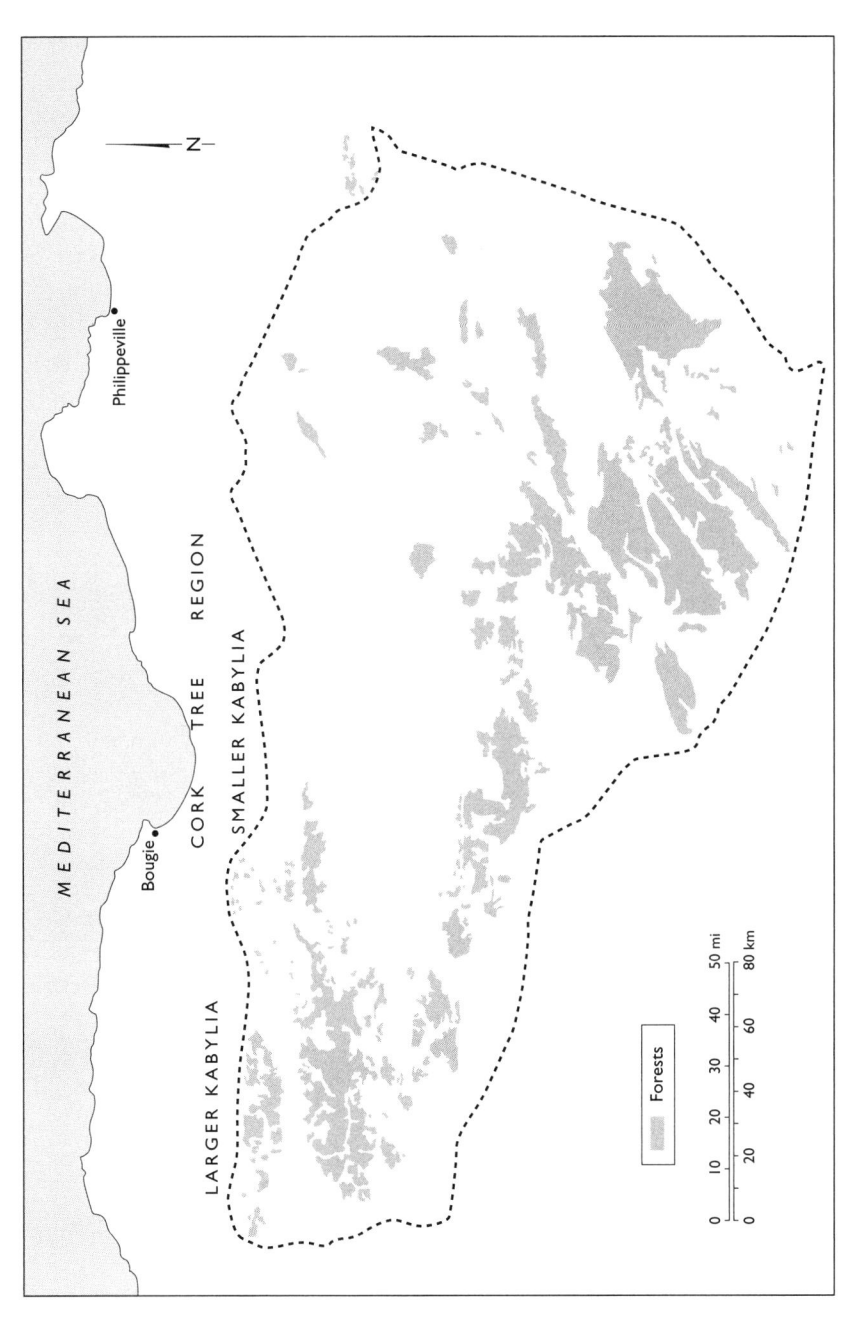

MAP 2. Forested Region III. Map drawn by Bill Nelson. Reprinted from *American Historical Review* 113, no. 2: 341–362.

From the period of the French conquest in 1830, forested lands were used and preserved for military purposes. The law of 16 June 1851 made the forests of Algeria the property of the state and proscribed certain rights to their indigenous inhabitants; most of this land was used for pasturage and the collection of wood. However, from 1846 the French government had started to grant long-term leases or concessions, thereby ceding large tracts of forests to wealthy French businessmen for specific periods of time, which ranged from forty to sixty years. These tracts, which often consisted of lucrative cork and Aleppo pine, were then exploited for commercial purposes, and Algeria quickly became one of the leading exporters of cork in the world. As a result, *concessionaires* (dealers) expropriated vast tracts of forested land and barred their use by the indigenous population.

The French applied the 1827 metropolitan forest code to all forested land administered by the French state in 1838 (when the Algerian forest service was created) without any modification, despite the real differences that existed in terms of the nature of the agricultural economy and forested land in metropolitan France and colonial Algeria. It did not take into account the existing forest economy, which relied both on livestock grazing and periodic brush fires to provide clearings for the planting of crops.[8] The 1827 law in many respects assumed the existence of uninhabited forests, which was hardly a reality in metropolitan France in the first half of the nineteenth century, and even less so in Algeria. The forest code of 1827 did not permit the grazing of sheep or goats, but allowed pigs, whose husbandry would have been largely unimaginable for Muslims. It severely curtailed the cultivation of plots in the forest, forbade the building of *gourbis* (huts) less than one kilometer from a forest, and, as in France, prosecuted those found gathering fallen wood, cork, or other material.[9] The 1827 forest code was strengthened by the passage of an 1874 fire law designed to prevent forest fires, which required the indigenous population to fight fires, while imposing collective fines and punishment for setting fires. Although Algeria never experienced a Guerre des Demoiselles—the protracted nineteenth-century war between forest dwellers dressed as women and the forest administration in metropolitan France—the number of forest violations and, even more significantly, the number of forest fires increased steadily in the last quarter of the nineteenth century and continued to grow up to World War I and beyond (see table).[10]

In 1900 Algeria possessed 3,247,692 hectares of forested land, 2,503,336 of which were administered by the French forest service (Eaux et Forêts). Only 468,495 hectares belonged to individuals, and much of the most lucrative forested land was exploited by the French.[11] The most prized of the forests ceded to French businessmen were the cork forests *(chêne liège)* in

NUMBER OF FOREST FIRES IN ALGERIA, 1865–1913

Year	Number	Surface hectares	Damage in francs	Observation
1865		160,000	2 million	Commission d'enquête
1873		73,313		
1874		2,777		
1875				Insignificant number
1876	120	55,172	441,881	
1877	134	40,538	1,807,061	Numerous Beni-Salah
1878	164	8,156	617,324	
1879	218	17,662	625,987	
1880	137	20,880	353,245	
1881	244	169,056	9,042,000	Commission d'enquête
1882	130	4,018	188,751	
1883	148	2,464	102,339	
1884	147	3,231	205,185	
1885	285	51,569	674,487	
1886	288	14,043	270,325	
1887	395	53,714	1,560,920	
1889	309	17,807	522,389	
1890	202	23,165	1,786,505	
1891	393	45,924	2,906,459	
1892	409	135,574	6,605,276	
1893	398	47,756	5,303,752	
1894	308	106,889	2,266,043	
1895	250	32,957	324,661	
1896	179	14,091	632,557	
1897	396	79,203	2,468,062	
1898	150	12,384	282,164	
1899	272	16,099	547,766	
1900	162	2,937	143,192	
1901	135	9,687	259,110	Numerous Beni-Salah
1902	475	141,141	3,668,780	Inquiry into 1902–1904 fires
1903	388	94,398	5,329,047	
1904	244	2,759	90,093	
1905	255	7,676	274,084	
1906	219	9,126	399,037	
1907	211	4,457	92,809	
1908	344	6,540	182,339	
1909	278	16,309	339,148	
1910	482	24,294	411,286	
1911	322	16,309	399,148	
1912	338	26,505	377,205	
1913	700	139,625	3,096,958	

Source: "Note sur les incendies de forêts en 1913," Archives nationales d'Outre Mer (ANOM), ALG, GGA, P/128. Reprinted from *American Historical Review* 113, no. 2: 341–362.

FIGURE 11. Algerian Forest Pavilion at the 1906 Marseille Colonial Exhibition. The Getty Research Institute, Los Angeles (970031).

the department of Constantine, from which the indigenous population was slowly expelled. These forests were lucrative, and their bounty was already on full display in the Algerian Forest Pavilion at the 1906 Colonial Exhibition in Marseille (Figure 11). They were in an area near the Mediterranean coast, where the vast majority of the French and European populations of Algeria resided, as well as in the Tell, which was "the principal center of colonization under the Romans" and where French colonization was most developed, which was in part because its climate was "essentially Mediterranean."[12]

French concerns about forest conservation coincided with the emergence of a "declensionist" environmental narrative among the French in Algeria from the 1850s on. According to this narrative, forests in North Africa were sites of memory, emblems of North Africa's golden Roman past—which had allegedly been destroyed by the Arab invasions of the seventh and eleventh centuries, when the Maghreb ceased to be the "granary of Rome."[13] According to what must now be acknowledged as a legend, which was based on inconclusive and in many cases fallacious historical, geographical, and environmental evidence, under Roman domination North Africa had once been a bountiful and peaceful land until its conquest by the Arabs and later by the Ottoman Empire. These views were largely based on French readings of Herodotus, Strabo, and Tacitus, on archeological evidence of irrigation networks and olive presses, and on Roman coins, which depicted bundles of wheat.[14] The legend was also based on the writings of the fourteenth-century North African historian Ibn Khaldun (1332–1406), whose work was translated into French by Baron de Slane in the 1850s and 1860s.[15] Various authors repeatedly cited Ibn Khaldun's description of Arab nomads as locusts who destroyed gardens and trees.[16] Some recent research ironically suggests, however, that the real beginning of soil degradation in North Africa might be better attributed to Roman practices of overcultivation, and that the greatest amount of deforestation in North Africa took place between 1890 and 1940, when the French virtually decimated Algeria's extensive cork forests for profit—thus a period well after the French had already constructed "their story of the environmental history of North Africa."[17]

Theodore Woolsey, a member of the U.S. Forest Service who conducted a comparative study of forests and forestry in Tunisia, Algeria, and Corsica in 1916, argued that there had been a "direct diminution of forest area through the sale of valuable cork-oak lands," noting that "one writer estimates that the forested areas near Constantine, Batna, Médéa, and Sétif have shrunk by from 10 to 60 per cent since 1871."[18] Nonetheless, José Germain and Stéphane Faye, among other contemporary commentators, believed that deforestation had occurred long before, and that it was France's mission to recover the region's former greatness while supplying grain and other agricultural produce to the metropole:

> Following the prosperous days of the Roman era, Algeria, Tunisia and Morocco . . . vegetated, barely surviving, cultivating piracy. . . . One by one, the former riches disappeared . . . all fell into ruin. Of the splendid golden age of Roman Mauretania only the sun-baked rocky desert remained, where the beneficent river had become a devastating torrent, where agriculture had atrophied, where livestock persisted and perished according to the vagaries of rainfall, and where the native sought to secure by force or ruse what his neighbor had produced instead of producing it himself.[19]

Forests were also frequently seen as sites of resistance on the part of Arabs, and the prevailing judgment in the colony was that a continuing series of forest fires from the 1860s to World War I were deliberately set.[20] To some extent colonists' perception of the *indigène* was little different from those of government administrators and bourgeoisie with respect to the French peasantry at the beginning of the nineteenth century in metropolitan France. Conflict concerning the use of forests was similar to what had occurred in metropolitan France, where pasturage and deforestation were said to account for a whole host of ills, including floods, from the French Revolution onward.

Diana Davis has argued that the declensionist narrative ultimately served three main purposes: "the appropriation of land and resources; social control (including the provision of labor); and the transformation of subsistence production into commodity production."[21] A closer look at the development of the narrative and the terms in which it came to be articulated suggests, however, that it was a reflection of much larger concerns and anxieties among settlers in Algeria. What was distinctive about calls for forest conservation in colonial Algeria was the way in which commentators linked deforestation to debates about hygienic issues, race, and climate change and to the possible decline of both empire and "civilization" itself.

Antoine-César Becquerel, a scientist who studied physics and meteorology and a member of the Institut de France, wrote in 1853: "One can already posit in principle that the absence of forests in a country that was once covered with them is the most certain sign of the passage of great conquerors, of an advanced civilization or of political turmoil."[22] The implication, which was taken up by a number of commentators in the nineteenth century, was that the greater the degree of deforestation, the closer a civilization was to its final days. Forests were at the center of a larger struggle to control the African continent, as evidenced by the growing fear of the gradual, and some argued inevitable, encroachments by the Sahara, which would destroy Algeria's Latin, Mediterranean character.

Algeria had a Mediterranean climate in areas where most French and European settlers lived and farmed, but a vast amount of its territory consisted of desert—indeed, one of the largest deserts in the world, the Sahara. As Ilhem Saida and others have indicated, the French had an ambiguous and complicated relationship to the desert. At times the desert had a positive, even spiritual or mystical valence, and at others it invoked terror.[23] The two climates of Algeria, that of the shores of the Mediterranean and that of the vast, empty desert of Africa, were at odds with one another, and some viewed the forests as essential to ensuring that the desert would not engulf the coast.

For this reason debates about reforestation and deforestation in both metropolitan and colonial Algeria centered first and foremost on the question of water. In France, there was a growing consensus that deforestation resulted in too much water, which produced floods, whereas in Algeria, by contrast, the phenomenon was deemed to result in too little water, which resulted in forest fires and climate change in the form of warmer temperatures.[24]

Many feared that these temperatures would ultimately hinder colonization by Europeans. One commentator argued that areas that had the most rainfall were forested and that rainfall had been diminishing progressively between 1836 and 1876 in areas that had been deforested.[25] The anxieties implicit in the desiccation narrative surrounding deforestation and reforestation also centered on questions of hygiene, climate, and health, all of which had been debated in the decades following the conquest of Algeria in 1830. Could men and women from colder climates acclimatize and adapt to warmer climates?[26] This was a question that was crucial to European settler colonialism, and it was one that occupied the British as well.[27] Indeed, acclimatization was central to debates about colonization more generally.[28]

Alfred Becquerel's *Traité élémentaire d'hygiène publique et privée* implicitly and explicitly considered the question of whether the French could adapt to the climates found in their colonies: "Can the man born and raised in more temperate or colder countries habituate himself to the modifications that warmer climates exert on his organs, and can he resist the diseases that these climates are susceptible of developing in him? It is in these terms that the question of acclimatization, so controversial today, must be posed."[29] Becquerel cited opposing evidence presented by doctors who had considered the question, quoting statistics concerning illness and death among European colonial troops in the tropics, India, and the Antilles. Many attributed the insalubrious climate, which led to European mortality, to the lack of rainfall, aggravated by deforestation, contributing to higher temperatures. Studies indicated that the highest rates of mortality in Algeria in 1844 and 1845 were among Europeans, in contrast to those among indigenous Muslims and Jews.[30] Becquerel suggested that while studies undertaken by Doctor Boudin, using official statistics, argued that acclimatization among European settlers was impossible, a "good study" by Martin and Foley contested his conclusion, arguing in favor of the "possibility of acclimatization in Algeria."[31] Nonetheless, official figures showed that the rates of mortality among children in hot climates represented an "enormous number," which was considerably greater than anywhere else. Most who argued against the ability of Europeans to adapt to warmer climates suggested that the number of deaths among settlers would necessarily exceed the number of births, which would gradually lead to depopulation without the arrival of new settlers, but Becquerel concluded that the jury was still out on the issue. He was, however, skeptical about the long-term prospects of settler colonialism, noting that "there is no people issuing from a country with a temperate climate, who came to conquer and establish itself in a country with a hot climate who have been able to implant themselves in a definitive manner, to prosper there and completely replace the native peoples."[32] Merely considering the statistics, he thought that many observers would probably pronounce "against the acclimatization of Europeans in countries with hot climates," but, he declared that this was not his view.[33] He argued that the studies had been inconclusive because they focused inordinate attention on colonial troops, who had distinctive problems and habits, and because they had not taken the problem of malaria as well as its root causes into account. Becquerel suggested that some Europeans could adapt more easily than others, and they included those from southern Europe, such as the French from the Midi, Italians, Portuguese, and Spanish, while the English and the Dutch "acclimatize with more difficulty."[34] Indeed, considerable attention was also given to the impact of the North African climate on women. Achille Fillias, a civil servant who popularized many of the theories that circulated at the time concerning the effect of climate on women's menstrual cycle and reproduction, claimed that pregnant women arriving in the Maghreb were more likely to abort than they were in Europe, for example, suggesting that they had greater difficulty in adapting to a warm climate.[35]

Becquerel also addressed the problem of nostalgia or homesickness in considering the problem of acclimatization. "Thus the chagrin of having left the native land, sometimes a certain degree of nostalgia" would have a necessary influence on adaptation.[36] Indeed, the problem of homesickness had been recognized since the earliest days of Algeria's conquest and would ultimately be at the heart of how the French tried to make the colony their own.[37]

※ ※ ※

THE FIGURE who did perhaps more than any other to address the problem of acclimatization, colonization, and the environmental challenges that Europeans faced when the declensionist narrative was at its height was Dr. Paulin Trolard. Trolard became director of the Institut Pasteur of Algiers in 1894, a post he held until he was forcibly removed in 1910, just before his death, for allegedly distributing bad vaccines.[38] He was also a publicist and was elected to the Conseil général of Alger. He took up the cause of reforestation in Algeria with a vengeance and was largely responsible for the foundation of the League for the Reforestation of Algeria in 1882, serving as its president for its over twenty-year existence.[39]

The League for the Reforestation of Algeria began with a membership of 1,200 in the three departments of Algeria—Alger, Constantine, and Oran—and its members consisted of French farmers and property holders and a very small number of Algerians.[40] It supported the study of the problem of reforestation and saw itself as a group that would pressure the French state to act to preserve Algeria's forested landscapes. In an appeal to Algerians in the first issue of the *Bulletin de la Ligue du Reboisement de l'Algérie*, Trolard wrote that "every deforested country is condemned to death!" and that areas in Algeria that were not destroyed by pasturage were destroyed by the "incendiary Arab" (Figure 12).[41]

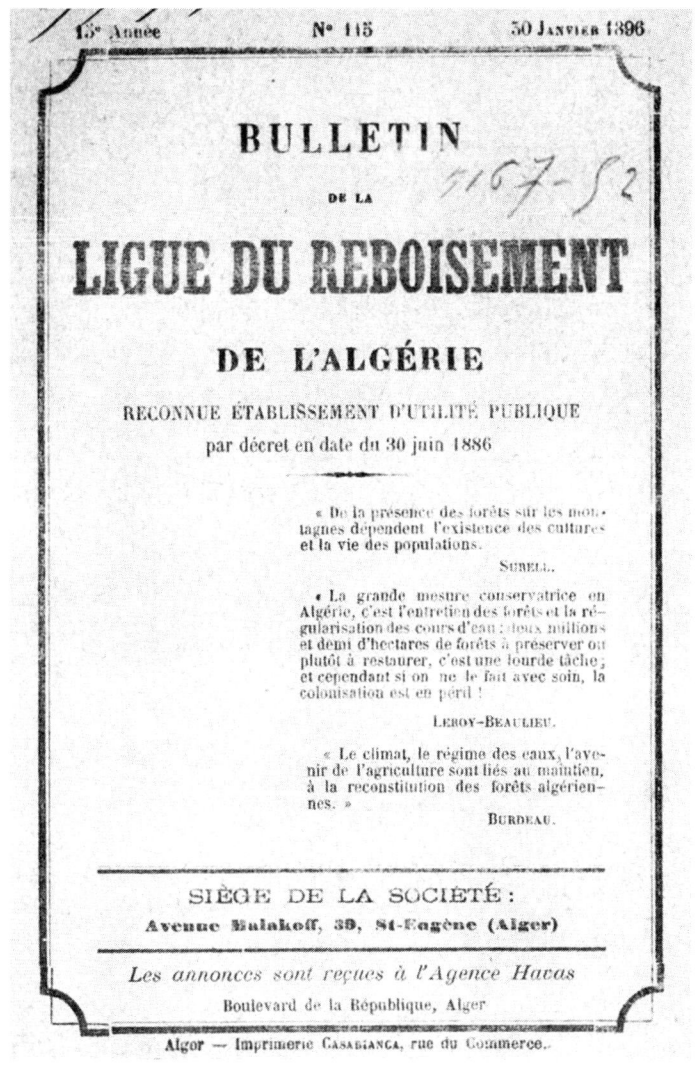

FIGURE 12. The first issue of the *Bulletin of the League for the Reforestation of Algeria* (Bulletin de la Ligue du Reboisement de l'Algérie), 30 January 1896.

Soon after, M. Reynaud, a government official who held a post in the Algerian forest service, wrote that "it is above all we Europeans who claim to bring modern civilization here" and to take charge of landscape conservation. He went on to state, "It belongs to us to repair the ruin caused by fatalism and error" through "the regularization and restoration of the climate of one part of the globe."[42] He also declared at a conference sponsored by the league held in the National Theater in Algiers that history had shown that without maintaining an equilibrium between agricultural and forested land, civilization would soon be destroyed:

> One has long sought to explain these ruins of empires regularly accumulated through the centuries by a supposed fatal law which would push the civilization of the East into the West; Bossuet wished to show the hand of Providence; but human reason refused to bend before these supernatural explanations. It is for our epoque to show the hand of man destroying his own work through the trouble he brings himself to the equilibrium between of forests and cultivated land. In thus modifying climate, he changed customs and practices, and destroyed the conditions which had rendered civilization possible.[43]

It was forests that preserved the culture of a "civilized" Mediterranean from being engulfed by a barren, uncivilized East and South. Indeed, there were all kinds of predictions that the Sahara and therefore sub-Saharan Africa were creeping toward the shores of the Mediterranean. Trolard warned metropolitan France that the French Empire would experience the same fate as the Roman Empire in North Africa if it failed to address the problem: "Is it possible to deny that French occupation is coming to an end and very rapidly; and that one can already fix the moment when it will have the same fate as the Roman occupation?"[44] Trolard thus called on France to restore North Africa to the splendor of its Roman past with the aid of Western science and landscape protection, believing that thereby France would become a new Rome.[45]

References to France becoming a new Rome and recovering the Roman Empire's greatness reflected not only a broader interest in North Africa's Latin past imbedded in the "granary of Rome" legend but also the myth of a new "Latin-Mediterranean race," who were the people destined to reestablish the greatness of North Africa. Discussions of this new, essentially European race became prevalent in a variety circles in the 1870s and 1880s and came to be intimately linked to the environmentalist concerns of those worried about the deforestation of North Africa.

Many found that mixed marriages among the French, Spanish, Italian, and Maltese settler populations helped to strengthen this supposed "race," and they were heartened by the high birthrates that resulted from these unions at a time when birthrates were falling in metropolitan France.[46]

Onésime Reclus, brother of the great French geographer Elisée Reclus and a frequent traveler to North Africa, made a case for France abandoning its colonial possessions in Asia in order to concentrate on the African continent, where a "neo French" race had been born.[47] Louis Bertrand, who was elected to the Académie française in 1925, did much to foster the importance of a new Latin Africa, and Jules Cambon, who became governor general of Algeria, praised Bertrand's interest in its settlers and his "insight into the lives of the Provençaux, the Catalans, the Maltese, and their like, who were at present merging together, as they had done in the time of Rome and Carthage, to form a resistant combination which resonated with the sounds of the Mediterranean."[48] Bertrand also extolled a Christian Africa, epitomized by the great North African saint Augustine, which had been destroyed by the Donatists and by Islam. Indeed, his goal was to return Algeria to its Latin, Christian, and Western origins.[49]

While there was no consensus regarding the virtues of the new "Latin race," and some even argued that only northern Italians had anything in common with the French, the danger posed by the possibility of being engulfed by a vast indigenous Muslim population who allegedly had nothing in common with Europeans and who were alleged to be in the process of destroying the environment was deemed by many Europeans in Algeria to be a very great peril.[50] The existence of this population made Algeria appear to the French settlers to be radically different from metropolitan France, a land they saw as being dominated by Islam, barbarous tribes, and pirates. This perception, according to Trolard and many others, posed almost insurmountable obstacles in terms of encouraging further colonization without the assurance of a propitious climate, which would be created by reforestation. An insalubrious climate would, in contrast and in his view, be an obstacle for the progress of civilization itself.[51]

M. Ollive, who was a member of the League for the Reforestation of Algeria, gave a speech in Sétif in which he argued that the long-dead empires in Asia Minor had been rich and populous and had constituted some of the most powerful in the world before the "Arab race" arrived and brought their practices of setting fires and grazing animals, which led to the disappearance of forests, which resulted in the rivers drying up and climate change.[52] The anti-Arab or anti-Muslim rhetoric became even more pronounced in the pages of the *Bulletin de la Ligue du Reboisement de l'Algérie* ten years later. In a report by J. Rochard on the relationship between deforestation and depopulation in France, he invoked the specter of past Muslim invasions and the havoc they wrought: "Muslims covered Europe in these ruins. The grass no longer grows where their horses have passed. North Africa, Greece, and most of Spain have seen their prosperity disappear with the vegetation that covered them."[53] He suggested, moreover, that deforestation was a cause of sterility, as evidenced in the barren and supposedly uninhabited areas of the steppes of Central Asia, the Sahara, and the Arabian desert.

A series of disastrous periodic fires beginning in the 1860s and continuing through World War I initiated a prolonged debate about deforestation and reforestation in which French *colons* (settlers), the forest service, and the French state increasingly came to see them as a result of deliberate arson perpetrated by "Arabs" to resist the French state.[54] They did not take into account the fact that fires regularly broke out in the hot, dry climate of late summer in North Africa and in other parts of the Mediterranean. Nor did they acknowledge the fire ecology of the region, which consisted of controlled burning within forests *(keçir)*.[55]

In 1878, following another set of devastating fires, an editorial in the *Courier de Bône,* commenting on the extensive damage in the forests of Beni-Saleh in the department of Constantine, expostulated that the periodic fires set by the *indigènes* represented the "most serious obstacle that colonization could confront in Algeria." It went on to assert that "neither the English in India, nor the Americans in the plains of the Far West[,] have encountered as rebellious and hostile an element as this Arab nation animated by Muslim fanaticism and contempt for the riches of the earth."[56]

The "clash of civilizations"/anti-Muslim rhetoric and the link made between Islamic fanaticism and environmental devastation came to be articulated in this context and was part of a broader anticlerical sentiment that came to pervade Catholic France at the end of the Second Empire and the early Third Republic. A commission composed of French businessmen granted concessions to exploit vast tracts of Algeria's abundant cork forests was formed to reflect on the problem of forest fires. It was in no doubt about where the trouble lay, writing that "in contrast to the Berber, the Arab is the personal enemy of trees. Everywhere that he establishes himself, he destroys them. This is so evident that, in no point of Africa or Asia, does one see trees on the territory of an Arab tribe."[57] They went on to claim that the cause of fires that swept the region was ill will "provoked by religious fanaticism," and even considered them as part of a larger Muslim conspiracy against Christianity. The report cited other examples of this conspiracy in the planning of a massacre of Christians in 1856 at Easter in Larissa and in the pillaging of the Christian district of Galata in Istanbul in 1859.[58]

Stereotypes of the Arab and the Berber pervaded the report. It asserted that the Kabyles were "friends of work and of trees" and looked on the European forest concessions as a source of income, whereas Arabs were enemies of both work and trees. It claimed that for some years Arab tribes had come to inhabit forested areas close to Syria and that a voyager who recently visited the area "predicts that there will be no trees in twenty-five years, insofar as the work of denuding the earth has already advanced."[59]

The power of the myth of Muslim depredations and the "bedouinization" of North Africa can be adduced in the historical narrative surrounding indigenous groups, notably the Kabyles—a supposedly non-Arab (Berber) population alleged to have been native to Algeria at the time of the Arab invasions of the seventh and eleventh centuries—and the nomadic population, who were the supposed descendants of the Arab invaders. Abbé Raynal's *L'Histoire philosophique et politique des établissements et du commerce des européens dans l'Afrique septentrionale,* which was published posthumously in Paris in 1826, propagated this myth. His account became particularly popular from the 1850s onward. The largely sedentary and farming Kabyle people, according to his narrative, were pushed into the forested mountain regions of the Maghreb, while the rich lowlands became denuded and inhabited by nomadic Arab pastoral groups. The Kabyle Berbers were said to be an independent people with a wild taste for liberty, and were the descendants of the Vandals, a Nordic, European population from across the Mediterranean. They were reputed to be handsome, originally with blond hair and blue eyes, and only incompletely converted to Islam.[60] During the course of the nineteenth century, French ethnographic texts, administrative reports, and travel literature helped to propagate this "Kabyle myth" and the belief that this mountainous people was superior to and fundamentally different from the lowland Muslim Arabs because of their fierce independence, egalitarianism, respect for property, and sedentary life.[61] This myth was largely accepted by French geographers in the interwar period and underpins the work of the great *annaliste* historian Fernand Braudel, who wrote, "To the east and to the south the Mediterranean suffered two invasions, in fact two series of prolonged upheavals that altered everything. These were the 'two gaping wounds' spoken of by Xavier de Planhol: The Arab invasions which began in the seventh century and the Turkish invasions which began in the eleventh, which had introduced the culture of nomadism into the region.[62] According to Braudel, the "Arab invader" avoided mountainous regions and "skirted the edge of the deserted mountains bordering the sea, where an abundant rainfall accounts for thick forests of antiquity long respected by man."[63] Reproducing the Kabyle myth, Braudel asserted that the forests "therefore served as refuges for the native populations before the Arab conquerors," and that "'Bedouinization' following the Arab conquest spread all over the land in between the mountains, whether early or lately settled, like a flood cutting off the mountain tops as islands."[64] The power of this narrative can also be seen in its pervasiveness, even in the English-speaking world. In 1915, for example, J. Russell Smith, a professor at the University of Pennsylvania, wrote in the *Bulletin of the American Geographical Society* that "Rome once ruled the world—all of it that was worth taking, but she never took the Bedouin. He fled into his desert pastures and left the farm lands to the conqueror. Then Rome fell, and the Bedouin who had helped bring it about came back into his own, turning the Roman farms into pastures."[65] Smith went on to acknowledge Latin Europe's mission to reclaim Rome's glory in North Africa. Perhaps also thinking of the Italians in Libya, he wrote, "And now Rome and her children, the other Romance countries, are taking another turn and are again driving the Bedouin back from the Mediterranean shores."[66]

The drive to stem the tide of deforestation was part of a larger attempt to claim Algeria's landscape as one that was Mediterranean and that eminently suited the *pied noir* (European settler) population in the Maghreb. This is reflected powerfully in literary forms as well and in the romanticization of the Mediterranean climate. Robert Randau, one of the principal authors in the so-called turn-of-the-century *algérianiste* literary movement, for example, has one of his main characters exclaim that he would never abandon Algeria for Paris: "No, Paris has wonderful sunsets on the Seine, and the night there is prodigious in its richness; but my ideal is not at all that of a bookworm.... I am an adventurer.... I have a sort of perverse love for tropical countries where nature is massive, heavy, sinister, and cynical."[67]

The French worried about desertification and the encroachment of the Sahara as early as the beginning of the conquest of Algeria in 1830. In the years that followed they expropriated, nationalized, and redistributed millions of hectares of land in what has been described as a "colossal territorial experiment."[68] Concerns about deforestation were accompanied by the implementation of policies to protect and promote other forms of vegetation beginning in the 1880s for similar reasons. For example, alfa (*halfa* in Arabic, or needle grass), a brush plant found in North Africa and the western and southern Mediterranean, became the object of study for the role it might play in protecting the young colony from the creeping sands of the Sahara, just as the planting of pines had in western France. Harvested for the production of certain textiles and fine paper, it had disappeared from much of northern Algeria by the 1880s but continued to grow in the south. In 1884 and 1885 a mission headed by Auguste Mathieu, *conservateur des forêts* of Oran, embarked on a study of the function of alfa in the region.[69] He was joined by two representatives from the Compagnie franco-algérienne and a naturalist from the Jardin d'acclimatation in Algiers. When Mathieu published the commission's findings, he concluded that alfa covered pastoral land that was often inhospitable to colonization because of persistent drought and extremes of temperature. It also held the sandy soil in place, provided shade, allowed the ground to retain moisture more effectively, and served as vegetation for livestock.[70] Its gradual disappearance was attributed to grazing and to the harvesting of the plant for commercial purposes. Mathieu proposed granting concessions to the Compagnie franco-algérienne for the harvesting of the plant in a controlled environment. He also argued for the creation of zones where the plant would be completely protected from human exploitation. His proposals were quickly adopted through a decree issued by the governor on 14 December 1888 that complemented a law passed in 1885 governing the cultivation and the rights to use forests in colonial Algeria.[71] What was unique about the decree was the way in which it saw ground shrubs playing a role that was similar to that of trees in consolidating topsoil—in this case sand—to prevent further erosion in mountainous areas and to serve as a barrier against the shifting sands of the Sahara. Ironically, an elevation in the status of alfa, which was an indigenous plant, transformed it into an instrument through which to manage the colonial environment and make it habitable for a settler population.[72]

A neglected part of the story of the drive for reforestation or the conservation of alfa is the degree to which it was also profoundly shaped by competition between the European powers after 1890. This was not just a question of standing up for "Western civilization" and Christendom, reclaiming the Mediterranean, or providing a justification for the dispossessing of an indigenous population and appropriating their land. It was also an extension of the fierce conflicts among the European rivals in the region. M. Ollive argued that reforestation was about France's survival as a great power. For him it was a question of whether or not the "French race" would be able to make further inroads into Africa, which was the challenge that destiny put before "yesterday the Great Nation, and perhaps tomorrow the protégés of the Slavs and the Saxons!"[73] He declared to his audience:

> Oh all of you ... you who have felt the tears of rage and of shame well up in your eyes, at the memory of the errors and crimes of those who, presiding over the destiny of our country, led us to Rosbach, to Waterloo, to Sédan; [who] made us lose America, the Indias and the scepter of the world. Will you hesitate when fortune shines [on us] again, permits us to repair the disasters of the past, no longer with the sword, but with the spade, no longer by spilling blood, but by working, protecting the land, a continent, which can again become the most beautiful in the world, the jewel [in the crown], the future of our race.[74]

In an article entitled "A Colony in Danger," published three years later, Trolard asked, "What will become of France when the Anglo-Saxon empire has bases in America and Australia, when in the Old World, pan-Slavism and pan-Germanism will have fulfilled their program?"[75] France should, in Trolard's view, therefore encourage more French to settle in Algeria, because the disappearance of Algeria would signal the decline of France itself.[76] To appeal to potential settlers, the state would have to make a concerted effort to entice them; the climate did not "suit the very large majority of French temperaments" because of its "extreme dryness" in some regions and its "excessive humidity" in others as well as its "proximity to the Sahara, which generates the sirocco."[77] Reforestation through scientific means would increase rainfall and reverse the effects of the North African climate. Trolard therefore called for the reforestation of no less than 4 million hectares of land in Algeria and suggested that once this task was accomplished it would be the beginning of France taking real possession of central Africa, which was the ambition of all modern nations.[78] In short, while the environmental discourse that linked reforestation, colonization, and civilization justified territorial possession by settlers and colonial rule over the "uncivilized" Arab nomad, it also came to be voiced in terms of a desire to preserve Algeria as a French and Mediterranean colony whose climate would foster the arrival of new settlers from France and a new Latin race.[79]

The specific ideology behind and justification for the drive for landscape conservation and reforestation in Algeria was largely absent from other parts of France's colonial empire. In Indochina, where there would be a much smaller settler population and where the landscape itself had no historical, sentimental, or nostalgic past associations in metropolitan France, the French were less concerned about how their conservation might foster a more hospitable climate for further colonization. This does not mean that the military administration did not attempt to manage forests for their lucrative value. The French were interested in the dense forests of teak and other woods as valuable natural resources. Indeed, the ultimate establishment of a protectorate in Cambodia in 1863, the pacification of Tonkin in 1883–1885, and the French push into Laos were in part motivated by the presence of forests. While the French colonial administration initially made it relatively easy for entrepreneurs to gain access to Indochina's prized tropical forests, they soon began to become conscious of their rapid depletion. A new decree, issued on 12 June 1891, recognized that previous decrees governing the exploitation of the colony's forests had not done enough to protect them, and a subsequent report affirmed that the new decree "responded to fears manifested by all those who saw, little by little, the forest disappear."[80] The decree represented an important departure in that for the first time it created forest reserves where any form of exploitation was forbidden in Cochin China, and it laid the blame for deforestation at the feet of European entrepreneurs. Afterward, however, peasants were increasingly held accountable for infractions, particularly those populating forested villages.[81] In sum, from 1862 to 1900 it was the governors who oversaw the forests of Indochina with the view of military provisioning. From 1866 onward the forests began to be open for colonial exploitation, and few constraints were placed on European entrepreneurs. It was only after 1891 that protective measures were put in place and the budget of the forest service increased.

※ ※ ※

IN CONTRAST TO INDOCHINA, much of the drive behind reforestation in Algeria came from the European settler population, who frequently clashed with the colonial administration and with Paris, as the career of Dr. Paulin Trolard suggests. Indeed, Trolard complained bitterly about the way in which the government in metropolitan France downplayed Algeria's importance in the French Empire and slighted French settlers there—a not infrequent *pied noir* refrain. In 1886 Trolard argued that the metropole ignored the importance of Algeria, which was a part of France, in favor of its possessions in Indochina and the Far East. It appeared to him to be more concerned with "sav[ing] the prestige of the flag in Tonkin" and "establish[ing] a few insignificant trading posts" than saving Algeria. He went on to wonder if to keep the "authority of its name intact in the Muslim world" it would refuse "to pluck from ruin and death two hundred thousand of its children, whom it brought to Algeria."[82]

The tensions between the European settler population in Algeria and the metropole ran high and were played out in political debates regarding Algeria's governance generally, and environmental policy more particularly, from the 1890s onward. In 1893 a senatorial commission, headed by Jules Ferry, was charged with assessing government policies in Algeria.[83] Seven senators, including Ferry, left France and spent fifty-three days in Algeria (from 19 April to 10 June 1892). They traveled 4,000 kilometers to gather testimony from both *pied noir* settlers and the Muslim population, and deliberately avoided contact with Algeria's political elite. Forest policy and its reform were central to the commission's agenda, and the commission's report called for relaxing the harsh penalties imposed on the native population for pasturing animals in forested areas, arguing that pastoralism was the basis of its livelihood. Ferry's commission went so far as to propose the creation of a new forest code that was applicable to the specific conditions in North Africa, but Algeria had to wait almost a decade before this code was enacted in 1903.

The limitations and lacunae of the sources in this period for Algeria present the historian with a formidable challenge: it is almost impossible to recover fully the "voices" of the indigenous populations, but their responses are reflected in a number of petitions filed with the colonial administration, and they did address themselves to Ferry's commission. After hearing a unanimous call from the indigenous population for tempering the excesses of overzealous forest officials, Jules Ferry issued a blistering attack on forest officials for the prosecution of Algerians for forest violations. He deplored their actions, arguing that whereas forest officials considered the Muslim population to be in a constant state of delinquency, it appeared to be facing destitution.[84] Trolard answered with a scathing critique of the commission's report by arguing that the Arabs themselves would die out after the French had disappeared: "With your own hands, senators, you will have dug their grave" through, he argued, "indulgence and solicitude for the nomadic population."[85] The Conseil général of Alger (of which Trolard was a member) published a protest against the commission's report, the pretext of which, in their view, was the "protection of the natives against the settlers," but whose aim was "the destruction of our departmental and communal liberties."[86]

The governor general of Algeria, Jules Cambon, was, however, sympathetic to Ferry's recommendations. In 1893 he noted to the administrator of the mixed commune of Boghari that the Algerians were fined over 100,000 francs by a civil court in Blida for grazing their livestock: "These populations are in a state of alarming misery," he observed, and they might end up perhaps abandoning the region to avoid forest officials.[87] Six months later Cambon wrote to the minister of agriculture in Paris and argued that the complaints of the indigenous population in Boghari were "well founded and worthy of every solicitude" from the government, which should remember how the "pre-existing rights of these populations have been reduced and distorted little by little by the progressive application of our metropolitan laws."[88]

In May 1895 a report to the governor general of Algeria from Aumale indicated that the disputes over forests had as their source "the antinomy that exists in the matter of property between customary or Muslim law and our French law."[89] Numerous conflicts emerged, including one involving a forest fire near Batna in the department of Constantine in 1908 in which the indigenous populations in the *douar* (village) El-Ksour stood accused. They responded in Arabic that the village was over three kilometers from the fire, not close by, and that the sheikh of the *douar* instructed them to fight the fire. They concluded, "We respectfully point out the indigenous population of douar El-Ksour has no interest in seeing the forest burn."[90]

Some government administrators on the ground also showed sympathy for the plight of the indigenous population. In 1895 the administrator of the commune of Ain Bessem in the department of Alger wrote to the prefect that one could not deny that "our natives show proof of submission and real patience in the presence of daily vexations to which they are . . . subjected on the part of the subaltern agents of the forest service."[91] He further observed that this "often brutal personnel," ignorant of local mores and the native language, which they did not attempt to learn, "only [see] in the native a dangerous neighbor," to be taxed and pressed into forced labor at will.[92] He concluded that "the frequency and importance of fires" were directly related to the increase in forest service personnel, who did more to create conditions for insurgency than to plant trees.[93]

In 1892 Jules Cambon made 227,000 hectares of forested land available for livestock herds that were threatened by drought, but he was forced to rescind some of these measures when exceedingly dry conditions resulted in fires that destroyed 135,000 hectares of forested land in the same year and 101,000 hectares in 1894.[94] Despite his attempts and those made by other government administrators to rein in the forest service, the situation of the indigenous population probably worsened during these years, judging by the number of petitions submitted by them to various French ministries and to the president of the republic. They became more numerous between 1895 and 1900,[95] as did the size of monetary fines and *procès-verbaux*, which increased from 12,388 in 1893 to 17,181 in 1898.[96] Moreover, the government appeared unable to stop what was an illegal de facto conversion by the forest service of fines into days of forced labor. In the words of one commentator, the service "has never wanted to persuade itself . . . that it was not in France, but in Algeria and in an Arab country."[97]

Algeria had to wait until 1900 and the appointment of a forest commission by the governor general for recommendations to be made that led to the passage of a forest code in 1903, which was to be specific to conditions in the region. Theodore Woolsey of the American national forest system suggested in 1916 that many of the difficulties that the French encountered in Algeria were "due to the fact that the Forest Service at first attempted to copy too closely for local necessities methods used in France."[98] In his address to the commission, Governor General Charles Jonnart observed that he knew of regions where the natives were sandwiched between lands opened for settlement and forests, but he was satisfied that the 1903 code was more "supple" and sensitive to the needs of the local population.[99] In reality, it retained the punitive aspects of the 1874 fire law with regard to the indigenous Algerian population.

The civil administration in Algeria sent mixed signals to both settlers and the indigenous population. Jonnart, who was largely responsible for introducing the 1903 forest code, to which Trolard objected, joined the Ligue du reboisement de l'Algérie in 1905 and presided over Algeria's first Arbor Day, when he declared that like the members of the league he was "absolutely convinced of the capital importance of reforestation, to which the future" of the colony was linked: "It's there, for French North Africa, a question of life or death."[100]

Conflicts and fires persisted, however. In 1903, seventy-three Algerians in Nemours sent a petition to the governor general to protest a proposal to create a reforestation project that would deny them the use of the land in the Bassin de L'Oued Touent.[101] At first both the governor general and the prefect wrote that the concerns of the Arab population should be taken into consideration, and the prefect of Oran even suggested that the project be abandoned in view of the protests.[102] Ultimately, however, the governor general, on the advice of officials in the forest service and the mayor of Nemours, firmly instructed the prefect to enforce the forest code.[103] In 1911 the *conseillers municipaux* of Nemours again petitioned the governor in the name of the villages of Sidi-Omar and Ouled-Ziri, arguing that the forest service had unlawfully seized 700 hectares of land without taking into account that they had rights over the land where their ancestors had lived for centuries, thereby reducing them to ruin and destitution.[104] The governor general closed the case in a letter to the forest service and to the prefect of Oran in which he instructed them to inform the petitioners that "it is not possible to give them satisfaction" and that the petition was rejected.[105]

※ ※ ※

THE ALGERIAN CASE suggests that in order to understand the motivations behind landscape protection in different geographical contexts one must take into account not only the ways in which landscapes become sites of memory or emblems of the past, but how and why some memories are privileged or erased. It also reminds us that landscapes are "imprinted with our tenacious, inescapable obsessions."[106] While there was no colonial consensus regarding how to manage Algeria's forests and establish a place for the *indigènes* in their own landscape, forest management and conservation were nonetheless governed by the desire to create an environment that would be suitable and sustainable for settler colonialism, which was less of a concern in other parts of the French Empire.

While some of the impetus behind landscape preservation was inspired by scientific thought in metropolitan France, it was taken up and largely propagated by the settler *pied noir* population in Algeria in novel and distinct ways. It was, perhaps not surprisingly, a settler cause, as opposed to an initiative generated in the metropole, and the "environmentalism" that settlers espoused justified territorial displacement, as Diana Davis has so eloquently argued.[107] However, the narrative of environmental degradation was not simply shaped by the attempt to expropriate land for the purpose of transforming "subsistence production into commodity production," because not all land in colonial Algeria was expropriated for this purpose, as evidenced by the case of the new national parks. Following World War I, for example, the governor general, Charles Lutaud, responding to pleas first voiced in 1912, decreed on 17 February 1921 that a series of national parks be created mainly in forested areas in the interest of preserving "the natural beauty of the colonies and developing tourism."[108] Article 1 of the decree declared that "forests or parts of forests whose botanical composition, picturesque beauty, or climatic conditions" made them particularly amenable would be set aside as "centers of scientific study and tourism."[109] All hunting and wood gathering by indigenous populations would be prohibited, while the government, as noted in article 8, would favor building hotels and other forms of accommodation. The colonial government thus established thirteen national parks in the departments of Alger and Constantine between 1923 and 1927.[110] These parks, from which all human settlement and land use would be banned, represented an attempt to preserve the ancient landscapes of Mediterranean North Africa and to serve as buffer zones in the face of encroachments by the Sahara.

An overriding sentiment of anxiety and potential loss pervaded environmental narratives of deforestation and landscape conservation in colonial Algeria. The environmentalism espoused in Algeria was inspired by settler anxieties regarding the perceived limits of further colonization and territorial expansion in the face of competition with other European empires, an intractable climate, the Sahara Desert, a far more numerous indigenous Muslim population, and the fate of Western "civilization" itself. This environmentalism also reflected a desire to claim Algeria as a Mediterranean landscape linked to Europe. John H. Elliott has argued in the context of the Atlantic world that "one of the paradoxes than runs through the whole history of metropolitan-colonial relationships" was that colonists, "even while coming to appreciate the qualities that made their environment unique, devoted a great deal of time and energy to making it resemble as closely as possible the environment that they had left behind."[111] This was no less true of Algeria, where at the end of the nineteenth century French *colons* allegedly attempted to recover a bountiful Christian and Mediterranean landscape and to complete the process of colonization. Like the Europeans of colonial New England, the *pieds noirs* of Algeria sought to effect "changes in the land" that led to restructuring the nature of land use as well as the organization of plant and animal communities.[112] That European settlers' search for the familiar was apparent in their attempt to create "neo-European" spaces as they did when they created colonial spas in other parts of the French Empire to heal the colonizer's body.[113] Such initiatives were inspired by a sentiment of nostalgia. However, in contrast to North America and other French or British colonial possessions, they ultimately viewed these changes as a form of historical "restoration," which was predicated on a sense of nostalgia for an imagined lost empire.

The environmental consciousness that emerged among European settlers in North Africa did not then constitute a kind of utopian yearning of the kind that Richard Grove identifies in the context of tropical Edens like Mauritius in the seventeenth and eighteenth centuries where Europeans searched for the "normative location for social Utopias and the simultaneous formulation of an environmental critique."[114] The "nascent environmentalism" of Bernardin de Saint-Pierre on Mauritius, and later of Edward Balfour in India, Ernst Dieffenbach in New Zealand, and Paul Strzelecki in Australia, inspired as it was by the "social reformism of physiocracy and the Enlightenment," had little to do with the "violence of environmentalism" that was inherent in the League for the Reforestation of Algeria in 1900.[115] Since its conquest, Algeria was long regarded as having a climate that was impossible for Europeans and one that required profound alteration by wresting the land from the Arab population, which allegedly defiled it and was incapable of responsible stewardship. The struggle for the environment was cast in terms of a clash of civilizations and hygiene. In 1862 Achille Fillias wrote that it was thought that "the climate of Algeria is the most murderous on the globe," and the number of immigrants was diminishing. He argued that this was because Arabs had left "detritus of all sorts" to accumulate for centuries, which created unhealthy miasmas for the soldier and settler. He suggested that little by little the soil had actually been purified and sanitary conditions were improving: "Today, thanks to the work undertaken or being undertaken, the climate of Algeria is truly and exceptionally healthy."[116] Dr. H. Agnély, who had been professor of medicine at Dijon and who was a cofounding member of the Société de climatologie algérienne, concurred in this assessment, citing Dr. Périer, the army's chief physician, who declared that the conditions of health were not equal "but superior to those of a great number of cities in France."[117]

Myths regarding natural landscapes appear to be an inherent part of their mastery, but also of the profound anxieties surrounding their potential loss, as recent work on the conquest and Russification of the central Asian steppes suggests.[118] The Algerian case reflected the all too familiar processes of expropriation that occurred in other parts of the world, from central Asia to North America and Australia. What was unique in Algeria, however, was not only some of the myths that were invoked but the anxieties the settler population expressed regarding the threat of competing empires, climate, race, and the progress of "civilization" itself at the end of the nineteenth century, suggesting, more generally, that there was a diversity of colonial environmental projects, shaped by differing forms of colonial domination and rule at different historical moments in time. In short, the Algerian case reveals some of environmentalism's darker sides and indicates that there was no linear, reformist, or enlightened historical path for environmentalism from the past into the future.

SEVEN

The Greening of Paris

> One ought to be careful about considering parks and gardens as a somewhat superfluous manifestation of great luxury. Quite to the contrary, large areas planted with trees and shrubs in the middle of urban agglomerations are indispensable to public hygiene, just like water and sunlight. A park, on the condition that it is sufficiently large, is a reserve of pure air, and the trees that surround and protect it form a very effective natural filter to eradicate unhealthy dust and purify the ambient atmosphere.
> —Eugène Hénard

DURING MUCH of the nineteenth century initiatives that were launched to preserve and conserve the natural environment focused on France's forests, rivers, and landscapes in both metropolitan and colonial France. However, as early as the 1820s and 1830s the environmental condition of France's urban spaces began to attract the attention of hygienists, doctors, government officials, and the lay public, who began to think about cities and towns in new ways. Pierre Emmanuel Bruneseau (1751–1819), an inspector for the city of Paris and founder of the city's sewer services, wrote at the beginning of the nineteenth century that most of the city's smaller streets had no ventilation or sunlight and that the "filthy ground" filled "the atmosphere with dangerous miasmas," while decaying debris continually piled up and a "quantity of effluvia" arose from "vegetable and animal substances."[1]

The nineteenth century witnessed the greening of urban spaces, the birth of the urban greenhouse, and the rise of the garden city. Concerns about the urban environment also gradually spearheaded a number of new projects designed to clean up the city and revitalize the suburbs, which led to their gradual "greening" during the course of the nineteenth century. Three of the most ambitious projects were first launched in the 1850s by Napoleon III to rebuild and reorder the capital city of Paris. While Napoleon III's vast scheme to rebuild Paris was in part inspired by the desire to make the city safe from revolution, it also addressed the problems of plumbing, sanitation, and ventilation, and focused its attention on the creation of public parks in the place of insalubrious cesspools to complement the surviving private and royal parks built by the aristocracy and the French monarchy in previous centuries. The second large-scale project was proposed by social reformers in the first decade of the twentieth century, when they sought to create new parks for the city of Paris and to build low-cost housing for the working class, integrating green space into their design. The third consisted of plans to establish a network of garden cities in the suburbs of Paris and in other parts of France. The French were, of course, not alone in reflecting on the place of nature in urban spaces during this period. Like the movement to protect landscapes, urban planning and the garden city movement were international initiatives, and France drew inspiration from Britain, Germany, and the United States.

※ ※ ※

TREATISES ON landscaped and picturesque gardens abounded from the eighteenth century onward, but they were primarily intended for monarchs and aristocratic clientele and had little impact on the discussion of the role of nature in the city.[2] However, during the nineteenth century a new garden aesthetic emerged that bore little relationship to the formal gardens of André Le Nôtre at Versailles, Chantilly, or Saint-Germain, although his style never died out and continued to be favored by French society, as the popularity during the early Third Republic of the father-and-son team of landscape artists Henri and Achille Duchêne suggests. They were responsible for a new genre, the "mixed garden," which reconciled the formal garden associated with Le Nôtre and the landscaped English park, and they designed 6,000 gardens in Europe and South America.[3] Arthur Mangin (1824–1887), a writer of popular books about the natural world, noted in 1867 that "today we understand the landscape garden differently from sixty years ago, and will probably understand it differently in a few years time.... As a result of this, the landscape fashion, which leaves the way open to any systematic innovation and the fantasy of individuals, can be said to conform to the liberal spirit of the nineteenth century."[4]

The new garden aesthetic emerged with the rise of the private middle-class garden. Many nineteenth-century treatises, which were written for a broader public, counseled against excessively formal garden designs and clearly thought in terms of small residential gardens attached to houses or apartment dwellings.[5] In this context it is not surprising that a new garden and flower aesthetic came to be articulated for the middle classes, whose gardens were too small to be amenable to formal landscaping. Pierre Boitard (1789–1859), a botanist who wrote popular books on natural history, also published more practical books on gardening for the bourgeois reader.[6] He introduced his readers to the variety of gardens and suggested how they should be composed, taking note of the emergence of the phenomenon of the picturesque kitchen garden attached to houses that belonged to the middle classes, which had been regarded with disdain by a number of observers and could be found almost exclusively in Paris's suburbs.[7]

In addition to the kitchen garden and the flower garden, floor boxes, window boxes, and huge vases of greenery were introduced into the apartments themselves during the nineteenth century.[8] The greening of the domestic interior led to a new appreciation of horticulture, which middle-class women took up in greater and greater numbers, and Boitard himself early on wrote *La botanique des dames,* in the form of letters to one Eugènie, in which he extolled the importance of botany and the aesthetic beauty of flowers.[9] This was followed by a spate of similar works from the 1820s to the turn of the century, including Hippolyte Hostein's 1840 *Flore des dames, ou nouveau langage des fleurs.*[10] This cult of flowers, moreover, contributed directly to the expansion of the Paris flower market, which was established on the Ile de la Cité in 1808 under the First Empire and which could not keep up with demand. The number of flower sellers on the streets of Paris—the majority of whom were women—increased considerably, and biweekly markets came to be set up in some parts of the city for the first time. Moreover, the buying of flowers themselves was no longer confined to the middle and upper classes. Even working-class girls, according to M. Debay, decorated their attic abodes with them.[11] By 1896 Gabriel Viaud-Bruant would write that "in no [other] time was the cult of flowers as alive as in our day."[12]

Alongside the cult of flowers, a new interest in botany and natural history emerged among the middle classes during the nineteenth century, which led to their commodification. For example, Jean-Baptiste Deyrolle, a French naturalist turned natural history dealer, opened a shop in Paris in 1831. It sold insects, tools for botanical collections, plant specimens, and equipment for natural history collections. His son, Emile Deyrolle, took over the business in 1866. It became an enormous success when he branched out to include books, pedagogical material, and even taxidermy, becoming a kind of commercial *cabinet des curiosités* (Figure 13).[13]

The introduction of the greenhouse into urban spaces also led to a new value placed on the vegetal world in urban settings. These greenhouses were diverse in their function and form. They included winter gardens, hothouses for rare plants, and temperate greenhouses, which were the successors of orangeries. While greenhouses were first introduced into France by the state and the aristocracy and were associated with the Museum of Natural His-

FIGURE 13. The boutique Deyrolle, 46 rue du Bac, Paris. Photographs copyright © Caroline Ford.

tory, as they proliferated in the nineteenth century they also became bourgeois spaces. Louis Neumann (1800–1858), who entered the school of botany at the Museum of Natural History in 1818, wrote a book on greenhouses in 1844 after collecting a large number of plants from the island of Réunion and bringing them back to the greenhouses of the museum, where he continued to work. He advocated their construction in wood.[14] Two years later, in 1846, a greenhouse was built with private capital on the Champs-Elysées in Paris and opened to the public. It met with immediate success. Each month 40,000 visitors paid one franc during the week and fifty centimes on Sundays to view its plants and flowers.[15] Almost ten years later, in 1855, *Le Magasin Pittoresque* wrote that the "temperate greenhouse is today the indispensable accessory of every country house" for the well-heeled family, and that ideally it should be an extension of the ground floor salon.[16] The *jardin d'hiver* (winter garden) was in effect a greenhouse where plants were to be displayed rather than cultivated. It functioned as an extension of a sitting room; one would go there to converse, read, play whist, and admire the plants. The *serre* (greenhouse) made an early appearance, for example, in Honoré de Balzac's 1831 novel *Le peau de chagrin,* in which Raphael de Valentin dines with Pauline in February in a greenhouse, which is described as a sort of sitting room filled with flowers. The greenhouse appeared again in 1842 in Balzac's *La fausse maîtresse,* but it was Eugène Sue's *Le juif errant* that popularized the *serre,* according to the Goncourt brothers.[17]

In some respects the popularity of the greenhouse created the vogue of the houseplant, and more especially the palm, during the nineteenth century. When Georges Duroy, the protagonist in Guy de Maupassant's second novel, *Bel-Ami*, visits his friend Charles Forestier in the salon of his Paris apartment, he has the sensation of entering a greenhouse because of the presence of large palms in the room's four corners, two rubber plants on either side of the fireplace, and two small flowering plants on the piano.[18] Such plants were captured in paintings of actual greenhouses from the period, such as Louise Abbéma's 1877 *Lunch in the Greenhouse* and Edouard Manet's *In the Greenhouse,* which was exhibited at the 1879 Paris Salon. Manet knew the greenhouse well. Situated on the rue d'Amsterdam near the St. Lazare train station, it belonged to the painter Otto Rosen, and Manet used it as a studio for nine months in 1878–1879.

While early greenhouses were attached to wealthy bourgeois houses or hôtels, they gradually came to be integrated, in modified ways, into the architecture of apartment buildings. The first such structure was built at 32 boulevard Malesherbes in 1860, where each apartment in the four-story building had what amounted to a miniature semicircular greenhouse in the form of a tower (Figure 14). Greenhouses also figured prominently in the many universal exhibitions that were held in Paris in the nineteenth and twentieth centuries, including those of 1867 and 1889, and they had an impact on the architecture of the restaurant from the 1860s on. These restaurants and brasseries often featured high glass ceilings and an array of palms. In Paris they included the popular Fermette Marboeuf and the restaurant Champeaux at the Place de la Bourse, and in Bordeaux, the hotel of Chapon Fin.[19]

While greenhouses, gardens, and flower markets in the city began to proliferate during the course of the nineteenth century, both the French state and the city of Paris undertook to transform the city in fundamental ways, and the period of the Second Empire was a turning point in this regard. The crusade launched by hygienists to clean up the city and free its population from disease, which began even before the 1850s, formed an integral part of the rebuilding of Paris in what became known as the Haussmannization of the city in the 1850s and 1860s.[20] The project was undertaken by the prefect of the department of the Seine, Baron Georges Haussmann, who oversaw the work. Soon after Haussmann took charge of the city, he put the engineer Adolphe Alphand in charge of public works in the Bois de Boulogne, and in 1857 Alphand became engineer in chief of the Service des promenades. After having played an important role in defending Paris during the Prussian siege of 1870, he was also appointed director of

FIGURE 14. The building at 32 boulevard Malesherbes, Paris, shows the integration of early greenhouses into city architecture. Photograph copyright © Caroline Ford.

public works for the city after the war, in May 1871, and was a key figure in the organization of the universal exhibitions of 1867, 1878, and 1889.[21] One of his first initiatives was to establish a number of greenhouses throughout the city for the acclimatization of exotic and rare plants, and he was seconded in this task by Jean-Pierre Barillet, the capital's gardener in chief. Together, they were responsible for the creation of parks in and outside the city, which included new gardens on the Champs-Elysées, the Trocadéro Gardens, the parc Montsouris, the parc Monceau, the Bois de Boulogne, and the Bois de Vincennes. He also had a considerable impact on similar projects in other French cities and on the creation of private gardens.

Prior to 1850 there were few parks and open spaces. The only municipal parks were the Place des Vosges—a garden of minute size that was built for Henri IV—and the promenade of the Champs-Elysées. Nationally owned gardens were few and far between and had formerly been attached to palaces; they included the Luxembourg Garden on the left bank of the Seine and the Tuileries Garden and the garden of the Palais Royal on the right bank. Most of the trees on streets and boulevards had disappeared between the French Revolution and the Revolution of 1848.[22]

Public urban playgrounds and parks emerged gradually in Paris from the late eighteenth century onward when private entrepreneurs began to create *jardins-spectacles* in gardens that had belonged to aristocratic émigrés and those who had been guillotined. These included a property belonging to Simon-Charles Boutin, an émigré who was guillotined in 1794, which was rented by an entrepreneur who converted it into a paying public park, the Tivoli.[23]

Both Napoleon III and Haussmann believed that parks would improve public health and contribute to the capital's aesthetic beauty. Indeed, while Napoleon III was away at war in Italy, Haussmann took it upon himself to remove the rotting vegetation and decrepit trees on the Champs-Elysées and to replant the cleared space of the oldest public promenade in Paris with trees and shrubs, while covering the area with baskets of flowers. He noted in his memoirs that it was a big surprise for the victorious sovereign to find this unexpected change in the city's landscape fully completed on his return.[24]

The city ultimately created twenty-two enclosed squares whose size varied from a quarter of an acre to six and a half acres, and when all of the parks were completed, the number of new green spaces expanded considerably in a mere span of twenty years.[25] The administration's first project, which was overseen by Alphand, was the Bois de Boulogne, at the western, wealthier end of the city. Soon after he focused its efforts on the eastern end by transforming the forest of Vincennes into a park. However, some of the most ambitious projects were undertaken in the center of the city itself, where three large parks were created. They included the park of Buttes-Chaumont, which had been the site of the municipality's open-air sewage dump, the gibbet of Montfaucon, and a number of quarries. Alphand used sixty-two acres to create a landscaped park that possessed a waterfall more than 100 feet high (using water from the Canal de L'Ourcq), a lake, and a grotto carved out of a former quarry, as well as numerous footpaths. At the eastern end of the city, the park was to serve the industrial quarters of La Villette and Belleville.

To the west, Alphand transformed twenty-one acres of a property that had belonged to the Orléans family, and which was purchased by the city, into the municipal park of Monceau. In contrast to the park of Buttes-Chaumont, it served a well-heeled clientele at the city's western end, and Alphand gave the park a similar waterfall, a lake, and a grotto. It was landscaped in such a way as to provide new lawns, a profusion of flower beds, trees, and shrubs.

The municipality did not turn its attention to the left bank of the Seine until the end of the Second Empire, when it bought thirty-nine acres of land on the hill of Montsouris in 1867. The Franco-Prussian War interrupted work on the project, and it is probably for this reason that it did not come to possess a waterfall or a grotto when work was resumed. It was finally completed in 1878. By the beginning of the Third Republic, Paris had 4,500 acres of municipal parks, whereas in 1850 the city had a scant 50 acres.

The proliferation of gardens, greenhouses, parks, and green spaces clearly transformed the city in positive ways, but the effects of Haussmannization, which included the clearing of slums and pushing the working class out of the city, were severely criticized by progressive architects, social reformers, and some philanthropists, as no new housing for the working poor was provided to replace what was pulled down. Haussmannization created a city divided along class lines, and even the new green spaces were intended to cater to particular social groups. Haussmann wrote that the peripheral parks, the Bois de Boulogne and the Bois de Vincennes, which were dear to the heart of Napoleon III, were the domain of the wealthy, and more particularly those who spent much of their leisure time displaying that wealth.[26] The *intra-muros* gardens that were open to the public welcomed a more popular clientele, but they existed alongside private gardens or squares that were enclosed by gates and iron fences.

※ ※ ※

SOCIAL REFORMERS and politicians began to reconsider how nature might be reintroduced in the city and domesticated, while improving the housing conditions of a working class that had been all but ignored in the plans of Napoleon III and Haussmann. To this end a series of organizations began to conduct studies related to public health, hygiene, and housing. They included the Société française d'hygiène and the Société de médecine publique et d'hygiène professionelle, both founded in 1877. Similar organizations came into being in Bordeaux and Le Havre in 1881, and a Société des habitations à bon marché was created in the 1890s.[27] These organizations were part of a larger movement of social reform and were linked to similar organizations abroad, and some later came to be associated with the Society for the Protection of the Landscapes of France.[28]

In 1902 the engineer and hygienist Edouard Fuster, who was a member of the Musée social, a private foundation established in 1894 by a group of social reformers, called for the creation of a federation devoted to problems of public hygiene, which led to the establishment the Alliance d'hygiène sociale in 1904. One of its purposes was to help eradicate insalubrious housing and the public health problems associated with it. The entrepreneur and politician Jules Siegfried (1837–1922), who was also a member of the Musée social, pressed for the creation of the Société des habitations à bon marché and the Société d'art populaire, which would be committed, like the Alliance d'hygiène sociale, to the creation of great expanses of greenery that would provide cities with air and light in the vicinity of new social housing, which would be built in conformity with the principles of public hygiene.[29]

Just as the Musée social was at the heart of one of the first international congresses devoted to the protection of landscapes, it played a central role in arguing for new social housing and the creation and preservation of green spaces in Paris in the wake of a decision taken in 1881 to claim and redevelop the zone of military fortifications surrounding Paris.[30] This was followed by a thirty-year tug-of-war between the French state and the city of Paris, but it first became the subject of fierce debate in the Chamber of Deputies.[31]

The Musée social early on developed a proposal for the development of the *enceinte fortifiée* (fortified zone), which was part of its larger vision for the extension of Paris and for urban renewal. In 1907 the Musée social decided to create its own Section d'hygiène urbaine et rurale, and Siegfried, who had been the chief architect of the so-called 30 November 1894 loi Siegfried, which facilitated the creation of social housing (*habitations à bon marché* or HBM), was its first president. Landscape preservationists were members of the section, and Fernand Cros-Mayrevieille and Charles Beauquier of the SPPF joined due to their interest in environmental preservation and the promotion of national heritage *(patrimoine)*.

Siegfried suggested that the Musée social, in alliance with the Alliance d'hygiène, the Société des habitations à bon marché, and the Société d'art populaire, influence public opinion regarding the preservation of open and green spaces in the capital, and indeed for all cities in France. He also wished to promote extending the boundaries of the city, an idea put forward by Jean-Claude Nicolas Forestier, a *conservateur* of Eaux et Forêts and director of parks and promenades for the city of Paris.[32]

One member of the section was an architect employed by the city of Paris, Eugène Hénard (1849–1923), who worked for the municipal bureau of public works. He proved influential in devising a plan for extending the boundaries of the city and for the transformation and development of Paris's fortifications.[33] He began his career designing schools before working on the universal expositions of 1889 and 1900. He then turned his attention to urban planning. Hénard was responsible for the founding of the Société française des architectes-urbanistes in 1912, which became the Société française d'urbanisme in 1919.[34] Hénard had the support of a group of young architects/urbanists, including Henri Prost, Jean-Claude Nicolas Forestier, Donat-Alfred Agache, Marcel Poëte, who also promoted the greening of the city.

A "Parisian from Paris," who "loved" his "native city profoundly," Hénard was deeply concerned about improving and increasing the number *espaces libres* (open green spaces) in the city.[35] He undertook a number of studies, published as *Etudes sur les transformations de Paris* between 1903 and 1909, and then, in 1906, wrote *Rapport sur l'avenir des grandes villes*. As part of his study of the transformation of Paris, he compared *espaces libres* in the cities of Paris and London in 1903. He found that between 1789 and 1900 park space had declined 64 percent, while the population of the city had tripled, and that Paris was in a "state of flagrant inferiority in relation to a good number of foreign cities" as a result of the lack of foresight on the part of governments that allowed for the destruction of green spaces and trees. He made, however, an exception for the fifteen years of Haussmann's administration in this regard. He saw Haussmann as the "only man who frankly contributed to increasing" green space in the city in a "notable way" and to "improving the great promenades of Paris," even if he had been criticized in other ways.[36] Hénard noted that in 1789 green spaces in the form of private and royal gardens as well as public promenades constituted 391 hectares, but that by 1900 two-thirds of the city's gardens had disappeared. What remained was 137 hectares of green space (Figure 15). Large tracts of land around Saint Lazare, which could have been developed into a park, were absorbed by the Gare du Nord. All of the convents that formed a circular crown around the city's old perimeter in the eighteenth century had been carved up and developed. While their gardens were not accessible to the public, Hénard argued that they had nonetheless contributed to a cleaner environment and that they could have easily been developed into public gardens or parks.[37]

Hénard observed that the density of Paris was greatest at its center and in the north and decreased as one moved toward and into its suburbs, necessitating green spaces, but that existing parks were badly distributed and

174   *The Greening of Paris*

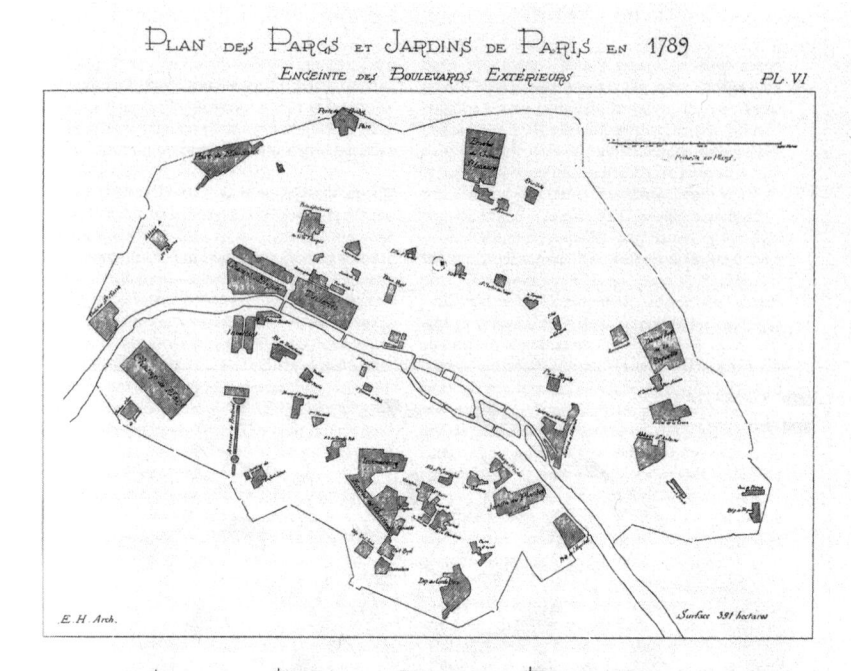

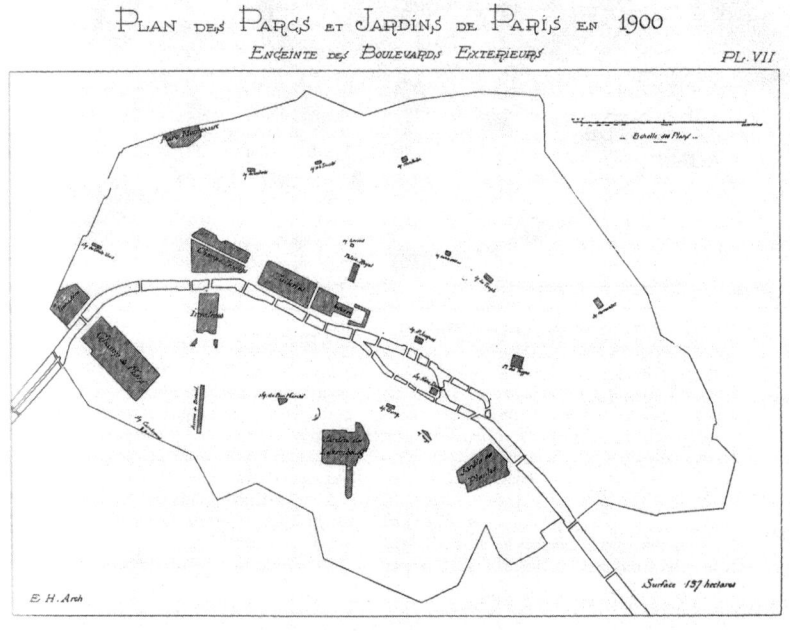

FIGURE 15. Eugène Hénard found that between 1789 and 1900 park space in Paris had declined 64 percent. "Plans des parcs et jardins de Paris en 1789 et 1900," in Eugène Hénard, *Etudes sur les transformations de Paris* (Paris, 1903–1909).

that the denser areas of the cities were deprived of them. He noted that there was unanimous agreement about the need to create green spaces but considerable debate about how to do so. One proposal would be to create large apartment blocks with interior green courtyards, or to let developers construct buildings as they wished, but to then create well-spaced public parks throughout the city. He noted that both initiatives had been taken in Germany and in Britain, where the garden city was favored. He reiterated, however, many times that this would be impossible due to Paris's population density.[38] Therefore, given the capital city as it was, Hénard believed that every measure should be taken to increase the number of public green spaces. Property owners could be given financial incentives to create small collective gardens, and the municipal council could introduce restrictions and requirements when the city sold municipal property for development. His solution for replacing Paris's fortifications envisioned an extensive new urban belt *(grande ceinture)* that would encircle the city, nine new peripheral parks and thirteen playing fields at the city's periphery, as well as apartment buildings that would be constructed in such a way as to allow for sunlight and for the planting of trees.[39] Indeed, he wrote of Paris's wide boulevards that "the introduction of vegetation gives these streets a character of incontestable gaiety. Trees in cities not only serve to provide a little shade, their role is larger and more important; they evoke the memory of nature, reminding us of the season, the invitation to rest. The tree, through its foliage, above all serves as a contrast to the coldness and immobility of stone edifices."[40]

While Hénard is remembered most for his plan for creating nine new parks on the city's former fortifications, which was adopted by the Musée social, he had larger ambitions. In the third chapter of *Etudes sur les transformations de Paris,* entitled "Les grands espaces libres: Les parcs et jardins de Paris et de Londres," he proposed creating nine new parks within the city itself as well eight small green squares that would not be less than one hectare. The interior parks included four south of the Seine (parc de Grenelle, parc de Maine, parc de la Maison Blanche, and parc de Croulebarbe) and five north of the Seine (parc de Saint Antoine, parc Voltaire, parc de Menilmont, parc Saint-Denis, and parc de Montmartre). The biggest of the nine parks, the parc Saint-Denis and the parc Voltaire, were in his mind the ones that needed to be created with the greatest urgency to relieve the congestion in these areas (Figure 16). Finally, while the population at the eastern and western ends of the city had access to two large parks *extramuros,* the Bois de Vincennes and the Bois de Boulogne, Hénard saw the need to create two parks of a similar size outside of the city at its northern and southern ends. With his system of parks in place, no Parisian—man,

FIGURE 16. Hénard proposed the creation of nine new parks within Paris. "Projet d'ensemble des parcs et jardins à établir dans Paris." Eugène Hénard, *Etudes sur les transformations de Paris* (Paris, 1903–1909).

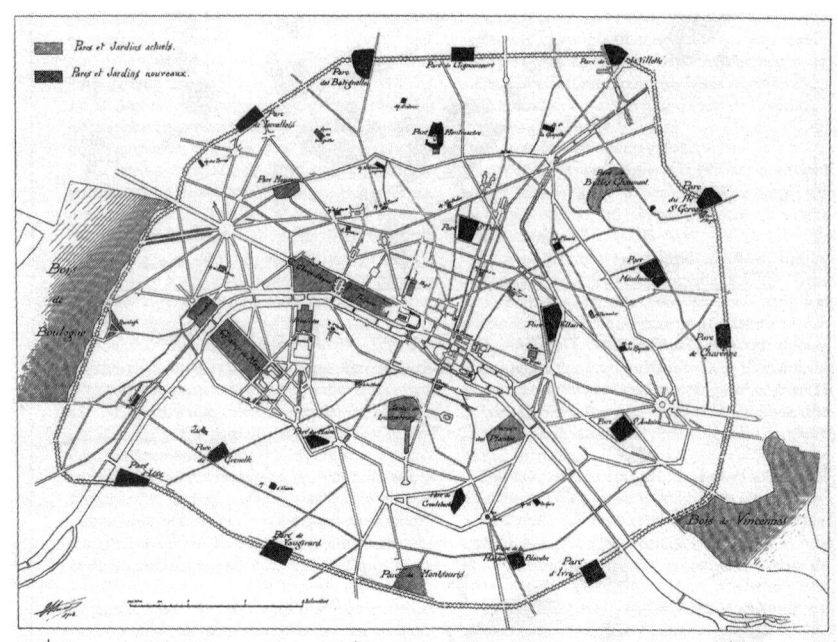

woman, or child—would be more than one kilometer away from one of the large parks or 500 meters from a garden or square. He argued that it was unnecessary to create luxurious gardens similar to those of the parc Monceau. It was simply enough to have a large expanse of sheltered green space planted with flowers and trees and smaller areas suitable for open-air sports.[41]

He realized that his proposal would be costly, especially the creation of parks in the city's center, but he believed that the rent that would come from the spaces reserved for sports would bring money to the municipal coffers, and he argued that it was vital for every inhabitant to be able to go on foot, at no extra cost, without exertion, and without losing time, to find "a piece of nature with sunlight, purified atmosphere and trees." He noted that in the previous thirty years 300 million francs had been spent to "give Paris clean water," so "it would not be exaggerated to spend half of that to give it air."[42]

Hénard recognized that the property owner or developer would always attempt to extract a maximum profit from his real estate and would sacrifice a green space to do so. As the denser districts of Paris could not be rebuilt without expropriating property, which would be impossible, it would be necessary to create parks that could be easily accessed by their inhabitants, and one could not count on the private sector to protect the environment. This was, in his view, the task of the public sector.[43]

For Hénard a park should offer the city's "inhabitants and visitors a refuge from the noise of the city and the dangers that characterized overcrowded places."[44] These included human waste of all kinds and dust that was constantly stirred up by cars and passersby. For a park to provide effective protection, it had to be large and bounded by thickets of trees with dense foliage that would block out the sides of the surrounding buildings and serve as a filter for the city's clouds of dust: "It must offer vast, sun-filled lawns, where children can play and run." Finally, according to Hénard, vehicles of any kind should be prohibited. In his estimation, such a park had to be at the very least ten hectares in size.[45]

Hénard envisioned the creation of three new peripheral parks south of the Seine, where currently there was only one, the parc de Montsouris.[46] The new parks would be the parc d'Issy, parc de Vaugirard, and parc d'Ivry. To the north of the Seine, which was the most dense area of the city, he envisioned six, including the parc de Charonne, parc du près St. Gervais, parc de la Villette, parc de Clignancourt, parc de Batignolles, and parc de Levallois. Each park was to be between nine and twelve hectares in size, the size of the only existing peripheral park created under Haussmann, the parc de Montsouris.

From the available 800 hectares that comprised the fortification zone, Hénard proposed using between 81 and 108 hectares for the creation of new parks, which represented 10 to 15 percent of the land and which would have increased the *espaces libres* from 60 to 80 percent. The remaining land would become a new type of ring road, the *boulevard à rédans* (stepped boulevard), which would be lined with buildings that would be recessed at intervals to provide for green space, and they would connect the peripheral parks. He would do this by reducing the space of interior courtyards, and he proposed the creation of open courtyards and small parks along boulevards.

Hénard's plan was ardently embraced by a number of organizations, and he was supported by Jean-Claude Forestier. One organization that took up Hénard's proposal was the Société du Nouveau Paris, which was founded in 1902, and one of whose purposes was to lead the movement for green spaces.[47] Hénard himself was a member of the organization and provided it with a blueprint for its campaign. In 1903 he was honored for his work by the organization and awarded the society's gold medal. The Société pour la conservation des espaces libres à Paris was also formed, along with a Comité pour la conservation et la création des espaces libres, whose meetings were held at the Musée social, where Jules Siegfried presided. Many of those who were part of the landscape preservation movement were associated with these organizations, including Henri Cazalis and Charles Beauquier.[48]

The creation of green spaces in the city became an issue that the Musée social directly introduced into the electoral arena during the municipal elections of 1908, and it adopted Hénard's plan. Drawings of the proposed parks, which were based on Hénard's plan, and extracts of the proposed legislation were incorporated into electoral posters—12,150 of them—signed by the Musée social, the Association des cités-jardins, the SPPF, and the Touring Club during the municipal elections.[49] The urban section of the Musée social also distributed a manifesto in advance of the elections to encourage voters to support candidates who favored the creation of *espaces libres*. It was entitled "Air, Parks, Sports! Let us save our green open spaces, let us save our fortifications":

> Why?
>   Because you cannot live in prisons of stone.
>   Because for your children it is necessary to have something other than the street.
>   Because we must all have light, space and sporting fields.
>   Because for half a century Paris has grown tremendously as its gardens have disappeared.
>   Because London, Berlin, Vienna, all the capitals have more green and open spaces than Paris.[50]

The Musée social paid groups of young militants to put the posters up, and Eugéne Hénard explained how they should intervene in public electoral meetings.[51] The Musée social, following Hénard's lead, argued that the population of the capital had tripled since 1855 and that the government had done little or nothing to create additional green spaces in the city, in contrast to London and Berlin.

The Musée social did not endorse specific candidates; it instead attempted to rally public support and opposed any proposal that would put the fortified zone in the hands of private real estate speculators. Socialists were still a force in municipal politics, and they made their support of preserving green spaces in the city clear. The socialist Albert Thomas (1878–1932) even contended that he and his compatriots refused to leave the question of the development of the fortified zone and the creation and preservation of green spaces to "an association of intellectuals, artists, philanthropists, some association for the protection of landscapes, some league against alcoholism, and some gentlemen from the Musée social."[52] Indeed, Thomas wrote a series of articles on the issue in *L'Humanité* in which he argued that a "revolutionary proletariat will not be formed within infected dwellings and cities lacking air," and he concluded that "we want the country to become more city-like and the city a little more country-like."[53] A cleaner and greener environment had clearly become a working-class cause as well.

The Musée social then held a large public meeting at the Sorbonne on the subject of "green open spaces in Paris," which was organized on 5 June 1908 before an audience of fifteen hundred and attended by government ministers. With the support of the Société des amis des arbres, the lawyer Henri Robert argued that trees across the city needed to be protected and preserved, and that the plan to preserve open spaces in developing the zone of fortifications at the perimeter of the city should be supported in the interest of the people, the working classes. The campaign was endorsed by fifteen local and national newspapers, including *Le Temps, Le Débat, Le Journal, Le Figaro, L'Eclair, Le Soleil, Le Petit Parisien, Le Matin,* and *Le Petit Journal.*

In April 1909 Hénard's plan for the development of the fortifications was republished in *Le Musée Social: Bulletin Mensuel* along with a suggested law authored by Jules Siegfried that would provide for the creation of a series of large parks, public squares, and a circular boulevard around the perimeter of the city. Both Hénard's plan and Siegfried's proposed law were then presented to the Chamber of Deputies and the Paris Municipal Council.

As the Municipal Council moved to the right during the "nationalist revival" preceding World War I, the proposed legislation stalled. The council ended up voting for an alternative proposal for the development of the fortifications drawn up by one of its own members, Louis Dausset, in December 1908. It called for the city's purchase from the state of the fortified zone, which would be sold in its entirety in lots for development, leaving, in effect, little or nothing in the form of unsold land available for the creation of parks.[54] The state signed off on the legislation in 1912, and it was finally ratified by parliament in 1919, at which point the fortifications began to be demolished. Even though Eugène Hénard opposed it, the Musée social eventually rallied to the plan, as the Dausset Law in principle provided for the creation of parks, even if much of the land could be rented to businesses.

※ ※ ※

IN 1911 the city of Paris created a commission for the extension of Paris composed of architects/urban planners, and municipal officials. It was headed by Louis Bonnier (1856–1946), a member of the Musée social's Section d'hygiène urbaine et rurale and an architect who was employed by the city of Paris. Although the commission issued a report in 1913, its recommendations were never implemented; however, it too advocated the creation of parks and squares. Its importance lay in the fact that it was the first attempt to consider the development of Paris and its suburbs together.

Following World War I, the Chamber of Deputies passed the so-called Cornudet Law, which was named after the deputy who proposed it (Honoré Cornudet), requiring all communes with a population greater than 10,000 and all cities that had been damaged during the war to formulate an urban plan for their extension, development, and beautification.[55] The law was then strengthened in 1924 by the creation of the Commission supérieure d'aménagement et d'extension des villes, which was attached to the Ministry of the Interior.

Although the demolition of the fortifications of Paris began in 1919, it was not completed until 1932, and the plans that had been so avidly discussed in the pre–World War I period had been put aside with respect to the outer periphery. The land was by and large sold off to private developers in parcels, and the sites on which the fortifications stood were turned into a circular peripheral highway, the *periphérique*, after World War II.

While Hénard's ambitious plan for the creation of nine new parks and the development of the fortifications was never realized, not all of the hopes of Hénard, Siegfried, and the broader public were entirely dashed, as some historians have suggested.[56] Much of the city's periphery was to undergo extensive rebuilding in the 1920s and 1930s under the auspices of the Office public des habitations à bon marché, which did in fact incorporate enlightened design concepts that responded to many of the concerns of those who debated the fate of the fortified zone over the previous twenty-year period.

The Cornudet Law laid the groundwork for the construction of what came to be called the "ceinture rose" or the "ceinture des Marechaux," a quarter of which was to be reserved for residential housing and three-quarters for green spaces.[57] HBMs and HLMs (*habitations à loyer modéré*, or moderate-rent housing) were given priority in the residential zones.[58] The Office public d'habitations de la ville de Paris, instead of private developers, was responsible for much of the construction around the ceinture des Marechaux—a set of circular boulevards that bear the name of the marshals of the Napoleonic empire—that was constructed near the "rue militaire," bordering the military zone established in 1840. Georges Risler, president of the Musée social and a member of the permanent committee of the Conseil supérieur des HBM, was the principal promoter of the development of the area in the interwar period. He took up the themes that he himself promoted before the Great War, including parks, squares, and playing fields. Most of the buildings were constructed between 1928 and 1935.[59] The project reconciled several seemingly contradictory goals: to build the greatest number of buildings while respecting the principles of public hygiene; to reconcile the new buildings' architecture with the city's older structures; and to integrate green spaces in the overall project. The buildings themselves were often constructed around large inner open-air courtyards that were filled with greenery. By 1936, 12,106 HBMs, 9,836 HLMs, and 2,957 larger-sized HBMs had been constructed.[60]

As urban renewal and plans for the extension of cities took root during this period, the concept of the garden city became increasingly important among social reformers, politicians, and architects in France. The garden city movement, a method of urban planning launched by the British activist Sir Ebenezer Howard in 1898, envisioned new urban communities that included parks or extensive green spaces.[61] The movement found an enthusiastic following in France at the beginning of the twentieth century and shaped subsequent city planning initiatives well into the interwar period and beyond.[62]

The cité-jardin movement was both a culmination of and a reaction to earlier initiatives that were launched to "naturalize" cities for both aesthetic and hygienic reasons. One of the earliest proponents of the garden city in France was Georges Benoit-Lévy (1880–1970), who at the age of twenty-three and having recently been awarded his law degree, received a grant from the Musée social to travel to England to study the industrial villages of Port Sunlight and Bourneville as well as the building site of England's first garden city, Letchworth, which was modeled on Ebenezer Howard's concept of the garden city. He returned to France a garden city convert and founded the Association des cités-jardins de France in 1903 with the support of the social reformers Charles Gide and Emile Cheysson, one of the founding members of the Musée social.[63] Howard's concept of the garden city bore some resemblance to Charles Fourier's phalanstery, a planned community containing a balance of residential housing, industry, agriculture, and green spaces, which would be surrounded by green belts. Howard's ideal was a city of 32,000 people, planned on a concentric pattern with radial boulevards. Benoit-Lévy enthusiastically embraced Howard's concept.

The Association des cités-jardins was dedicated to the creation of new cities, following the English example. Charles Gide saw the creation of garden cities as a means for workers to lose their taste for "base pleasures of cities and crowds," and the café-concert.[64] There was in a sense a moral purpose that was absent from arguments that were made about the creation of public green spaces in the city. Indeed, Benoit-Lévy and Cheysson called on employers and factory owners to finance the new garden cities: "It is for industrialists to create the new cities, it is for them to make them healthy and beautiful," and it is from them that "we must wait for social improvements."[65] He paid only lip service to the idea of urban renewal and to the expansion of existing cities—causes to which the Musée social and a number of younger architects of the period were so committed—in stating that the association also devoted itself to the "conservation and extension of open spaces in big cities."[66] Throughout his association with the garden city movement he insisted on the role of employers in the creation of new cities, which ultimately put him at odds with other supporters of the movement who came to reinterpret how the garden city would be implemented in France. The Musée social, for example, distanced itself from his conception of the garden city as primarily an industrial city, and he distanced himself from the Musée social. In 1908, for example, when Jules Siegfried used the occasion of a conference given by Benoit-Lévy at the Musée social to launch the new Section d'hygiène urbaine et rurale, he asked Benoit-Lévy to be its secretary. Benoit-Lévy declined and did not participate in the work of the section again.[67]

Some advocates of green open spaces thought that the idea of the garden city as espoused by Benoit-Lévy went too far. Eugène Hénard is a case in point. The idea of a city in which half of the total surface would consist of gardens, with an immense park at its center, was, to him, extreme: "In the very praiseworthy intention to improve cities, it is necessary to be careful about destroying all [their] advantages. A big city is a place of intense activity, it is not a place of rest."[68] He believed that at the core of a great city was commercial and intellectual activity, and that the green spaces should be distributed outward, so he ridiculed the idea of re-creating the country in the city: "To give every inhabitant a square of land to cultivate his vegetables and raise his chickens, that is to return to rustic life [*la vie champêtre*]; it suffices, to obtain this result, to return to the village."[69] Hénard argued that it would be more reasonable to create a large number of well-distributed public parks. For him, the cité-jardin was, in fact, best suited to manufacturing and industrial centers where the worker, after leaving the factory, would go home to his own house, a place of rest and relaxation. He argued that one could not do this in cities inhabited by millions of people and where intellectual, artistic, scientific, industrial, commercial, and financial elites were concentrated. One could, in his view, find a means of making the city less compact and environmentally noxious: "One has tried to obtain this result in Paris, notably in certain boulevards by bringing back the alignment of buildings and imposing on property owners the constraint of leaving a little garden of a few meters, planted with trees, shrubs, and flowers."[70] In Hénard's view, the result, while pleasing to eye, was not successful, as this discouraged commercial activity, and he cited the commune of Neuilly, in the northwest of Paris, with its charming villas, where "activity is almost non-existent."[71] His plan for Paris, which integrated green spaces through the distribution of public parks and the careful design of apartment buildings on *boulevards à rédans,* addressed, in his view, the environmental challenges of modern life without sacrificing the culture of the city.

Social reformers associated with the Musée social and architects also shied away from the English model of the garden city, which Benoit-Lévy espoused, but they embraced its focus on ventilation, light, and green spaces, which were central to urban renewal, and incorporated it into the "Parisian urban debate."[72] Emile Cheysson and Jules Siegfried, who, in addition to being members of the Musée social, sat on the Fondation Rothschild's board of directors as "experts" on HBMs, had these considerations in mind in judging architectural projects that were put before the foundation.

The Fondation Rothschild, which was founded in 1904, was an organization whose goal was to improve the living conditions of the working class, particularly in Paris. One of the principal means of achieving this was to build HBMs in working-class districts.[73] Its first undertaking was a large apartment dwelling that came to embody some of the principles of the garden city movement, without adopting the English model. The government and city of Paris enthusiastically welcomed Alphonse, Edmond, and Gustave de Rothschild's proposal to invest 10 million gold francs in the housing project and to purchase a triangular city block bounded by the rue de Prague, the rue Charles Baudelaire, and the rue Théophile Roussel in the twelfth arrondissement, which was in the working-class faubourg Saint Antoine, to construct a building that would ultimately house 324 apartments.[74] Following an architectural competition, the foundation selected a proposal entitled "For the People," submitted by the architect Augustin Rey, as the winning entry in 1905. The architect proposed constructing the buildings around three large open-air courtyards (closed courtyards were the rule in Parisian urban dwellings); perforated walls were part of the design to improve ventilation and let in light. As no corridors were part of the plan, all apartments opened onto staircase landings. Particular attention was given to the building's eighteen staircases, which were also open and light-filled. The building itself was covered with white stucco, and the exterior walls were punctuated by large windows that opened onto balconies that had large window boxes. When the building was inaugurated, the press called it "the Louvre of social housing" (Figure 17).

FIGURE 17. Dubbed "the Louvre of social housing," 8 rue de Prague, Paris, was designed by Augustin Rey to provide light and air to city dwellers. Photograph copyright © Caroline Ford.

In an appraisal of Rey's plan, H. Franz wrote in *The Studio* in 1906 that three-fourths of the Parisian population continued to live in virtual wells, the air of which remained virtually unchanged, or in narrow, ill-ventilated streets, and that Rey had addressed this problem by abolishing these inner courtyards and replacing them with "real squares with wide openings onto the public highways, so that the air should circulate freely everywhere amongst the trees—for the creation of these open spaces is inseparably associated with the planting of trees, those great purifiers of the air." He noted that "we find plantations of wide-spreading trees indicated throughout the plan both in the courtyards and on the street frontages."[75]

Rey's plan and the Rothschild project had an enormous impact on how both working-class and middle-class housing would be built in subsequent years. Ecological, aesthetic, and hygienic considerations were at the center of subsequent projects, including those launched by the Rothschild Foundation itself, which included the social housing projects in the rue de Bargue (206 apartments) in 1912 and the rue Marcadet (420 apartments) in 1912–1919. When a law was passed in 1914 to create the Office public d'HBM, the specialists associated with the Rothschild Foundation were invited to join the council of the administration.

While the English model of the garden city, with its individual cottages and gardens, never made significant inroads into the urban spaces of Paris, as the projects pursued by the Rothschild Foundation suggest, it did have an impact on its suburbs, the *banlieues,* in the interwar period. The debates surrounding the demolition and development of the city's fortifications led social reformers, nascent urbanists, architects, and politicians to consider the impact of urban growth on Paris's larger metropolitan areas, ultimately resulting in projects that reshaped the suburban landscape.

The suburbs, in Eugène Hénard's words, formed "a belt of housing areas connected to each other" and could be viewed as a direct extension of the city.[76] While the surface area of Paris *intra-muros* was 7,802 hectares in 1910, the surface area of its suburbs was 8,694 hectares.[77] The suburbs comprised a series of municipalities. The best-known were Neuilly, Levallois, Asnières, Clichy, Aubervilliers, Pantin, Vincennes, Saint-Mandé, Charenton, Montrouge, and Vanves, and they had been separated from the city by an uninhabited fortified and military zone that was not wider than 375 meters. Hénard predicted that the villages and small cities beyond Paris and its suburbs, which made up the department of the Seine, would soon be linked with the city and in need of development *(aménagement),* as would its suburbs. However, Hénard, himself a Parisian, did not turn his attention to this question, and he never showed any real interest in the garden city, which would soon be the model for urban planning in suburban Paris.

It was a building cooperative that launched the first French garden city in the Parisian suburb of Draveil. The newspaper *L'Humanité* announced in 1909 that *pères de familles,* influenced by socialism, decided to form a cooperative to build housing for their families in the countryside surrounding Paris. The cité-jardin was formed from forty-two hectares of land bought from a neighboring eighteenth-century château. It was not completed until 1928.[78]

The concept of the cité-jardin was taken up by a number of different politicians and social reformers, but none was more ardent than a socialist politician whose name was intimately bound up with construction of social housing within Paris and beyond as an administrator and then as president of the Office départemental des habitations à bon marché de la Seine (OHBM). Henri Sellier (1883–1943), who was born into the working-class aristocracy—his father was a foreman at the arsenal—was able to receive a degree in law from the faculty in Paris, and he pursued a degree at the Ecole des hautes études commerciales. He joined Jean Allemane's Parti socialiste révolutionnaire at the age of fifteen and in 1910 was elected *conseiller général* of the Puteaux, a commune in the western suburbs of Paris; but his career really began in 1914, when he became administrator of the

OHBM, which was dedicated to the creation of affordable housing for the popular classes.[79]

After the war Sellier was elected mayor of Suresnes and remained so until he was removed from office during the German occupation in 1941, two years before his death. Suresnes was another commune in the western suburbs of Paris, adjoining the Bois de Boulogne. Sellier always had an interest in urban planning, and with the urbanist and historian of Paris, Marcel Poëte, founded the Ecole des hautes études urbaines et d'administration municipale in 1919, which became the Institut d'urbanisme de l'Université de Paris in 1924, and in 1935 he was elected senator of the department of the Seine.

Sellier's lifelong interest in urban renewal and social housing, which was reflected in his *Crise du logement et l'intervention en matière d'habitation populaire dans l'agglomération parisienne,* was translated into direct action after World War I.[80] He embraced the concept of the cité-jardin, but preferred to use the term *banlieue-jardin,* as it was in the suburbs that he set out to implement his aim of creating a green paradise for the working class.[81]

Sellier launched an initiative to form a Commission d'extension de Paris, which was duly created in 1911, and it was reinforced by the establishment of a Commission des habitations ouvrières et du plan d'extension in 1913. In 1911 the Comité départementale des HBM et de la prévoyance sociale de la Seine established an architectural competition for the design of cités-jardins. Recognizing that it was impossible to construct a new city in a department as populated as the Seine along the lines of Ebenezer Howard's garden cities, Emile Cacheux, one of the commission's members, argued that it was nonetheless possible to create HBMs with plenty of air and an abundance of light. The cooperative society Campagne à Paris, which was founded in 1906, shared first prize with the cité-jardin of Epinay. The latter conformed best to what Cacheux had in mind. The Comité départmental des HBM et de la prévoyance social de la Seine also gave awards to the cité-jardin of Ivry-sur-Seine, which was under construction, and the projects for garden cities in Rosnay-sous-Bois, Châtenay-Malabry, Choisy, and Châtillon.[82] Other entries included the cité-jardin of Petit-Groslay in the commune of Blanc-Mesnil in the department of Seine-et-Oise, which was both a fifty-hectare housing estate and a park. Begun in 1910, the project employed the internationally renowned architect and landscape designer Edouard Redont (1862–1942), who created a radial design, setting his buildings around a central man-made lake. He dotted the garden city with squares and playing fields and planted thousands of trees.[83]

During the interwar period the building of cités-jardins was at its height. Between 1921 and 1939, fifteen were constructed in the suburbs of Paris, which resulted in 10,704 collective units and 2,549 houses in Dugny, Drancy, Nanterre, Cachan, Arcueil, Les Lilas, Genevilliers, Bagnolet, Stains, Le Pré Saint-Gervais, Champigny, Le Plessis Robinson, Suresnes, and Drancy-la-Muette. The individual houses adopted the model of cottages in English garden cities, and careful attention was paid to their gardens and landscaping. In order to have the maximum number of old-growth trees, communes sought out property that had once been parks attached to châteaus—Stains, Châtenay-Malabry, and Plessis-Robinson being cases in point. Alongside oaks, chestnuts, poplars, and maples, lawns were planted and encircled by regular hedges. Collective housing was favored in most locales, as a greater number of people could be housed, so the model of urban social housing design in the form of apartment buildings became prevalent in many places, with the same attention paid to gardens and landscaping.[84] While the cité-jardin assumed different forms and architectural styles ranging from the picturesque, which employed regionalist idioms, to the modern, architects sought to make the housing, whether collective or individual, and the nature into which it was placed a coherent whole.

While most of the garden cities built during the interwar period were undertaken by the OHBM, some were the result of private initiatives. The garden city of Orgement in the department of Seine-et-Oise is a case in point. It was located on a plateau overlooking the Seine, four and a half miles from Paris. The first cornerstone was laid in 1929 by Louis Loucheur, who was minister of labor, and in 1930 its first inhabitants took possession of the housing. The buildings occupied 10 percent of the total area, which covered ninety acres. Apartment buildings were grouped around a park and five squares, and "everywhere there [were] fruit trees, the remains of the former fields in which the city was built."[85]

In the public sector one of Sellier's crowning achievements was the cité-jardin built in Suresnes, the city of which he was mayor for over twenty years. It was built to house 8,000–10,000 inhabitants and represented an attempt by its architect, Alexandre Maistrasse, to integrate the cité-jardin into the preexisting urban space.[86] Of course, the plan evolved over time, and other architects joined the project. Ultimately, the cité-jardin had two principal axes (east-west and north-south) planted with trees. Nature was introduced into the project in different ways. Tree-filled green spaces were at the center of the main blocks. Square Léon Bourgeois, with its 10,200 square meters of open space, was a good example of this. Streets and paths were bordered by lawns, and flowering plants placed at strategic intervals were shaded by trees. Some of the individual houses also had their own gardens.

There was a clear attempt to use the cité-jardin of Suresnes and those built in other suburbs of Paris as a means of improving the lived environment through the creation of green spaces, but it is misleading to understand the garden city idea "solely or even mainly in terms of the environmental impact."[87] For some bourgeois social reformers the cité-jardin had a moral purpose and could be used as an instrument of social control and a means of transforming a "red belt" into a less threatening "green belt." Urbanists saw parallels between the *banlieues* and France's colonies. Both could and did serve as laboratories of social control and experimentation.[88] Nonetheless, some workers and socialist politicians embraced social housing, green initiatives, and cités-jardins. Indeed, in 1908 Albert Thomas reproached fellow socialists in *Cahiers du Socialiste* for not taking more of an interest in social questions such as the creation of more green spaces in the city of Paris. For him, not doing so merely left the door open to the paternalist initiatives of employers: "But it is no less appalling to see the work, so important for the future of the working class, of healthy low cost housing, abandoned to the timid initiatives of philanthropists or conservatives like Georges Picot, or the demand for open green spaces and playing fields formulated only by esthetes and artists from the 'Society for the Protection of Landscapes' or sportsmen from the 'Touring Club.'"[89]

Yet in many respects it was in the battle to save the "lungs of Paris" that the interests of part of the Left, the working class, and bourgeois reformers converged. It was here that the hygienic considerations of some socialists and members of the Section d'hygiène urbaine et rurale came to be joined with the aesthetic considerations of the SPPF and the Touring Club, though they often regarded each other with suspicion. Indeed, Jean Lahor (pseudonym for Dr. Henri Cazalis), one of the founders of the SPPF, argued that everything—art, hygiene, even medicine and morality—was only an aesthetic.[90]

While the motivations behind initiatives to bring nature to the city during the course of the nineteenth century were diverse, what these initiatives revealed was an ever-growing awareness of the effect of the environment on the health and welfare of the city's inhabitants. Roger Marx, a proponent of *l'art social* who promoted art for the people, which was embraced by many of the architects associated with the campaign for green spaces and the suburban cités-jardins in the interwar period, summed up the nature of this environmental consciousness well in his influential manifesto, *L'art social*. There he recalled Pierre-Joseph Proudhon's injunction to transform France into a vast garden composed of woods of all kinds, old-growth trees, springs, and streams. He made specific reference to the campaign to develop the fortifications of Paris into green spaces, noting that "nature is not only the source of all inspiration," but it is also vital to progress: "The mutilations that we inflict on it only serve to show better the price of its benefits; the consciousness of the links between man and the environment [*milieu*] becomes clearer; the protection of the earth and edifices, the green space 'lung of the city' and the old stones that narrate its history, are inspired and defended by the same devotion and the same ideal."[91] In short, he argued that destruction of the natural world made the link between human beings and their environment clearer and inspired initiatives to protect the earth and the structures on it, including green spaces and the old stones that narrate the city's past. Writing almost a hundred years after François-Antoine Rauch, he asked, "Is it not moreover true that works of art and of nature constitute an indivisible whole?"[92]

Conclusion

> To act on the environment, man does not place himself outside of this environment.
>
> —Lucien Febvre

IN 1931, the year in which France hosted both an international colonial exhibition and the Second International Congress for the Protection of Nature saw the birth of a new publication, *La Terre et la Vie*, which absorbed the *Bulletin de la Société Nationale d'Acclimatation de France* and the *Bulletin de la Société des Amis du Muséum Nationale d'Histoire Naturelle et du Jardin des Plantes*. At the same time it merged with the *Revue d'Histoire Naturelle*. The creation of the journal was to lay the foundations for the fusion of several organizations devoted to the protection of nature into the Société nationale de protection de la nature, which laid the groundwork for the Fédération française des sociétés de protection de la nature, formed in the 1960s. In the first issue of *La Terre et la Vie* Louis Mangin, director of the Natural History Museum, observed:

> The search for the joys of the countryside, the taste for animals and plants is very widespread in all classes of society, and above all, perhaps in the popular classes. The exodus of city dwellers to the countryside on Sundays or holidays is proof of it. One understands the sentiment of this exuberant and joyful population from the perspective of a good day in the woods, meadows, and fields illuminated by the sun, who the same evening or the next day return home, their arms full of flowers, or, according to the season, fruit, mushrooms or even stones gathered in the course of the walk.[1]

In contrast, many historians have generally regarded the 1960s as a turning point in terms of the development of a widespread appreciation of the natural world among all social classes in France. This was reflected in the foundation of a green party; the Ministère de la protection de la nature et de l'environnement (Ministry for the Protection of the Environment); and a wide range of environmental groups, including Les amis de la terre, led by a twenty-five-year-old activist, the *soixante-huitard* (sixty-eighter) Brice Lalonde, who would go on to become France's leading environmentalist; as well as in the appearance of a number of books and films on the subject of the environment. Books on the subject included Jean Dorst's *Avant que nature meure* (1965), Pierre Aguesse's *Clefs pour l'écologie* (1971), Pierre George's *L'environnement* (1971), Serge Moscovici's *La société contre la nature* (1972), Marcel Clébant's *Croisade pour la mer* (1972), René Dubos's *Nous n'avons qu'une terre* (1972), and André Gorz's *Ecologie et politique* (1974). Films and documentaries included *Nature morte* (1968), *La France de demain* (1972), *Le retour du saumon* (1974), *Au rhythme de la nature* (1974), and *Les parcs nationaux* (1977). Subsequently, in the 1980s and 1990s, there was the persistent rallying cry "Tous verts!," the title of a book about environmental subjects written by one of the newspaper *Le Monde*'s chief journalists.[2]

The relatively late institutionalization of the field of environmental history has also been seen by some as another reflection France's late embrace of environmental causes, even though environmental history had firm roots in French geography and the natural sciences, and it drew on approaches taken by some historians associated with the *Annales* school.[3] One commentator has even linked France's late interest in the protection of the natural world to the role of Catholicism, the country's dominant religion, arguing that nature protection as a movement was by and large Protestant in inspiration.[4] This thesis, advanced by Jean Viard in the 1980s, still holds sway among some historians, as Mark Stoll's 2013 consideration of the issue attests. Stoll cites Protestant writers, thinkers, and scientists, including Elisée Reclus, Théodore Monod, and Jean Dorst, for their contributions to ecological thought in nineteenth- and twentieth-century France. He argues that while ecological thinking was not absent among Catholics in France, their conception of nature was different, and he explains "the national preference, shared by the Greens, for inhabited and domesticated spaces," as opposed to "wild and natural spaces."[5]

The historian Michael Bess has stressed France's ambivalent attitudes toward the environment in the twentieth century and attributed them to a particular attachment to new technologies during the period of the *trente glorieuses* (the thirty years of unprecedented economic expansion following the end of World War II). France's heavy investment in nuclear power, which shaped its identity as a nation in the postwar period, was for him a clear indication of this.[6] Bess has as a result characterized France as a "light-green" society in its double embrace of technological modernity and ecological values, and he stresses France's unique path into the twentieth century in its attempt to reconcile technology with environmental concerns.[7]

Moreover, the term *environnement,* as it is currently understood, did not enter the French language until quite late. It was introduced by geographers associated with the school of Paul Vidal de la Blache around 1921 as a technical term before falling into temporary desuetude. According to *Le Grand Robert de la langue française,* it gained currency only in the 1960s, when it was (re)introduced from the English-speaking world. It acquired a meaning that signified the natural (physical, chemical, biological) and cultural conditions that could act on living organisms and on human beings, and it came to replace terms that were most often used by geographers previously, most notably the word *milieu.*[8]

The term *environnement* has thus been regarded as an "Anglo-Saxon" or American import. For Andrée Corvol, even to speak of the environment in the context of the period of the eighteenth century is anachronistic. *Paysage* or landscape, nature, and *milieu* were more familiar terms for many in France until the late twentieth century, and these terms do not, according to Corvol and others, "recover the same reality."[9] Emma Spary also explicitly rejects the term "environmentalism" in discussing ideas about nature in eighteenth-century France because she believes that it obscures the specific meanings of theories regarding climate in the eighteenth century, which cannot be directly linked to nineteenth- or twentieth-century understandings.[10]

For all these reasons many historians have downplayed the importance of the nineteenth and early twentieth centuries in terms of understanding the emergence of an environmental consciousness and movement. The campaign in 1969 to save one of France's most treasured parks, the Vanoise, from falling into the hands of Pierre Schnebelen, a developer who wanted to build a ski resort, is frequently cited as a major turning point, marking a widespread and unprecedented public engagement with the cause of environmental protection. The newly sworn-in president of the Republic, Georges Pompidou, received a massive number of letters protesting the government's approval of Schnebelen's plans. He quickly rescinded that approval and declared himself to be a staunch defender of nature, reinforcing this by announcing his plan to create a cabinet-level ministry, the Ministry for the Protection of the Environment, which was officially established in 1971.

Public interest in the environment was backed up by opinion polls in the 1960s and 1970s. The French were asked in a 1967 survey how they looked at the year 2000 when it came to environmental issues, and 70 percent of respondents were pessimistic and thought that most environmental problems would not be solved by then. In 1976 another poll posed the question whether the public thought that technological progress was "rendering our lifestyle so artificial as to endanger the survival of the coming generation."[11] Seventy-six percent answered in the affirmative, and only 18 percent answered negatively.

Opinion polls such as those instituted after World War II did not exist in the nineteenth century. What would French men and women have said before World War I? We cannot know, but we can surmise from the intense public discussions and debates about deforestation, floods, and climate change that took place from the time of the French Revolution up to World War II that the public was not indifferent to these problems—far from it—and groundbreaking environmental reforms were enacted. Unfortunately, to refer to this period as a "pre-history of ecological awareness" does not bear witness to the richness of the historical sources on the question.[12] It is problematic at best to think that people in the past would not perceive the environmental devastation around them. How they interpreted it, and whether they thought they could do something about it, and if so what, is another issue.

It is clear that a broad range of different individuals from all social classes expressed their concerns and anxieties about the state of the environment in new ways in the century and a half following the French Revolution. These anxieties and concerns were not confined to naturalists or intellectuals. For this reason this book has not focused primarily on savants or scientists, as many historians regarding the period in question have been wont to do. It has focused instead on proselytizers, publicists, and impresarios—and sometimes even dreamers and eccentrics—and their role in disseminating environmental knowledge, as they understood it, and in generating debate. It has also explored responses to events on the ground from a larger public, and the record shows that many of those who advocated for environmental reform were successful, even if those reforms, in some cases, were implemented after their deaths.

In short, there is ample evidence of both the emergence of an environmental consciousness and its democratization in the period between the French Revolution and World War II. One reason this awareness has been downplayed, and in some cases dismissed, is that many of the advocates for environmental reform in this period had a conception of nature in which human beings had a place, rather than one that viewed nature as autonomous, as "wilderness," as independent of humans. Wilderness or a pristine nature is predicated on a binary conception of the world, one divided into the natural and the human, "nature" and "culture." The advocates of environmental reform in the nineteenth and early twentieth century did sometimes set out to protect landscapes that were inhabited, and they acknowledged that those landscapes had been shaped by humans in both positive and negative ways.[13] On the other hand, French scientists and naturalists came to argue for the creation of *réserves naturelles intégrales* in France's colonies in the interwar period, for a nature that would be left untouched by humans.[14] This was in contrast to their European neighbors, who tended to advocate national parks and game reserves, which would be open to hunters and the public at large.

It is telling that the French word used to translate "wilderness" is *désert*. A "wilderness experience" in French is a *séjour en milieu sauvage*. Indeed, in a 1998 French survey regarding attitudes toward the environment, the majority of the French saw human beings as an integral part of nature. When asked, "Do you agree that men and women are a part of nature?," 76 percent responded that they completely agreed, 20 percent that they rather agreed, and only 1 percent that they disagreed.[15] The American environmental historian William Cronon has questioned the reified notion of a pristine nature, which in his view led to an exaggerated separation of the human from the nonhuman. He identifies what he called a "false duality" in a controversial essay entitled "The Trouble with Wilderness," in which he argues that "our challenge is to stop thinking of such things according to a set of bipolar moral scales in which the human and the non-human, the unnatural and the natural, the fallen and the unfallen, serve as our conceptual map for understanding and valuing the world."[16] For this reason it is important not to impose a rigid and uncompromising definition on the word "environmentalism" and to avoid a narrow understanding of what constituted an environmental awareness predicated on particular conceptions of nature and measured in terms of how well earlier advocates of the protection of nature conform to present-day green activists.[17] This makes the historian blind to the ways in which an environmental consciousness emerges, comes to be expressed, and changes in particular cultural and historical contexts over time.

In the French context, the environmental consciousness that came into being had distinctive features. Environmental protection focused first and foremost on France's forested landscapes, and this focus ultimately extended to its colonies. It simultaneously emerged in urban settings, and environmental reform was propagated by a diverse group of individuals and organizations, which included engineers, who had been called upon to resolve major problems engendered by environmental disaster since the eighteenth century; naturalists and scientists associated with Museum of Natural History; mountain climbers; social reformers; nature walkers; artists; people displaced by flooding; and workers and their advocates in search of a greener and better living environment in cities and towns. This constituency was by definition diverse. Their voices were cacophonous. They comprised a mix of all social classes, and they were frequently at odds with one another in terms of their political views.

Public engagement in environmental questions could be observed as early as the eighteenth century in France. In 1731, for example, François Blumenstein, an owner of several lead mines in the Lyonnais, attempted to convince his angry neighbors that their crops were being damaged by a drought rather than by the mines' noxious waste.[18] These neighbors asserted their right to complain to public authorities. There were already some embryonic institutions in place to deal with such complaints. In Lyon, the second largest city in France and one that possessed a number of industries, the *commissaire de police de la ville et des faubourgs* visited the sites of the complaints he received in order to draw up a report, after which action against alleged offenders would or would not be taken. Archives and records in Lyon from the 1770s onward reveal that complaints were lodged against butchers, carpenters, a difficult cheese merchant, starch makers, tanners, and handlers of various animal products. In addition, the city launched its own initiatives. When reclamation projects at the confluence of the Rhône and Saône Rivers created a large, swampy expanse that may have had consequences for public health, the municipality called for the installation of various furnaces to dry and purify the air.

Public complaints and governmental initiatives as well as the 1669 forest ordinance reveal that even in the early modern period there was a growing awareness of environmental damage, even if its causes were not fully articulated or understood. After a period of liberalization during the French Revolution, it was in the nineteenth century that awareness of the environmental costs of certain kinds of changes in the land and landscape came to be felt, as evidenced by the widespread obsession with flooding that came to be expressed in letters, literary works, photography, painting, and governmental reports.

One of the first measures taken to control the damaging environmental effects of industrial and economic ventures in the nineteenth century was the Napoleonic decree of 15 October 1810, which was the first comprehensive legislation in Europe to regulate the activities of manufacturing concerns that were considered "dangerous, insalubrious or incommodious." Paris was given a special status in the legislation, and it was applied to parts of the Napoleonic empire, including the Netherlands.[19] The initial preface to the fourteen articles of the legislation referred to popular grievances against manufacturing concerns. The articles actually distinguished between different types of enterprises and the risks they posed. The setting up of a manufacturing establishment in the first category necessitated a public inquiry, which had to be advertised within a five-kilometer radius, and required a governmental decree. A prefect could authorize the creation of a factory of the second category with the recommendation of a town's mayor and feedback from the public, and manufacturing concerns of the third type could simply be authorized by mayors. The legislation had an appeal procedure, and the last three articles cited existing offenders. The decree was clearly inadequate, and new chemical forms of pollution were not fully appreciated. Some argue that its author, Jean-Antoine Chaptal, a chemist and a minister of the interior under Napoleon, was moreover probusiness in his inclinations.[20] Nonetheless, it was the first European legislation of its kind and served as a foundation for later legislation.

Following this early legislation, scientific societies and academies embarked on projects to protect wild species in the 1830s and the 1840s. The Society for the Protection of Animals was founded in Paris on 2 December 1845, and the movement spread. Similar societies were established in Lyon (1853), Pau (1858), Cannes (1877), Le Havre (1880), Dunkerque (1882), Rouen (1886), and Biarritz (1890). In 1850, shortly after the creation of the Society for the Protection of Animals came into being, the Grammont Law was passed (2 July 1850), under which any person who was found guilty of abusing domestic animals would be fined or imprisoned.[21] A more specialized organization, the French League for Ornithology, was founded in 1892 in Aix-en-Provence, under the auspices of the Ministry of Agriculture. This led to an international ornithological congress for the protection of birds useful to agriculture in 1897, and to the International Convention for the Protection of Birds Useful to Agriculture, which was first drafted in France and signed in Paris on 19 March 1902 by twelve European nations.

The nineteenth century also saw the creation of a new school of forestry, a new forest administration, and the promulgation of the Forest Code of 1827, which, for all its faults, was a landmark in terms of protective legislation. Much of the popular groundswell that gave rise to such legislation peaked in the 1850s and 1860s, during the Second Empire. It was during Napoleon III's rule that Paris was rebuilt and a vast system of parks and green spaces was created under the eye of the department of the Seine's prefect, Baron Haussmann. This resulted in the creation of one of the city's largest parks *intra-muros,* that of the Buttes-Chaumont, which was 24 hectares in size, and two large forest parks, the Bois de Boulogne (50 hectares) and the Bois de Vincennes (730 hectares), flanking the city to the east and west.[22] These initiatives were complemented by the laws of 28 July 1860 and 9 June 1864, which provided for a massive project to reforest France's mountains; and soon after the founding of the Third Republic in 1871, yet another law was proposed, which had the title Restoration and Conservation of Mountain Lands, which was passed on 4 April 1882. This law "recognized forestry as obligatory public work" and also provided for the "reservation" of grazing grounds on terrain that was not damaged enough to merit expropriation, and whose boundaries would be set by decree for a period of not more than ten years.[23]

In many respects it was during the Second Empire, one of the most politically reactionary, authoritarian regimes of the nineteenth century, that some of the major landmarks in environmental legislation in the postrevolutionary period were passed, including the first legislation to protect a site as a natural monument, in the artistic reserve of Fontainebleau in 1861. This raises the question of how one might consider the politics of environmental reform in the nineteenth and early twentieth centuries. It has generally been associated with the Left in the late twentieth and early twenty-first centuries. In grappling with the terms "environmentalist," "ecological," and "green," Michael Bess, for example, posits that in France the word "écologiste" means what "environmentalist" means in English: "an activist devoted to a program of social change."[24] He goes on to use a "historically specific" definition of French environmentalism whose "political and moral orientation," in his view, is "solidly anchored in the language and habits of the liberal European Left."[25] Was this the case in the nineteenth and early twentieth centuries? Was it a left-wing cause? François-Antoine Rauch and Jean-Baptiste Rougier de la Bergerie represent interesting points of departure in terms of answering these questions. Both began as supporters of the French Revolution, but each came to criticize the liberal policies that were enacted with respect to forest reform, which, they argued had disastrous consequences. Rauch criticized these policies from the start, whereas Rougier de la Bergerie, an early supporter of revolutionary forest reform, withdrew his support, but he also despaired of the regimes that succeeded it, namely, the Consulate, First Empire, Restoration, and July Monarchy, even though it was during the Restoration that the forest administration was reorganized and a new forest code was written. Other supporters of environmental reform and protection were allied to various political groups—and later to parties—which did not, by and large, put the environment on their programmatic agenda. In short, calls for environmental reform came from a diverse set of individuals, ranging from Charles Beauquier, the first president of the SPPF, who was a member of the Radical Socialist Party, to Jean Charles-Brun, president of the Fédération régionaliste française, who has often been viewed as a conservative.[26] In short, like the French preservationist movement more generally, proponents of environmental reform "escape any simple political categorisation."[27]

The environmental reform movement in France's colonies drew inspiration from the metropole, but the situation there was complicated by the weight of French colonial domination. On the one hand, the French state, businessmen, and settlers were involved in expropriation and extraction of natural resources. While Richard Grove observed that it was in the colonies that French colonial governors began to be aware of the finitude of natural resources as early as the seventeenth and eighteenth centuries, French settlers and administrators came to blame indigenous populations for environmental degradation and used this as a justification for both expropriation and reclamation projects, including reforestation. The darker side of environmentalism could be observed across the French Empire, where violence ruled. On the other hand, the colonies served as a place for environmental experimentation. It was in the colonies that a system of national parks and natural and forest reserves was established, which served as a model for the six national parks that were established in France in the 1960s.[28]

In assessing the motives behind environmental reform in both metropolitan and colonial France, historians have measured them in terms of either the concept of conservation, which involves the management of natural resources, or that of preservation, which implies protecting and sometimes restoring nature to a presumed "natural" state. What is clear is that both approaches were employed in metropolitan and colonial France. Eaux et Forêts officials were in the business of conservation, and frequently clashed with preservationists such as the Barbizon school painters at Fontainebleau and the SPPF, even though all acted in the name of the protection of nature. In cities urban planners who envisioned new parks and squares also spoke the language of protection and preservation as they created totally new green spaces. In France's colonies organizations like the Société d'acclimatation, which was founded in 1854, initially spoke the language of conservation and preservation, in the interests of the economic needs of the metropole, which was translated into a policy of *mise en valeur* (development to marshall natural resources), celebrated by Albert Sarraut, the governor general of Indochina from 1912 to 1914.[29] A director of the Museum of Natural History summed up this position in the following terms:

> The inhabitants of the old world have their eyes fixed on these virgin regions where nature is so rich and whose resources nevertheless lie unused . . . it is necessary to increase the patrimony of the generations that succeed us, in working to exploit the resources of territories recently acquired by France and

where the reserves of the future sleep .... It is now about taking advantage of these new possessions, and for that, it is necessary to know what they produce, by what races of men they are inhabited, what their flora is.[30]

By the first decade of the twentieth century, after a long period of colonial conquest and expansion had passed, and France dealt more and more with the actual administration of the empire, the naturalists associated with the Museum of Natural History began to distance themselves from the colonial administration and became more critical of the concept of *mise en valeur*. Louis Mangin, director of the museum, came to preside over the first international congress devoted to the protection of nature, which was held in Paris in 1923. The naturalists' changing position became clear in the interwar period, when they pushed for the creation of *réserves naturelles intégrales*, which were defined in the following terms in 1937:

> The expression "réserve naturelle intégrale" designates an area placed under public control and on whose expanse all forms of hunting or fishing, all tree and agricultural farming or mining, all excavations or prospecting, surveys, earthworks or constructions, all work tending to modify the aspect of the terrain or the vegetation, all acts of a kind that damages or disturbs the fauna or flora, any introduction of zoological or botanical species, whether indigenous, imported, wild, or domesticated, will be strictly prohibited; where it will be forbidden to enter, circulate, or to camp without special, written authorization from the competent authorities, and in which scientific research can only be performed with the permission of these authorities.[31]

This new and radical conception of nature protection was a far cry from those held by naturalists in the Société nationale d'acclimatation in the nineteenth century. Put alongside the proposals of various organizations and individuals calling for environmental reform throughout this entire period, it indicates the degree to which environmental perceptions were never wholly fixed. They did and would change, and look toward the future.

Notes

Introduction

1. Jean-Baptiste Rougier de la Bergerie, *Mémoire et observations sur les abus des défrichemens et la destruction des bois et forêts; avec un projet d'organisation forestière* (Auxerre: Laurent Fournier, 1800), 65. Rougier de la Bergerie published this work under the name Citizen Rougier-Labergerie, perhaps in an attempt to disguise his noble origins during the revolutionary and Napoleonic periods. Unless otherwise noted, all translations from the French are mine.
2. Clarence J. Glacken, *Traces on the Rhodian Shore: Nature and Culture in Western Thought from Ancient Times to the End of the Eighteenth Century* (Berkeley: University of California Press, 1967), 705. See also Ludmilla J. Jordanova, "Environmentalism in the Eighteenth Century," in *Nature and Science: Essays in the History of Geographical Knowledge,* ed. Felix Driver and Gillian Rose, special issue, Historical Geography Research Series 28 (February 1992): 19–26.
3. David Blackbourn has recently explored this phenomenon in the context of Germany in *The Conquest of Nature: Water, Landscape, and the Making of Modern Germany* (London: Jonathan Cape, 2006).
4. This view has been reevaluated in Charles-François Mathis and Jean-François Mouhot, eds., *Une protection de l'environnement à la française? (XIXe–XXe siècles)* (Seyssel: Champ Vallon, 2013).
5. See Donald Worster, *Nature's Economy: A History of Ecological Ideas,* 2nd ed. (Cambridge: Cambridge University Press, 1994), and Pascal Acot, *Histoire de l'écologie* (Paris: Presses Universitaires de France, 1988), where French sources are few, though Frank N. Egerton has recently been more inclusive in this regard. Egerton, *Roots of Ecology: Antiquity to Haeckel* (Berkeley: University of California Press, 2012).

6. Some historians understand preservation as the protection of nature or nature in the wild from the destructive hand of humans.
7. Acot, *Histoire de l'écologie;* Jean-Marc Drouin, *Réinventer la nature: L'écologie et son histoire* (Paris: Desclée de Brower, 1991); Marie-Claire Robic et al., eds., *Du milieu à l'environnement: Pratiques et répresentations du rapport homme/nature depuis la Renaissance* (Paris: Economica, 1992); Patrick Matagne, *Aux origines de l'écologie: Les naturalistes en France de 1800 à 1914* (Paris: Editions du CTHS, 1999).
8. See Kapil Raj, *Relocating Modern Science: Circulation and the Construction of Knowledge in South Asia and Europe, 1650–1900* (Basingstoke: Palgrave Macmillan, 2010), and Kapil Raj, "Circulation and Locality in Early Modern Science," *British Journal for the History of Science* 42 (2010): 513–517.
9. These works were quickly translated into English. Alain Corbin, *The Foul and the Fragrant: Odor and the French Social Imagination* (Cambridge, Mass.: Harvard University Press, 1986); Corbin, *The Lure of the Sea: The Discovery of the Seaside in the Western World, 1750–1840,* trans. Jocelyn Phelps (Cambridge, Mass.: Harvard University Press, 1994); Corbin, *Village Bells: Sound and Meaning in the Nineteenth-Century French Countryside,* trans. Martin Thom (New York: Columbia University Press, 1998).
10. See Constance Classen, *Worlds of Sense: Exploring the Senses in History and across Cultures* (London: Wiley, 1993), and Mark M. Smith, *Sensing the Past: Seeing, Hearing, Smelling, Tasting, and Touching in History* (Berkeley: University of California Press, 2008).
11. Alfred Crosby, "The Past and Present of Environmental History," *American Historical Review* 100, no. 4 (October 1995): 1188.
12. David Blackbourn, "A Sense of Place: New Directions in German History" (1998 Annual Lecture, German Historical Institute London, 1999), 16–17.
13. David Blackbourn, "'Conquests from Barbarism': Taming Nature in Frederick the Great's Prussia," in *Nature in German History,* ed. Christof Mauch (New York: Berghahn, 2004), 11.
14. Ibid.
15. Cited in Richard White, "Environmental History, Ecology and Meaning," *Journal of American History* 76, no. 4 (March 1990): 1113, from Maurice Godelier, *The Mental and the Material: Thought, Economy and Society* (London: Verso, 1988).
16. Andrée Corvol, ed., *Les sources de l'histoire de l'environnement,* vol. 3, *Le XXe siècle* (Paris: L'Harmattan, 2003).
17. Lucien Febvre, *La terre et l'évolution humaine* (Paris: La Renaissance du Livre, 1922), and Marc Bloch, *Les caractères originaux de l'histoire rurale* (Oslo: Aschehoug, 1931). For a discussion of the terms *milieu* and *environnement* among scholars in France, see Jean-Louis Tessier, "Du milieu à l'environnement: L'émergence d'un concept dans le discours des géographes français," in *Les français dans leur environnement,* ed. René Neboit-Guilhot and Lucette Davy (Paris: Nathan, 1996). Also see Robert Delort and François Walter, *Histoire de l'environnement européen* (Paris: Presses Universitaires de France, 2001), and Florian Charvolin, *L'invention de l'environnement en France: Chroniques anthropologiques d'une institutionalisation* (Paris: La Découverte, 2003).

18. James Beattie, *Empire and Environmental Anxiety: Health, Science, Art, and Conservation in South Asia and Australasia, 1800–1920* (London: Palgrave Macmillan, 2011), 1.
19. Quoted in Svetlana Boym, *The Future of Nostalgia* (New York: Basic Books, 2001), 3. See Johannes Hofer, *Dissertio medica de Nostalgia, oder Heimveh* (Bâle: Jakob Betsche, 1688).
20. Thomas Dodman, "Un pays pour la colonie: Mourir de nostalgie en Algérie française, 1830–1880," *Annales. Histoire, Sciences Sociales* 3 (July–September 2011): 744. Also see Jean Starobinski, "Le concept de la nostalgie," *Diogène* 54 (1966): 92–115; George Rosen, "A 'Forgotten' Psychological Disorder," *Clio Medica* 10, no. 1 (1975): 28–51; Michael Roth, "Dying of the Past: Medical Studies of Nostalgia in Nineteenth-Century France," *History and Memory* 1, no. 1 (1991): 5–29; André Bolzinger, *Histoire de la nostalgie* (Paris: Campagne Première, 2007).
21. Boym, *The Future of Nostalgia*, xiii.
22. David Lowenthal discusses this characterization in "Nostalgia Tells It Like It Wasn't," in *The Imagined Past: History and Nostalgia*, ed. Christopher Shaw and Malcolm Chase (New York: St. Martin's Press, 1989), 27. Focusing on literary sources, Jennifer Ladino proposes an alternative perspective in "Longing for Wonderland: Nostalgia for Nature in Post-frontier America," *Iowa Journal of Cultural Studies* 5 (Fall 2004), and in Jennifer K. Ladino, *Reclaiming Nostalgia: Longing for Nature in American Literature* (Charlottesville: University of Virginia Press, 2012). For a more general discussion of nostalgia as a concept, see Boym, *The Future of Nostalgia*.
23. Ladino, *Reclaiming Nostalgia*. Also see Linda M. Austin, *Nostalgia in Transition, 1780–1917* (Charlottesville: University of Virginia Press, 2007); Lawrence Buell, "Ecoglobal Affects: The Emergence of the U.S. Environmental Imagination on a Planetary Scale," in *Shades of the Planet: American Literature as World Literature*, ed. Wai Chee Dimock and Lawrence Buell (Princeton, N.J.: Princeton University Press, 2007), 227–248. William Cronon and Raymond Williams have discussed how environmentalism can be nostalgic in problematic ways in Cronon, "The Trouble with Wilderness, or Getting Back to the Wrong Nature," in *Uncommon Ground: Rethinking the Human Place in Nature*, ed. William Cronon (New York: W. W. Norton, 1995), 65–90; and Williams, *The Country and the City* (London: Chatto and Windus, 1973).
24. See, for example, John M. MacKenzie, "Empire and the Ecological Apocalypse: The Historiography of the Imperial Environment," in *Ecology and Empire: Environmental History of Settler Societies*, ed. Tom Griffiths and Libby Robin (Seattle: University of Washington Press, 1997), 215–228; Ramachandra Guha, *The Unquiet Woods: Ecological Change and Peasant Resistance in the Himalaya* (Delhi: Oxford University Press, 1989); S. Ravi Rajan, *Modernizing Nature: Forestry and Imperial Eco-development, 1800–1930* (Oxford: Oxford University Press, 2006); and William Beinart and Lotte Hughes, *Environment and Empire* (Oxford: Oxford University Press, 2007).
25. Most notably, Eric T. Jennings, *Curing the Colonizers: Hydrotherapy, Climatology, and French Colonial Spas* (Durham, N.C.: Duke University Press, 2006). For Britain, see Mark Harrison, *Climates and Constitutions: Health, Race,*

Environment, and the British Empire in India, 1600–1800 (Oxford: Oxford University Press, 1999), and Beattie, *Empire and Environmental Anxiety*, 39–71, 100–122.

26. Will D. Swearingen, *Moroccan Mirages: Agrarian Dreams and Deceptions, 1912–1986* (Princeton, N.J.: Princeton University Press, 1987); Diana K. Davis, *Resurrecting the Granary of Rome: Environmental History and French Colonial Expansion in North Africa* (Athens: Ohio University Press, 2007); Adel Selmi, "L'émergence de l'idée du parc national en France: De la protection à l'expérimentation coloniale," in *Histoire des parcs nationaux: Comment prendre soin de la nature?*, ed. Raphaël Larrère et al. (Versailles: Editions Quae, 2009), 43–58.

27. Richard White, "The Nationalization of Nature," *Journal of American History* 86, no. 3 (December 1999): 976. By contrast, Ian Tyrrell has made a case for a transnational approach to environmental history in *True Garden of the Gods: Californian-Australian Environmental Reform, 1860–1930* (Berkeley: University of California Press, 1999).

28. John Croumbie Brown, *Reboisement in France: or, Records of the Replanting of the Alps, the Cevennes and the Pyrenees with Trees, Herbage and Bush with a View to Arresting and Preventing the Destructive Consequences and Effects of Torrents* (London: Henry S. King, 1876). See Richard Grove, "Scotland in South Africa: John Croumbie Brown and the Roots of Settler Environmentalism," in Griffiths and Robin, *Ecology and Empire*, 139–153.

29. Bernard Kalaora and Chloe Vlassopoulos, *Pour une sociologie de l'environnement: Environnement, société, politique* (Seyssel: Champ Vallon, 2013), 15.

30. *Revue Forestière Française*, no. 5 (15 April 1955): 337.

31. Jean-François Mouhot and Charles-François Mathis, "Du manque de visibilité de l'écologisme et de ses penseurs au XXe siècle," in *Penser l'écologie politique en France au XXe siècle*, special issue, *Ecologie et politique* 44 (2012): 13–27. Historians of France have paid less attention to the impact of industrialization on the environment in the nineteenth century than have historians of Britain, Geneviève Massard-Guilbaud's valuable *Histoire de la pollution industrielle: France, 1789–1914* (Paris: Editions de l'école des hautes études en sciences sociales, 2010) notwithstanding. See, for example, James H. Winter, *Secure from Rash Assault: Sustaining the Victorian Environment* (Berkeley: University of California Press, 1999); Peter Thorsheim, *Inventing Pollution: Coal, Smoke and Culture in Britain since 1800* (Athens: Ohio University Press, 2006); and Charles-François Mathis, *"In Nature We Trust": Les paysages anglais à l'ère industrielle* (Paris: Presses de l'Université de Paris-Sorbonne, 2010).

32. For a discussion of the role that French engineers played during times of environmental crisis, see Paul Allard, "Le rôle des ingénieurs des Ponts et Chaussées au XIXe siècle dans la gestion des crises environnementales," in *Temps et espaces des crises de l'environnement*, ed. Corinne Beck, Yves Luginbühl, and Tatiana Muxart (Versailles: Editions Quae, 2006), 249–261.

33. Yves Luginbühl, "Nature, paysage, environnement, obscurs objets du désir de totalité," in Marie-Claire Robic et al., *Du milieu à l'environnement*, 11–56.

34. Alain Corbin, *Le miasme et la jonquille: L'odorat et l'imaginaire social, XVIIIe–XIXe siècles* (Paris: Flammarion, 1986), 134.
35. Quoted in Louis Chevalier, *Laboring Classes and Dangerous Classes in Paris during the First Half of the Nineteenth Century*, trans. Frank Jellinek (New York: H. Fertig, 1973), 210.
36. Quoted in ibid., 212.
37. While the establishment of this institution was a landmark in terms of environmental legislation, it turned out to be lenient in terms of enforcement. See Jean-Pierre Baud, "Les hygiènistes face aux nuisances industrielles dans la première moitié du XIXe siècle," *Revue Juridique de l'Environnement* 3 (1981): 205–220.
38. Quoted in ibid., 218.
39. Haussmann was particularly concerned with water pollution and turned to his chief engineers. On Haussmannization, see David H. Pinkney, *Napoleon III and the Rebuilding of Paris* (Princeton, N.J.: Princeton University Press, 1958).
40. Richard H. Grove, *Green Imperialism: Colonial Expansion, Tropical Island Edens and the Origins of Environmentalism, 1600–1800* (Cambridge: Cambridge University Press, 1995), 3.
41. Alain Corbin, *Le territoire du vide: L'occident et le désir du rivage, 1750–1840* (Paris: Flammarion, 1988); Peter H. Hansen: *Summits of Modern Man: Mountaineering after the Enlightenment* (Cambridge, Mass.: Harvard University Press, 2013).
42. See Bernard Kalaora, *Le musée vert ou le tourisme en forêt: Naissance et développement d'un loisir urbain; le cas de Fontainebleau* (Paris: Anthropos, 1981); Jean-Claude Polton, *Tourisme et nature au XIXe siècle* (Paris: Comité des Travaux Historique et Scientifique, 1994); Nicholas Green, *The Spectacle of Nature: Landscape and Bourgeois Culture in Nineteenth-Century France* (Manchester, UK: Manchester University Press, 1990); Simon Schama, *Landscape and Memory* (New York: Knopf, 1995), 546–560; and Greg M. Thomas, *Art and Ecology in Nineteenth-Century France: The Landscapes of Théodore Rousseau* (Princeton, N.J.: Princeton University Press, 2000).

1. François-Antoine Rauch's New Harmony of Nature

Epigraph: Quoted in G. R. Larrère, *"L'harmonie hydrovégétale et météorologique" ou L'utopie forestière de F. A. Rauch* (Paris: INRA, 1985), 57.

1. Charles-François Mathis and Jean-François Mouhot, "Introduction générale," in Mathis and Mouhot, *Une protection de l'environnement à la française*, 11. Mathis and Mouhot reemphasize the prominence of the German, American, and northern European "founding fathers" of ecology and environmentalism.
2. Rauch appears neither in Worster's *Nature's Economy* nor in Frank B. Egerton's more recent *Roots of Ecology*.
3. François-Antoine Rauch, *Plan nourricier, ou recherches sur les moyens à mettre en usage pour assurer à jamais le pain au peuple français* (Paris: Didot, 1792).
4. Rauch explained, "If one finds that I often repeat myself, I warn [you], that neither having had the vain pretension of writing for the learned, to whom I

can only pay homage, nor of producing a refined book, since French is not my mother tongue," his intent was "to gather together in a popular form and within the reach of all my compatriots, a large number of facts and useful observations." Ibid., 4.
5. Letter, Rauch to minister of public works, 22 June 1817, Archives nationales (hereafter A.N.) F/14/2308. Much of his own autobiographical account of himself can be found in a letter he addressed to the minister of public works to ask for financial assistance. "It is, Monsieur le Comte, with sincere humility and for the first time in my life that I open up my heart regarding my private life; I believe in the need to do so, because I have already cruelly suffered at the hands of men . . . I do it, because I am speaking to a just man . . . who is my natural judge, to whom I must open my soul, in order to deserve the prospect of his charity."
6. Mona Ozouf, "Régénération," in *Dictionnaire critique de la Révolution française,* ed. François Furet and Mona Ozouf (Paris: Flammarion, 1988), 821.
7. As Mary Ashburn Miller has argued, revolutionary leaders, playwrights, journalists, and festival organizers very often used metaphors taken from the natural world to make sense of the changes taking place around them. Floods, lightning bolts, volcanic eruptions, and earthquakes all became a part of the political vocabulary and ceremony of the period. Miller, *A Natural History of Revolution: Violence and Nature in the French Revolutionary Imagination, 1789–1794* (Ithaca, N.Y.: Cornell University Press, 2011), 2.
8. Quoted in Jean Petot, *Histoire de l'administration des ponts et chaussées 1599–1815* (Paris: M. Rivière, 1958), 360. Also see Antoine Picon, *L'invention de l'ingénieur moderne: L'Ecole des ponts et chaussées 1747–1851* (Paris: Presses de l'Ecole nationale des ponts et chaussées, 1992), 649. The original manuscript is part of the archives of the Ecole des ponts et chaussées (MS 1835).
9. *Procédés de la fabrication des armes blanches, publiés par l'ordre du Comité de salut public* (Paris: Imprimerie du Département de la Guerre, 1793).
10. E. C. Spary, *Utopia's Garden: French Natural History from the Old Regime to the French Revolution* (Chicago: University of Chicago Press, 2000), 102–117.
11. Ibid., 127–128. See John Ellis, *Description du mangostan et du fruit à pain,* trans. Balillière de Laisern (Rouen: P. Machuel, 1779), and Louis-Antoine de Bougainville, *Voyage autour du monde par le frégate du roi La Boudeuse et la flûte l'Etoile, en 1766, 1767, 1768 & 1769,* 2nd ed., 2 vols. (Neuchâtel: Société Typographique, 1772).
12. Spary, *Utopia's Garden,* 130.
13. Rauch, *Plan nourricier,* 90–91.
14. See, for example, Carol E. Harrison, "Planting Gardens, Planting Flags: Revolutionary France in the South Pacific," *French Historical Studies* 34, no. 2 (Spring 2011): 243–277.
15. Spary, *Utopia's Garden,* 131.
16. A.N. AJ/15/847.
17. A.N. AJ/15/848, Report by Thouin entitled "Jardin Kinski," 12 March 1794 (23 ventôse, year 2 of the Republic). Article 6 of a decree passed by the National Convention on 16 germinal, year 2 provided for the collection of plants

that were not indigenous to France from the city of Paris and the surrounding countryside. In addition to authorizing the confiscation and inventorying of plants and seeds and bringing them to the newly renamed Muséum national, the National Convention also issued a decree that provided for the creation of botanical gardens throughout France's departments. A number of projects came to be discussed as well as a proposal to create a "jardin national des plantes" in Abbeville. A.N. AJ/15/848, "Projet d'établissement d'un jardin national des plantes à Abbeville," 18 fructidor, year 2 of the Republic.

18. A.N. AJ/15/848, Report by Thouin.
19. A.N. AJ/15/848, "Inventory of Objects Found at Port Libre, rue de la Bourbe, Faubourg Jacques, in a room and in Part of the Garden Occupied by the Condemned Dumas Labrousse," 21 August 1794. According to the report, Labrousse left a file of notes and manuscripts relative to a voyage to the Cape of Good Hope, where he stayed for six years. Given the circumstances in which their author found himself, as a prisoner condemned to death, it is not surprising that Thouin should find them "in great disorder, incomplete," and "written in a handwriting" that was "not easy to read" and hence of "mediocre utility."
20. Antoine Parmentier, *Examen chimique des pommes de terre, dans lequel on traite des parties constituentes du blé* (Paris: Didot, 1773), and Parmentier, *Manière de faire le pain des pommes de terre* (Paris: Imprimerie Royale, 1779).
21. "I think that the government would render a great service to humanity and to mill owners, by enlightening them about their own interests and obliging them to adopt the new method." Rauch, *Plan nourricier,* 18–19.
22. Ibid., 112–113.
23. "But if it turned out, Mr. President, that no [other] Frenchman could be found who is friend enough to his country to devote himself to this work with all of its ties to the public good; in spite of my youth, I would have the courage to undertake it, in the hope of teaching great and useful truths to my country about this important matter." Ibid., 114.
24. Ibid., 117.
25. Elizabeth Fox-Genovese, *The Origins of Physiocracy* (Ithaca, N.Y.: Cornell University Press, 1976).
26. Letter from chief engineer to the minister of the interior, 7 December 1797 (17 frimaire, year 6 of the Republic), A.N. F/14/2308.
27. Rauch fostered deep resentment toward the chief engineer, noting in 1814 that "the hate of a chief [engineer], who is no longer, has weighed on my destiny for 22 years." Letter from Rauch to directeur général, Ponts et Chaussées, 31 August 1814, A.N. F/14/2308.
28. Letter from J.-A. Rauch to Emmanuel Crétet, conseiller d'état and directeur général, Ponts et Chaussées, 30 October 1804 (8 brumaire, year 13 of the Republic), A.N. F/14/2308. He claimed that he was "coldly sacrificed to the ambition of a profoundly nasty man," one who "never knew the sweet inspirations of virtue."
29. He characterized the transfer as an "incomprehensible order" that would separate him from his wife, child, octogenarian mother, and infirm brother. Ibid. Another internal report, dated 5 April 1800 (15 germinal, year 8 of the

Republic), noted that Rauch had acquired a "rural property" which interfered with his functions. A.N. F/14/2308.
30. Letter from J.-A. Rauch to the minister of the interior, 1 July 1799, A.N. F/14/2308. Rauch went on to write a series of letters for several years to figures as diverse as François de Neufchateau, Lucien Bonaparte, minister of the interior (in 1800), and Jean-Antoine Chaptal, minister of the interior (in 1802), concerning his case.
31. Letter from Rauch to Chaptal, 21 frimaire, year 9 of the Republic, A.N. F/14/2308. He added that he had been deprived of his salary for the preceding two years.
32. Report by minister of the interior, 10 August 1802 (22 thermidor, year 10 of the Republic), A.N. F/14/2308.
33. François-Antoine Rauch, *Harmonie hydro-végétale: Ou recherches sur les moyens de recréer avec nos forêts la force des températures et la regularité des saisons par les plantations raisonnées*, 2 vols. (Paris: Levrault, 1801), 1:8.
34. Ibid., 1:6–7.
35. Ibid., 1:1.
36. Ibid., 1:5.
37. Ibid., 1:1, 5–6.
38. Ibid., 1:2.
39. The alternative title of the work is *Recherches sur les moyens de recréer avec nos forêts la force des températures et la régularité des saisons, par des plantations raisonnées*.
40. Rauch, *Harmonie hydro-végétale*, 1:6.
41. Ibid., 1:191.
42. Ibid., 1:345–346.
43. Alexandre Lenoir, *Musée impérial des monumens français* (Paris: Hacquart, 1810); Mona Ozouf, *La fête revolutionnaire, 1789–99* (Paris: Gallimard, 1976).
44. This view was articulated early on by the Viennese art historian Alois Riegl, a member of the Royal Central Commission for Researching and Preserving Monuments and author of a work that was to have a considerable impact on the field of historic conservation, *Der Moderne Denkmalkultus, sein Wesen, seine Entstehung* (Vienna: Braumüller, 1903). Dominque Poulot, among others, believes that this conception of heritage is a Western or European phenomenon, which was then exported to other parts of the globe. Poulot, *Une histoire du patrimoine en occident* (Paris: Presses Universitaires de France, 2006).
45. Rauch, *Harmonie hydro-végétale*, 1:347.
46. Ibid., 1:347–388.
47. Picon, *L'invention de l'ingénieur moderne*, 57.
48. Ibid., 21.
49. See, for example, Henri Grégoire, *Essai historique et patriotique sur les arbres de la liberté* (Paris: Desenne, 1793-1794), and Chatelain, *Discours prononcé aux enfants de la patrie, en plantant l'arbre de la liberté* (Paris: Imprimerie de Renaudière jeune, 1793).
50. Rauch, *Harmonie hydro-végétale*, 2:290.
51. Ibid., 2:291.

52. Ibid., 2:290.
53. Rauch, *Régénération de la nature, ou recherches sur les moyens de recréer, dans tous les climats, les anciennes températures et l'ordre primitif des saisons, par des plantations raisonnées,* 2 vols. (Paris: Didot, 1818).
54. Ibid., 1:xiii.
55. Ibid., 1:xv.
56. Ibid., 1:xv–xvi.
57. "The system of army corps, and that of deciding the fate of peoples through battles, are also only systems of appalling massacres, which are an outrage to humanity and religion. Fortresses and permanent armies which demolish governments and nations, in uselessly destroying precious resources [contributing] to social well-being, will soon be evaluated in this new meeting of sovereigns, that religion, wisdom, and goodness are again going to assemble with the generous view of improving the destiny of the peoples entrusted to their paternal care." Ibid., 1:380–381.
58. At the end of the second volume he explicitly thanks the minister of the interior and the Comte de Chabrol, undersecretary of state. Ibid., 2:384.
59. *Annales Européennes,* Prospectus (Paris, n.d. [1818]), 1–2.
60. Ibid., 5. Rauch had evidently moved to Paris in the years between his retirement in 1806 and the publication of *Régénération de la nature* and the prospectus in 1818.
61. The publisher of the first volume of *Annales Européennes* was the Parisian publishing house J.-M. Eberhart in the rue St-Jacques, and Rauch was listed as residing at no. 20 Place Royale (Place des Vosges). He would move again many times within Paris between 1821 and his death in 1837.
62. A footnote observes that this passage was written a year earlier, and that it had been retained, in spite of the "events of the moment." *Annales Européennes* 1 (1821): 1.
63. Ibid., 8.
64. Michael A. Osborne, *Nature, the Exotic, and the Science of French Colonialism* (Bloomington: Indiana University Press, 1994).
65. *Annales Européennes* 2 (1821): 241.
66. Ibid., 484–485.
67. The extract from *Le Moniteur* is quoted in its entirety. *Annales Européennes* 3 (1822): 6–8.
68. The circular from the minister of the interior was reprinted in its entirety in ibid., 15–17. Rauch expressed regret that the circular did not ask the prefects to assess a time span greater than thirty years, preferring a century's hindsight.
69. Ibid., 75.
70. Ibid., 365.
71. *Annales Européennes* 4 (1824): 121, 377.
72. *Société de fructification générale de la terre et des eaux de la France* (Paris: C. J. Trouvé, n.d.). This brochure is attributed to the author of *Annales Européennes.*
73. *Annales Européennes* 6 (1824): 378.
74. *Annales Européennes* 7 (1826): 9–33.

75. "If it be permitted in my capacity as an old friend and 'camarade de corps' of Bernardin St. Pierre, to present for your attention the long and useful works in which I have been engaged to solicit your kindness, at the age of sixty-nine, [to provide] the honor that I believe to have merited." Letter from Rauch to the minister of the interior, 25 March 1831, A.N. F/14/2308.
76. Letter from Rauch to M. Legrand (Ministère de ponts et chaussées), 10 August 1832, A.N. F/14/2308.
77. Letter from Ministère de ponts et chaussées to Rauch, 18 August 1832, A.N. F/14/2308.
78. "Deboisements en Asie, en Afrique, en Amérique et en Europe; des maux physiques qu'ils entraînent à leur suite," *Annales Européennes* 1 (1821): 114.
79. R. Grove, *Green Imperialism*; Glacken, *Traces on the Rhodian Shore*.
80. Desertification theories were, of course, by no means new. As A. T. Grove and Oliver Rackham have argued, desertification already existed in the imagination of Dante in the fourteenth century. What was new was how these theories were employed and linked to other natural phenomena. A. T. Grove and Rackham, *The Nature of Mediterranean Europe: An Ecological History* (New Haven, Conn.: Yale University Press, 2001), 9.
81. Spary, *Utopia's Garden*, 151.

2. Saving the Forests First

Epigraph: Alexandre Moreau de Jonnès, *Premier mémoire en réponse à la question proposée par l'Académie royale de Bruxelles: Quels sont les changemens que peut occasioner le déboisement de forêts considérables sur les contrées et communes adjacentes*... (Brussels: P. J. De Mat, 1825), i.

1. R. Grove, *Green Imperialism*, 474.
2. Glacken, *Traces on the Rhodian Shore*, 491; John Croumbie Brown, *The French Forest Ordinance of 1669; with Historical Sketch of Previous Treatment of Forests in France* (Edinburgh: Oliver and Boyd, 1883).
3. Quoted in Glacken, *Traces on the Rhodian Shore*, 492.
4. *Les eaux et forêts du 12e au 20e siècle* (Paris: CNRS, 1987), 165–179.
5. Keiko Matteson, *Forests in Revolutionary France: Conservation, Community, and Conflict, 1669–1848* (Cambridge: Cambridge University Press, 2015), 50.
6. Georges Louis Leclerc de Buffon, "Sur la conservation et le rétablissement des forêts," in *Supplément à histoire naturelle,* 7 vols. (Paris: Imprimerie Royale, 1775), 2:249–271; Buffon, "Sur la culture et l'exploitation des forêts," ibid., 2:271–290.
7. *Les eaux et forêts,* 213.
8. Bernard Kalaora and Antoine Savoye, *Forêt et sociologie: Les forestiers de l'Ecole de Le Play, défenseurs des populations de montagne (1860–1913)* (Paris: INRA, 1984), 1.
9. For a discussion of the revolutionary and postrevolutionary legislation and debates surrounding forests, see Matteson, *Forests in Revolutionary France,* 106–206.
10. *Les eaux et forêts,* 265–266.

11. Ibid., 267.
12. "Décret sur l'administration forestière," title 1, article 6, in *Collection complète des lois, décrets, ordonnances, réglemens, avis du Conseil-d-Etat*, ed. J. B. Duvergier, 2nd ed., vol. 3 (Paris: Chez A. Guyot et Scribe, 1834–1838), 272.
13. See Marie-Noëlle Grand-Mesnil, "La loi du 29 septembre 1791," in *Révolution et espaces forestières: Colloque du 3 et 4 juin 1987*, ed. Denis Woronoff (Paris: L'Harmattan, 1988), 200–205.
14. Jules Michelet, *Histoire de France*, 2nd ed., 17 vols. (Paris: Hachette, 1835), 2:53.
15. Denis Woronoff, "La dévastation révolutionnaire des fôrets," in Woronoff, *Révolution et espaces forestières*, 46; Jean-Pierre Husson, "Les paysages forestiers lorrains, rôle et impact de l'épisode révolutionnaire (étude de géographie historique)," in Woronoff, *Révolution et espaces forestières*, 63–70.
16. Peter McPhee, *Revolution and Environment in Southern France, 1780–1930: Peasants, Lords, and Murder in Corbières* (Oxford: Oxford University Press, 1999).
17. Woronoff, "La dévastation révolutionnaire," 52.
18. "Jean-Baptiste Rougier de la Bergerie (Yonne)," *Dictionnaire des législateurs 1791–92*, ed. Edna Hindie Lemay, 2 vols. (Fernay-Voltaire: Centre international d'étude du XVIIIe siècle, 2007), 2:662–664.
19. Rougier de la Bergerie, *Mémoire et observations sur les abus des défrichemens et la destruction des bois et forêts*, 53. Rougier de la Bergerie explicitly acknowledged the error of his ways on pages 69–70.
20. Rougier de la Bergerie, *Traité d'agriculture pratique, ou annuaire des cultivateurs du département de la Creuse et pays circonvoisins, avec des vues générales sur l'économie rurale* (Paris: n.p., 1795), 385. Emphasis in the original.
21. Ibid., 379.
22. Henri Grégoire, *Convention nationale: Troisième rapport sur le vandalisme fait au nom du Comité d'instruction publique* (Paris: Imprimerie Nationale, 1794). On Abbé Grégoire and the vandalism of the French Revolution, see Joseph L. Sax, "Heritage Preservation as Public Duty: The Abbé Grégoire and the Origins of an Idea," *Michigan Law Review* (April 1990): 1142–1169. Also see Astrid Swenson, *The Rise of Heritage: Preserving the Past in France, Germany and England, 1789–1914* (Cambridge: Cambridge University Press, 2013).
23. Rougier de la Bergerie, *Mémoire et observations sur les abus des défrichmens*.
24. "Jean-Baptiste Rougier de la Bergerie (Yonne)," 2:664.
25. Rougier de la Bergerie, *Mémoire et observations sur les abus des défrichemens*, 3.
26. Ibid., 4.
27. Ibid., 11–12.
28. Ibid., 23.
29. Ibid., 53.
30. Ibid., 61.
31. Ibid., 66.
32. Ibid., 69.
33. Ibid., 62.
34. Ibid., 69–75.

35. Rougier de la Bergerie, *Histoire de l'agriculture française, considérée dans ses rapports avec les lois, les cultes, les moeurs, et le commerce* (Paris: Mme. Huzard, 1815); Rougier de la Bergerie, *Les forêts de la France, leurs rapports avec les climats, la température et l'ordre des saisons; avec la prosperité de l'agriculture et de l'industrie* (Paris: A. Bertrand, 1817).
36. Rougier de la Bergerie, *Les forêts de la France*, 7.
37. Ibid., 117.
38. Ibid., 178.
39. Matteson, *Forests in Revolutionary France*, 156.
40. Ibid., 171.
41. *Notice des travaux scientifiques d'Alex. Moreau de Jonnès* (Paris: Imprimerie Bourgogne et Martinet, 1842).
42. See, for example, Moreau de Jonnès, *Des effets du climat des Antilles sur le système moteur* (Paris: de Mignaret, n.d.), and Moreau de Jonnès, *France avant ses premiers habitants et origines nationales de ses populations* (Paris: Guillaumin, 1856).
43. Moreau de Jonnès, *Premier mémoire*. Jonnès was also a correspondent at the Academy of Sciences in Paris.
44. Ibid., v.
45. Ibid., 62.
46. Ibid., 164.
47. Ibid., 181.
48. Ibid., 182.
49. See Richard Grove's survey of the question in the early modern period in "Historical Review of Early Institutional and Conservationist Responses to Fears of Artificially Induced Global Climate Change: The Deforestation-Dessication Discourse, 1500–1860," *Chemosphere* 20, no. 5 (September 1994): 1001–1013.
50. Buffon believed, however, that it was easier to raise temperatures than to decrease them; Buffon, "Des époques de la nature," in *Histoire naturelle, générale et particulière, Supplément*, vol. 5 (Paris: Imprimerie Royale, 1769–1770), 240.
51. Buffon, "Sur la conservation et le rétablissement des forêts" and "Sur la culture et l'exploitation des forêts," 2:249–290.
52. Glacken, *Traces on the Rhodian Shore*, 671.
53. Spary, *Utopia's Garden*, 254.
54. C. F. de Nieuport, "Analyse synoptique de mémoire qui précède," in Moreau de Jonnès, *Premier mémoire*, 205.
55. Ibid., 206.
56. Other than his *mémoire* on deforestation, Bosson, the pharmacist, has left little trace in the historical record, though he was listed as a member of the Société libre d'agriculture, des sciences, arts et belles-lettres du département de l'Eure. *Bulletin Trimestriel de la Société Académique de Boulogne-sur-Mer* 9 (Evreux: Ancelle Fils, 1838): 20.
57. M. Bosson, *Second mémoire en réponse à cette question* (Brussels: P. J. De Mat, 1825), 3–4.
58. Ibid., 15.

59. Jacques-Joseph Baudrillart, *Instruction sur la culture du bois, à l'usage des forestiers: Ouvrage traduit d'allemand de G. I. Hartig, maître des forêts de la principauté de Solms, et membre honoraire de la Société de physique de Berlin* (Paris: Levrault, 1805); Jacques-Joseph Baudrillart, *Nouveau manuel forestier, à l'usage des agens forestiers de tous grades, des arpenteurs, des gardes des bois impériaux, des préposés de la marine pour la recherche des bois propres aux constructions navales . . . traduit sur la 4e édition de l'ouvrage allemande de M. de Burgsdorf, grand maître des forêts de la Prusse . . . et adapté à notre système d'administration d'après l'ordre du gouvernement* (Paris: Arthus-Bertrand, 1808).
60. Matteson, *Forests in Revolutionary France*, 167.
61. Quoted in *Les eaux et forêts*, 477–478.
62. Quoted in ibid., 479.
63. Gérard Buttoud, *Les conservateurs des eaux et forêts sous la Troisième République (1870–1940): Matériaux biographique pour une sociologie historique de la haute administration forestière française* (Nancy: Ecole nationale du génie rural des eaux et forêts, 1981); Kalaora and Savoye, *Forêt et sociologie*, 13.
64. Jean-Claude Richez, "Science allemande et forestière française: L'expérience du rive gauche du Rhin," in *Révolution et l'espace forestière*, ed. Denis Woronoff (Paris: L'Harmattan, 1989), 232–246.
65. Kalaora and Savoye, *Forêt et sociologie*, 7.
66. *Annales Forestières* 1 (Paris, 1842): 6.
67. Rougier de la Bergerie, *Mémoire au roi et aux chambres législatives sur la destruction des bois et sur les graves conséquences qui peuvent en résulter* (Paris: G.-A. Dentu, 1831).
68. Ibid., 1.
69. Ibid., 1–2.
70. *Les eaux et forêts*, 488.
71. His son Alexander Edmond Becquerel became a professor of applied physics whose research centered on solar radiation and phosphorescence, while his grandson Antoine Henri Becquerel won the Nobel Prize in Physics in 1903.
72. Antoine-César Becquerel, *Des climats et de l'influence qu'exercent les sols boisés et non boisés* (Paris: Firmin Didot, 1853).
73. Alfred Maury, *Histoire des grandes forêts de la Gaule et de l'ancienne France; précédée de recherches sur l'histoire des forêts de l'Allemagne, de l'Angleterre et de l'Italie, et de considérations sur le caractère des forêts des diverse parties du globe* (Paris: A. Leleux, 1850).
74. Becquerel, *Des climats*, 293.
75. Ibid., 300.
76. Alexandre Surell, *Etude sur les torrents des Hautes-Alpes* (Paris: Carilion-Goeury & V. Dalmont, 1841). (See Chapter 3 for a discussion of Surell.) Becquerel, however, incorrectly identifies him as Alphonse Surel.
77. Becquerel, *Des climats*, 361.
78. Corbin, *Le miasme et la jonquille*, 1.
79. Ibid., 152.
80. Joseph-Jean-Nicholas Fuster, *Des maladies de la France dans leurs rapports avec les saisons, ou histoire médicale et météorologique de la France* (Paris: Dufart,

1840) and *Des changements dans le climat de la France: Histoire de ses révolutions météorologiques* (Paris: Capelle, 1845). His first work was awarded a prize of 3,000 francs by the Académie des sciences in Paris. Fuster was also the cofounder of *Revue Thérapeutique du Midi: Journal de Médecine, de Chirugie et de Pharmacie Pratique* and was its editor in 1850–1851.

81. Brown, *Forests and Moisture; or, The Effects of Forests on Humidity of Climate* (Edinburgh: Oliver and Boyd, 1877), 212. Brown cites Becquerel, among others.
82. *Revue des Eaux et Forêts* 1 (January 1862): 2.
83. Quoted in Kalaora and Savoye, *Forêt et sociologie*, 19.
84. Alfred Puton, *Code de la législation forestière* (Paris: J. Rothschild, 1883), 393–400.
85. John M. Merriman, "The Demoiselles of the Ariège, 1829–1831," in *1830 in France*, ed. John M. Merriman (New York: New Viewpoints, 1975); Peter Sahlins, *Forest Rites: The War of the Demoiselles in Nineteenth-Century France* (Cambridge, Mass.: Harvard University Press, 1994); Tamara L. Whited, *Forests and Peasant Politics in Modern France* (New Haven, Conn.: Yale University Press, 2000), 40–42.
86. Quoted in Bernard Kalaora and Antoine Savoye, *La forêt pacifiée: Les forestiers de l'Ecole de Le Play, experts des sociétés pastorales* (Paris: L'Harmattan, 1986), 31.
87. Quoted in ibid., 31–32.
88. Charles de Ribbe, *La Provence au point de vue des bois, des torrents et des inondations avant et après 1789* (Paris: Guillaumin, 1857).
89. Charles de Ribbe, *Le deboisement et le reboisement* (Paris: Charles Douniol, 1858); de Ribbe, *Des incendies de forêts dans la région des Maures et de l'Esterel (Provence)* (Paris: Librarie Agricole, 1865).
90. Zéphirin Jouyne, *Reboisement des montagnes: Reboisement, difficultés, causes des inondations et moyens de les prévenir* (Digne: Repos, 1850).
91. Zéphirin Jouyne, *Vues sur l'agriculture des Basses-Alpes et des départements méridionaux* (Marseille: A. Ricard, 1823).
92. Jouyne, *Reboisement des montagnes*, vi–vii.
93. *Les codes de la législation forestière contenant le code forestier, l'ordonnance réglementaire du 1er août 1827; le code du reboisement des montagnes, le code des dunes, le code de la chasse . . .* , 3rd ed. (Paris: La Revue des Eaux et Forêts, 1856).
94. Quoted in Whited, *Forests and Peasant Politics in Modern France*, 63.
95. Kalaora and Savoye, *La forêt pacifiée*, 59.
96. Ibid., 62–64.
97. Whited, *Forests and Peasant Politics in Modern France*, 88.
98. John Croumbie Brown, *Pine Plantations on the Sand-Wastes of France* (Edinburgh: Oliver and Boyd, 1878).
99. Nicolas-Théodore Brémontier, *Mémoire sur les dunes et particulièrement celles qui se trouvent entre Bayonne et la pointe de Grave à l'embouchure de la Gironde* (Paris: Imprimerie de la République, 1796).

100. Pierre-Charles Chassiron, *Rapport sur les différents mémoires de M. Brémontier* (Paris: Mme. Huzard, 1806); also, numerous articles appeared in the *Annales de Ponts et Chaussées* and the *Annales Forestières*.
101. Quoted in Brown, *Pine Plantations on the Sand-Wastes of France*, 5.
102. Ibid., 13. Arthur Mangin, *Le désert et le monde sauvage* (Tours: Alfred Mame, 1866).
103. Quoted in Brown, *Pine Plantations on the Sand-Wastes of France*, 13.
104. *Les eaux et forêts*, 565–566.

3. The Torrents of the Nineteenth Century

Epigraph: Charles Chauvelot, *Quelques mots sur les inondations de 1856* (Paris: Ledoyen, 1856), 4.

1. Anonymous, *Couronne poétique au sujet des inondations de 1840 contenant des vers de M. de Lamartine, de Mmes. Desbordes-Valmore, Clara Mollard et autres* (Paris: Maison; Lyon: Chambet, 1841), 3.
2. Léon Boitel, *Lyon inondée en 1840 et á diverses époques: Histoire de toutes les inondations qui ont affligé Lyon* (Lyon: L. Boitel, 1840).
3. Chauvelot, *Quelques mots sur les inondations de 1856*, 4.
4. Maurice Champion, *Les inondations en France depuis le VIe siècle jusqu'à nos jours,* 6 vols. (Paris: V. Dalmont [Dunod], 1858–1863).
5. This is a point made by Denis Coeur in his history of floods in Grenoble, *La plaine de Grenoble face aux inondations: Genèse d'une politique publique du XVIIe au XXe siècle* (Versailles: Quae, 2008), xiii.
6. Charles Walker, "Shaking the Unstable Empire: The Lima, Quito, and Arequipa Earthquakes, 1746, 1783 and 1797," in *Dreadful Visitations: Confronting Natural Catastrophe in the Age of the Enlightenment*, ed. Alessa Johns (New York: Routledge, 1999), 114. For some more recent reflections on natural disasters, see Christof Mauch and Christian Pfister, eds., *Natural Disasters, Cultural Responses: Case Studies toward a Global Environmental History* (Lanham, Md.: Lexington Books, 2009).
7. For a discussion of natural disasters in the early modern period, see Maurice Lever, *Canards sanglants: Naissance du fait divers* (Paris: Fayard, 1993), and Françoise Lavocat, ed., *Pestes, incendies, naufrages: Ecritures du désastre au dix-septième siècle* (Turnhout: Brepols, 2011).
8. Simon Schama, *The Embarrassment of Riches: An Interpretation of Dutch Culture in the Golden Age* (Berkeley: University of California Press, 1988), 15–50.
9. Maurice Champion, *Les inondations en France du VIe siècle à nos jours,* 6 vols. (repr., Paris: CEMAGREF, 2000), 1:xv. He was also the author of *La fin du monde et les comètes au point de vue historique et anecdotique* (Paris: A. Delahaye, 1859).
10. On the Little Ice Age, see Geoffrey Parker, *Global Crisis: War, Climate Change and Catastrophe in the Seventeenth Century* (New Haven, Conn.: Yale University Press, 2013), 1–25.

11. Emmanuel Le Roy Ladurie, *Histoire du climat depuis l'an mil* (Paris: Flammarion, 2009). For the lower Rhône during this period, see G. Pichard, "Les crues sur le Bas-Rhône de 1500 à nos jours: Pour une histoire hydro-climatique," *Méditerranée*, nos. 3–4 (1995): 105–116.
12. Shelby T. McCloy, "Flood Relief and Control in Eighteenth-Century France," *Journal of Modern History* 13, no. 1 (March 1941): 5.
13. Champion, *Les inondations en France*, 1:85; Charlotte Lacour-Veyranne, *Les colères de la Seine* (Paris: Paris-Musées, 1994), 25, 47.
14. McCloy, "Flood Relief and Control in Eighteenth-Century France," 6.
15. Auguste Pawlowski and Albert Radoux, *Les crues de la Seine (VI–XXe siècles): Causes, mécanisme, histoire, dangers, la lutte contre le fléau* (Paris: Berger-Levrault, 1910), 64–65; Philippe Buache, "Observations sur l'étendue et la hauteur de l'inondation du mois de décembre 1740," *Mémoires de l'Académie Royale des Sciences*, 7 January 1741, 335–337.
16. Hélène Noizet, Sandrine Robert, and Laurent Mirlou, "Cartographie des crues centennales à Paris (1740, 1910)," in *Zones humides et villes d'hier et aujourd'hui: Des premières cités aux fronts d'eau contemporaines*, ed. Corinne Beck et al. (Villeneuve d'Ascq: Presses Universitaire de Charles de Gaulle–Lille 3, 2011), 91–104; Pawloski and Radoux, *Les crues de la Seine*, 118.
17. McCloy, "Flood Relief and Control," 1–2.
18. Champion, *Les inondations en France*, 1:172; François-Jean Bralle, *Précis des faits et observations relatifs à l'inondation qui a eu lieu dans Paris en frimaire et nivôse de l'an X de la République française* (Paris: B. Pottier, 1803).
19. Champion, *Les inondations en France*, 4:95.
20. Ibid., 4:105.
21. A. Berger, *Inondations de 1846: Relation complète et officielle* (Paris: L. Maison, 1846).
22. Roger Dion, *Histoire des levées de la Loire* (Paris: Habouzit, 1961), 223.
23. Champion, *Les inondations en France*, 3:109.
24. Quoted in ibid., 3:114.
25. Anonymous, *Histoire de l'inondation de 1846, de ses causes et de ses ravages* (Paris: Maistrasse et Wiart, 1846), 74. Mlle. Rachel (1821–1858) was one of the most admired actresses before the rise of Sarah Bernhardt.
26. Denis Coeur, "Les inondations de mai–juin 1856 en France: Dommages et conséquences," *La Houille Blanche: Revue Internationale de l'Eau*, no. 2 (April 2007): 44.
27. Jacques Bethemont, "1856: De la gestion d'une catastrophe au bon usage d'une crise," *La Houille Blanche: Revue Internationale de l'Eau*, no. 1 (January 2007): 22–32; Rouillé-Courbe, *Inondations, départements d'Indre et Loire, 1846–1856* (Tours: Guilland Verger, 1858). Also see Ch. Stephan, *Récit des inondations en France pendant les mois de mai et juin 1856* (Lyon: F. Cajani, 1857); J.-B. Coulon and L. Auché, *Inondations de 1856 dans la vallée de la Loire* (Saumur: P. Gaudet, 1857); Octave Féré, *Les inondations de 1856* (Paris: H. Boisgard 1856); Anonymous, *Le fléau de Dieu, ou les inondations de 1856 par un catholique* (Paris: Vivès, 1856); Léon Cazeaux, *Les inondations de Tours en 1856* (Tours: De Placé 1856); Denis Coeur and Andelatif Djerboua, "La crue de 1856: Reconstitu-

tion et analyse d'un événement hydrologique de référence," *La Houille Blanche: Revue Internationale de l'Eau*, no. 2 (April 2007): 27–37; and E. Geneslay, *La Loire: Crues et embâcles* (Paris: Nouvelles Editions Latines, 1971).
28. Bethemont, "1856: De la gestion d'une catastrophe," 27.
29. Coeur, "Les inondations de mai–juin 1856," 44.
30. Ibid., 45–46.
31. Champion, *Les inondations en France*, 3:177–183; Charles Robin, *Inondations de 1856: Voyage de l'empereur* (Paris: Garnier frères, 1856).
32. Annie Mejean, "Utilisation politique d'une catastrophe: Le voyage de Napoleon III en Provence durant la grande crue de 1856," *Revue historique* 597 (January–March 1996): 133–152.
33. Robin, *Inondations de 1856*, 11.
34. Mejean, "Utilisation politique d'une catastrophe," 141; *Le Moniteur*, 2 June 1856.
35. Paul Allard, "La presse et les inondations dans la région du Bas-Rhône en 1840 et 1856," in *Récits et représentations des catastrophes depuis l'antiquité*, ed. René Favier and Anne-Marie Granet-Abisset (Grenoble: Publications de la MSH-Alpes, 2005), 73–92.
36. "Circulaire du ministre de l'agriculture, du commerce, et des travaux publics aux préfets au sujet du programme d'études à engager sur le régime des cours d'eau," 26 July 1856, A.N. F/14/7548.
37. *Le Moniteur*, 16 February 1857.
38. Report, 11 August 1857, A.N. F/14/7566. Responses to the circular and information on floods in the nineteenth century are filed in forty boxes in the Archives nationales, F/14/7546–F/14/7586.
39. Ministère de l'agriculture, du commerce et des travaux publics, *Documents statistiques sur les dépenses faites de 1814 à 1865 pour travaux extraordinaire des ponts et chaussées* (Paris: Imprimerie Impériale, 1866). Also see A.N. F/14/7552 for general information regarding floods between 1862 and 1869.
40. Ministère de l'agriculture, du commerce et des travaux publics, *Documents statistiques*, 3. The state spent a total of 27,701,179 francs on the 1856 flood, while the 1846 flood cost about half as much (14,108,550 francs).
41. A substantial literature on the relationship between torrents, floods, and deforestation began to be published following some of the worst floods, in 1840, 1846, 1856, and 1875. Berger, *Inondations de 1846*; François Vallès, *Etudes sur les inondations, leurs causes et leurs effets, les moyens à mettre en oeuvre pour combattre leurs inconvénients et profiter de leurs avantages* (Paris: V. Valmont, 1857); Claude-Antoine Rozet, *Moyens de forcer les torrents des montagnes de rendre à l'agriculture une partie du sol qu'ils ravagent, et d'empêcher les grandes inondations des fleuves et des principales rivières* (Paris: Maillet-Bachelier, 1856); de Ribbe, *La Provence au point de vue des bois des torrents*; E. de Chamberet, *Des inondations en France* (Paris: Mallet-Bachelier, 1856); Champion, *Les inondations en France*; Boitel, *Lyon inondé en 1840*; Léon Boitel, *Inondations du Rhône et de la Saône à diverses époques* (Lyon: Chez les principaux libraires, 1840); Armand Landrin, *Les inondations* (Paris: Hachette 1880). The flooding of the Garonne in 1875 left Toulouse and the area

surrounding the city devastated. It was estimated that over 3,000 people lost their lives. Brown, *Reboisement in France,* 329ff.

42. For biographical information and the employment history of both Fabre (1748–1834) and Surell (1813–1887), see A.N. F/14/2223/1 and A.N. F/14/2326/2, respectively.

43. Jean-Antoine Fabre, *Essai sur la théorie des torrens et des rivières, contenant les moyens les plus simple d'en arrêter les ravages* (Paris: Bidault, 1797); Glacken, *Traces on the Rhodian Shore,* 698–702.

44. Glacken, *Traces on the Rhodian Shore,* 698.

45. Quoted in Brown, *Reboisement in France,* 70–71. He further noted that Arthur Young had commented on the richness of the region in his travels through France on the eve of the French Revolution.

46. Surell, *Etude sur les torrents des Hautes-Alpes,* 2nd ed., vol. 1 (Paris: Dunod, 1870), viii. The first edition was published in 1841 in Paris by Carilion-Goeury & V. Dalmont.

47. Alexandre Surell, *Etude sur les torrents des Hautes-Alpes,* 2nd ed., vol. 2 (Paris: Dunod, 1872).

48. "Attached like a leper to the soil of its mountains, it gnaws away at its sides, and disgorges them in the plains [below] in the form of debris." Surell, *Etude sur les torrents* (Paris: Carilion-Goeury & V. Dalmont, 1841), 1:iv. Moreover, Surell argued that deforestation and the subsequent degradation of the soil led to out-migration and to the disappearance of village communities.

49. Surell, *Etude sur les torrents,* 2nd ed., 1:269.

50. Ibid., 1:272.

51. Pierre-Henri Dugied, *Projet de boisement des Basses-Alpes* (Paris: Imprimerie Royale, 1819).

52. Surell, *Etude sur les torrents,* 2nd ed., 1:166.

53. Ibid., 1:194.

54. Ibid., 1:284.

55. Alexandre Surell, *Etude sur les torrents des Hautes-Alpes* (repr., Nîmes: Lacour, 2002).

56. Letter from Vallès to the minister of public works, de Bourneville, 26 March 1857, A.N. F/14/7565. He also communicated his study's table of contents and noted that the study had received an honor from the Academy.

57. Vallès, *Etudes sur les inondations,* 419.

58. Ibid.

59. François Vallès, *Réponse aux critiques publiées dans les Annales Forestières contre l'ouvrage de M. Vallès sur les inondations* (Batignolles: de Hennuyer, 1858), 22–23.

60. A.N. F/14/7565.

61. François Vallès, *The Influence of Forests on Rainfall and Inundations,* trans. Charles J. Allen (Washington, D.C.: Government Printing Office, 1873).

62. Champion, *Les inondations en France,* 1:vii.

63. Ibid., 1:ix.

64. Champion, *Les inondations en France,* 4:6; "L'histoire ne laisse aucun doute à cet égard; ne prouve-t-elle pas que dans le temps ancien, alors que le sol, non

seulement montagneux, mais encore celui des plains, étaient couverts presque partout des forêts impénétrables, l'inondation existait comme aux époques modernes."
65. Paul Veyret, "Un centenaire: L'Etude sur les torrents des Hautes-Alpes de Surell," *Revue de Géographie Alpine* 31, no. 4 (1943): 513–524.
66. Surell, *Etude sur les torrents des Haute-Alpes,* 2nd ed., 1:13–14.
67. Allard, "Le rôle des ingénieurs des Ponts et Chaussées au XIXe siècle," 249–261.
68. For a detailed discussion of the implementation of this legislation, particularly in the departments of the Savoie and Ariège, see Whited, *Forests and Peasant Politics in Modern France.*
69. A.N. F/14/7552.
70. A.N. F/14/7552, F/14/7566, and F/14/7567.
71. Léopold Graffin, *Un inondé à ses concitoyens* (Paris: Librairie des Sciences Sociales, 1866), 14.
72. A. Bonabry, *Inondations, causes principales et préservatifs* (Cahors: Crayssac, 1875). He identified himself as a member of the Chambre des études littéraires, scientifiques, et artistiques du Lot, of the Société française d'hygiène, etc.
73. A. Bonabry, *Polémique entre l'administration des ponts et chaussées et l'auteur du mémoire: Inondations, causes principales et préservatifs* (Cahors: Chez l'auteur, 1880), 19–20.
74. Ibid., 29. Bonabry was not the first to accuse the state's engineers of faulty practices. Thirty years earlier, in 1837, Armand Duchatellier wrote, "We think that in this regard our engineers and our governments are on the wrong road." Duchatellier, *Des inondations et du régime des eaux en France: Devoirs du gouvernement envers le pays* (Nantes: Mellinet, 1847).
75. The study of how individuals and communities experienced and survived natural catastrophes such as floods remains a relatively undeveloped area of historical inquiry, though it is the subject of a recent ethnographic study of a flood in the Aude in 1999. See Julien Langumier, *Survivre à l'inondation: Pour un ethnologie de la catastrophe* (Lyon: ENS, 2008).
76. *Le clergé français pendant les inondations de 1840, traits de dévouement, de courage et de charité chrétienne suivi d'une couronne poétique avec des vers de M. Lamartine . . .* (Lyon: Chambert, 1841).
77. See Malcolm Daniel, "Edouard Baldus, artiste photographe," in *Edouard Baldus, photographe: Le guide de l'exposition,* ed. Françoise Heilbrun et al. (Paris: Réunion des Musées Nationaux, 1996), 17–97; and Françoise Heilbrun, "Edouard Baldus, photographe du patrimoine français et architectural," in ibid., 12–15.
78. The photographer Claude-Marie Ferrier was sent at the same time to the Loire valley to document the flood's ravages there. Daniel, "Edouard Baldus," 68–69.
79. Ernest Lacan, "Photographies historiques," *La Lumière,* 21 June 1856, 97. Also see Lacan, "Les inondations de 1856: Epreuves de M. Baldus," *La Lumière,* 9 August 1856, 125; and Lacan, *Esquisses photographiques* (Paris: Grassart, 1856), 184–190.
80. P.-C. Ordinaire, *L'inondation de 1840 sur le littoral de la Saône et du Rhône: Documents historiques* (Macon: Charpentier fils, 1840).

81. Auguste Jouhaud, *Les inondés de Lyon, mélodrame en trois actes* (Paris: L.-A. Gallert, 1840); Eugène Cranney, *L'inondation de Lyon, episode des désastres du Midi, en deux actes et trois tableaux* (Paris: G. Roux et O. Cassanet, 1841); Francis Cornu and Anicet Bourgeois, *Marie, ou l'inondation, drame en 5 actes et 8 tableaux* (Paris: Michel Lévy frères, 1847).
82. Anonymous, *Couronne poétique au sujet des inondations de 1840*.
83. C. L. Supernant, *Les inondations de la Loire, 18 octobre 1846* (Laôn: E. Fleury et A. Chervegny, 1847), 50.
84. Pawlowski and Radoux, *Les crues de la Seine*; Lacour-Veyranne, *Les colères de la Seine*; Gustave Bord, *Les inondations du bassin de la Seine (1658–1910)* (Paris: Chez l'auteur, 1910). The most recent comprehensive work in English on this subject is Jeffrey H. Jackson, *Paris under Water: How the City of Light Survived the Great Flood of 1910* (New York: Palgrave Macmillan, 2010).
85. The Zouaves were soldiers in an army corps that was formed in Algeria in 1830 and which initially consisted of Frenchmen and North Africans, most notably Berbers. They wore a distinctive uniform and were known to be particularly fierce and disciplined fighters. They played an especially important role in the Crimean War.
86. A second set of plaques marks the great Parisian floods of 1740 and 1910 close to the Bastille at 28, rue de Charenton at the Hospice des Quatre-Vingts.
87. Jackson, *Paris under Water*, 195.
88. Pascal Popelin, *Le jour où l'eau reviendra: 100 ans après la grande crue de 1910* (Paris: Gawsewitch, 2009).
89. Ibid., 87–95.
90. Ibid., 99–100.
91. Ibid., 97–98.
92. Ibid., 111–112.
93. Pawlowski and Radoux, *Les crues de la Seine*, 64.
94. Allard, "Le rôle des ingénieurs des Ponts et Chaussées au XIXe siècle dans des crises environmentales."
95. Andreï Makine, *Le testament français* (Paris: Mercure de France, 1995).
96. Sarah Smith, *The Knowledge of Water* (New York: Ballantine Books, 1996).
97. François Beaudoin, *Paris/Seine ville fluviale: Son histoire des origines à nos jours* (Paris: Editions de la Martinière, 1993), 15.

4. Environment and Landscape as Heritage

Epigraph: Quoted in Jean Lahor, *Une société à créer pour la protection des paysages français* (Paris: Alphonse Lemerre, 1901), 3.
1. Rauch, *Harmonie hydro-végétale*, 1:345–346.
2. For a discussion of the preservationist movement in comparative context, see Swenson, *The Rise of Heritage*.
3. Dominique Poulot, *Musée, nation, patrimoine, 1789–1815* (Paris: Gallimard, 1997); Pierre Nora, ed., *Les lieux de mémoire*, 7 vols. (Paris: Gallimard, 1984–1992).

4. Nabila Oulebsir, *Les usages du patrimoine: Monuments, musées et politique coloniale en Algérie (1830–1930)* (Paris: Editions de la MSH, 2004), 20.
5. Normand's summary of the society's project is quoted in Swenson, *The Rise of Heritage*, 98. Normand, "Société des amis des monuments parisiens: Constituée dans le but de veiller sur les monuments d'art et sur la physionomie monumentale de Paris," *Bulletin-Société Historique et Cercle Saint-Simon* 2 (1884): 306.
6. Swenson, *The Rise of Heritage*, 99.
7. Herman Lebovics, *Mona Lisa's Escort: André Malraux and the Reinvention of French Culture* (Ithaca, N.Y.: Cornell University Press, 1999).
8. Gustave Flaubert, *Sentimental Education*, trans. Robert Baldick (New York: Penguin, 1964), 323.
9. Ibid., 324.
10. Kalaora, *Le musée vert*, 108.
11. Jean-Claude Polton, *Tourisme et nature*, 157–158. For the development of tourism in Fontainebleau, see Bernard Kaloara, *Le musée vert*.
12. Green, *The Spectacle of Nature*, 65–66.
13. Daniel Mornet argued that the French aristocracy had been making these rural excursions as early as the 1760s in *Le sentiment de la nature en France de J.-J. Rousseau à Bernardin de Saint-Pierre* (Paris: Hachette, 1907), 45–63. For the development of tourism in France and Europe more generally, see Marc Boyer, *Histoire générale du tourisme du XVI au XXI siècle* (Paris: L'Harmattan, 2005); Alain Corbin, *L'avènement des loisirs, 1850–1960* (Paris: Aubier, 1995); Stephen Harp, *Au Naturel: Naturism, Nudism, and Tourism in Twentieth-Century France* (Baton Rouge: Louisiana State University Press, 2015); and, for a regional context, Patrick Young, *Enacting Brittany: Tourism and Culture in Provincial France, 1871–1939* (Burlington, Vt.: Ashgate, 2012).
14. Polton, *Tourisme et nature*, 133, 253.
15. Ibid., 114.
16. Charles Rémard, *Le guide de voyageur à Fontainebleau* (Fontainebleau: E. Durant, 1820); E. Jamin, *Quatre promenades dans la forêt de Fontainebleau, ou description physique et topographique de cette forêt royale* (Fontainebleau: H. Rabotin, 1837).
17. Polton, *Tourisme et nature*, 130. For a brief sketch of Denecourt's life, see Schama, *Landscape and Memory*, 546–560; Jean-Claude Polton, *Claude-François Denecourt (1788–1875): "L'amant de la forêt de Fountainebleau"* (Fountainebleau: Sentiers Bleus, 2011).
18. Claude-François Denecourt, *Guide du voyageur dans la forêt de Fontainebleau, ou choix de promenades les plus pittoresques* (Fontainebleau: Chez l'auteur, 1839) and *Guide voyageur dans le château de Fontainebleau, ou précis historique et descriptif de ce magnifique séjour de plaisance* (Fontainebleau: Chez l'auteur, 1840).
19. Charles Colinet (1839–1906) was junior to Denecourt by forty years. He began to accompany the older man on his walks and continued his work after his death. Some paths in the forest are still marked Denecourt-Colinet.

20. Green, *The Spectacle of Nature*, 173.
21. Ibid., 177.
22. Fernand Desnoyers, ed., *Hommage à C. F. Denecourt: Fontainebleau, paysages, légendes, souvenirs, fantaisies* (Paris: Hachette, 1855), 347–348.
23. Quoted in Françoise Cachin, "Le paysage du peinture," in *Les lieux de mémoire*, ed. Pierre Nora, 3 vols. in 7, vol. 1, *Nation*, pt. 1 (Paris: Seuil, 1984–1986), 476.
24. Quoted in Kalaora, *Le musée vert*, 165.
25. Cited in ibid.
26. Ibid., 132.
27. Desnoyers, *Hommage*. A dinner was organized in a Paris café in July 1855 at which the volume was presented to Denecourt. Green, *The Spectacle of Nature*, 213.
28. Desnoyers, *Hommage*, 1.
29. Kalaora, *Le musée vert*, 157–158. Emphasis in the original.
30. Périer bought Rousseau's *Effet d'hiver et de soleil couchant* for 2,000 francs, for example. Ibid., 109. Born, like Rousseau, in 1812, Paul Périer was both a wealthy shipowner and a banker in Paris in the 1830s. He became one of Rousseau's most ardent patrons. Greg M. Thomas, *Art and Ecology in Nineteenth-Century France: The Landscapes of Théodore Rousseau* (Princeton, N.J.: Princeton University Press, 2000.), 108.
31. The church depicted in the distance in *Angelus* is in Chailly-en-Bière, near Barbizon.
32. Greg Thomas, *Art and Ecology in Nineteenth-Century France*, 5.
33. Quoted in Lowenthal, *The Past Is a Foreign Country*, 114.
34. *L'Artiste: Journal de la Littérature et des Beaux Arts*, 2nd series, 3 (1839): 290.
35. Ibid.
36. Ibid., 292.
37. Ibid.
38. Greg Thomas, *Art and Ecology in Nineteenth-Century France*, 167.
39. Ibid., 47.
40. Ibid., 10.
41. Polton, *Tourisme et nature*, 118–119.
42. Emile Michel, *La forêt de Fontainebleau dans la nature, dans l'histoire, dans la littérature et dans l'art* (Paris: H. Laurens, 1909), 192.
43. Brown, *Pine Plantations on the Sand-Wastes of France*, 99.
44. Quoted in Greg Thomas, *Art and Ecology*, 214–215.
45. Ibid., 215.
46. Ibid., 217.
47. Anonymous, "La réserve de la forêt de Fontainebleau," *Revue des Eaux et Forêts* 16 (1877): 14.
48. Quoted in Brown, *Pine Plantations on the Sand-Wastes of France*, 98.
49. *Bulletin des Lois*, supplement to vol. 18, no. 764 (Paris, 1862): 577–578.
50. Greg Thomas, *Art and Ecology*, 178. Between 1831 and 1847, 5,000 of the forest's 17,000 hectares were to be planted with pines, and by 1859, 4,000 hectares were planted with pines that were under forty years old.

51. Philippe Fritsch, "Les séries artistiques dans la forêt de Fontainebleau: Genèse d'une perception," in *La forêt: Perceptions et représentations*, ed. Andrée Corvol, Paul Arnould, and Micheline Hotyat (Paris: L'Harmattan, 1997).
52. Jane Carruthers, *The Kruger National Park: A Social and Political History* (Pietermaritzburg: University of Natal Press, 1995), 5.
53. Lowenthal, *The Past Is a Foreign Country*, xxiv. Tom Griffiths makes a similar point in his masterful *Hunters and Collectors: The Antiquarian Imagination in Australia* (Cambridge: Cambridge University Press, 1996), which explores the evolution of European environmental sensibilities in Australia.
54. Donald Pisani, "Forests and Conservation, 1865–1890," in *American Forests: Nature, Culture, and Politics*, ed. Char Miller (Lawrence: University Press of Kansas, 1997), 26; William Cronon, "The Trouble with Wilderness, or Getting Back to the Wrong Nature," 76.
55. Dominique Lejeune, *Les "alpinistes" en France à la fin du XIXe et au début du XXe siècle (vers 1875–vers 1919): Etude d'histoire sociale, étude de mentalité* (Paris: CTHS, 1988), 45–46.
56. Ibid.
57. *Bulletin de la Société pour la Protection des Paysages de France*, nos. 2–3 (April–September 1902): 50.
58. Ibid.
59. Jean Lahor, *Une société à créer pour la protection des paysages français*, 3.
60. He praised Americans for being "utilitarian democrats" who should be honored for creating Yellowstone Park, taking it away "from beasts of prey, the industrialists and merchants, who were going to acquire and certainly ruin it." At the same time, he pointed out that "these same Americans" were degrading the "noble rocks of Niagara with pill advertisements or other commercial creations," just as the Swiss had been doing in selling chocolates. Ibid., 6.
61. Ibid., 8.
62. Ibid., 9.
63. Swenson, *The Rise of Heritage*, 111; Jean-Michel Leniaud, *Les archipels du passé: Le patrimoine et son histoire* (Paris: Fayard, 2002), 219.
64. On the concept of the *petite patrie* and the importance of locality in modern France, see Jean-François Chanet, *L'école républicaine et les petites patries* (Paris: Aubier, 1995); Stéphane Gerson, *Pride of Place: Local Memories and Political Culture in Nineteenth-Century France* (Ithaca, N.Y.: Cornell University Press, 2003); and Patrick Young and Philip Whalen, eds., *Place and Locality in Modern France* (London: Bloomsbury, 2014).
65. D. Trom, "Natur und nationale Identität: Der Streit um den Schutz der 'Natur' um die Jahrhundertwende in Deutschland und Frankreich," in *Nation und Emotion: Deutschland und Frankreich im Vergleich, 19. Und 20. Jahrhundert* (Göttingen: Vandenhoeck und Ruprecht, 1995), 147–167; Celia Applegate, *A Nation of Provincials: The German Idea of Heimat* (Berkeley: University of California Press, 1990); Thomas M. Lekan, *Imagining the Nation in Nature: Landscape Preservation and German Identity, 1885–1945* (Cambridge, Mass.: Harvard University Press, 2004).

66. Charles Beauquier, *Philosophie de la musique* (Paris: Baillière, 1865), 158.
67. Quoted in "Notre société à la Chambre des Députés," *Bulletin de la Société pour la Protection de Paysages de France,* nos. 2–3 (April–September 1902): 26.
68. Ibid., 27.
69. Quoted in *Bulletin de la Société pour la Protection des Paysages de la France,* no. 2, 15 April 1906, 1. Faure is an example of the way in which those associated with landscape protection found themselves in several different kinds of networks. He was a minister of public instruction and fine arts in the government of Aristide Briand in 1910 and 1911, as well as president of the Radical Party in 1903 and 1904. He had created a literary and artistic society in Paris in 1872, Le Cigale, for writers and artists from southern France, and he was a member of the Félibrige, a literary and cultural association dedicated to the promotion and preservation of the Occitan language and literature.
70. Fernand Cros-Mayrevieille, *De la protection des monuments historiques ou artistiques, des sites et des paysages: Evolution historique* (Paris: Larose, 1907), 6.
71. Ibid., 30.
72. On the environmental damage caused by the war, see Chris Pearson, *Mobilizing Nature: The Environmental History of War and Militarization* (Manchester, UK: Manchester University Press, 2012).
73. Pierre Leroux de la Roche, *La protection des sites et des paysages* (Paris: Presses Modernes, 1932). Indeed, Leroux de la Roche's law thesis was framed in these terms.
74. Ibid., 6.
75. Ibid., 8.
76. Henri Texier, *La protection des paysages et de la nature: Technique et philosophie de la conservation des beautés naturelles,* fascicule du *Bulletin de la Société pour la Protection des Paysages et de l'esthétique générale de la France,* no.4 (July 1937).
77. Leroux de la Roche, *La protection des sites et des paysages,* 6.
78. Ibid.
79. Raoul de Clermont, *Evolution et réglementation de la protection de la nature* (Paris: Sociéte d'éditions géographiques, maritimes et coloniales, 1932), 3. For the Heimatschutz movement, see Lekan, *Imagining the Nation in Nature.*

5. The Internationalization of Nature Protection

Epigraph: Quoted in P. Vayssière, "Réserves naturelles et parcs nationaux," in *Contribution à l'étude des réserves naturelles et des parcs nationaux,* ed. André Aubreville et al. (Paris: Paul Lechevalier, 1937), 1.

1. Dr. T. Graim, "La coopération internationale pour la protection de la nature," in *Deuxième Congrès international pour la protection de la nature (Paris, 20 juin–4 juillet 1931), procès verbaux, rapports et voeux, publié sous la direction de A. Gruvel,* ed. Charles Valois and Georges Petit (Paris: Société d'éditions géographiques, maritimes et coloniales, 1932), 335. Also see Mark Cioc, *The Game of Conservation: International Treaties to Protect the World's Migratory*

Animals (Athens: Ohio University Press, 2009), 14; and John M. MacKenzie, *The Empire of Nature: Conservation and British Imperialism* (Manchester, UK: Manchester University Press, 1988), 201ff.
2. Swenson, *The Rise of Heritage*, 3.
3. Convention for the Preservation of Wild Animals, Birds and Fish in Africa, 19 May 1900, in *Correspondence relating to the Preservation of Wild Animals in Africa* (London, 1906) (Parliamentary Papers, vol. 79, 25), no. 55, article 2, section 5; British Public Record Office (PRO) FO 881/7395 B: Protocols of the 3rd session, 27 April 1900.
4. Cioc, *The Game of Conservation*, 38–39.
5. *Premier Congrès international pour la protection des paysages (Paris, 17–20 octobre 1909)*, ed. Raoul de Clermont, Fernand Cros-Mayrevieille, and Louis de Nussac (Paris: Société pour la protection des paysages de France, 1910). The Musée social, which was founded in 1894, was a private foundation devoted to the study of political economy. The brainchild of Frédéric Le Play and Emile Cheysson, it had its headquarters at 5 rue Las Cases in Paris. See Janet R. Horne, *A Social Laboratory for Modern France: The Musée Social and the Rise of the Welfare State* (Durham, N.C.: Duke University Press, 2002), and Collette Chambelland, ed., *Le Musée social en son temps* (Paris: Editions de l'Ecole normale supérieure, 1998).
6. Clermont, Cros-Mayrevieille, and de Nussac, *Premier Congrès*, 10.
7. Ibid., 19.
8. William Mark Adams, *Against Extinction: The Story of Conservation* (London: Earthscan, 2004), 47.
9. Quoted in Chris Pearson, *Mobilizing Nature: The Environmental History of War and Militarization in Modern France* (Manchester, UK: Manchester University Press, 2008), 91. See Henry Malherbe, *The Flaming Sword of France: Sketches from an Observation Post of the French Artillery near Verdun*, trans. Lucy Menzies (London: J. M. Dent, 1918), 3.
10. Alan Kramer, *War Damage in Western Europe: Culture and Mass Killing in the First World War* (Oxford: Oxford University Press, 2007), 6–30. For a discussion of how soldiers perceived the landscapes of war and the environmental destruction around them, see Dorothee Brantz, "Environments of Death: Trench Warfare on the Western Front, 1914–18," in *War and the Environment: Military Destruction in the Modern Age*, ed. Charles E. Closmann (College Station: Texas A&M University, 2009), 68–86.
11. *Premier Congrès international pour la protection de la nature, faune et flore, sites et monuments naturels (Paris, 31 mai–2 juin 1923), rapports, voeux, réalisations, compte rendu*, ed. Raoul de Clermont, Albert Chappellier, Louis de Nussac, Fernand Le Cerf, and Charles Valois (Paris: Guillemot et de Lamothe, 1926).
12. Philippe Jaussaud and Edouard-Raoul Brygoo, *Du jardin au muséum en 516 biographies* (Paris: Muséum national de l'histoire naturelle, 2004), 369–370.
13. At the Congrès littéraire et artistique international held in Liège in 1906, Raoul de Clermont drafted a resolution proposing that necessary measures be taken for the creation of national parks destined to save animals, plants, and minerals from destruction. Yamina Larabi, Piotr Diaszkiewicz, and Patrick Blandin,

"Premier Congrès pour la protection de la nature, faune et flore, sites et monuments naturels: Hommage à Raoul de Clermont (1863–1942)," *Courrier de l'environnement de l'INRA,* no. 52 (2004): 117.

14. De Clermont et al., *Premier Congrès international pour la protection de la nature,* 268–269.
15. Ibid., 278–279.
16. Ibid., 245.
17. Chevalier received his doctorate in 1901 and undertook a long series of voyages to Africa, Indochina, and Brazil. He also assisted Albert Sarraut, who had been governor general of Indochina, in the reorganization of France's agricultural services in 1917. Jaussaud and Brygoo, *Du jardin au muséum,* 135–136.
18. De Clermont et al., *Premier Congrès international pour la protection de la nature,* 303.
19. Ibid., 31.
20. Ibid., 318.
21. Ibid., 319.
22. Ibid., 317.
23. Valois and Petit, *Deuxième Congrès international,* 14–15.
24. Ibid., 35.
25. Ibid.
26. Ibid., 3–4.
27. Ibid., 45.
28. Ibid.
29. Ibid., 52, 54.
30. Adams, *Against Extinction,* 91–92.
31. Ibid., 49.
32. Ibid., 92.
33. Cioc, *The Game of Conservation,* 1.
34. Quoted in Vayssière, "Réserves naturelles et parcs nationaux," 1.
35. Ibid., 2.
36. Quoted in G. Petit, "Protection de la nature et questions de définition," in Aubreville et al., *Contribution à l'étude des réserves naturelles,* 8. Petit had been on a research trip for the museum to Madagascar between 1920 and 1922. He obtained his doctorate in the natural sciences in 1925 and returned to Madagascar between 1925 and 1927 before being named as a delegate for the museum at the 1932 international conference in London. Jaussaud and Brygoo, *Du jardin au muséum,* 416.
37. Arnold Pictet, "Les équilibres naturels de vie et la protection de la nature: Contribution à l'étude scientifique des parcs nationaux et des réserves naturelles," *Mémoires de l'Académie royale de Belgique,* 2nd series, vol. 17 (Brussels: Palais des Académies, 1938).
38. Charles Valois, "Le parc national du Pelvoux," in Aubreville et al., *Contribution à l'étude des reserves naturelles,* 85.
39. It was this impulse that guided measures taken to reforest vast tracts of land in France from the 1860s to the 1880s. Tamara L. Whited, *Forests and Peasant Politics in Modern France.*

40. M. G. Tallon, "La réserve zoologique et botanique de Camargue," in Aubreville et al., *Contribution à l'étude des reserves naturelles*, 39–57; Mme. A. Feuillée-Billot, "La réserve des Sept-Iles," ibid., 59–64; Pierre Chouard, "La réserve naturelle de Neouvieille dans les Pyrenées centrales," ibid., 65–74; P. Marié, "Les réserves naturelles des Basses-Alpes," ibid., 75–83.
41. Selmi, "L'émergence de l'idée du parc national en France," 50.
42. Valois and Petit, *Deuxième Congrès international*, 3–4.
43. A. Joubert, "Constitution et choix de réserves naturelles: Réserves biologiques forestières," in Aubreville et al., *Contribution à l'étude des réserves naturelles*, 29.
44. P. de Peyerimhoff, "'Parcs nationaux' d'Algérie," in Aubreville et al., *Contribution à l'étude des réserves naturelles*, 127.
45. Osborne, *Nature, the Exotic, and the Science of French Colonialism*; Christophe Bonneuil, *Du jardin d'essais à la station expérimentale* (Paris: CIRAD, 1993); Yannick Mahrane, Frédéric Thomas, and Christophe Bonneuil, "Mise en valeur, préserver ou conserver? Génèse et déclin du préservationnisme dans l'empire colonial français (1870–1960)," in *Une protection de l'environnement à la française? (XIXe–XXE siècles)*, ed. Charles-François Mathis and Jean-François Mouhot (Seyssel: Champ Vallon, 2013), 62–80.
46. Osborne, *Nature, the Exotic, and the Science of French Colonialism*, 34–55.
47. Ibid., 53.
48. Selmi, "L'émergence de l'idée du parc national en France," 52.
49. Joubert, "Constitution et choix de réserves naturelles," 30.
50. Quoted in de Peyerimhoff, "Les 'parcs nationaux' d'Algérie," 128–129.
51. Ibid, 129.
52. Ibid., 129–131. The 7,225 hectares included about a thousand hectares in the southern territories bordering the Sahara at the summit of Djebel Mzi and Djebel Aïssa.
53. Ibid., 132.
54. Ibid., 138.
55. L. Lavauden, "Tunisie et les réserves naturelles," in Aubreville et al., *Contribution à l'étude des réserves naturelles*, 139.
56. "The destruction, to which Arabs are accustomed, but to which they don't, alas! have a monopoly, has been going on for centuries in this whole region." Ibid., 147.
57. L. Joleaud, "Réserves naturelles du Maroc," in Aubreville et al., *Contribution à l'étude des réserves naturelles*, 151–157.
58. See, for example, Carruthers, *The Kruger National Park*.
59. De Peyerimhoff, "Les 'parcs nationaux' d'Algérie," 132.
60. See Chapter 6. Also see Davis, *Resurrecting the Granary of Rome*; Diana K. Davis, "Desert 'Wastes' of the Maghreb: Desertification Narratives in French Colonial Environmental History of North Africa," *Cultural Geographies* 11 (2004): 359–387.
61. De Clermont et al., *Premier Congrès international pour la protection de la nature*, 318.
62. A. Aubreville, "La protection de la flore en Afrique occidentale française," in Aubreville et al., *Contribution à l'étude des réserves naturelles*, 223–225.

228   Notes to Pages 134–138

63. G. Petit, "Les 'réserves naturelles' de Madagascar," in Aubreville et al., *Contribution à l'étude des reserves naturelles*, 229.
64. Henri Perrier de la Bathie, "Les reserves naturelles de Madagascar," *La Terre et la Vie*, no. 7 (August 1931): 427–442.
65. Adel Selmi argues that while the foresters had the upper hand in French West Africa, the scientists were the masters in Madagascar. Selmi, "L'émergence de l'idée du parc national en France," 56.
66. De Peyerimhoff, "Les 'parcs nationaux' d'Algérie," 138.
67. De Peyerimhoff seems to recognize this irony in placing "national parks" in quotation marks in the title of his essay "Les 'parcs nationaux' d'Algérie."
68. De Clermont et al., *Premier Congrès international pour la protection de la nature*, 318–319.
69. Valois and Petit, *Deuxième Congrès international*, 45.
70. Eric T. Jennings, *Curing the Colonizers: Hydrotherapy, Climatology, and French Colonial Spas* (Durham, N.C.: Duke University Press, 2006); Jennings, *Imperial Heights: Dalat and the Making and Undoing of French Indochina* (Berkeley: University of California Press, 2011); Dr. [Paulin] Trolard, *Les eaux thermominérales de l'Algérie, rapport presenté au gouverneur général* (Mustapha: Imprimerie Algérienne, 1901). For British India, see Judith Kenny, "Climate, Race and Imperial Authority: The Symbolic Landscape of the British Hill Station in India," *Annals of the Association of American Geographers* 85 (1995): 694–714; and Dane Kennedy, *The Magic Mountains: Hill Stations and the British Raj* (Berkeley: University of California Press, 1996).
71. See Bernhard Gissibl's discussion of the impact of imperial environmental nationalism in this regard in "German Colonialism and the Beginning of International Wildlife Preservation in Africa," *GHI Bulletin Supplement* 3 (2006): 121–143.

6. Reforestation and the Anxieties of Empire in Colonial Algeria

Epigraph: Albert Camus, *Œuvres*, ed. Raphaël Enthoven (Paris: Gallimard, 2013), 1244.

1. The ways in which Europeans managed natural landscapes and resources in the building of overseas empires have become the focus of an abundant historical literature in recent years. See Davis, *Resurrecting the Granary of Rome*; David Arnold and Ramachandra Guha, eds., *Nature, Culture and Imperialism: Essays on the Environmental History of South Asia* (Delhi: Oxford University Press, 1996); Paul Carter, *The Road to Botany Bay: An Essay in Spatial History* (London: Faber and Faber, 1987); and David Arnold, *The Tropics and the Traveling Gaze: India, Landscape, and Science, 1800–1856* (Delhi: Permanent Black, 2005). William Beinart has also traced the origins of conservationism in South Africa from the eighteenth century on. Beinart, *The Rise of Conservation in South Africa: Settlers, Livestock, and the Environment, 1770–1950* (Oxford: Oxford University Press, 2003). For a discussion of indigenous responses, see, for example, Guha, *The Unquiet Woods*; Ajay Skaria, *Hybrid Histories: Forests, Frontiers, and Wildness in Western India* (Delhi: Oxford University

Press, 1999); James Beattie, *Health, Science, Art and Conservation in South Asia and Australasia* (London: Palgrave Macmillan, 2011). To a lesser extent, historians have also addressed indigenous responses to these European initiatives and perceptions.

2. For British policies regarding colonial forests, see, for example, Dane Kennedy, *The Magic Mountains: Hill Stations and the British Raj* (Berkeley: University of California Press, 1996); Ravi Rajan, "Imperial Environmentalism or Environmental Imperialism: European Forestry, Colonial Foresters and the Agendas of Forest Management in British India, 1800–1900," in *Nature and the Orient: The Environmental History of South and Southeast Asia,* ed. Richard Grove, Vinita Damodaran, and Satpal Sangwan (Delhi: Oxford University Press, 1998), 324–371; and Richard Tucker, "Non-timber Forest Products Policy in the Western Himalayas under British Rule," in ibid., 459–483. Initiatives in Algeria also differed from those undertaken in other parts of the French Empire. For Indochina, see Frédéric Thomas, *Histoire du régime et des services forestiers français en Indochine de 1862 à 1945* (Hanoi: Thé Giói, 1999) and "Ecologie et gestion forestière dans l'Indochine française," *Revue Française d'Outre Mer* 85, no. 139 (April–May 1998): 59–86.

3. This is a point made by Nicholas Thomas in *Colonialism's Culture: Anthropology, Travel, and Government* (Princeton, N.J.: Princeton University Press, 1994) and by Ann Laura Stoler in "Rethinking Colonial Categories: European Communities and the Boundaries of Rule," *Comparative Studies in Society and History* 31, no. 1 (1989): 134–161. Also see Eric T. Jennings's discussion of this issue in "From Indochine to Indochina: The Lang Bian/Dalat Palace Hotel and French Colonial Leisure, Power and Culture," *Journal of Asian Studies* 37, no. 1 (2003): 161–163. In her excellent study of narratives of environmental decline in North Africa, Diana Davis tends, in contrast, to see French environmental policy as fundamentally the same in Algeria and the protectorates of Morocco and Tunisia as well as being chiefly determined by a single project, which was to expropriate land for commodity production. Davis, *Resurrecting the Granary of Rome.*

4. For stimulating new reflections on the varieties of European settler colonialism, see Susan Pedersen and Caroline Elkins, eds., *Settler Colonialism in the Twentieth Century* (London: Routledge, 2005). For the French approach to the environment in other colonial contexts, see Jeffrey Kauffmann, "La Question des Raketa: Colonial Struggles with the Prickly Pear Cactus in Southern Madagascar, 1900–23," *Ethnohistory* 48 (2001): 87–123; and Gense Sodikof, "Forced Forest Labor Regimes in Colonial Madagascar, 1926–1936," *Ethnohistory* 52 (2005): 407–435.

5. Henri Marc and André Knoertzer, *Le code forestier algérien* (Paris: Soubiron, 1931).

6. Theodore S. Woolsey, *French Forests and Forestry: Tunisia, Algeria, Corsica* (New York: J. Wiley and Sons, 1917), 47; P. Boudy, *Economie forestière nord-africaine,* 4 vols., vol. 4, *Description forestière de l'Algérie et de la Tunisie* (Paris: Larose, 1955), 1. Also see Achille Fillias, *Géographie physique et politique de l'Algérie: Dictionnaire géographique et historique de toutes les localités* (Algiers:

Tissier, 1862); Fillias, *Notice sur les forêts de l'Algérie* (Algiers: de Cursach, 1878); Henri Lefebvre, *Les forêts de l'Algérie* (Algiers-Mustapha: Giralt, 1900); and Henri Marc, *Notes sur les forêts de l'Algérie* (Algiers: Adolphe Jourdan, 1916).

7. Charles-Robert Ageron, *Les algériens musulmans et la France (1871–1919)*, 2 vols. (Paris: Presses Universitaires de France, 1968), 1:103–106; David Prochaska, "Fire on the Mountain: Resisting Colonialism in Algeria," in *Banditry, Rebellion, and Social Protest in Africa*, ed. Donald Crummey (London: J. Currey, 1986), 230–235; Davis, *Resurrecting the Granary of Rome*, 28–32. Paul Marès remarked in a publication associated with the Universal Exhibition in Paris in 1878 that "the natives have still kept, under our domination . . . the disastrous custom of setting fires." Marès, *Histoire des progrès de l'agriculture en Algérie* (Algiers: J. Lavagne, 1878), 13.

8. For a history of fire and environmental practices in Algeria, see Stephen J. Pyne, *Vestal Fire: An Environmental History, Told through Fire, of Europe and Europe's Encounter with the World* (Seattle: University of Washington Press, 1997), 120–125.

9. Prochaska, "Fire on the Mountain," 235.

10. These fires generated an extensive literature on their probable cause during this period, most of which was published in Algeria. See M. Ch. de Chabannes (*concessionnaire*, Ouled-Djemma, cercle de Bougie), *Lettre sur les incendies périodiques des forêts en Algérie adressée à M. le baron G. Martineau des Chesnez* (Algiers, 1866); Gouvernement général de l'Algérie, *Mésures à prendre à l'occasion des incendies des forêts, rapport présenté à son excellence le gouverneur général de l'Algérie au nom de la commission de Conseil du gouvernement* (Algiers: Duclaux, 1866); J. Reynard, *Restauration des forêts et des paturages du sud de l'Algérie* (Algiers: Adolphe Jourdan, 1880); Département de Constantine, Conseil général, session d'octobre 1881, *Incendies des forêts du département de Constantine (août 1881), rapport de M. Treille* (Constantine: Braham, 1881); *Réponse des conseillers généraux indigènes au rapport de M. Treille sur les incendies* (Constantine, 1881); Paulin Trolard, *La cause des forêts de l'Algérie devant la réunion d'études algériennes* (Paris: 12, galerie d'Orléans, [1900]); René Rousseau, *Contribution à l'étude de la question forestière en Algérie* (Algiers: Minerva, 1931).

11. M. Rebattu, "Le régime forestier en Algérie," *Bulletin de la Réunion d'Etudes Algériennes* 2, nos. 3–4 (March–April 1900): 57.

12. Achille Fillias, *Histoire et progrès de l'agriculture en Algérie* (Algiers: J. Lavagne, 1878), 10. The Tell was a zone worked by sedentary farmers, whereas nomads inhabited the other two zones.

13. See Diana Davis's extended and thorough discussion of how this narrative came to be constructed in Algeria from the Arab conquest to the twentieth century in *Resurrecting the Granary of Rome*, especially chapters 3 and 4. For the place of this Roman heritage in the French imagination, see Patricia M. E. Lorcin, "Rome and France in Africa: Recovering Colonial Algeria's Latin Past," *French Historical Studies* 25, no. 2 (Spring 2002): 327. Nabila Oulebsir explores the

French initiatives to save the archeological vestiges of North Africa's Roman past as French *patrimoine* in *Les usages du patrimoine*.
14. See Davis, "Desert 'Wastes' of the Maghreb," 362. A number of historians have debunked the "granary of Rome" myth. See Swearingen, *Moroccan Mirages;* B. D. Shaw, "Climate, Environment and History: The Case of Roman North Africa," in *Climate and History,* ed. T. Wrigley, M. Ingram, and G. Farmer (Cambridge: Cambridge University Press, 1981), 379–403; and G. Barker, "A Tale of Two Deserts: Contrasting Desertification Histories on Rome's Desert Frontiers," *World Archeology* 33, no. 1 (2002): 488–507. Also see Diana K. Davis, "Potential Forests: Degradation Narratives, Science, and Environmental Policy in Protectorate Morocco, 1912–56," *Environmental History* 10, no. 2 (2005): 211–238.
15. Ibn Khaldun, *Les prolégomènes d'Ibn Khaldoun,* trans. W. M. de Slane, 2 vols. (Paris: Imprimerie Imperiale, 1863–1865), and *Histoire des Berbères,* trans. Baron de Slane, 4 vols. (Algiers: Imprimerie du Gouvernement, 1852–1856). Also see Yves Lacoste, *Ibn Khaldoun: The Birth of History and the Past of the Third World* (London: Verso, 1985).
16. Davis, "Desert 'Wastes' of the Maghreb," 364.
17. Ibid., 370. Some have suggested that massive deforestation occurred worldwide during the nineteenth century, which coincided with the expansion of European empires. Richard P. Tucker and J. F. Richards, eds., *Global Deforestation and the Nineteenth-Century World Economy* (Durham, N.C.: Duke University Press, 1983).
18. Woolsey, *French Forests and Forestry,* 50.
19. Quoted in Swearingen, *Moroccan Mirages,* 29. See André Fribourg, *L'Afrique latine—Maroc, Algérie, Tunisie* (Paris: Plon-Nourrit, 1922); José Germain and Stéphane Faye, *Le nouveau monde français: Maroc Algérie, Tunisie* (Paris: Plon-Nourrit, 1924); Stéphane Gsell, *Histoire ancienne de l'Afrique du nord,* vol. 8, *Jules César et l'Afrique: Fin des royaumes indigènes* (Paris: Hachette, 1928).
20. Prochaska, "Fire on the Mountain," 229–252.
21. Davis, *Resurrecting the Granary of Rome,* 166.
22. Becquerel, *Des climats et de l'influence qu'exercent,* iii. His son Alfred Becquerel drew on his father's work in publishing his *Traité élémentaire d'hygiène privée et publique* (Paris: Labé, 1851), which was in its sixth edition by 1877 and in its seventh in 1883, giving currency to these ideas. Antoine-César Becquerel's work was also read by George Perkins Marsh for his work *Man and Nature: or, Physical Geography as Modified by Human Action* (Cambridge, Mass.: Harvard University Press, 1965), which was first published in 1864.
23. See Ilhem Saida, *Mysticisme et désert: Thèse de doctorat en recherches sur l'imaginaire* (Manouba: Editions Sahar, 2006); Jean-Claude Vatin, "Désert construit et inventé, Sahara perdu ou retrouvée: Le jeu des imaginations," in *Le Maghreb dans l'imaginaire: La colonie, le désert, l'exil,* ed. Jean-Robert Henry et al. (Aix-en-Provence: Edisud, 1986), 107–127.
24. For a discussion of the impact of forests on moisture and climate during this period, see Caroline Ford, "Nature, Culture and Conservation in France and

Her Colonies," *Past and Present*, no. 183 (May 2004): 173–198. For the "theory of ruined landscapes" in the Mediterranean, see A. Grove and Rackham, *The Nature of Mediterranean Europe*.
25. Dr. [Paulin] Trolard, *Les forêts de l'Algérie et la colonisation: Mémoire presentée au ministre de l'agriculture* (Algiers: Imprimerie Casablanca, 1890), 28.
26. Alexis de Tocqueville took up the question in his "Second Report on Algeria," written in 1847. De Tocqueville, *Writings on Empire and Slavery*, ed. and trans. Jennifer Pitt (Baltimore: Johns Hopkins University Press, 2001), 176.
27. Eric T. Jennings, in *Curing the Colonizer*, has demonstrated that it was no accident that the French developed a network of colonial spas in the empire and that Vichy was a central metropolitan place to cure the colonial body exposed to the rigors of tropical climates. Also see M. Harrison, *Climates and Constitutions*. The relationship among climate, politics, and human nature was, of course, an old question, and one that Aristotle, Buffon, and Montesquieu addressed. Glacken, *Traces on the Rhodian Shore*.
28. Michael Osborne suggests that acclimation was "the essential science of colonization." Osborne, *Nature, the Exotic, and the Science of French Colonialism*, xiv.
29. Alfred Becquerel, *Traité élémentaire d'hygiène privée et publique*, 2nd ed. (Paris: Labé, 1854), 259.
30. Ibid., 259–261.
31. Ibid., 261.
32. Ibid., 262.
33. Ibid.
34. Ibid., 264.
35. Achille Fillias, *Etat actuel de l'Algérie: Géographie physique et politique de l'Algérie; Dictionnaire géographique et historique de toutes les localités* (Algiers: Tissier, 1862), 13.
36. Becquerel, *Traité élémentaire d'hygiène privée et publique*, 2nd ed., 265.
37. "Thomas Dodman, "Un pays pour la colonie: Mourir de nostalgie en Algérie française, 1830–1880," *Annales. Histoire, Sciences Sociales* 3 (2011): 743–784.
38. Dr. [Paulin] Trolard, *L'Institut Pasteur d'Alger: Sa fondation, sa réorganisation, mon expulsion* (Algiers: de Fontana frères, 1910). This work was published posthumously by his sons, who argued that Trolard's unjustified dismissal for allegedly distributing contaminated vaccines hastened his death.
39. Trolard was a prolific publicist and wrote, among other works, *La forêt, conseil aux indigènes* (Algiers: Imprimerie de l'Association Ouvrière P. Fontana et Cie, 1883), which was published in French and Arabic; *La question forestière en Algérie et le programme du reboisement du gouvernement général* (Algiers: Imprimerie Casablanca, 1885); *La question juive* (Blida: A. Mauguin, 1907); *Les incendies forestiers en Algérie* (Algiers: Publications de la Ligue du Reboisement de l'Algérie, 1892); *Le testament d'un assimilateur* (Algiers: J. Torrent, 1903); and *La question forestière algérienne devant le Sénat* (Algiers: Imprimerie Casablanca, 1893).
40. Anne Bergeret, "Discours et politiques forestières coloniales en Afrique et Madagascar," *Revue Française d'Outre Mer* 80, no. 298 (1993): 23–47.

41. Dr. [Paulin] Trolard, "Appel aux Algériens!," *Bulletin de la Ligue du Reboisement de l'Algérie*, no. 1 (15 January 1882): 2.
42. M. Reynaud, in *Bulletin de la Ligue du Reboisement de l'Algérie*, no. 5 (15 May 1882): 91–92.
43. Ibid.
44. Trolard, "Appel aux Algériens!," 5. Trolard had his critics. The head of the Société de climatologie in Algiers, O. MacCarthy, questioned his reading of Roman history, arguing that the Roman Empire did not disappear due to droughts but because of political revolutions that forced the Romans out. *Bulletin de la Ligue du Reboisement de l'Algérie,* no. 61 (15 December 1886): 1186. He argued that Trolard presented Algeria in a "fantastical and exaggerated light" (1182). MacCarthy, a Frenchman of Irish origin who immigrated to Algeria as the leader of 800 colonists in 1848, was a local savant and a formidable critic. Sanford H. Bederman, "Oscar MacCarthy, 1815–1894," in *Geographers: Biobibliographical Studies,* ed. T. W. Freeman, 26 vols. (London: Mansell, 1984), 8:57–60.
45. *Bulletin de la Ligue du Reboisement de l'Algérie*, no. 61 (15 December 1886): 1182.
46. The geographer Onésime Reclus, who coined the term *francophonie* in the 1880s, saw the Italians and Spanish of North Africa as natural allies in the conquest of the African continent in *Lachons l'Asie, prenons l'Afrique: Ou renaître? et comment durer?* (Paris: Librairie Universelle, 1904), but he curiously anticipated the future mixing of all races: "Humanity in the future will not be only blond or brown-haired. Whether one likes it or not, all peoples will be mixed." Reclus, *L'Atlantide, pays d'Atlas: Algérie, Maroc, Tunisie* (Paris: La Renaissance du Livre, 1918), 14. Reclus spent a considerable amount of time in North Africa and reflected on the problem of colonial expansion in much of his work.
47. Reclus, *Lachons l'Asie,* 73.
48. Quoted in Lorcin, *Imperial Identities: Stereotyping, Prejudice and Race in Colonial Algeria* (London: I. B. Tauris, 1995), 198. Bertrand, who first came to Algeria in 1891 to assume a post at the lycée of Algiers, visited the Roman ruins of Tipasa in 1895 and declared that he rediscovered ancestors who spoke his language and believed in his gods, so that he was no longer a "lost Rumi in an Islamic land" (200). *Rumi* was the term used by Arabs and Berbers to designate foreigners, especially Christians. It is derived from the Arabic *rum,* meaning land dominated by Rome. This designation survives among the native population of the Maghreb. In her study of collective memory in Tunisia, the anthropologist Jocelyne Dakhlia found that the people of the Jérid spoke of the Romans as the "ancient French" and explained that archeologists and tourists came to North Africa in search the traces of their ancestors. Dakhlia, *L'oubli de la cité: La mémoire collective à l'épreuve du lignage dans le jérid tunisien* (Paris: La Découverte, 1990), 56–57.
49. Lorcin, *Imperial Identities,* 200; Bertrand, "Le centenaire du cardinal Lavigerie," in *Devant Islam* (Paris: Plon-Nourrit, 1926), 83.
50. "Inhabited by indigenous populations hostile or quasi refractory to all European civilisation, Algeria will always manifest an ethnic heterogeneity which

will not be in accordance with the aspirations of France with regard to its grand African possession." M. Paoli, "La question des étrangers en Algérie," *Bulletin de la Réunion d'Etudes Algériennes,* nos. 2–3 (February–March 1906): 93. Trolard was skeptical about the new Latin race and preferred encouraging emigration from France, but the issue of climate was also all-important for this project. Dr. [Paulin] Trolard, *De la mentalité algérienne (à propos de la question des étrangers)* (Blida: A. Mauguin, 1905), 17.

51. Albert Billiard, "Le péril étranger," *Bulletin de la Réunion d'Etudes Algériennes,* nos. 8–9 (October–November 1905): 270–273.
52. *Bulletin de la Ligue du Reboisement de l'Algérie,* no. 8 (15 September 1882): 184.
53. J. Rochard, "Rapport sur le rapport de M. Jeannel relatif au deboisement, considéré comme cause de la dépopulation de la France," *Bulletin de la Ligue du Reboisement de l'Algérie,* no. 104 (15 January 1892): 1920.
54. Prochaska, "Fire on the Mountain," 229–252. Also see Henry Sivak, "Legal Geographies of Catastrophe: Forests, Fires, and Property in Colonial Algeria," *Geographical Review* 103, no. 4 (October 2013): 556–574.
55. Pyne, *Vestal Fire,* 120–125; A. Grove and Rackham, *The Nature of Mediterranean Europe,* chap. 13.
56. *Courrier de Bône,* 29 August 1878, 3.
57. Archives Nationales d'Outre Mer (hereafter ANOM), ALG GGA P/128, *Incendies en Algérie, années 1860, 1863 et 1865: Rapport de la commission d'enquête nommée par l'assemblée générale des concessionnaires de forêts de chênes-lièges* (Paris: A. Chaix, 1866), 29.
58. Ibid., 34.
59. Ibid., 30.
60. Ageron, *Les algériens musulmans et la France,* 1:268.
61. For a discussion of the development of the Kabyle myth, see ibid., 1:267–292, and Lorcin, *Imperial Identities,* 2–6. See de Tocqueville, *Writings on Empire and Slavery,* 171–172.
62. Fernand Braudel, *The Mediterranean in the Age of Philip II,* 2 vols., trans. Siân Reynolds (New York: Harper and Row, 1976), 1:95–96. Braudel based his observations on the work of Xavier de Planhol, a geographer and Islamologist who held a post at the Sorbonne. See Planhol, "Caractères généraux de la vie montagnarde dans le Proche-Orient et dans l'Afrique du Nord," *Annales de Géographie,* no. 384 (1962): 113–129; and Planhol, "Nomades et pasteurs," *Annales de l'Est* 1 (1961): 291–310 and 2 (1962): 295–318. Braudel taught for several years in lycées in Algeria as a very young man and began his thesis on the Mediterranean, which Lucien Febvre hoped would focus on "La Méditerranée des Barbaresques," but which was later to become *The Mediterranean in the Age of Philip II.* Braudel's experiences and interest in Algeria in his youth have hardly been explored. See Oulebsir, *Les usages du patrimoine,* 325.
63. Braudel, *The Mediterranean,* 96–97.
64. Ibid., 97.
65. J. Russell Smith, "The Desert's Edge," *Bulletin of the American Geographical Society* 47, no. 11 (1915): 813. This narrative—without the purple prose—persisted into the 1940s and 1950s in the North American academic commu-

nity. See, for example, A. N. Sherwin-White, "Geographical Factors in Roman Algeria," *Journal of Roman Studies* 34, pts. 1 and 2 (1944): 1–10; and Rhoads Murphey, "The Decline of North Africa since the Roman Occupation: Climatic or Human?," *Annals of the Association of American Geographers* 41, no. 2 (1951): 116–132.

66. J. Smith, "The Desert's Edge," 813.
67. Robert Randau, *Les algérianistes: Roman de la patrie algérienne,* 2nd ed. (Paris: E. Sansot, 1911), 310.
68. Hakim Bourfouka and Nicolas Krautberger, "Préserver la nature de l'Algérie française—L'alfa est-il colon comme les autres?," in Mathis and Mouhot, *Une protection de l'environnement à la française?,* 47. For recent assessments of colonial policy in the area of environmental disaster and the legal administration of forests, see Henry Sivak, "Law, Territory, and the Legal Geography of French Rule in Algeria: The Forestry Domain, 1830–1903" (PhD diss., University of California, Los Angeles, 2008), and Brock Cutler, "Evoking the State: Environmental Policy and Colonial Disaster in Algeria, 1840–1870" (PhD diss., University of California, Irvine, 2011).
69. Bourfouka and Krautberger, "Préserver la nature de l'Algérie française," 54–55. Mathieu was a specialist in botany, meteorology, and *restauration de terrains de montagne* in metropolitan France and had been associate director of the Ecole forestière de Nancy.
70. Ibid., 55.
71. Quoted in Bourfouka and Krautberger, "Préserver la nature de l'Algérie française," 58.
72. Ibid., 59.
73. *Bulletin de la Ligue du Reboisement de l'Algérie,* no. 10 (15 October 1882): 204.
74. Ibid. The Société d'acclimatation of Algeria gave Ollive a first class medal for his speech on reforestation. *Bulletin de la Société du Reboisement de l'Algérie,* no. 21 (15 September 1883): 424.
75. *Bulletin de la Ligue du Reboisement de l'Algérie,* nos. 49–50 (15 November 1886): 1176. Alexis de Tocqueville, who visited Algeria twice, voiced similar views as early as 1841. See "Travail sur l'Algérie," in *Sur l'Algérie* (Paris: Flammarion, 2003).
76. In a striking statement he declared, "Algeria will be colonized entirely, or it will not be. Algeria must be populated almost entirely with Frenchmen, or it will not be French." Trolard, *La colonisation et la question forestière* (Algiers: Imprimerie Casablanca, 1891), 15.
77. Ibid., 18, 19.
78. Ibid., 94.
79. *Bulletin de la Ligue du Reboisement de l'Algérie,* no. 104 (15 January 1892): 1916–1922.
80. Quoted in F. Thomas, *Histoire du régime et des services forestières en Indochine,* 23.
81. Ibid., 39.
82. *Bulletin de la Ligue du Reboisement de l'Algérie,* no. 60 (15 November 1886): 1172–1173.

83. Ageron, *Les algériens musulmans et la France*, 1:447–477.
84. Ibid., 1:451.
85. Trolard, *La question forestière algérienne devant le Sénat*, 57.
86. Ageron, *Les algériens musulmans et la France*, 1:456.
87. Letter, 11 January 1893, ANOM, ALG GGA P/89.
88. Letter, 13 June 1893, ANOM, ALG GGA P/89.
89. ANOM, ALG GGA P/89.
90. Letter, 2 September 1908, ANOM, ALG GGA P/91.
91. Letter, 26 February 1895, ANOM, ALG GGA, P/89.
92. Ibid. He also noted that one forest official himself kept thirty-five goats on forested land.
93. Ibid.
94. Ageron, *Les algériens musulmans et la France*, 1:489–490.
95. Ibid., 1:491.
96. Ibid., 1:493.
97. M. Le Moigne quoted in Rebattu, "Le régime forestier en Algérie," 59.
98. Woolsey, *French Forests and Forestry*, 50.
99. Ibid., 51–52.
100. *Bulletin de la Ligue du Reboisement de l'Algérie*, no. 6 (2nd series) (30 November 1905): 111.
101. 20 February 1903, ANOM, ALG, GGA 5/O/14. Protests over the project began in 1896, and the matter was not closed until 1911.
102. Letter, Subprefect of Oran to Prefect, 30 April 1904, and letter, Governor General to the Prefect of Oran, 2 July 1904, ANOM, ALG GGA, 5/O/14.
103. Letter, Governor General to the Prefect of Oran, 10 October 1906, ANOM, ALG GGA 5/O/14.
104. Petition, 15 October 1911, ANOM, ALG GGA 5/O/14.
105. Letter, Governor General to Directeur des Forêts and Prefect of Oran, ANOM, ALG, GGA 5/O/14.
106. Schama, *Landscape and Memory*, 18.
107. Davis, *Resurrecting the Granary of Rome*. William Cronon makes a similar point with respect the creation of national parks and wilderness areas in the United States. Cronon, "The Trouble with Wilderness; or, Getting Back to the Wrong Nature," 79.
108. P. de Peyerimhoff, "Les 'parcs nationaux' d'Algerie," in *Contribution à l'étude des réserves naturelles*, by A. Aubreville et al., 132.
109. Ibid.
110. For colonial Algeria's "national parks," see Gouvernement général de l'Algérie, Service des eaux et forêts, Commissariat général du Centenaire, *Les parcs nationaux en Algérie* (Algiers: Jules Carbonel, 1930).
111. John H. Elliott, "Introduction: Colonial Identity in the Atlantic World," in *Colonial Identity in the Atlantic World, 1500–1800*, ed. Nicholas Canny and Anthony Pagden (Princeton: Princeton University Press, 1987), 9–10. William Cronon makes a similar point and highlights the divergent perceptions of landscape among settlers in North America and Native Americans in the seventeenth century. Cronon, *Changes in the Land: Indians, Colonists and the Ecology of New England*, 1st rev. ed. (New York: Hill and Wang, 2003).

112. Ibid., xv.
113. Antsirabe, Madagascar's spa retreat, was admired for its "Frenchness," because of its physical resemblance to the Massif Central. Jennings, *Curing the Colonizer,* 141.
114. R. Grove, *Green Imperialism,* 481.
115. Ibid. I borrow the term "violence of environmentalism" from Ajay Skaria, who explores the conflicts between the British and the Dangis in western India. Skaria, *Hybrid Histories,* 192.
116. Fillias, *Etat actuel de l'Algèrie,* 10. He also contended that the climate of Algeria was analogous to that of the Midi in France (p. 1).
117. Dr. H. Agnély, *Le climat de l'Algérie* (Algiers: J.-B. Dubois, 1866), 22.
118. Willard Sunderland, *Taming the Wild Field: Colonization and Empire on the Russian Steppe* (Ithaca, N.Y.: Cornell University Press, 2004).

7. The Greening of Paris

Epigraph: Eugène Hénard, *Etudes sur l'architecture et les transformations de Paris et autres écrits sur l'architecture et l'urbanisme,* ed. Jean-Louis Cohen (Paris: Editions de la Villette, 2012), 95. This essay on parks and gardens in Paris and London was originally published in the form of pamphlets, which were bound together as Eugène Hénard, *Etudes sur les transformations de Paris* (Paris: Editions Motteroz, 1903–1909).

1. Quoted in Louis Chevalier, *Classes laborieuses, classes dangereuses à Paris pendant la première moitié du dix-neuvieme siècle* (1958; facsimile, Paris: Perrin, 2007), 255.
2. See, for example, René-Louis de Girardin, *De la compositions des paysages ou les moyens d'embellir la nature autour des habitations, en joignant l'agréable à l'utile* (Seyssel: Champ Vallon, 1992), which was first published in 1775, and J. Lalos, *De la composition des parcs et jardins pittoresques,* 5th ed. (Paris: L'auteur, 1832), which was first published in 1817.
3. Claire Frange, ed., *Le style Duchêne: Henri et Achille Duchêne, architectes paysagistes* (Neuilly: Editions du Labyrinthe, 1998).
4. Quoted in Monique Mosser, "Through the Lens: The Gardens of the Duchênes, between History and Creation," ibid., 172. See Arthur Mangin, *Les jardins: Histoire et description* (Tours: Mame, 1867), 323–324.
5. See Marcel Fouquier and Achille Duchêne, *Des divers styles de jardins: Modèles de grandes et petites résidences, sur l'art décoratif des jardins, jardins européens et jardins orientaux* (Paris: Emile Paul, 1914), and John Claudius Loudon, *Traité de la composition et de l'exécution des jardins d'ornement* (Paris: Encyclopédie portative, 1830).
6. Boitard also wrote a fictional natural history of Paris, *Paris avant les hommes, l'homme fossile etc.: L'histoire naturelle du globe terrestre illustre* (Paris: Passart, 1861), which recounted the story of an ape-like human living in the Paris region; it was published after his death in 1861, as were a host of other works.
7. Pierre Boitard, *Manuel complet de l'architecte des jardins, ou l'art de les composer et les décorer* (Paris: Roret, 1834), 29. Boitard was also the author of other books on gardening, which were popular judging by the number of

editions that were published during the nineteenth century. See Boitard, *Traité de la composition et de l'ornement des jardins,* 3rd ed. (Paris: Audot, 1825); Boitard, *L'art de composer et décorer les jardins,* 2 vols., 3rd ed. (Paris: Roret, 1847); and Victor Bréant and Pierre Boitard, *Manuel illustré du jardinier-fleuriste ou traité de la culture des fleurs et arbustes d'agrément* (Paris: Delarue, 1860). He was also the chief editor of the *Journal des Jardins,* which began to be published in 1828.

8. Pierre Boitard, *Le jardinier, des appartements et des petits jardins,* 3rd ed. (Paris: Audot, 1836).
9. Pierre Boitard, *La botanique des dames* (Paris: Audot, 1821).
10. Hippolyte Hostein, *Flore des dames, ou nouveau langage des fleurs, precédée d'un cours élémentaire du botanique* (Paris: B. Neuhaus, 1840).
11. Corbin, *The Foul and the Fragrant: Odor and the French Social Imagination* (Cambridge, Mass.: Harvard University Press, 1986), 193, and Auguste Debay, *Les parfums et les fleurs* (Paris: Dentu, 1861).
12. Quoted in Philip Knight, *Flower Poetics in Nineteenth-Century France* (Oxford: Clarendon Press, 1986), 1; Gabriel Viaud, *Les fleurs dans notre littérature contemporaine* (Poitiers: L'Horticulture Poitevine, 1896), 13. Viaud celebrated plant life in a number of works, including *L'arbre de vie* (Paris: E. Giguière, 1912), *Riche nature* (Paris: Arnat, n.d.), and *Baptême des fleurs* (Paris: Société française d'imprimerie, 1901).
13. The family business survives to this day and is located at 46, rue du Bac in the seventh arrondissement of Paris.
14. Louis Neumann, *L'art de construire et gouverner les serres,* 2nd ed. (Paris: Audot, 1846).
15. Bernard Marrey and Jean-Pierre Monnet, *La grande histoire des serres et de jardins d'hiver: France 1780–1900* (Paris: Graphite, 1984), 43.
16. Ibid., 101.
17. Ibid., 120–121.
18. Guy de Maupassant, *Bel-Ami,* 7th ed. (Paris: Havard, 1885).
19. Marrey and Mornet, *La grande histoire des serres,* 157, 183–186.
20. Fabienne Chevallier, *Le Paris moderne: Histoire des politiques d'hygiène, 1855–1898* (Rennes: Presses Universitaires de Renne, 2010).
21. He also authored a number of works on the new green spaces in the city. See Adolphe Alphand, *Arboretum et fleuriste de la ville de Paris* (Paris: Rothschild, 1875) and *Promenades de Paris* (Paris: Rothschild, 1868).
22. Pinkney, *Napoleon III and the Rebuilding of Paris,* 7–8.
23. For a discussion of the development of leisure gardens, see Sung-Young Park, "The Body and the Building: Architecture, Urbanism and Hygiene in Early Nineteenth-Century Paris" (PhD diss., Harvard University, 2014), 250–256. Also see Gilles-Antoine Langlois, *Folies, tivolis, et attractions: Les premiers parcs et loisirs parisiens* (Paris: Delegation à l'Action Artistique de la Ville de Paris, 1991), and Richard S. Hopkins, *Planning the Green Spaces in Nineteenth-Century Paris* (Baton Rouge: Louisiana State University Press, 2015).
24. Françoise Choay, "Pensées sur la ville, arts de la ville," in *Histoire de la France urbaine,* ed. Georges Duby, 5 vols., vol. 4, *La ville de l'âge industriel: Le cycle haussmannien* (Paris: Seuil, 1983), 170.

25. Ibid.
26. Ibid.
27. Roger-Henri Guerrand, *Les origines du logement social en France, 1850–1914* (Paris: Editions de la Villette, 2010), 147.
28. Horne, *A Social Laboratory for Modern France.*
29. The Société internationale d'art populaire et d'hygiène was created by Jean Lahor (Henri Cazalis), who played such an important role in the establishment of the SPPF, which indicates the extent to which the membership of various preservationist organizations overlapped during this period.
30. Marie Charvet, "La question des fortifications de Paris dans les années 1900: Esthètes, sportifs, réformateurs sociaux, élus locaux," *Genèses* 16 (June 1994): 23–44; Marie Charvet, *Les fortifications de Paris: De l'hygiènisme à l'urbanisme* (Rennes: Presses Universitaires de Rennes, 2005). Also see Georges Risler, *Les espaces libres dans les grandes villes et les cités-jardins* (Paris: Rousseau, 1910), and Robert de Sousa, *L'avenir de nos villes: Etudes pratiques d'esthétique urbaine* (Paris: Berger et Levrault, 1913).
31. Emile Crozet-Fourneyron, *Déclassement et mise en valeur des fortifications et des zones militaires (22 mars 1888)* (Paris: Quantin, n.d.).
32. Janet R. Horne, "Dans l'intérêt public: Espaces verts et visions de plantification urbaine au Musée social, 1907–1920," in *Cités-Jardins: Genèse et actualité d'une utopie*, ed. Ginette Baty-Tornikian (Paris: Editions Recherches/Ipraus, 2001), 75–76.
33. Eugène Hénard and Jules Siegfried, "Les espaces libres à Paris: Les fortifications remplacées par une ceinture des parcs," *Le Musée Social: Mémoires et Documents* 4 (1909): 73–92; Hénard, *Etudes sur les transformations de Paris* (Paris: Editions Motteroz, 1903–1909). He also discussed the question of parks and open spaces from a comparative perspective at the Seventh International Congress of Architects, which was held in London at the Royal Institute of British Architects in 1908. Hénard, "Planification des rues et des espaces ouverts," in *Etudes sur l'architecture et les transformations de Paris*, 283–299.
34. Jean-Paul Flamand, *Loger le peuple: Essai sur l'histoire du logement social* (Paris: La Découverte, 1989), 118; Peter M. Wolf, *Eugène Hénard and the Beginning of Urbanism in Paris, 1900–14* (The Hague: International Federation for Housing and Planning, 1968); Nicolas Lemas, *Eugène Hénard et le futur urbain: Quelle politique pour l'utopie?* (Paris: L'Harmattan, 2008).
35. Hénard, *Etudes sur l'architecture et les transformations de Paris*, 94.
36. Ibid., 105–106.
37. Ibid., 102.
38. "Les banlieues de Paris et la nouvelle ceinture verte," in Hénard, *Etudes sur l'architecture et les transformations de Paris*, 308. This essay was first published in *Der Städtebau* in 1910.
39. Eugène Hénard, *Etudes sur les transformations de Paris*, and Hénard, *Les espaces libres à Paris: Les fortifications remplacée par une ceinture des parcs* (Paris: A. Rousseau, 1909). Also see Wolf, *Eugène Hénard*; Anthony Sutcliffe, *The Autumn of Central Paris: The Defeat of Town Planning, 1850–1970* (Montreal: McGill University Press, 1971); and Kory Olson, "A New Paris? Eugène

Hénard's Vision of Paris's Future," *Contemporary French and Francophone Studies* 14, no. 4 (September 2010): 431–440.
40. Eugene Hénard, *Etudes sur les transformations de Paris et autres écrits sur l'urbanisme* (Paris: L'Equerre, 1982), 29.
41. Hénard, *Etudes sur l'architecture et les transformations de Paris*, 105.
42. Ibid., 108.
43. Hénard, "Les banlieues de Paris et la nouvelle ceinture verte," 309.
44. Ibid.
45. Ibid.
46. The Luxembourg Gardens, Jardin des Plantes, and Champ de Mars were open green spaces, and Hénard classified them as *parcs anciens*, but, unlike the parc Montsouris, they did not fit his description of the ideal park.
47. Quoted in Wolf, *Eugène Hénard*, 67.
48. Emile Pierret, *Vers la lumière et la beauté: Essai d'esthétique sociale* (Paris: Renaissance Française, 1909), 275–278.
49. Horne, "Dans l'intérêt publique," 77. A copy of the poster was reproduced in "La campagne éléctorale municipale de 1908," *Le Musée Social: Mémoires et documents* (July 1908): 198–199.
50. Quoted in Giovanna Osti, "La section d'hygiène urbaine et rural au Musée social," in *La banlieue oasis: Henri Sellier et les cités-jardins, 1900–1940*, ed. Katherine Burlen (Saint Denis: Presses Universitaires de Vincennes, 1987), 66.
51. Ibid.
52. Albert Thomas, "Espaces libres et fortifications," *Cahiers du Socialiste*, no. 4 (Paris, 1908): 17.
53. Quoted in Horne, *A Social Laboratory for Modern France*, 258.
54. Hénard's critique of Dausset's proposal was published as a response to M. P. Lafollye in *L'Architecture* on 11 December 1909. See Hénard, "Les espaces libres et les fortifications: Le projet Dauset et le projet du Musée social," in *Etudes sur l'architecture et les transformations de Paris*, 300–304.
55. Anna Hours and Jean-Pierre Piechaud, *Penser la metropole parisienne: Plaidoyer pour un projet citoyen et postcarbone* (Paris: L'Harmattan, 2010), 34; Flamand, *Loger le peuple*, 179–180.
56. One of the most damning assessments was put forward by Norma Evenson: "What many had anticipated as a well planned residential district, embodying abundant greenery, and reflecting enlightened design concepts, had evolved into a dense wall of mediocrity encircling the city." This assessment, however, is belied by a stroll in this area. Norma Evenson, *Paris: A Century of Change, 1878–1978* (New Haven, Conn.: Yale University Press, 1981), 278.
57. "Ceinture rose" referred to the red brick with which many of the buildings were constructed.
58. Flamand, *Loger le peuple*, 215.
59. Georges Risler, "Les espaces libres dans les grandes villes et cité-jardins," *Musée Social: Mémoires et Documents* (1910): 355–404; Risler, *Les espaces libres dans les grandes villes et les cités-jardins*.
60. Roger Quilliot and Roger-Henri Guerrand, *Cent ans d'habitation social: Une utopie réaliste* (Paris: Albin Michel, 1989), 94.

61. The text that launched the movement was Ebenezer Howard's 1898 *Garden Cities of Tomorrow*. See Howard, *Garden Cities of Tomorrow* (Cambridge, Mass.: MIT Press, 1965). On Howard, see Robert Beevers, *The Garden City Utopia: A Critical Biography of Ebenezer Howard* (New York: St. Martin's Press, 1988), and Stephen Chambers, "The Garden and the City: Dispositifs architecturaux et progrès social dans le modèle urbain d'Ebenezer Howard," in Baty-Tornikian, *Cités-Jardins,* 13–25.

62. Kermit C. Parsons and David Schuyler, eds., *From Garden City to Green City: The Legacy of Ebenezer Howard* (Baltimore: Johns Hopkins University Press, 2002).

63. Susanna Magri, "Le Musée social, Georges Benoit-Lévy et les cités-jardins, 1900–1909," in Baty-Tornikian, *Cités-Jardins,* 84–85. Benoit-Lévy also went to the United States to study American garden cities with a grant from the Musée social and published *Les cités-jardins d'Amérique* (Paris: Henri Jouve, 1905).

64. Magri, "Le Musée social," 85.

65. Georges Benoit-Lévy, *La cité-jardin* (Paris: Henri Jouve, 1904), 7–8.

66. Georges Benoit-Lévy, *La cité-jardin*, vol. 3, *Art et coopération dans les cités-jardins* (Paris: Editions des Cités-Jardins, 1911), 165.

67. Anthony Sutcliffe, "Le contexte urbanistique de l'oeuvre d'Henri Sellier: La transcription du modèle anglais de la cité-jardin," in Burlen, *La banlieue oasis,* 76.

68. Eugène Hénard, "Planification des rues et des espaces ouvertes," in Hénard, *Etudes sur l'architecture et les transformations de Paris,* 295. He gave this presentation at the Seventh International Congress of Architects in London.

69. Ibid.

70. Ibid., 296.

71. Ibid.

72. Sutcliffe, "Le contexte urbanistique de l'oeuvre d'Henri Sellier," 76.

73. Flamand, *Loger le peuple,* 112.

74. Marie-Jeanne Dumont, "La Fondation Rothschild et les premières habitations à bon marché de Paris, 1900–1925," unpublished research report, Ministère de l'urbanisme et du logement, Direction de l'architecture, Paris, 1984, 36.

75. "The Rothschilds' Artizans' Dwellings in Paris, Designed by Augustin Rey, Described by H. Frantz," *The Studio: An Illustrated Magazine of Fine and Applied Art,* no. 156 (March 1906): 115–116.

76. Eugène Hénard, "Les banlieues de Paris et la nouvelle ceinture verte," in *Etudes sur l'architecture et les transformations de Paris,* 306.

77. The urban population stood at 2,722,731 in 1910, whereas the suburban population was 747,500. Ibid., 307.

78. Quilliot and Guerrand, *Cent ans d'habitat social,* 86.

79. It was not considered to be a suburb in 1910 administratively, though many western communes were so in reality. Eugène Hénard wrote that many western communes were "incontestably linked to Paris," even though they were a part of the department of Seine-et-Oise. Hénard, "Les banlieues de Paris et la nouvelle ceinture verte," 307.

80. Henri Sellier, *La crise du logement* (Paris: OPHBM, 1921).

81. Quillot and Guerrand, *Cent ans d'habitat social*, 84.
82. Benoît Pouvreau, Marc Couronné, Marie-Françoise Laborde, and Guillaume Gaudry, *Les cités-jardins de la banlieue du nord-est parisien* (Paris: Editions Le Moniteur, 2007), 39–41.
83. The design of the garden city was, however, changed after one part of it was acquired by the Compagnie des chemins de fer du Nord in 1911. Ibid., 42–43.
84. For La Cité de la Muette, whose architects, Marcel Lods and Eugène Beaudoin, looked more toward the *grands ensembles* characterizing social housing in the post–World War II period, see Robert Brian Weddle, "Urbanism, Housing and Technology in Inter-war France: The Case of the Cité de la Muette" (PhD diss., Cornell University, 1998), and Alise Hansen, "A Lieu d'Histoire, à Lieu de Mémoire, and à Lieu de Vie: The Multidirectional Potential of the Cité de la Muette," *French Historical Studies* 37, no. 1 (Winter 2014): 119–120.
85. Georges Risler, *Better Housing for Workers in France* (Paris: Centre d'informations documentaires, 1937), 22.
86. Amina Sellali, "La cité-jardin de Suresnes: L'architecture au service d'une politique urbaine d'avant-garde," in Baty-Tornikian, *Cités-Jardins*, 122.
87. Jean-Pierre Gaudin, "The French Garden City," in *The Garden City: Past, Present and Future*, ed. Stephen V. Ward, vol. 1 (London: Chapman and Hall, 1992), 67.
88. Gwendolyn Wright, *The Politics of Design in French Colonial Urbanism* (Chicago: University of Chicago Press, 1991), 53; Tyler Stovall, "From Red Belt to Black Belt: Race, Class and Urban Marginality in Twentieth-Century Paris," *L'Esprit Créateur* 41, no. 3 (2001): 9–23.
89. Quoted in Giovanna Osti, "La section d'hygiène urbaine et rurale du musée social," 66.
90. On Lahor, see Stéphanie Pallini Strohm, "Jean Lahor: De l'art pour le peuple à l'art populaire," in *L'art social en France de la Révolution à la grande guerre*, ed. Neil McWilliam, Catherine Méneux, and Julie Ramos (Rennes: Presses Universitaires de Rennes, 2014), 263–280.
91. Roger Marx, *L'art social* (Paris: Charpentier, 1913), 5.
92. Ibid.

Conclusion

Epigraph: Lucien Febvre, *La terre et l'évolution humaine* (Paris: La Renaissance du Livre, 1922), 439.

1. Louis Mangin, "Introduction," *La terre et la Vie: Revue d'Histoire Naturelle* 1 (1931): 3.
2. The early years of the *trente glorieuses*, the 1940s and 1950s, also witnessed some important environmental initiatives, including the creation of the International Union for the Conservation of Nature, which came out of a meeting of scientists and conservationists at Fontainebleau in 1948. Roger Heim, the director of the Museum of Natural History, published *Destruction et protection de la nature* in 1952, and Jacques Cousteau brought ocean environments

to a broad public in his film *The Silent World*, which was shown at the Cannes Film Festival in 1956, and in his subsequent work.
3. There has been some debate about the existence of "environmental history" before its formal institutionalization in France—environmental history *avant la lettre*—and about whether the *Annales* school played a significant role in shaping the field. For some recent assessments of this question, see Fabien Locher and Grégory Quénet, "L'histoire environnementale: Origines, enjeux et perspectives d'un nouveau chantier," *Revue d'Histoire Moderne et Contemporaine* 56, no. 4 (2009): 7–38; Verena Winiwarter et al., "Environmental History in Europe from 1994 to 2004: Enthusiasm and Consolidation," *Environment and History* 10, no. 4 (November 2004): 501–530; and Kalaora and Vlassopoulos, *Pour une sociologie de l'environnement*, 1–54. A more recent discussion of this question, which has also been evaluated in terms of European environmental history more generally, can be found in Grégory Quénet, *Qu'est ce que l'histoire environnementale?* (Seyssel: Champ Vallon, 2014). Also see Caroline Ford, "Nature's Fortunes: New Directions in the Writing of European Environmental History," *Journal of Modern History* 79, no. 1 (March 2007): 112–133.
4. Jean Viard, "Protestante, la nature?," in *Protection de la nature: Histoire et idéologie*, ed. A. Cadoret (Paris: L'Harmattan, 1985), 161–173; Michael Bess, Marc Cioc, and James Sievert, "Environmental History Writing in Southern Europe," *Environmental History* 5, no. 4 (October 2000): 545–556. For an alternative perspective, see James Sievert, *The Origins of Nature Conservation in Italy* (Bern: Peter Lang, 2000). For a discussion of evaluations of France as an "ungreen" nation, see Michael Bess, "Greening the Mainstream: Paradoxes of Antistatism and Anticonsumerism in the French Environmental Movement," *Environmental History* 5, no. 1 (January 2000): 6–26.
5. Mark Stoll, "Les influences religieuses sur le mouvement écologiste français," in *Une protection de l'environnement à la française? (XIXe–XXe siècles)*, ed. Charles-François Mathis and Jean-François Mouhot (Seyssel: Champ Vallon, 2013), 326.
6. Gabrielle Hecht, *The Radiance of France: Nuclear Power and National Identity after World War II* (Cambridge, Mass.: MIT Press, 1998).
7. Michael Bess, *The Light-Green Society: Ecology and Technological Modernity in France, 1960–2000* (Chicago: University of Chicago Press, 2003).
8. For a discussion of the term, see Patrick Matagne, "L'homme et l'environnement," in *Les sources de l'histoire de l'environnement*, vol. 2, *Le XIXe siècle*, ed. Andrée Corvol (Paris: L'Harmattan, 1999), 71–83.
9. Andrée Corvol, "Avertissement," in *Nature, environnement et paysage: L'héritage du XVIIIe siècle, guide de recherche archivistique et bibliographique*, ed. Andrée Corvol and Isabelle Richefort (Paris: L'Harmattan, 1995), v. Also see R. Delort, "Pour une histoire de l'environnement," in *Pour une histoire de l'environnement*, ed. Corinne Beck and Robert Delort (Paris: CNRS, 1993), 5–8.
10. "However, the term 'environment' has become so loaded with modern biological and ecological implications that its use risks creating a false understanding

of the particular purposes that theories of climate served for eighteenth-century writers." Spary, *Utopia's Garden*, 151.
11. Quoted in Bess, *The Light-Green Society*, 87.
12. Ibid., 57.
13. Anonymous, "La réserve de la forêt de Fontainebleau," *Revue des Eaux et Forêts* 16 (1876): 14.
14. Caroline Ford, "Imperial Preservation and Landscape Reclamation: National Parks and Natural Reserves in French Colonial Africa," in *Civilizing Nature: National Parks in Global Perspective*, ed. Bernhard Gissibl et al. (New York: Berghahn Books, 2012), 69–83; Yannick Mahrane, Frédéric Thomas, and Christophe Bonneuil, "Mettre en valeur, préserver ou conserver? Genèse et déclin du préservationnisme dans l'empire colonial français," in Mathis and Mouhot, *Une protection de l'environnement à la française*, 62–80.
15. Philippe Collomb and France Guérin Pace, *Les français et l'environnement: L'enquête "populations-espaces de vie-environnement"* (Paris: Presses Universitaires de France, 1998), 27.
16. William Cronon, "The Trouble with Wilderness: or, Getting Back to the Wrong Nature," in Cronon, *Uncommon Ground*, 89. He cites the tropical rain forest as an icon of the unfallen sacred wilderness, "yet protecting the rain forest in the eyes of First World environmentalists all too often means protecting it from the people who live there" (82).
17. Michael Bess, for example, uses contemporary green activism as a yardstick to measure Geoffroy Saint-Hilaire's environmental credentials: "Nevertheless, the words 'protection of nature' in the organization's name should not mislead us; for the mentality of Geoffroy Saint-Hilaire and his successors was (not surprisingly) rather far removed from a contemporary green activist." Bess, *The Light-Green Society*, 65.
18. Pierre Claude Reynard, "Public Order and Privilege: Eighteenth-Century Roots of Environmental Regulation," *Technology and Culture* 43, no. 1 (January 2002): 1.
19. Geneviève Massard-Guilbaud, "La régulation des nuisances industrielles urbaines (1808–1940)," *Vingtième Siècle* 64 (1999): 53–65; Massard-Guilbaud, *Histoire de la pollution industrielle en France, 1789–1914* (Paris: Editions de l'Ecole des hautes études en sciences sociales, 2010).
20. Chaptal is more frequently considered in terms of his efforts to promote French industrialization. Jeff Horn and Margaret C. Jacob, "Jean-Antoine Chaptal and the Cultural Roots of French Industrialization," *Technology and Culture* 39, no. 4 (October 1998): 671–698.
21. Maurice Agulhon, "Le sang des bêtes: Le problème de la protection des animaux en France au XIXe siècle," in *Histoire vagabonde* (Paris: Gallimard, 1988), 243–282.
22. Hénard, *Etudes sur l'architecture et les tranformations de Paris*, 98.
23. Theodore Salisbury Woolsey, *Studies in French Forestry* (London: Wiley, 1920), 142.
24. Bess, *The Light-Green Society*, 60.
25. Ibid., 61.

26. Julian Wright, however, presents a more nuanced view of Brun in *The Regionalist Movement in France, 1890–1914: Jean-Charles Brun and French Political Thought* (Oxford: Oxford University Press, 2003).
27. Swenson, *The Rise of Heritage*, 112.
28. They include Vanoise National Park (1963), Port-Cros National Park (1963), Pyrenees National Park (1967), Cévennes National Park (1970), Ecrins National Park (1973), and Mercantour National Park (1979). Selmi, "L'émergence de l'idée du parc national en France," 43–58.
29. Christophe Bonneuil, *Des savants pour l'empire: La structuration des recherches scientifiques coloniales au temps de la "mise en valeur" des colonies françaises* (Paris: Orstom, 1991).
30. Quoted in Mahrane, Thomas, and Bonneuil, "Mettre en valeur," 64.
31. G. Petit, "Protection de la nature et questions de 'définitions,'" in Aubreville et al., *Contribution à l'étude des réserves naturelles et des parcs nationaux*, 9.

Bibliography

Archival Sources

Archives Nationales (Paris)

ARCHIVES—AGRICULTURE

F/10/1722—Plantations nouvelles-dunes
F/10/2296—Inondations de 1907, 1909–1910

ARCHIVES DES TRAVAUX PUBLIQUES

F/14/2223/1—Personnel (Fabre)
F/14/2308—Personnel (Rauch)
F/14/2326—Personnel (Surell)
F/14/7546–7586—Inondations, 1808–1889
F/14/14667—Dommages causés par les inondations, 1867
F/14/14723–14733—Annonces des crues, 1853–1936
F/14/16575–16596—Travaux de défense contre les inondations

ARCHIVES DU MUSEUM D'HISTOIRE NATURELLE

AJ/15/847–848—Jardins et serres, an II–1923

Archives Nationales d'Outre Mer (Aix-en-Provence)

ALGERIA

ALG GGA F/80/971–990—Forêts, Chasse, Pêche
ALG GGA 5/O/14—Correspondance

ALG GGA P/59—Forêts, reboisement
ALG GGA P/60—Forêts, organisation des services, 1850–1905
ALG GGA P/61–82, 89–90—Forêts, incendies
ALG GGA P/89–91—Forêts, contentieux
ALG GGA P/128–129—Forêts, incendies
ALG GGA P/131—Forêts, organisation, 1884–1886
ALG GGA P/140—Forêts, incendies, 1930–1931
ALG GGA P/147–148—Forêts, contentieux
ALG GGA 1/I/181—Administration des musulmans, forêts

Periodicals

Annales Européennes, 1821–1827
Au delà des Mers: Revue mensuelle, Organe du Groupe Colonial et Cynégétique du Touring Club de France, 1932
Bulletin de la Ligue du Reboisement de l'Algérie, 1882–1915
Bulletin de la Société Nationale d'Acclimatation de France, 1882–1938
Bulletin de la Société pour la Protection des Paysages de France, 1902–1939
Journal of the Society for the Preservation of the Fauna of the Empire, 1904–1913, 1921–1940
Revue des Eaux et Forêts, 1862–1930
La Terre et la Vie: Revue d'Histoire Naturelle, 1931–1940
Touring Club de France—Revue Mensuelle, 1891–1919

Primary Sources

Ageron, Charles-Robert. *Les algériens musulmans et la France (1871–1919)*. 2 vols. Paris: Presses Universitaires de France, 1968.

Agnely, Dr. H. *Le climat de l'Algérie*. Algiers: J.-B. Dubois, 1866.

Alphand, Alphonse. *Arboretum et fleuriste de la ville de Paris*. Paris: Rothschild, 1875.

———. *Promenades de Paris*. Paris: Rothschild, 1868.

American Committee for International Wildlife Protection. Special publication. *African Game Protection* 1, no. 3. Cambridge, Mass.: American Committee for International Wildlife Protection, 1933.

———. Special publication. *The London Convention for the Protection of African Fauna and Flora*, no. 6. Cambridge, Mass.: American Committee for International Wildlife Protection, 1935.

Anonymous. *Couronne poétique au sujet des inondations de 1840 contenant des vers de M. de Lamartine, de Mmes. Desbordes-Valmore, Clara Mollard et autres*. Paris: Maison; Lyon: Chambet, 1841.

———. *Des inondations, de leurs causes et de leurs remèdes par un habitant du Val de la Loire*. Orléans: Alphonse Gatineau, 1866.

———. *Le fléau de Dieu, ou les inondations de 1856 par un catholique*. Paris: Vivès, 1856.

———. *Histoire de l'inondation de 1846, de ses causes et de ses ravages*. Paris: Maistrasse et Wiart, 1846.

———. *Inondations de 1856 pendant les mois de mai et juin 1856*. Lyon: Cajani, 1856.

———. *Inondations du Midi: Récits complets des désastres épouvantables*. . . . Paris: Le Bailly, 1875.

Aubreville, André. *La forêt coloniale: Les forêts de l'Afrique occidentale française*. Vol. 9 of *Annales de l'Académie des sciences coloniales*. Paris: Editions Geographiques maritimes et coloniales, 1938.

Aubreville, André, et al. *Contribution à l'etude des réserves naturelles et des parcs nationaux*. Paris: Paul Lechevalier, 1937.

Babinet, M. *De la pluie et des inondations*. Paris: Firmin Didot, 1866.

Banchereau, Jules. *Les forêts et les inondations*. Orléans: Auguste Gout, 1911.

Baranger, René. *Etude de la Camargue d'après le manuscrit de M. Poulle, ingénieur des Ponts et Chaussées de la ville d'Arles datant de 1835*. Clichy: Chez l'auteur, 1985.

Battistini, Eugène François Louis. *Les forêts de chêne-liège de l'Algérie*. Algiers: Heintz, 1937.

Baudrillart, Jacques-Joseph. *Traité général des eaux et forêts, chasses et pêches: Recueil chronologique des réglements forestiers*. 2 vols. Paris: Huzard, 1921.

Becquerel, Alfred. *Traité élémentaire d'hygiène privée et publique*. 2nd ed. Paris: Labé, 1854.

———. *Traité élémentaire d'hygiène privée et publique*. 3rd ed. Paris: P. Asselin, 1864.

Becquerel, Antoine-César. *Des climats et de l'influence qu'exercent les sols boisés et non boisés*. Paris: Firmin Didot, 1853.

Benoit-Lévy, Georges. *La cité-jardin*. Paris: Henri Jouve, 1904.

———. *La cité-jardin*. Vol. 3, *Art et coopération dans les cités-jardins*. Paris: Editions des Cités-Jardins, 1911.

Berger, A. *Inondations de 1846: Relation complète et officielle*. Paris: L. Maison, 1846.

Boitard, Pierre. *L'art de composer et décorer les jardins*. 2 vols. 3rd ed. Paris: Roret, 1847.

———. *La botanique des dames*. Paris: Audot, 1821.

———. *Le jardinier, des appartements et des petits jardins*. 3rd ed. Paris: Audot, 1836.

———. *Manuel complet de l'architecte des jardins, ou l'art de les composer et de les décorer*. Paris: Roret, 1834.

———. *Traité de la composition et de l'ornement des jardins*. 3rd ed. Paris: Audot, 1825.

Boitel, Léon. *Inondations du Rhône et de la Saône à diverses époques*. Lyon: Chez les principaux libraires, 1840.

———. *Lyon inondé en 1840 et à diverses époques: Histoire de toutes les inondations qui ont affligé Lyon*. Lyon: L. Boitel, 1840.

Bonabry, A. *Inondations, causes pricipales et préservatifs*. Cahors: Crayssac, 1875.

———. *Polémique entre l'administration des ponts et chaussées et l'auteur du mémoire: Inondations, causes principales et préservatifs*. Cahors: Chez l'auteur, 1880.

Bord, Gustave. *Les inondations du bassin de la Seine (1658–1910)*. Paris: Chez l'auteur, 1910.

Bosson, M. *Second mémoire en réponse à cette question*. Brussels: P. J. De Mat, 1825.

Boudy, P. *Economie forestière nord-africaine*. 4 vols. Vol. 4, *Description forestière de l'Algérie et de la Tunisie*. Paris: Larose, 1955.

Bralle, François-Jean. *Précis des faits et observations relatifs à l'inondation qui a eu lieu dans Paris en frimaire et nivôse de l'an X de la République française*. Paris: B. Pottier, 1803.

Bréant, Victor, and Pierre Boitard. *Manuel illustré du jardinier-fleuriste, ou traité de la culture des fleurs et arbustes d'agrément*. Paris: Delarue, 1860.

Brémontier, Nicolas-Théodore. *Mémoire sur les dunes et particulièrement celles qui se trouvent entre Bayonne et la pointe de Grave à l'embouchure de la Gironde*. Paris: Imprimerie de la République, 1796.

Brown, John Croumbie. *Forests and Moisture; or, The Effects of Forests on Humidity of Climate*. Edinburgh: Oliver and Boyd, 1877.

———. *The French Forest Ordinance of 1669; with Historical Sketch of Previous Treatment of Forests in France*. Edinburgh: Oliver and Boyd, 1883.

———. *Pine Plantations on the Sand-Wastes of France*. Edinburgh: Oliver and Boyd, 1878.

———. *Reboisement in France: or, Records of the Replanting of the Alps, the Cevennes, and the Pyrenees with Trees, Herbage and Bush, with a View to Arresting and Preventing the Destructive Consequences and Effects of Torrents*. London: Henry S. King, 1876.

Buache, Philippe. "Observations sur l'étendue et la hauteur de l'inondation du mois de décembre 1740." *Mémoires de l'Académie Royale des Sciences*, 7 January 1741, 335–337.

Buffon, Georges-Louis Leclerc de. "Sur la conservation et le rétablissement des forêts." In *Supplément à l'histoire naturelle*, 7 vols., 2:249–271. Paris: Imprimerie Royale, 1775.

———. "Sur la culture et l'exploitation des forêts." In *Supplément à l'histoire naturelle*, 7 vols., 2:271–290. Paris: Imprimerie Royale, 1775.

Bulard, Charles. *Sécheresse et inondations: Avant de reboiser protégeons nos forêts contre les incendies*. Algiers: P. Fontana, 1882.

Cazeaux, Léon. *Les inondations de Tours en 1856*. Tours: De Placé, 1856.

Chamberet, E. de. *Des inondations en France*. Paris: Mallet-Bachelier, 1856.

Chambet, Charles Joseph. *Les inondations de Lyon du Rhône et de la Saône en 1856*. Paris: Ballay et Conchon, 1856.

Champion, Maurice. *Les inondations du Rhône et de la Loire*. Paris: Panckouke, 1856.

———. *Les inondations en France depuis le VIe siècle jusqu'à nos jours*. 6 vols. Paris: V. Dalmont (Dunod), 1858–1863.

Chassiron, Pierre-Charles. *Rapport sur les différents mémoires de M. Brémontier*. Paris: Mme. Huzard, 1806.

Chauvelet, Charles. *Quelques mots sur les inondations de 1856*. Paris: Ledoyen, 1856.

Clermont, Raoul de. *Evolution et réglementation de la protection de la nature*. Paris: Société d'éditions géographiques, maritimes, et coloniales, 1932.

Commission française d'études des calamités. *Première Conférence international pour la protection contre les calamités naturelles*, Paris, 13–17 septembre 1937. Paris: Secrétariat de la commission, 1938.

Cornu, Francis, and Anicet Bourgeois. *Marie, ou l'inondation, drame en 5 actes et 8 tableaux*. Paris: Michel Levy frères, 1847.

Coulon, J.-B., and L. Auché. *Inondations de 1856 dans la vallée de la Loire*. Saumur: P. Gaudet, 1857.

Cranney, Eugène. *L'inondation de Lyon, épisode des désastres du Midi, en deux actes et trois tableaux*. Paris: G. Roux et O. Cassanet, 1841.

Cros-Mayrevieille, Fernand. *De la protection des monuments historiques ou artistiques, des sites et des paysages: Evolution historique*. Paris: Larose, 1907.

Crozet-Fourneyron, Emile. *Déclassement et mise en valeur des fortifications et des zones militaires (22 mars 1888)*. Paris: Quantin, n.d.

Dalmon, H. *Un parc national en forêt de Fontainebleau*. Roanne: Souchier, 1914.

Daubrée, Lucien. *Statistique et atlas des forêts de France*. Paris: Imprimerie Nationale, 1912.

De Girardin, René-Louis. *De la compositions des paysages, ou les moyens d'embellir la nature autour des habitations, en joignant l'agréable à l'utile*. Seyssel: Champ Vallon, 1992. (Originally published in 1775)

Delachénaye, B. *Abécédaire de flore, ou langage des fleurs*. Paris: Didot, 1811.

De Laforest, Hippolyte. In *Souvenirs poétiques du Bourbonnais: Les inondations, octobre 1846*. Moulins: M. Place, 1846.

De Laprade, Victor. *Histoire du sentiment de la nature; Prolégomènes*. Paris: Didier, 1882.

De la Roche, Pierre Leroux. *La protection des paysages*. Paris: Presses Modernes, 1932.

De la Tour, Mme. Charlotte. *Le langage des fleurs*. 12th ed. Paris: Garnier, 1876.

Denecourt, Claude-François. *Ah! Si l'empéreur le savait!* Paris: Simon Raçon, 1860.

———. *Guide du voyageur dans la forêt de Fontainebleau, ou choix de promenades les plus pittoresques*. Fontainebleau: Chez l'auteur, 1839.

———. *Guide voyageur dans le château de Fontainebleau, ou précis historique et descriptif de ce magnifique séjour de plaisance*. Fontainebleau: Chez l'auteur, 1840.

De Ribbe, Charles. *Le deboisement et le reboisement*. Paris: Charles Douniol, 1858.

———. *La Provence au point de vue des bois, des torrents et des inondations avant et après 1789*. Paris: Guillaumin, 1857.

Desnoyers, Fernand., ed. *Hommage à C. F. Denecourt: Fontainebleau, paysages, légendes, souvenirs, fantaisies*. Paris: Hachette, 1855.

Deuxième Congrès international pour la protection de la nature (Paris, 30 juin–4 juillet 1931). Paris: Société d'editions géographiques, maritimes et coloniales, 1932.

Diderot, Denis. "Climat." In *Encyclopédie ou dictionnaire raisonné des sciences, des arts et des métiers par une société de gens to lettres*, 3:533–536. Geneva: Cramer, 1772.

———. "Forêt." In *Encyclopédie ou dictionnaire raisonné des sciences, des arts et des métiers par une société de gens to lettres*, 7:129–132. Paris: Le Breton, 1757.

Dion, Roger. *Essai sur la formation du paysage rural français*. Tours: Arrault, 1934.

Dralet, M. *Traité du régime forestier ou analyse méthodique et raisoné*. Paris: Bertrand, 1812.

Duchatellier, Armand. *Des inondations et du régime des eaux en France: Devoirs du gouvernement envers le pays*. Nantes: Mellinet, 1847.

Dugied, Pierre Henri. *Projet de boisement des Basses-Alpes*. Paris: Imprimerie Royale, 1819.

Duhamel du Monceau, Henri-Louis. *Des semis et plantations des arbres et de leur culture*. Paris: Guerin et Delatour, 1760.

Dureau de la Malle, Adolphe. *Réfutation de l'ouvrage du docteur Fuster "Sur les changements dans le climat de France, histoire de ses révolutions météorologiques."* Paris: Bachelier, 1846.

Fabre, Jean-Antoine. *Essai sur la théorie des torrens et des rivières, contenant les moyens les plus simple d'en arrêter les ravages*. Paris: Bidault, 1797.

Faure, Gabriel. *Paysages littéraires*. Paris: Charpentier, 1918.

Féré, Octave. *Les inondations de 1856*. Paris: H. Boisgard, 1856.

Fouquier, Marcel, and Achille Duchêne. *Des divers styles de jardins: Modèles de grandes et petites résidences, sur l'art décoratif des jardins, jardins européens et jardins orientaux*. Paris: Emile Paul, 1914.

François, Georges. *L'Afrique occidentale française*. Paris: Larose, 1907.

Frantz, H. "The Rothschilds' Artizans' Dwellings in Paris, Designed by Augustin Rey, Described by H. Frantz." *The Studio: An Illustrated Magazine of Fine and Applied Art*, no. 156 (March 1906): 115–116.

Fribourg, André. *L'Afrique latine—Maroc, Algérie, Tunisie*. Paris: Plon-Nourrit, 1922.

Fuster, Joseph-Jean-Nicolas. *Des changements dans le climat de la France: Histoire de ses révolutions météorologiques*. Paris: Capelle, 1845.

———. *Des maladies de la France dans leurs rapports avec les saisons, ou histoire médicale et météorologique de la France*. Paris: Dufart, 1840.

Gallouédec, Louis. *La Loire: Etude de fleuve*. Paris: Hachette, 1910.

Germain, José, and Stéphane Faye. *Le nouveau monde français: Maroc, Algérie, Tunisie*. Paris: Plon-Nourrit, 1924.

Gouvernement général de l'Algérie, Service des eaux et forêts, Commissariat général du Centenaire. *Les parcs nationaux en Algérie*. Algiers: Jules Carbonel, 1930.

Graffin, Léopold. *Un inondé à ses concitoyens*. Paris: Librairie des Sciences Sociales, 1866.

Grandidier, A., and G. Grandidier. *Histoire physique, naturelle et politique*. Vol. 4, *Ethnographie de Madagascar*. Paris: Hachette, 1938.

Gravius, Georges. *Les incendies de forêts en Algérie: Leurs causes vraies et leurs remèdes*. Constantine: Louis Marle, 1866.

Gsell, Stéphane. *Histoire ancienne de l'Afrique du nord*. Vol. 8, *Jules César et l'Afrique: Fin des royaumes indigènes*. Paris: Hachette, 1928.

Guichard, Jules. *Extrait du Journal officiel du 3 mars 1891, Discours de M. Jules Guichard, senateur de l'Yonne, séance du 2 mars 1891, discussion sur la situation de l'Algérie*. Paris: Imprimerie des journaux officiels, 1891.

Guyot, Charles. *L'enseignement forestier en France: L'Ecole de Nancy*. Nancy: Crepin Leblond, 1898.

Heim, Roger. *Destruction et protection de la nature*. Paris: Armand Colin, 1952.

Hénard, Eugène. *Les espaces libres à Paris: Les fortifications remplacée par une ceinture des parcs*. Paris: A. Rousseau, 1909.

———. *Etudes sur l'architecture et les transformations de Paris et autres écrits sur l'architecture et l'urbanisme*. Edited by Jean-Louis Cohen. Paris: Editions de la Villette, 2012.

———. *Etudes sur les transformations de Paris*. Paris: Editions Motteroz, 1903–1909.

Hénard, Eugène, and Jules Siegfried. "Les espaces libres à Paris: Les fortifications remplacées par une ceinture des parcs." *Le Musée Social: Mémoires et documents* 4 (1909): 73–92.

Hostein, Hippolyte. *Flore des dames, ou nouveau langage des fleurs, précédée d'un cours élementaire de botanique*. Paris: B. Neuhaus, 1840.

Huffel, Gustave. *Histoire des forêts françaises*. Nancy: Ecole forestière, 1925.

Humbert, Henri. *La disparition des forêts à Madagascar*. Paris: Gaston Doin, 1927.

Hun, L. *Des inondations et des moyens de les prévenir*. Paris: Annales Forestières, 1856.

Incendies en Algérie, années 1860, 1863 et 1865: Rapport de la commission d'enquête nommée par l'assemblée générale des concessionaires de forêts de chènes-lièges. Paris: A. Chaix, 1866.

Jacquot, Andre. *La forêt: Son rôle et les sociétés*. Paris: Berger-Levrault, 1911.

Jamin, E. *Quatre promenades dans la forêt de Fontainebleau, ou description physique et topographique de cette forêt royale*. Fontainebleau: H. Rabotin, 1837.

Jouhaud, Auguste. *Les inondés de Lyon, mélodrame en trois actes*. Paris: L.-A. Gallert, 1840.

Jouyne, Zéphirin. *Reboisement des montagnes: Reboisement, difficultés, causes des inondations et moyens de les prévenir*. Digne: Repos, 1850.

———. *Vues sur l'agriculture des Basses-Alpes et des départements méridionaux*. Marseille: A. Ricard, 1823.

Labillardière, Jacques Julien Houton de. *Relation du voyage à la recherche de la Pérouse fait par ordre de l'assemblée constituente*. 2 vols. Paris: H. J. Jansen, 1799.

Lacan, Ernest. *Esquisses photographiques*. Paris: Grassart, 1856.

Lafond, Andre-Auguste-Eugène-Laurent-Marie. *Fixation des dunes: Le paysage des dunes et les travaux de défense contre l'Océan (Charente-inférieure et Vendee)*. Paris: Imprimerie Nationale, 1900.

Lahor, Jean. *Une société à créer pour la protection des paysages français*. Paris: Alphonse Lemerre, 1901.

Lalos, J. *De la composition des parcs et jardins pittoresques.* 5th ed. Paris: Chez l'auteur, 1832.
Landrin, Armand. *Les inondations.* Paris: Hachette, 1880.
Le Blanc, Paul. *Les inondations de l'Allier dans l'arrondissement de Brioude.* Brioude: L. Watel, 1905.
Lenoir, Alexandre. *Musée impérial des monumens français.* Paris: Hacquart, 1810.
Lenthéric, Charles. *Le Rhône: Histoire d'un fleuve.* 2 vols. Paris: Plon, 1892.
Le Play, Frédéric. *Des forêts considerées dans leur rapports avec la constitution physique du globe et l'économie des sociétés.* Fontenay: E.N.S., 1996.
Leroux de la Roche, Pierre. *La protection des sites et des paysages.* Paris: Presses Modernes, 1932.
Ligue du Reboisement [de l'Algérie]. *La forêt: Conseils aux indigènes,* supplement to *Bulletin de la Ligue du Reboisement de l'Algérie,* no. 16. Algiers: Fontana, 1883.
Ligue du Reboisement de l'Algérie. *L'Arbre (citations): Programme du Comité central de la ligue.* Algiers: Imprimerie Casablanca, 1884.
———. *De la promulgation en Algérie de la loi du 4 avril 1882 sur la conservation et la restauration des terrains en montagne.* Algiers: Imprimerie Casablanca, n.d. [1883].
Lorentz, Bernard. *Cours élémentaire de culture des bois, créé à l'Ecole royale forestière de Nancy.* Paris: Mme. Huzard, 1837.
Lorette, Didier. *La forêt française après les tempêtes: Bilan et perspectives.* Bordeaux: Editions synthèse agricole, 2001.
Loudon, John Claudius. *Traité de la composition et de l'exécution des jardins d'ornement.* Paris: Encyclopédie portative, 1830.
Louvel, M. *Les forêts de l'ouest de Madagascar.* Paris: Challamel, 1914.
Mangin, Arthur. *Histoire des jardins, anciens et modernes.* Tours: Mame, 1888.
———. *Les jardins: Histoire et description.* Tours: Mame, 1867.
Marc, Henri. *Notes sur les forêts de l'Algérie.* Algiers: Adolphe Jourdan, 1916.
Marc, Henri, and André Knoertzer. *Le code forestier algérien.* Algiers: Soubiron, 1931.
Marès, Paul. *Histoire des progrès de l'agriculture en Algérie.* Algiers: J. Lavagne, 1878.
Marquise, Pierre de. *Compte rendu du Congrès international pour l'étude et la protection des oiseaux organisé à Bruxelles, au Palais des Académies, les 6, 7, et 9 juin 1927.* Gand: Hoste, 1927.
Massart, Jean. *Pour la protection de la nature en Belgique.* Brussels: Lamertin, 1912.
Maury, Alfred. *Histoire des grandes forêts de la Gaule et de l'ancienne France; précédée de recherches sur l'histoire des forêts de l'Allemagne, de l'Angleterre et de l'Italie, et de considérations sur le caractère des forêts des diverse parties du globe.* Paris: A. Leleux, 1850.
Ministère de la guerre, de l'agriculture et des colonies. *Mission forestière coloniale.* 2nd ed. Vol. 2, *Les bois de Gabon.* Paris: Larose 1929.
———. *Mission forestière coloniale.* Vol. 3, *La question forestière coloniale.* Paris: Larose, 1919.
Moreau de Jonnès, Alexandre. *Premier mémoire en réponse à la question proposée par l'Académie royale de Bruxelles: Quels sont les changemens que peut oc-*

casioner le déboisement de forêts considérables sur les contrées et communes adjacentes. . . . Brussels: P. J. De Mat, 1825.
Mornet, Daniel. *Le sentiment de la nature en France de J.-J. Rousseau à Bernardin de Saint Pierre*. Paris: Hachette, 1907.
Neumann, Louis. *L'art de construire et gouverner les serres*. 2nd ed. Paris: Audot, 1846.
Olivier, Marcel. *Six ans de politique social à Madagascar*. Paris: Grasset, 1931.
Ordinaire, P.-C. *L'inondation de 1840 sur le littoral de la Saône et du Rhône: Documents historiques*. Macon: Charpentier fils, 1840.
Pawlowski, Auguste, and Albert Radoux. *Les crues de la Seine (VI–XXe siècles): Causes, mécanisme, histoire, dangers, la lutte contre le fléau*. Paris: Berger-Levrault, 1910.
Pensa, Henri. *L'Algérie: Voyage de la délégation de la commission sénatoriale d'études des questions algériennes présidé par Jules Ferry*. Paris: Rothschild, 1894.
Perrier de la Bathie, Henri. "Les reserves naturelles de Madagascar." *La terre et la vie*, no. 7 (August 1931): 427–442.
Petit, Georges et al. *Contribution à l'étude faunistique de la réserve naturelle du Manampetsa (Madagascar)*. Paris: Masson, 1935.
Pick, E. de l'Isère. *Almanach pour 1857: Almanach impérial, grandes inondations de 1856*. Paris: Librairie Napoléonienne, 1857.
Pissot, M. A. *A propos des défrichements et des inondations*. Batignolles: Hennuyer, n.d.
Premier Congrès international pour la protection de la nature, faune et flore, sites et monuments naturels (Paris, 31 mai–2 juin 1923), rapports, voeux, réalisations, compte rendu. Edited by Raoul de Clermont, Albert Chappellier, Louis de Nussac, Ferdinand Le Cerf, and Charles Valois. Paris: Guillemot et de Lamothe, 1926.
Premier Congrès international pour la protection des paysages: Compte rendu revu et annoté par Raoul de Clermont, Fernand Cros-Mayrevieille and Louis de Nussac. Paris: Société pour la protection des paysages de France, 1910.
Puton, Alfred. *Code de la législation forestière*. Paris: J. Rothschild, 1883.
Randau, Robert. *Les algérianistes: Roman de la patrie algérienne*. 2nd ed. Paris: E. Sansot, 1911.
Rauch, François-Antoine. *Harmonie hydro-végétale et météorologique: Ou recherches sur les moyens de recréer avec nos forêts la force des températures et la regularité des saisons par les plantations raisonnées*. 2 vols. Paris: Levrault, 1801.
———. *Plan nourricier, ou recherches sur les moyens à mettre en usage pour assurer à jamais le pain au peuple français*. Paris: Didot, 1792.
———. *Procédés de la fabrication des armes blanches, publiés par l'ordre du comité de salut public*. Paris: Imprimerie du Département de la Guerre, 1793.
———. *Régénération de la nature végétale, ou recherches sur les moyens de recréer, dans tous les climats, les anciennes températures et l'ordre primitif des saisons, par des plantations raisonnées*. 2 vols. Paris: Didot, 1818.
Rebattu, M. "Le régime forestier en Algérie." *Bulletin de la réunion des études algériennes* 2, nos. 3–4 (March–April 1900): 57–88.

Réclus, Onésime. *L'Atlantide, pays d'Atlas: Algérie, Maroc, Tunisie*. Paris: La Renaissance du Livre, 1918.

———. *Lachons l'Asie, prenons l'Afrique: Ou renaître? et comment durer?* Paris: Librairie Universelle, 1904.

Rémard, Charles. *Le guide de voyageur à Fontainebleau*. Fontainebleau: E. Durant, 1820.

Reynard, J. *Le deboisement et le reboisement*. Paris: C. Douniol, 1858.

———. *Restauration des forêts et des paturages du sud de l'Algérie*. Algiers: Adolphe Jourdan, 1880.

Risler, Georges. *Better Housing for Workers in France*. Paris: Centre d'informations documentaires, 1937.

———. "Les espaces libres dans les grandes villes et cité-jardins." *Musée Social: Mémoires et Documents* (1910): 355–404.

———. *Les espaces libres dans les grandes villes et les cités-jardins*. Paris: Rousseau, 1910.

Robin, Charles. *Inondations de 1856: Voyage de l'empereur*. Paris: Garnier frères, 1856.

Rougier de la Bergerie, Jean-Baptiste. *Les forêts de la France, leurs rapports avec les climats, la température et l'ordre des saisons; avec la prosperité de l'agriculture et de l'industrie*. Paris: A. Bertrand, 1817.

———. *Histoire de l'agriculture française, considérée dans ses rapports avec les lois, les cultes, les moeurs, et le commerce*. Paris: Mme. Huzard, 1815.

———. *Mémoire au roi et aux chambres législatives sur la destruction des bois et sur les graves conséquences qui peuvent en résulter*. Paris: G.-A. Dentu, 1831.

———. *Mémoire et observations sur les abus des défrichemens et la destruction des bois et forêts; avec un projet d'organisation forestière*. Auxerre: Laurent Fournier, 1800.

———. *Traité d'agriculture pratique, ou annuaire des cultivateurs du département de la Creuse et pays circonvoisins, avec des vues générales sur l'économie rurale*. Paris: n.p., 1795.

Rouille-Courbe. *Inondations, départements d'Indre et Loire, 1846–1856*. Tours: Guilland Verger, 1858.

Roupnel, Gaston. *Histoire de la campagne française*, 3rd ed. Paris: Grasset, 1932.

Rousseau, René. *Contribution à l'étude de la question forestière en Algérie*. Algiers: Minerva, 1931.

Rozet, Claude-Antoine. *Moyens de forcer les torrents des montagnes de rendre à l'agriculture une partie du sol qu'ils ravagent, et d'empêcher les grandes inondations des fleuves et des principales rivières*. Paris: Maillet-Bachelier, 1856.

Saint-Pierre, Bernardin de. *Etudes de la nature*. 4 vols. Paris: Didot, 1789.

Sarraut, Albert. *La mise en valeur des colonies françaises*. Paris: Payot, 1923.

Société de fructification générale de la terre et des eaux de la France. Paris: C. J. Trouvé, n.d.

Sorel, Lucien. *La protection des paysages naturels et des perspectives monumentales*. Domfront: F. Marsat, 1932.

Sousa, Robert de. *L'avenir de nos villes: Etudes pratiques d'esthétique urbaine*. Paris: Berger et Levrault, 1913.

Stephan, Ch. *Récit des inondations en France pendant les mois de mai et juin 1856.* Lyon: F. Cajani, 1857.
Supernant, C. L. *Les inondations de la Loire, 18 octobre 1846.* Laôn: E. Fleury et A. Chervegny, 1847.
Surell, Alexandre. *Etude sur les torrents des Hautes-Alpes.* Paris: Carilion-Goeury & V. Dalmont, 1841.
———. *Etude sur les torrents des Hautes-Alpes.* 2nd ed. Vol. 1. Paris: Dunod, 1870.
———. *Etude sur les torrents des Hautes-Alpes.* 2nd ed. Vol. 2. Paris: Dunod, 1872.
Tassy, Louis. *Lorentz et Parade.* Paris: Bureau de la Revue des Eaux et Forêts, 1866.
Texier, Henri. *La protection des paysages et de la nature: Technique et philosophie de la conservation des beautés naturelles.* Fascicule du *Bulletin de la Société pour la Protection des Paysages et de l'esthétique générale de la France,* no. 4 (July 1937).
Thomas, Jean-Bazile. *Inondations et reboisement (extrait du Moniteur des Eaux et Forêts, dec. 1846).* Paris: Edouard Proux, 1847.
Thomé, Auguste. *De la cause des inondations et du moyen de les prévenir.* Valence: J. Marc Aurel, 1846.
Tocqueville, Alexis de. *Writings on Empire and Slavery.* Edited and translated by Jennifer Pitt. Baltimore: Johns Hopkins University Press, 2001.
Touring Club de France. *Grand tourisme en Algérie et en Tunisie.* Paris: n.p., 1910.
Travaux du Congrès forestier international de Grenoble (22–30 juillet 1925): Le problème forestier. Paris: Presses Universitaires de France, 1926.
Trolard, Dr. [Paulin]. *La cause des forêts de l'Algérie devant la réunion d'études algériennes.* Paris: 12, galerie d'Orléans, [1900].
———. *La colonisation et la question forestière.* Algiers: Imprimerie Casablanca, 1891.
———. *De la mentalité algérienne (a propos de la question des étrangers).* Blida: A. Mauguin, 1905.
———. *Les eaux thermo-minérales de l'Algérie: Rapport présenté au governeur général.* Mustapha: Imprimerie Algérienne, 1901.
———. *La forêt, conseil aux indigènes.* Algiers: Imprimerie de l'Association Ouvrière P. Fontana et Cie, 1883.
———. *Les forêts de l'Algérie et la colonisation: Mémoire presentée au ministre de l'agriculture.* Algiers: Imprimerie Casablanca, 1890.
———. *L'Institut Pasteur d'Alger: Sa fondation, sa réorganisation, mon expulsion.* Algiers: de Fontana frères, 1910.
———. *Lettres de Dr. P. Trolard pour sa candidature à la direction de l'Ecole de la médecine, Alger, juin 1904, février 1905.* Algiers: Imprimerie Casablanca, 1906.
———. *La question forestière algérienne devant le Sénat.* Algiers: Imprimerie Casablanca, 1893.
———. *La question forestière en Algérie et le programme de reboisement du gouvernement général.* Algiers: Imprimerie Casablanca, 1885.
———. *La question juive.* Blida: A. Mauguin, 1907.
———. *Le testament d'un assimilateur.* Algiers: J. Torrent, 1903.
Trottier. *Météorologie forestière: Influence des arbres sur la pluie, l'évaporation et la température.* Algiers: Aillaud, 1873.

Vallès, François. *Etudes sur les inondations, leurs causes et leurs effets, les moyens à mettre en oeuvre pour combattre leurs inconvénients et profiter de leurs avantages*. Paris: V. Valmont, 1857.

———. *Réponse aux critiques publiées dans les Annales Forestières contre l'ouvrage de M. Vallès sur les inondations*. Batignolles: Hennuyer, 1858.

———. *The Influence of Forests on Rainfall and Inundations*. Translated by Charles J. Allen. Washington, D.C.: Government Printing Office, 1873.

Vasselot de Régné, Médéric de. *Notice sur les dunes de la Coubre (Charente-Inférieure)*. Paris: Imprimerie Nationale, 1878.

Viaud, Gabriel. *Baptême des fleurs*. Paris: Société française d'imprimerie, 1901.

———. *Riche nature*. Paris: Arnat, n.d.

Vinson, Auguste. *Voyage à Madagascar au couronnement de Radama II*. Paris: Librarie Encyclopédique de Roret, 1865.

Wachi, Paul-Alphonse-Amable [Kiva, pseud.]. *La question des forêts en Algérie*. Paris: Collombon et Brulé, 1885.

Secondary Sources

Acot, Pascal. *Histoire de l'écologie*. Paris: Presses Universitaires de France, 1988.

Adams, William Mark. *Against Extinction: The Story of Conservation*. London: Earthscan, 2004.

Ageron, Charles-Robert. *Les algériens musulmans et la France (1871–1919)*. 2 vols. Paris: Presses Universitaires de France, 1968.

———. *Histoire de l'Algérie contemporaine, 1830–1994*. 10th ed. Paris: Presses Universitaires de France, 1994.

Agulhon, Maurice. "Le sang des bêtes: Le problème de la protection des animaux en France au XIXe siècle." In *Histoire vagabonde*. Paris: Gallimard, 1988.

Allard, Paul. "La presse et les inondations dans la région du bas-Rhône en 1840 et 1856." In *Récits et représentations des catastrophes depuis l'antiquité*, edited by René Favier and Anne-Marie Granet-Abisset, 73–92. Grenoble: Publications de la MSH-Alpes, 2005.

———. "Le rôle des ingénieurs des Ponts et Chaussées au XIXe siècle dans la gestion des crises environnementales." In *Temps et espaces des crises de l'environnement*, edited by Corinne Beck, Yves Luginbühl, and Tatiana Muxart, 249–261. Versailles: Editions Quae, 2006.

Ambroise-Rendu, Marc. *1910 Paris inondé*. Paris: Hervas, 1997.

Anderson, David, and Richard Grove, eds. *Conservation in Africa: People, Policies, and Practice*. Cambridge: Cambridge University Press, 1987.

Arnold, David. *The Problem of Nature: Environment, Culture and European Expansion*. Oxford: Blackwell, 1996.

———. *The Tropics and the Traveling Gaze: India, Landscape, and Science, 1800–1856*. Delhi: Permanent Black, 2005.

Arnold, David, and Ramachandra Guha, eds. *Nature, Culture and Imperialism: Essays on the Environmental History of South Asia*. Oxford: Oxford University Press, 1996.

Austin, Linda M. *Nostalgia in Transition, 1780–1917*. Charlottesville: University of Virginia Press, 2007.
Badre, Louis. *Histoire de la forêt française*. Paris: Arthaud, 1983.
Barker, G. "A Tale of Two Deserts: Contrasting Desertification Histories on Rome's Desert Frontiers." *World Archeology* 33, no. 1 (2002): 488–507.
Barrué-Pastor, M. "Cent ans de législation montagnarde: Des images contradictoires de la nature." In *Du rural à l'environnement: La question de la nature aujourd'hui*, edited by Mathieu Jollivet, Nicole Jollivet, and Marcel Jollivet, 225–233. Paris: L'Harmattan, 1989.
Baud, Jean-Pierre. "Les hygiènistes face aux nuisances industrielles dans la première moitié du XIXe siècle." *Revue Juridique de l'Environnement* 3 (1981): 205–220.
Beattie, James. *Empire and Environmental Anxiety: Health, Science, Art, and Conservation in South Asia and Australasia, 1800–1920*. London: Palgrave Macmillan, 2011.
Beck, Corinne, and Robert Delort, eds. *Pour une histoire de l'environnement*. Paris: CNRS, 1993.
Beck, Corinne, Yves Luginbühl, and Tatiana Muxart, eds. *Temps et espaces des crises de l'environnement*. Versailles: Editions Quae, 2006.
Bender, Barbara, ed. *Landscape: Politics and Perspectives*. Oxford: Berg, 1993.
Bergeret, Anne. "Discours et politiques forestières coloniales en Afrique et Madagascar." *Revue Française d'Outre Mer* 80, no. 298 (1993): 23–47.
Bernard, Claire. "Les débuts de la politique de reboisement dans la vallée du fleuve Sénégal (1920–45)." *Revue Française d'Outre Mer* 80, no. 298 (1993): 49–82.
Bernard, Héliane. *La terre toujours réinventée: La France rurale et les peintres, 1920–55; une histoire de l'imaginaire*. Lyon: Presses Universitaires de Lyon, 1990.
Berque, Augustin. *Cinq propositions pour une théorie du paysage*. Seyssel: Champ Vallon, 1994.
Bess, Michael. "Greening the Mainstream: Paradoxes of Antistatism and Anticonsumerism in the French Environmental Movement." *Environmental History* 5, no. 1 (January 2000): 6–26.
———. *The Light-Green Society: Ecology and Technological Modernity in France, 1960–2000*. Chicago: University of Chicago Press, 2003.
Bess, Michael, Marc Cioc, and James Sievert. "Environmental History Writing in Southern Europe." *Environmental History* 5, no. 4 (October 2000): 545–556.
Bethement, Jacques. "1856: De la gestion d'une catastrophe au bon usage d'une crise." *La Houille Blanche: Revue Internationale de l'Eau*, no. 1 (January 2007): 22–32.
Blackbourn, David. *The Conquest of Nature: Water, Landscape, and the Making of Modern Germany*. London: Jonathan Cape, 2006.
Bloch, Marc. *Les caractères originaux de l'histoire rurale*. Oslo: Aschehoug, 1931.
Bonneuil, Christophe. *Des savants pour l'empire: La structuration des recherches scientifiques coloniales au temps de la "mise en valeur" des colonies françaises, 1917–1945*. Paris: Orstom, 1991.

---. *Du jardin d'essais colonial à la station expérimentale, 1880–1930: Eléments pour une histoire du Cirad*. Paris: Cirad, 1993.
Boyer, Marc. *Histoire générale du tourisme du XVI au XXI siècle*. Paris: L'Harmattan, 2005.
Boym, Svetlana. *The Future of Nostalgia*. New York: Basic Books, 2001.
Braudel, Fernand. *The Mediterranean in the Age of Philip II*. 2 vols. Translated by Siân Reynolds. New York: Harper and Row, 1976.
Broc, Numa. *Les montagnes vues par les géographes et les naturalistes de la langue française au XVIII siècle: Contribution à l'histoire de la géographie*. Paris: Bibliothèque nationale, 1969.
Buchy, Marlène. "Histoire forestière de l'Indochine (1850–1954): Perspectives de recherche." *Revue Française d'Outre Mer* 80, no. 299 (1993): 219–250.
Buell, Lawrence. "Ecoglobal Affects: The Emergence of the U.S. Environmental Imagination on a Planetary Scale." In *Shades of the Planet: American Literature in World Literature*, edited by Wai Chee Dimock and Lawrence Buell. Princeton, N.J.: Princeton University Press, 2007.
Buttoud, Gérard. *Les conservateurs des eaux et forêts sous la Troisième République (1870–1940): Matériaux biographique pour une sociologie historique de la haute administration forestière française*. Nancy: Ecole nationale du génie rural des eaux et forêts, 1981.
Cabedoce, Béatrice, and Philippe Pierson, eds. *Cent ans d'histoire des jardins ouvriers 1896–1996: La Ligue française du coin de terre et du foyer*. Grâne: Créaphis, 1996.
Cadoret, A., ed. *Protection de la nature: Histoire et idéologie, de la nature à l'environnement*. Paris: L'Harmattan, 1985.
Carruthers, Jane. *The Kruger National Park: A Social and Political History*. Pietermaritzburg: University of Natal Press, 1995.
Cauquelin, Anne. *L'invention du paysage*. Paris: Plon, 1989.
Cebron de Lisle, Philippe. "L'eau à Paris au XIXe siècle." Doctoral thesis, Université de Paris-IV, 1991.
Chambers, Stephen. "The Garden and the City: Dispositifs architecturaux et progrès social dans le modèle urbain d'Ebenezer Howard." In *Cités-jardins: Genèse et actualité d'une utopie*, edited by Ginette Baty-Tornikian, 13–25. Paris: Editions Recherches/Ipraus, 2001.
Chanet, Jean-François. *L'école républicaine et les petites patries*. Paris: Aubier, 1995.
Charvet, Marie. *Les fortifications de Paris: De l'hygièmisme à l'urbanisme*. Rennes: Presses Universitaires de Rennes, 2005.
---. "La question des fortifications de Paris dans les années 1900: Esthètes, sportifs, réformateurs sociaux, élus locaux." *Genèses* 16 (June 1994): 23–44.
Charvolin, Florian. *L'invention de l'environnement en France: Chroniques anthropologiques d'une institutionalisation*. Paris: La Découverte, 2003.
Chevalier, Louis. *Laboring Classes and Dangerous Classes in Paris during the First Half of the Nineteenth Century*. Translated by Frank Jellinek. New York: H. Fertig, 1973.
Chevallier, Fabienne. *Le Paris moderne: Histoire des politiques d'hygiène (1855–1898)*. Rennes: Presses Universitaires de Rennes, 2010.

Choay, Françoise. "Pensées sur la ville, arts de la ville." In *Histoire de la France urbaine*, edited by Georges Duby. 5 vols. Vol. 4, *La ville de l'âge industriel: Le cycle haussmannien*, 156–237. Paris: Seuil, 1983

Cioc, Marc. *The Game of Conservation: International Treaties to Protect the World's Migratory Animals*. Athens: Ohio University Press, 2009.

Classen, Constance. *Worlds of Sense: Exploring the Senses in History and across Cultures*. London: Wiley, 1993.

Coeur, Denis. "Les inondations de mai–juin 1856 en France: Dommages et conséquences." *La Houille Blanche: Revue Internationale de l'Eau*, no. 2 (April 2007): 44–51.

———. *La plaine de Grenoble face aux inondations: Genèse d'une politique publique du XVIIe au XXe siècle*. Versailles: Editions Quae, 2008.

Coeur, Denis, and Andelatif Djerboua. "La crue de 1856: Reconstitution et analyse d'un événement hydrologique de référence." *La Houille Blanche: Revue Internationale de l'Eau*, no. 2 (April 2007): 27–37.

Collomb, Philippe, and France Guérin Pace. *Les français et l'environnement: L'enquête "populations-espaces de vie-environnement."* Paris: Presses Universitaires de France, 1998.

Conan, Michel. "Généalogie du paysage." *Le débat* 65 (May–August 1991): 29–42.

Corbin, Alain. *L'avènement des loisirs, 1850–1960*. Paris: Aubier, 1995.

———. *Les cloches de la terre: Paysage sonore et culture sensible dans les campagnes au XIXe siècle*. Paris: Albin Michel, 1994.

———. *L'homme dans le paysage*. Paris: Editions Textuel, 2001.

———. *Le miasme et la jonquille: L'odorat et l'imaginaire social, XVIIIe–XIXe siècles*. Paris: Flammarion, 1986.

———. *Le territoire du vide: L'occident et le désir du rivage, 1750–1840*. Paris: Flammarion, 1988.

———. *Village Bells: Sound and Meaning in the Nineteenth-Century French Countryside*. Translated by Martin Thom. New York: Columbia University Press, 1998.

Corvol, Andrée. *Forêt et paysage: Xe–XXIe siècles*. Paris: L'Harmattan, 2011.

———, ed. *La forêt: Perceptions et représentations*. Paris: L'Harmattan, 1997.

———. *L'homme aux bois: Histoire des relations de l'homme et de la forêt, XVII–XXe siècle*. Paris: Fayard, 1987.

———, ed. *La nature en révolution, 1750–1800*. Paris: L'Harmattan, 1993.

———, ed. *Les sources d'histoire de l'environnement*. Vol. 2, *Le XIXe siècle*. Paris: L'Harmattan, 1999.

———, ed. *Les sources d'histoire de l'environnement*. Vol. 3, *Le XXe siècle*. Paris: L'Harmattan, 2003.

Corvol, Andrée, and Isabelle Richefort, eds. *Nature, environnement et paysage: L'héritage du XVIIIe siècle, guide de recherche archivistique et bibliographique*. Paris: L'Harmattan, 1995.

Cosgrove, Denis E. *Social Formation and the Symbolic Landscape*. 2nd ed. Madison: University of Wisconsin Press, 1998.

Cosgrove, Denis, and Stephen Daniels. *The Iconography of Landscape*. Cambridge: Cambridge University Press, 1988.

Cronon, William. *Changes in the Land: Indians, Colonists and the Ecology of New England.* 1st rev. ed. New York: Hill and Wang, 2003.

———, ed. *Uncommon Ground: Rethinking the Human Place in Nature.* New York: W. W. Norton, 1995.

Crosby, Alfred. "The Past and Present of Environmental History." *American Historical Review* 100, no. 4 (October 1995): 1177–1189.

Cutler, Brock. "Evoking the State: Environmental Disaster and Colonial Policy in Algeria, 1840–1870." PhD diss., University of California, Irvine, 2011.

Dagognet, François. *Mort du paysage? Philosophie et esthétique du paysage, actes du colloque de Lyon.* Seyssel: Champ Vallon, 1982.

Dakhlia, Jocelyne. *L'oubli de la cité: La mémoire collective à l'épreuve du lignage dans le Jérid tunisien.* Paris: La Découverte, 1990.

Daniel, Malcolm. "Edouard Baldus, artiste photographe." In *Edouard Baldus, photographe: le guide de l'exposition,* edited by Françoise Heilbrun et al., 17–97. Paris: Réunion des Musées Nationaux, 1994.

Daniels, Stephen. *Fields of Vision: Landscape Imagery and National Identity in England and the United States.* London: Blackwell, 1993.

Davis, Diana K. "Desert 'Wastes' of the Maghreb: Desertification Narratives in French Colonial Environmental History of North Africa." *Cultural Geographies* 11 (2004): 359–387.

———. "Potential Forests: Degradation Narratives, Science, and Environmental Policy in Protectorate Morocco, 1912–56." *Environmental History* 10, no. 2 (2005): 211–238.

———. *Resurrecting the Granary of Rome: Environmental History and French Colonial Expansion in North Africa.* Athens: Ohio University Press, 2007.

Delort, Robert, and François Walter. *Histoire de l'environnement européen.* Paris: Presses Universitaires de France, 2001.

Delumeau, Jean, and Yves Lequin. *Les malheurs des temps: Histoire des fléaux et des calamités en France.* Paris: Larousse, 1987.

Dion, Roger. *Histoire des levées de la Loire.* Paris: Habouzit, 1961.

Dodman, Thomas. "Un pays pour la colonie: Mourir de nostalgie en Algérie française, 1830–1880." *Annales. Histoire, Sciences Sociales* 3 (2011): 743–784.

Drouin, Jean-Marc. *Réinventer la nature: L'écologie et son histoire.* Paris: Desclée de Brower, 1991.

Dubost, Françoise. *Les jardins ordinaires.* 2nd ed. Paris: L'Harmattan, 1997.

———. *Vert patrimoine: La constitution d'un nouveau domaine patrimonial.* Paris: Editions de la Maison des Sciences de l'Homme, 1994.

Duby, Georges. "Quelques notes pour une histoire de la sensibilité au paysage." *Etudes rurales* (January–December 1991): 11–14.

Dumont, Marie-Jeanne. "La Fondation Rothschild et les premières habitations à bon marché de Paris, 1900–1925." Unpublished research report, Paris, Ministère de l'urbanisme et du logement, Direction de l'architecture, 1984.

Egerton, Frank N. *Roots of Ecology: Antiquity to Haeckel.* Berkeley: University of California Press, 2012.

Favier, René, and Anne-Marie Abisset-Granet, eds. *Récits et représentations des catastrophes depuis l'antiquité.* Grenoble: MSH Alpes, 2005.

Febvre, Lucien. *La terre et l'évolution humaine.* Paris: La Renaissance du Livre, 1922.

Flamand, Jean-Paul. *Loger le peuple: Essai sur l'histoire du logement social.* Paris: La Découverte, 1989.

Ford, Caroline. "Imperial Preservation and Landscape Reclamation: National Parks and Natural Reserves in French Colonial Africa." In *Civilizing Nature: National Parks in Global Perspective,* ed. Bernhard Gissibl et al., 69–83. New York: Berghahn Books, 2012.

———. "Nature, Culture and Conservation in France and Her Colonies." *Past and Present,* no. 183 (May 2004): 173–198.

———. "Nature's Fortunes: New Directions in the Writing of European Environmental History." *Journal of Modern History* 79, no. 1 (March 2007): 112–133.

———. "Reforestation, Landscape Conservation, and the Anxieties of Empire in French Colonial Algeria." *American Historical Review* 113, no. 2 (April 2008): 341–362.

Fox-Genovese, Elizabeth. *The Origins of Physiocracy.* Ithaca, N.Y.: Cornell University Press, 1976.

Frange, Claire, ed. *Le style Duchêne: Henri et Achille Duchêne, architectes paysagistes.* Neuilly: Editions du Labyrinthe, 1998.

Fritsch, Philippe. "Les séries artistiques dans la forêt de Fontainebleau: Genèse d'une perception." In *La forêt: Perceptions et représentations,* edited by Andrée Corvol, Paul Arnould, and Micheline Hotyat. Paris: L'Harmattan, 1997.

Garnier, Emmanuel. *Les dérangements du temps: 500 ans de chaud et de froid en Europe.* Paris: Plon, 2010.

Gaudin, Jean-Pierre. "The French Garden City." Vol. 1, *The Garden City: Past, Present and Future,* edited by Stephen V. Ward, 52–68. London: Chapman and Hall, 1992.

Gerson, Stéphane. *Pride of Place: Local Memories and Political Culture in Nineteenth-Century France.* Ithaca, N.Y.: Cornell University Press, 2003.

Glacken, Clarence J. *Traces on the Rhodian Shore: Nature and Culture in Western Thought from Ancient Times to the End of the Eighteenth Century.* Berkeley: University of California Press, 1967.

Goody, Jack. *The Culture of Flowers.* Cambridge: Cambridge University Press, 1983.

Grand-Mesnil, Marie-Noëlle. "La loi du 29 septembre 1791." In *Révolution et espaces forestières: Colloque du 3 et 4 juin 1987,* edited by Denis Woronoff, 200–205. Paris: L'Harmattan, 1988.

Green, Nicholas. *The Spectacle of Nature: Landscape and Bourgeois Culture in Nineteenth-Century France.* Manchester, UK: Manchester University Press, 1990.

Gregory, Derek. "(Post)colonialism and the Production of Nature." In *Social Nature: Theory, Practice, and Politics,* edited by Noel Castree and Bruce Braun, 84–111. Oxford: Oxford University Press, 2001.

Griffiths, Tom. *Hunters and Collectors: The Antiquarian Imagination in Australia.* Cambridge: Cambridge University Press, 1996.

Griffiths, Tom, and Libby Robbins, eds. *Ecology and Empire: Environmental History of Settler Societies.* Seattle: University of Washington Press, 1997.

Grove, A. T., and Oliver Rackham. *The Nature of Mediterranean Europe: An Ecological History.* New Haven, Conn.: Yale University Press, 2001.

Grove, Richard. *Ecology, Climate, and Empire: Colonialism and Global Environmental History, 1400–1940.* Cambridge: White Horse Press, 1997.

———. *Green Imperialism: Colonial Expansion, Tropical Island Edens and the Origins of Environmentalism, 1600–1900.* Cambridge: Cambridge University Press, 1995.

———. "Historical Review of Early Institutional and Conservationist Responses to Fears of Artificially Induced Global Climate Change: The Deforestation-Dessication Discourse, 1500–1860." *Chemosphere* 20, no. 5 (September 1994): 1001–1013.

———. "Scotland in South Africa: John Croumbie Brown and the Roots of Settler Environmentalism." In *Ecology and Empire: Environmental History of Settler Societies,* ed. Tom Griffiths and Libby Robin, 139–153. Seattle: University of Washington Press, 1997.

Guerrand, Roger-Henri. *Les origines du logement social en France, 1850–1914.* Paris: Editions de la Villette, 2010.

Guha, Ramachandra. *The Unquiet Woods: Ecological Change and Peasant Resistance in the Himalaya.* Delhi: Oxford University Press, 1989.

Hansen, Alyse. "A Lieu d'Histoire, à Lieu de Mémoire, and à Lieu de Vie: The Multidirectional Potential of the Cité de la Muette." *French Historical Studies* 37, no. 1 (Winter 2014): 119–120.

Hansen, Peter H. *Summits of Modern Man: Mountaineering after the Enlightenment.* Cambridge, Mass.: Harvard University Press, 2013.

Harp, Stephen L. *Au Naturel: Naturism, Nudism, and Tourism in Twentieth-Century France.* Baton Rouge: Louisiana State University Press, 2015.

Harrison, Carol E. "Planting Gardens, Planting Flags: Revolutionary France in the South Pacific." *French Historical Studies* 34, no. 2 (Spring 2011): 243–277.

Harrison, Mark. *Climates and Constitutions: Health, Race, Environment, and the British Empire in India, 1600–1800.* Oxford: Oxford University Press, 1999.

Hayden, Sherman Strong. *The International Protection of Wildlife: An Examination of the Treaties and Other Agreements for the Preservation of Birds and Mammals.* New York: Columbia University Press, 1942.

Hecht, Gabrielle. *The Radiance of France: Nuclear Power and National Identity after World War II.* Cambridge, Mass.: MIT Press, 1998.

Heilbrun, Françoise et al., eds. *Edouard Baldus, photographe: Le guide de l'exposition.* Paris: Réunion des Musées Nationaux, 1996.

Hopkins, Richard S. *Planning the Green Spaces of Nineteenth-Century Paris.* Baton Rouge: Louisiana State University Press, 2015.

———. "Sauvons le Luxembourg: Urban Greenspace as Private Domain and Public Battleground, 1865–1867," *Journal of Urban History* 37, 1 (2011): 43–58.

Horn, Jeff, and Margaret C. Jacob. "Jean-Antoine Chaptal and the Cultural Roots of French Industrialization." *Technology and Culture* 39, no. 4 (October 1998): 671–698.

Horne, Janet R. "Dans l'intérêt public: Espaces verts et visions de plantification urbaine au Musée social, 1907–1920." In *Cités-jardins: Genèse et actualité d'une utopie,* edited by Ginette Baty-Tornikian, 73–82. Paris: Editions Recherches/Ipraus, 2001.

———. *A Social Laboratory for Modern France: The Musée Social and the Rise of the Welfare State.* Durham, N.C.: Duke University Press, 2002.

Husson, Jean-Pierre. "Les paysages forestiers lorrains, rôle et l'impact de l'épisode révolutionnaire (étude de géographie historique)." In *Révolution et espaces forestières,* edited by Denis Woronoff, 63–70. Paris: L'Harmattan, 1989.

Ibo, Guéhi Jonas. "La politique coloniale de protection de la nature en Côte d'Ivoire (1900–1958)." *Revue Française d'Outre Mer* 80, no. 298 (1993): 83–104.

Jackson, Jeffrey H. *Paris under Water: How the City of Light Survived the Great Flood of 1910.* New York: Palgrave Macmillan, 2010.

Jaussaud, Philippe, and Edouard-Raoul Brygoo. *Du jardin au Muséum en 516 biographies.* Paris: Muséum national de l'histoire naturelle, 2004.

Jennings. Eric T. *Curing the Colonizers: Hydrotherapy, Climatology, and French Colonial Spas.* Durham, N.C.: Duke University Press, 2006.

———. "From Indochine to Indochina: The Lang Bian/Dalat Palace Hotel and French Colonial Leisure, Power and Culture." *Journal of Asian Studies* 37, no. 1 (2003): 161–163.

Johns, Alessa, ed. *Dreadful Visitations: Confronting Natural Catastrophe in the Age of the Enlightenment.* New York: Routledge, 1999.

Jordanova, Ludmilla J. "Environmentalism in the Eighteenth Century." In *Nature and Science: Essays in the History of Geographical Knowledge,* edited by Felix Driver and Gillian Rose. Special issue, Historical Geography Research Series 28 (February 1992): 19–26.

Kalaora, Bernard. *Le musée vert ou le tourisme en forêt: Naissance et développement d'un loisir urbain; le cas de Fontainebleau.* Paris: Anthropos, 1981.

Kalaora, Bernard, and Antoine Savoye. *Forêt et sociologie: Les forestiers de l'Ecole de Le Play, défenseurs des populations de montagne (1860–1913).* Paris: INRA, 1984.

———. *La forêt pacifiée: Les forestiers de l'Ecole de Le Play, experts des sociétés pastorales.* Paris: L'Harmattan, 1986.

Kalaora, Bernard, and Chloe Vlassopoulos. "Les natures de paysage au Ministère de l'environnement." *Le débat* 65 (May–August 1991): 120–128.

———. *Pour une sociologie de l'environnement: Environnement, société, politique.* Seyssel: Champ Vallon, 2013.

Kennedy, Dane Keith. *The Magic Mountains: Hill Stations and the British Raj.* Berkeley: University of California Press, 1996.

Knight, Philip. *Flower Poetics in Nineteenth-Century France.* Oxford: Clarendon Press, 1986.

Koenig, Sebastien J., et al. "The Variability of Floods in AD 1500." *Climate Change* 101, nos. 1–2 (2010): 235–256.

Kory, Olson. "A New Paris? Eugène Henard's Vision of Paris's Future." *Contemporary French and Francophone Studies* 14, no. 4 (September 2010): 431–440.

Lacoste, Yves. *Ibn Khaldoun: The Birth of History and the Past of the Third World.* London: Verso, 1985.

———. *Paysages politiques: Braudel, Gracq, Réclus*. Paris: Librarie Générale Française, 1990.
Lacour-Veyranne, Charlotte. *Les colères de la Seine*. Paris: Paris-Musées, 1994.
Ladino, Jennifer K. *Reclaiming Nostalgia: Longing for Nature in American Literature*. Charlottesville: University of Virginia Press, 2012.
Langlois, Gilles-Antoine. *Folies, tivolis, et attractions: Les premiers parcs et loisirs parisiens*. Paris: Delegation à l'Action Artistique de la Ville de Paris, 1991.
Larrère, G. R. *L'harmonie hydrovégétale et météorologique ou l'utopie forestière de F. A. Rauch*. Rungis: ENRA, 1985.
Ledoux, Bruno. *Les catastrophes naturelles en France*. Paris: Payot, 1995.
Lejeune, Dominique. *Les "alpinistes" en France à la fin du XIXe et au début du XXe siècle (vers 1875–vers 1919): Etude d'histoire sociale, étude de mentalité*. Paris: CTHS, 1988.
———. *Les sociétés de géographie en France et l'expansion coloniale au XIXe siècle*. Paris: Albin Michel, 1993.
Lekan, Thomas M. *Imagining the Nation in Nature: Landscape Preservation and German Identity, 1885–1945*. Cambridge, Mass.: Harvard University Press, 2004.
Lemas, Nicolas. *Eugène Hénard et le futur urbain: Quelle politique pour l'utopie?* Paris: L'Harmattan, 2008.
Leniaud, Jean-Michel. *Les archipels du passé: Le patrimoine et son histoire*. Paris: Fayard, 2002.
Le Roy Ladurie, Emmanuel. *Times of Feast, Times of Famine: A History of Climate from the Year 1000*. Translated by Barbara Bray. New York: Doubleday, 1971.
Locher, Fabien, and Grégory Quénet. "L'histoire environnementale: Origines, enjeux et perspectives d'un nouveau chantier." *Revue d'Histoire Moderne et Contemporaine* 56, no. 4 (2009): 7–38.
Lorcin, Patricia M. E. *Imperial Identities: Stereotyping, Prejudice and Race in Colonial Algeria*. London: I. B. Tauris, 1995.
———. "Rome and France in Africa: Recovering Colonial Algeria's Latin Past." *French Historical Studies* 25, no. 2 (Spring 2002): 295–329.
Lowenthal, David. "Nostalgia Tells It Like It Wasn't." In *The Imagined Past: History and Nostalgia*, edited by Christopher Shaw and Malcolm Chase. New York: St. Martin's Press, 1989.
———. *The Past Is a Foreign Country*. Cambridge: Cambridge University Press, 1985.
Luginbühl, Yves. *Paysages: Textes et représentations du siècle des lumières à nos jours*. Lyon: La Manufacture, 1989.
MacKenzie, John. *The Empire of Nature: Hunting, Conservation and British Imperialism*. Manchester, UK: Manchester University Press, 1988.
———, ed. *Imperialism and the Natural World*. Manchester, UK: Manchester University Press, 1990.
Magri, Susanna. "Le Musée social, Georges Benoit-Lévy et les cités-jardins, 1900–1909." In *Cités-jardins: Genèse et actualité d'une utopie,* edited by Ginette Baty-Tornikian, 83–92. Paris: Editions Recherches/Ipraus, 2001.
Marrey, Bernard, and Jean-Pierre Monnet. *La grande histoire des serres et des jardins d'hiver: France, 1780–1900*. Paris: Graphite, 1984.

Massard-Guilbaud, Geneviève. *Histoire de la pollution industrielle: France, 1789–1914.* Paris: Editions de l'Ecole des hautes études en sciences sociales, 2010.

———. "La régulation des nuisances industrielles urbaines (1808–1940)." *Vingtième Siècle* 64 (1999): 53–65.

Matagne, Patrick. *Aux origines de l'écologie: Les naturalistes en France de 1800 à 1914.* Paris: Editions du CTHS, 1999.

———. "The Politics of Conservation in France in the 19th Century." *Environment and History* 4, no. 3 (October 1998): 359–367.

Mathis, Charles-François, and Jean-François Mouhot, eds. *Une protection de l'environnement à la française? (XIXe–XXe siècles).* Seyssel: Champ Vallon, 2013.

Matteson, Keiko. *Forests in Revolutionary France: Conservation, Community, and Conflict, 1669–1848.* Cambridge: Cambridge University Press, 2015.

Mauch, Christof, and Christian Pfister, eds. *Natural Disasters, Cultural Responses: Case Studies toward a Global Environmental History.* Lanham, Md.: Lexington Books, 2009.

McCloy, Shelby T. "Flood Relief and Control in Eighteenth-Century France." *Journal of Modern History* 13, no. 1 (March 1941): 1–18.

McPhee, Peter. *Revolution and Environment in Southern France: Peasants, Lords, and Murder in the Corbières.* Oxford: Oxford University Press, 1999.

Mejean, Annie. "Utilisation politique d'une catastrophe: Le voyage de Napoleon III en Provence durant la grande crue de 1856." *Revue Historique* 597 (January–March 1996): 133–152.

Miller, Mary Ashburn. *A Natural History of Revolution: Violence and Nature in the French Revolutionary Imagination, 1789–1794.* Ithaca, N.Y.: Cornell University Press, 2011.

Mission du patrimoine ethnologique, collection ethnologie de la France, cahier 9. *Paysage au pluriel: Pour une approche éthnologique des paysages.* Paris: Editions de la Maison des Sciences de l'Homme, 1995.

Mosser, Monique, and Georges Teyssot. *The Architecture of Western Gardens: A Design History from the Renaissance to the Present Day.* Cambridge, Mass.: MIT Press, 1991.

Murphey, Rhoads. "The Decline of North Africa since the Roman Occupation: Climatic or Human?" *Annals of the Association of American Geographers* 41, no. 2 (1951): 116–132.

Nash, Linda. *Inescapable Ecologies: A History of Environment, Disease and Knowledge.* Berkeley: University of California Press, 2006.

Neboit-Guilhot, René, and Lucette Davy, eds. *Les français dans leur environnement.* Paris: Nathan, 1996.

Noizet, Hélène, Sandrine Robert, and Laurent Mirlou. "Cartographie des crues centennales à Paris (1740, 1910)." In *Zones humides et villes d'hier et aujourd'hui: Des premières cités aux fronts d'eau contemporaines,* edited by Corinne Beck et al., 91–104. Villeneuve d'Ascq: Presses Universitaire de Charles de Gaulle–Lille 3, 2011.

Nourry, Louis-Michel. *Les jardins publics en province: Espace et politique au XIXe siècle.* Rennes: Presses Universitaires de Rennes, 1997.

Osborne, Michael. *Nature, the Exotic, and the Science of French Colonialism.* Bloomington: Indiana University Press, 1994.

Osti, Giovanna. "La section d'hygiène urbaine et rural au Musée social." In *La banlieue oasis: Henri Sellier et les cités-jardins, 1900–1940*, edited by Katherine Burlen, 59–66. Saint Denis: Presses Universitaires de Vincennes, 1987.

Oulebsir, Nabila. *Les usages du patrimoine: Monuments, musées et politique coloniale en Algérie (1830–1930)*. Paris: Editions de la MSH, 2004.

Ozouf, Mona. *La fête révolutionnaire, 1789–1799*. Paris: Gallimard, 1976.

———. "Régéneration." In *Dictionnaire critique de la Revolution française*, edited by François Furet and Mona Ozouf. Paris: Flammarion, 1988.

Park, Sun-Young. "The Body and the Building: Architecture, Urbanism and Hygiene in Early Nineteenth-Century Paris." PhD diss., Harvard University, 2014.

Parker, Geoffrey. *Global Crisis: War, Climate Change and Catastrophe in the Seventeenth Century*. New Haven, Conn.: Yale University Press, 2013.

Parsons, Kermit, and David Schuyler, eds. *From Garden City to Green City: The Legacy of Ebenezer Howard*. Baltimore: Johns Hopkins University Press, 2002.

Paysages au pluriel: Pour une approche ethnologique des paysages. Paris: Editions de la Maison des Sciences de l'Homme, 1995.

Pearson, Chris. *Mobilizing Nature: The Environmental History of War and Militarization in Modern France*. Manchester: Manchester University Press, 2008.

Petot, Jean. *Histoire de l'administration des Ponts et Chaussées 1599–1815*. Paris: M. Rivière, 1958.

Pichard, G. "Les crues sur le Bas-Rhône de 1500 à nos jours: Pour une histoire hydro-climatique." *Méditerranée*, nos. 3–4 (1995): 105–116.

Picon, Antoine. *L'invention de l'ingénieur moderne: L'Ecole des ponts et chaussées 1747–1851*. Paris: Presses de l'Ecole nationale des ponts et chaussées, 1992.

Pinkney, David H. *Napoleon III and the Rebuilding of Paris*. Princeton, N.J.: Princeton University Press, 1958.

Polton, Jean-Claude. *Claude-François Denecourt (1788–1875): "L'amant de la forêt de Fountainebleau."* Fountainebleau: Sentiers Bleus, 2011.

———. *Tourisme et nature au XIX siècle*. Paris: Comité des Travaux Historiques et Scientifiques, 1994.

Popelin, Pascal. *Le jour où l'eau reviendra: 100 ans après la grande crue de 1910*. Paris: Gawsewitch, 2009.

Pouchepadass, Jacques, ed. "Colonisations et environnement" *Revue Française d'Histoire d'Outre Mer* 80, nos. 298–299 (1993): 5–22.

Poulot, Dominique. *Une histoire du patrimoine en occident*. Paris: Presses Universitaires de France, 2006.

Pouvreau, Benoît, Marc Couronné, Marie-Françoise Laborde, and Guillaume Gaudry. *Les cités-jardins de la banlieue du nord-est parisien*. Paris: Editions Le Moniteur, 2007.

Prest, John. *The Garden of Eden: The Botanic Garden and the Re-creation of Paradise*. New Haven, Conn.: Yale University Press, 1981.

Pritchard, Sarah. *Confluence: The Nature of Technology and the Remaking of the Rhône*. Cambridge, Mass.: Harvard University Press, 2011.

Prochaska, David. "Fire on the Mountain: Resisting Colonialism in Algeria." In *Banditry, Rebellion, and Social Protest in Africa*, edited by Donald Crummey, 229–252. London: J. Currey, 1986.

Puyo, Jean-Yves. "Sur le mythe colonial de l'inépuisabilité des resources forestières (Afrique occidentale française/Afrique equatoriale française, 1900–1940." *Cahiers de Géographie du Québec* 45 (2001): 479–496.
Pyne, Stephen J. *Vestal Fire: An Environmental History, Told through Fire, of Europe and Europe's Encounter with the World*. Seattle: University of Washington Press, 1997.
Quénet, Grégory. *Qu'est que l'histoire environnementale?* Seyssel: Champ Vallon, 2014.
Quilliot, Roger, and Roger-Henri Guerrand. *Cent ans d'habitation social: Une utopie réaliste*. Paris: Albin Michel, 1989.
Raj, Kapil. *Relocating Modern Science: Circulation and the Construction of Knowledge in Europe and South Asia, 1650–1900*. London: Palgrave Macmillan, 2010.
Rajan, S. Ravi. *Modernizing Nature: Forestry and Imperial Eco-development, 1800–1930*. Oxford: Oxford University Press, 2006.
Rauch, André. "Les vacances et la nature revisitée (1830–1939)." In *L'avènement des loisirs, 1850–1960*, edited by Alain Corbin. 2nd ed. Paris: Flammarion, 2000.
Reynard, Pierre Claude. "Public Order and Privilege: Eighteenth-Century Roots of Environmental Regulation." *Technology and Culture* 43, no. 1 (January 2002): 1–28.
Richez, Jean-Claude. "Science allemande et foresterie française: L'expérience du rive gauche du Rhin." In *Révolution et l'espace forestière*, edited by Denis Woronoff, 232–246. Paris: L'Harmattan, 1989.
Robic, Marie-Claire, et al., eds. *Du milieu à l'environnement: Pratiques et représentations du rapport homme/nature depuis la Renaissance*. Paris: Economica, 1992.
Roger, Alain. *Court traité du paysage*. Paris: Gallimard, 1997.
Rollins, William H. *A Greener Vision of Home: Cultural Politics and Environmental Reform in the German Heimatschurz Movement: 1904–1918*. Ann Arbor: University of Michigan Press, 1997.
Sahlins, Peter. *Forest Rites: The War of the Demoiselles in Nineteenth-Century France*. Cambridge, Mass.: Harvard University Press, 1994.
Schama, Simon. *The Embarrassment of Riches: An Interpretation of Dutch Culture in the Golden Age*. Berkeley: University of California Press, 1988.
———. *Landscape and Memory*. New York: Knopf, 1995.
Sellali, Amina. "La cité-jardin de Suresnes: L'architecture au service d'une politique urbaine d'avant-garde." In *Cités-jardins: Genèse et actualité d'une utopie*, edited by Ginette Baty-Tornikian, 117–132. Paris: Editions Recherches/Ipraus, 2001.
Selmi, Adel. "L'émergence de l'idée du parc national en France: De la protection à l'expérimentation coloniale." In *Histoire des parcs nationaux: Comment prendre soin de la nature?*, edited by Raphaël Larrère et al., 43–58. Versailles: Editions Quae, 2009.
Shaw, B. D. "Climate, Environment and History: The Case of Roman North Africa." In *Climate and History*, edited by T. Wrigley, M. Ingram, and G. Farmer, 379–403. Cambridge: Cambridge University Press, 1981.

Sherwin-White, A. N. "Geographical Factors in Roman Algeria." *Journal of Roman Studies* 34, pts. 1 and 2 (1944): 1–10.
Sievert, James. *The Origins of Nature Conservation in Italy.* Bern: Peter Lang, 2000.
Simon, Laurent et al. "Forestry Disputes in Provincial France during the Nineteenth Century: The Case of the Montagne de Lure." *Journal of Historical Geography* 33, no. 2 (2007): 335–351.
Sivak, Henry. "Law, Territory, and the Legal Geography of French Rule in Algeria: The Forestry Domain, 1830–1903." *Geographical Review* 103, no. 4 (October 2012): 556–574.
———. "Law, Territory, and the Legal Geography of French Rule in Algeria: The Forestry Domain, 1830–1903." PhD diss., University of California, Los Angeles, 2008.
Skaria, Ajay. *Hybrid Histories: Forests, Frontiers, and Wildness in Western India.* Delhi: Oxford University Press, 1999.
Smith, J. Russell. "The Desert's Edge." *Bulletin of the American Geographical Society* 47, no. 11 (1915): 813–831.
Smith, Mark M. *Sensing the Past: Seeing, Hearing, Smelling, Tasting, and Touching in History.* Berkeley: University of California Press, 2008.
Spary, E. C. *Utopia's Garden: French Natural History from the Old Regime to the French Revolution.* Chicago: University of Chicago Press, 2000.
Stafford, Barbara Maria. *Voyage into Substance: Art, Science, Nature, and the Illustrated Travel Account, 1760–1840.* Cambridge, Mass.: MIT Press, 1984.
Stoler, Ann Laura. "Rethinking Colonial Categories: European Communities and the Boundaries of Rule." *Comparative Studies in Society and History* 31, no. 1 (1989): 134–161.
Sunderland, Willard. *Taming the Wild Field: Colonization and Empire on the Russian Steppe.* Ithaca, N.Y.: Cornell University Press, 2004.
Sutcliffe, Antony. *The Autumn of Central Paris: The Defeat of Town Planning, 1850–1970.* Montreal: McGill University Press, 1971.
———. "Le contexte urbanistique de l'oeuvre d'Henri Sellier: La transcription du modèle anglais de la cité-jardin." In *La banlieue oasis: Henri Sellier et les cités-jardins, 1900–1940,* edited by Katherine Burlen, 67–79. Saint Denis: Presses Universitaires de Vincennes, 1987.
Swearingen, Will D. *Moroccan Mirages: Agrarian Dreams and Deceptions, 1912–1986.* Princeton, N.J.: Princeton University Press, 1987.
Swensen, Astrid. *The Rise of Heritage: Preserving the Past in France, Germany and Britain, 1789–1914.* Cambridge: Cambridge University Press, 2013.
Thomas, Frédéric. "Ecologie et gestion forestière dans l'Indochine française." *Revue Française d'Outre Mer* 85, no. 139 (April–May 1998): 59–86.
———. *Histoire du régime et des services forestiers français en Indochine de 1862 à 1945.* Hanoi: Thé Gioi, 1999.
———. "Protection des forêts et environmentalisme colonial: Indochine, 1860–1945." *Revue d'Histoire Moderne et Contemporaine* 56, no. 4 (2009): 104–136.
Thomas, Greg M. *Art and Ecology in Nineteenth-Century France: The Landscapes of Théodore Rousseau.* Princeton, N.J.: Princeton University Press, 2000.

Thomas, Nicholas. *Colonialism's Culture: Anthropology, Travel, and Government.* Princeton, N.J.: Princeton University Press, 1994.

Tucker, Richard P., and J. F. Richards, eds. *Global Deforestation and the Nineteenth-Century World Economy.* Durham, N.C.: Duke University Press, 1983.

Vatin, Claude. "Désert construit et inventé, Sahara perdu ou retrouvée: Le jeu des imaginations." In *Le Maghreb dans l'imaginaire: La colonie le désert, l'exil,* edited by Jean-Robert Henry et al., 107–127. Aix-en-Provence: Edisud, 1986.

Veyret, Paul. "Un centenaire: Etudes sur les torrents des Hautes-Alpes de Surell." *Revue de Géographie Alpine* 31, no. 4 (1943): 513–524.

Viard, Jean. *Les tiers espace: Essai sur la nature.* Paris: Méridiens Klincksieck, 1990.

———. "Protestante, la Nature?" In *Protection de la nature: Histoire et idéologie,* ed. A. Cadoret. Paris: L'Harmattan, 1985, 161–173.

Walter, François. *Catastrophes: Une histoire culturelle, XVI–XXIe siècle.* Paris: Seuil, 2008.

Weber, Florence. *L'honneur des jardiniers: Les potagers dans la France du XX siècle.* Paris: Belin, 1998.

White, Richard. "Environmental History, Ecology and Meaning." *Journal of American History* 76, no. 4 (March 1990): 1111–1116.

———. "The Nationalization of Nature." *Journal of American History* 86, no. 3 (December 1999): 976–986.

Whited, Tamara L. *Forests and Peasant Politics in Modern France.* New Haven, Conn.: Yale University Press, 2000.

Williams, Raymond. *The Country and the City.* London: Chatto and Windus, 1973.

Winiwarter, Verena, et al. "Environmental History in Europe from 1994 to 2004: Enthusiasm and Consolidation." *Environment and History* 10, no. 4 (November 2004): 501–530.

Wolf, Peter M. *Eugène Hénard and the Beginning of Urbanism in Paris, 1900–14.* The Hague: International Federation for Housing and Planning, 1968.

Woronoff, Denis. "La dévastation révolutionnaire des forêts." In *Révolution et espaces forestières: Colloque des 3 et 4 juin 1987,* edited by Denis Woronoff. Paris: L'Harmattan, 1989.

Worster, Donald. *Nature's Economy: A History of Ecological Ideas.* 2nd ed. Cambridge: Cambridge University Press, 1994.

———. *The Wealth of Nature: Environmental History and the Ecological Imagination.* Oxford: Oxford University Press, 1993.

Young, Patrick. *Enacting Brittany: Tourism and Culture in Provincial France, 1871–1939.* Burlington, Vt.: Ashgate, 2012.

———. "A Tasteful Patrimony? Landscape, Preservation, and Tourism in the Sites and Monuments Campaign, 1900–1935." *French Historical Studies* 32, no. 3 (Summer 2009): 447–477.

Young, Patrick, and Philip Whalen, eds. *Place and Locality in Modern France.* London: Bloomsbury, 2014.

Acknowledgments

This book has been long in the making, as the original questions that I posed expanded over time, and I owe many debts of gratitude. It has benefited from generous institutional as well as financial support from both the University of British Columbia, where the project began, and the University of California, Los Angeles, where it was completed. An Izaak Walton Killam Memorial Fellowship and a Hampton Grant from UBC helped me to launch my research, and a Research Grant from UCLA's Faculty Senate provided support at a crucial moment. I am also grateful for the external funding that I received over the years from the Social Science and Humanities Research Council of Canada and the John Simon Guggenheim Memorial Foundation in the form of a fellowship in 2011–2012.

Numerous scholars, colleagues, and friends have also been generous with their time in discussing aspects of this project from its inception to its conclusion. They include Peter McPhee, Kapil Raj, Alice Conklin, Derek Gregory, Tim Tackett, Graeme Wynn, Bernhardt Gissibl, Fabien Locher, Christophe Bonneuil, Andrée Corvol, Ramachandra Guha, and Chris Pearson. I am also very grateful to Phil Nord, who has been tremendously supportive of my work and my career over the years. I learned a great deal from the presentation of aspects of this book in a number of venues, which include the UCLA department seminar, the German Historical Institute in Washington, D.C., the Humanities Center at Stanford, the University of Oregon, the Ecole des hautes études en sciences sociales, and the seminar of the Réseau universitaire des chercheurs en histoire environnementale in France. Friends, including Jocelyne Baverel, Elisabeth Gleason, Diana Lary, and Alex Woodside, and the "Indian" branch of my family have been wonderfully supportive, and I must thank Kathleen McDermott, my editor at Harvard University Press, for her professionalism and, more especially, her patience as my research took new twists and turns.

Of course, the staff at the libraries and archives I used in my research need a word of acknowledgment for their assistance. They include those at the Bibliothèque nationale de France, the Bibliothèques de la ville de Paris, the Archives nationales, the Archives nationales d'Outre Mer in Aix-en-Provence, and the British Library in London.

Chapter 6 was originally published as "Reforestation, Landscape Conservation, and the Anxieties of Empire in French Colonial Algeria" in *American Historical Review* 113, no. 2: 341–362, copyright © 2008 American Historical Association. It appears here by permission of the publisher, in slightly expanded form.

Finally, I must above all thank my spouse and partner in life, Sanjay Subrahmanyam, to whom this book is dedicated, for enriching my work through ongoing conversations and his own scholarly example. His companionship and unfailing support made this large and unwieldy undertaking all the more enjoyable.

Index

Academy of Sciences (Paris), 35, 58, 62, 70, 76, 89
Acclimatization, 8, 19, 20, 33, 130, 147–148, 169; and nostalgia, 148. *See also* Settler colonialism
Advertising, 108–109; and environmental degradation, 108
Africa, 8, 13–14, 20, 25, 31, 33, 36, 41, 53, 114–115, 123–124, 126–128, 129, 131–133, 136, 139, 146, 150–152, 155–156, 162; Afrique Occidentale Française (AOF), 134; French Equatorial Africa, 121, 134; French West Africa, 121, 127, 134–135; North Africa, 9, 14, 120, 127, 129, 130–132, 134, 136, 138, 144–145, 148, 150–154, 156, 158, 160–162. *See also* Maghreb
Aix-en-Provence, 62, 196
Alger (department), 131, 148, 159, 161
Algeria, 9, 11, 14, 58, 93–94, 111, 126, 128–133, 135, 137–140, 142–163; cork forests and trees in, 131, 142, 145, 152; land tenure in, 139; pasturage in, 142, 157
Algiers, 94, 130, 140, 148, 150, 154, 158, 161
Allier (department), 71
Allier (river), 90
Alphand, Adolphe, 168, 170–171
Alpine Club of France, 13, 93, 107, 110–111, 122, 136. *See also* Club alpin français
Aménagement du territoire, 5–6, 56
Americas, 33, 41; North America, 106, 112–113, 115, 155–156, 162–163, 192; South America, 112, 165
Arabs, 144–145, 152–153, 156, 158–160, 162. *See also* Berbers; Muslims
Arago, François, 57–58, 79
Architects, 11, 14, 93, 171; and the urban environment, 173, 181–183, 185, 187–188
Ardèche (department), 35, 49
Ariège (department), 49, 61
Arles, 72–73
Asia, 20, 25, 33, 41, 53, 151–152, 163
Aude (department), 49, 62, 83
Avignon, 71–73, 83–85

Baldus, Edouard, 73, 83–85
Ballif, Abel, 109–110
Barbizon, 96, 100–101; Barbizon school of painters, 13, 92, 101–102, 108, 127, 198
Bas-Rhin (department), 19, 30
Basses-Alpes (department), 49, 62–63, 77
Baudelaire, Charles, 100, 183

Baudrillart, Jacques-Joseph, 55
Beauquier, Charles, 109, 116, 172, 178, 197; and the Beauquier Law on the protection of natural sites and monuments, 110–112, 116–117, 119, 127
Becquerel, Alfred, 147–148
Becquerel, Antoine-César, 45, 57–59, 65, 146
Belgium, 114–116, 119, 121–124
Belgrand, Eugène, 79, 89
Benoit-Lévy, Georges, 181–183
Berbers, 152–153; and Kabyle myth, 153. See also Arabs; Muslims
Bernadin de Saint-Pierre, Henri, 20, 33, 40, 162
Bess, Michael, 191–192, 197
Bitche, 17, 39, 76
Boitard, Pierre, 165–166
Bordeaux, 72, 78, 168, 171
Bouches-du-Rhône (department), 49, 73
Bourbon Restoration, 11, 17, 30, 39, 55, 64, 97, 197
Bralle, François-Jean, 71
Braudel, Fernand, 153
Breadfruit, 19–20
Brémontier, Nicholas-Théodore, 63–64
Briand, Aristide, 89
Britain, 7–9, 49, 112, 115–116, 119, 121–124, 137, 165, 175, 181
Brittany, 58, 64, 117
Brown, John Croumbie, 8, 60, 63, 103
Buache, Philippe, 70, 90
Buffon, Georges-Louis Leclerc de, 19, 22, 33, 44, 47, 51, 53; on climate change and deforestion, 53, 60

Camargue, 72, 121, 128
Cambon, Jules, 151, 158–159
Cazalis, Henri, 108, 178, 188
Champion, Maurice, 67, 70–71, 79–80
Chaptal, Jean-Antoine, 24, 196
Charles-Brun, Jean, 108, 197
Cher (department), 119
Cher (river), 90
Chevalier, Auguste, 120
Cheysson, Emile, 181–183
Cholera, 11, 59
Clermont, Raoul de, 111, 113, 116, 119, 122
Climate, 16–17, 19, 32, 36, 39, 41–42, 51–52, 60, 139, 144, 146–148, 150–152, 154, 156, 161–163, 192; climate change, 1, 12, 53, 58–59, 65, 67, 92, 146, 193; effects on children, women, and different nationalities, 148; impact of forests on, 17, 30–31, 41, 58–60, 63, 65, 122, 133, 146; and *stations climatiques,* 136. See also Acclimatization; Climatology; Meteorology
Climatology, 29, 59, 68
Club alpin français, 78, 106. See also Alpine Club of France
Colbert, Jean-Baptiste, 43–45, 50, 65
Colonial Exhibition of Marseille (1906), 144
Colonial expansion: environmental anxieties about, 6, 8, 11, 13–14, 198; environmental degradation, 8; nostalgia, 7. See also Settler colonialism
Commission for the Protection of Colonial Fauna, 121–122, 134
Conseil de salubrité du département de la Seine, 10–11, 59
Conservationism, 3, 14–15, 128; conservation of forests, 144, 146; of historical monuments and sites, 93–94; of landscapes, 150, 156, 161
Constantine (department), 76, 131, 139, 144, 148, 152, 158, 161
Convention for the Preservation of Wild Animals, Birds, and Fish in Africa (London Convention of 1900), 114, 124
Convention Relative to the Preservation of Fauna and Flora in Their Natural State (London Convention of 1933), 14, 123–124, 126, 132, 134
Corbin, Alain, 4–5, 10, 12
Corsica, 117, 120, 136, 145
Côtes-du-Nord (department), 46, 128
Crimean War, 72–73, 87
Cronon, William, 106, 194
Cros-Mayrevieille, Fernand, 111, 116, 172
Cult of flowers, 14, 166. See also Horticulture
Cult of nature, 7, 100, 132

Davis, Diana, 146, 161
Deforestation, 8, 11–12, 21, 25, 29–31, 33, 35–36, 39, 41–47, 49–51, 53–54, 57, 59–60, 62, 65, 82, 92, 133–134, 136, 152, 157, 193; in Algeria, 133, 139, 145–147, 150, 154, 161; causes of, 58, 77, 79, 80; and climate change, 12, 30, 41, 51–54, 58–59, 65, 79–80, 146; and coastline erosion, 65; and the decline of civilizations, 146, 150; and *écobouage,* 50; the effect of the French Revolution

on, 41, 44, 46–47; and flooding, 12, 54, 59, 65, 76–78, 146; and forest fires, 146; and its impact on pastoral populations, 61; and Madagascar, 134; and rainfall, 52–53, 147; and urbanization, 50. *See also* Reforestation
Degeneration, 18–19
Denecourt, Claude-François, 97–100, 104
Déparcieux, Antoine, 70, 90
Deyrolle, Jean-Baptiste and Emile, 166–167
Diaz de la Pena, Narcisse, 100–101, 105
Diebolt, Georges, 87–88
Dieuze, 22–23, 40
Dijon, 73, 162
Doubs (department), 48, 108–109, 116
Drôme (department), 62, 77, 111
Dunes, 64; and erosion, 64. *See also* Brémontier, Nicholas-Théodore
Dupré, Jules, 101–102

Earthquakes, 67, 68; in Lisbon, 69; in London, 68–69; in southern Italy, 69. *See also* Natural disasters
Eaux et Forêts, 6, 9, 12, 46, 65, 81, 90, 92, 102, 109, 111, 119, 128, 132, 142, 172, 198; and Ecole nationale des eaux et forêts, 122
Écobouage, 50. *See also* Deforestation
Ecole de Nancy, 55–56
Ecole nationale des eaux et forêts, 55
Ecology, 2–4, 7, 12–16, 68, 101, 139, 184, 191–193
Engineers, 11, 13, 18, 22, 28, 32, 40, 56, 60, 64–65, 74, 76, 80–82, 89, 90–91, 107, 194
Environment: anxiety about, 1–2, 6, 8, 10, 12, 17, 42, 133, 161, 193; and protection of, 2, 15, 49, 80–81, 121, 125, 160–164, 194; war's impact on, 31, 118. *See also* Environmentalism
Environmental consciousness, 2–3, 8–9, 12, 17, 41, 43–44, 90, 138–139, 162, 188, 192–194
Environmental history, 3–6, 8–9, 16, 145, 191
Environmentalism, 2, 7, 17, 41, 161–163, 192, 194, 198; politics of, 2, 15, 197
European expansion, environmental effects of, 41, 120, 122–125, 163

Fabre, Jean-Antoine, 76–78
Fédération régionaliste française, 108, 116, 197
Ferry, Jules, 157–158

Fillias, Achille, 148, 162
First International Congress for the Protection of Landscapes (1909), 13–14, 116–118, 119, 124–125
First International Congress for the Protection of Nature (1923), 14, 118–119, 124–125, 136
Flaubert, Gustave, 95, 99, 100
Floods, 6, 12, 31, 42, 66–92, 146, 193, 195; causes of, 75–80; damages, 70–75, 89; and deforestation, 12, 35, 75–80; literary, pictorial, and photographic representations of, 12, 73, 75, 82–86; media coverage of, 73, 75, 82; popular responses to, 81–82; prevention of, 74–75, 90; state's role in, 74–75, 78
Fondation Rothschild, 183. *See also* Rothschild Foundation
Fontainebleau, 13, 92, 94–106, 109, 117, 119, 127, 197, 198; as a national museum, 99
Forest fires, in Algeria, 142–143, 145, 152, 159–160
Forestier, Jean-Claude Nicolas, 172–173, 177
Fourier, Charles, 78, 181
French forest law: French Forest Ordinance of 1669, 43–45, 55, 195; 29 September 1791 law, 45, 50, 58; coastline plantation decree of 14 December 1814, 64; Forest Code of 1827, 55, 58–59, 61, 65, 142, 196; 28 July 1860 reforestion law, 60–63, 81, 196; 9 June 1864 reforestation law, 60, 81; decree of 12 June 1891 in Indochina, 156; Algerian Forest Code of 1903, 139, 159–160. See also *Restauration des Terrains en Montagne* (RTM)
French Revolution, 5, 7, 12, 17, 18, 20, 22, 27, 29, 31, 40–41, 44–46, 48–53, 55–56, 59–60, 63–65, 77, 80, 86, 93, 105, 115, 146, 170, 193, 195, 197; and Committee of Public Safety, 18; Council of the Five Hundred, 47; Directory, 47; environmental effects of, 48–51; First Republic, 18; and National Convention, 21, 48; and Terror, 47–48
Fuster, Joseph-Jean-Nicolas, 59

Gard (department), 49, 62
Gardens, 14, 20–21, 28, 145, 164–166, 168–169, 170–171, 173, 175–176, 178, 182, 185, 187; botanical gardens, 126; and garden cities, 14, 165, 175, 181–183, 185, 186–188

Garonne (river), 67, 71, 73, 86
Gascony, 63–64
Gautier, Théophile, 98, 100
Gay-Lussac, Joseph Louis, 58
Germany, 8, 11, 16, 77, 89, 108, 113–119, 121, 165, 175; German influence on French forestry, 56
Gironde (department), 64, 73
Glacken, Clarence, 1, 4, 41, 76
Greenhouses, 14, 164, 166–169, 171; hothouses, 166; house plants, 168; orangeries, 166; temperate greenhouses, 166–167; winter gardens, 166
Grove, Richard, 11, 41, 162, 198
Gruvel, Abel, 121–122

Haeckel, Ernst, 2, 16
Haussmann, Georges, 11, 168, 170–171, 173, 177, 196
Hautes-Alpes (department), 76–77, 80, 127
Haut-Rhin (department), 32, 35, 50
Heim, Roger, 134
Heimat, 108–109; and Heimatschutz, 113, 115
Hénard, Eugène, 164, 173–179, 182–183, 185
Hérault (department), 62, 83
Heritage, 7, 15, 28, 48, 92–94, 106–109, 115, 123, 172. See also *Patrimoine*
Holland, 39, 49, 69, 70
Horticulture, 14, 130, 166. See also Cult of flowers
Howard, Ebenezer, 181, 186
Humbert, Henri, 134
Humboldt, Alexander von, 2, 16, 63
Hygiene, 10, 32, 41, 117, 147, 162, 164, 171–172, 181, 184, 188; and hygienists, 9, 10–11, 59, 96, 164, 168, 172

Indochina, 121, 156, 157, 198
Industrialization, 9, 11, 41, 96, 107–108
Institut de France, 10, 58–59, 146
International Colonial Exhibition (1931), 121–122, 133, 190
International Convention for the Protection of Birds Useful to Agriculture (1902), 114, 196
Isère (department), 49, 62, 73, 77, 127
Italy, 69, 89, 115, 117–119, 121, 124, 128, 170

Jamin, Etienne, 97
Jardin des Plantes, 19, 190

Jardin du Roi, 2, 19, 129
Joanne, Adolphe, 97, 107
Jonnart, Charles, 159–160
July Monarchy, 11, 17, 57, 62, 93, 96–97, 101, 103, 197

Kruger National Park, 124, 126

La Bérarde, 127. See also Parc du Pelvoux
Lahor, Jean, 188. See also Cazalis, Henri
Lamartine, Alphonse de, 66, 86, 100
Landes, 63–64
League for the Protection of Birds, 110, 115, 119, 122
League for the Reforestation of Algeria, 148–149, 151, 162. See also Ligue du reboisement de l'Algérie
Lebrun, Albert, 122–123
Le Nôtre, André, 165
Le Play, Frédéric, 61–63, 65
Ligue du reboisement de l'Algérie, 149, 151, 160. See also League for the Reforestation of Algeria
Little Ice Age, 70
Loire (river), 12, 67, 70–73, 81, 90
Loire (valley), 73
Loiret (department), 58, 73
Lorentz, Bernard, 55–56
Lorraine, 17, 76
Louis XIV (King of France), 43–44
Louis XVI (King of France), 45, 47
Louis XVIII (King of France), 55
Louis Philippe (King of the French), 71
Lutaud, Charles, 130–131, 161
Lyon, 71–73, 83–86, 100, 195–196

Madagascar, 121, 126–128, 134–136
Maghreb, 133, 139, 144, 148, 153–154; and granary of Rome narrative, 144
Mangin, Arthur, 64, 104, 165
Mangin, Louis, 119–120, 122, 125, 134, 136, 190, 199
Marne (department), 35, 48, 89
Marrier de Bois d'Hyver, Achille, 98, 103
Mathieu, Auguste, 154–155
Mauritius, 11, 162
Mediterranean, 53, 70, 133, 137, 139, 144, 146, 150–156, 161–162
Meteorology, 57, 146. See also Climate
Michelet, Jules, 46, 100
Midi, 46, 49, 80, 148
Milieu, 6, 15, 189, 192, 194
Millet, Jean-François, 13, 100–101, 105

Ministère de la protection de la nature et de l'environnement, 191. *See also* Ministry for the Protection of the Environment
Ministry for the Protection of the Environment, 6, 191
Montfaucon, 10–11, 170
Monuments, 26–28, 39, 42, 48, 93, 97, 102, 104, 112, 115; historical, 3, 27–28, 48, 84, 93–94, 98–99, 104, 108, 110–111; natural, 7, 13, 26–29, 39, 48, 92, 94, 102, 104, 106, 108–112, 119–121, 125, 135
Moreau de Jonnès, Alexandre, 43, 44–45, 52–54, 65
Morocco, 135, 139–140, 145
Morvan, 89–90
Moselle (department), 17, 22, 23, 39
Musée national des monuments français, 48, 93. *See also* Museum of French National Monuments
Musée social, 116, 172, 175, 178–183; Section d'hygiène urbaine et rurale, 172, 180, 182, 188
Muséum national d'histoire naturelle, 19. *See also* Museum of Natural History
Museum of French National Monuments, 27, 94. *See also* Musée national des monuments français
Museum of Natural History, 2, 9, 20, 33, 53, 58, 119–122, 124–127, 129–130, 132, 134–137, 166–167, 194–195, 198–199. *See also* Muséum national d'histoire naturelle
Muslims, 142, 147, 151, 157; and anti-Muslim rhetoric, 151, 152; French views on, 132, 151, 153. *See also* Arabs; Berbers

Napoleon Bonaparte (First Consul and then Emperor of France), 24, 25, 30–31, 47, 51, 52, 55, 71, 196; abdication and exile to Elba, 64; and Civil Code, 56; and Napoleonic decree of 15 October 1810, 6, 195; and Napoleonic wars, 31, 97, 115
Napoleon III (Emperor of France), 60, 71, 73–75, 81, 83, 99, 103, 105, 164, 170–171, 196
Natural disasters, 6, 67–69, 127; religious explanations of, 69. *See also* Earthquakes
Natural History Society of North Africa, 130–132

Naturalists, 1–2, 20, 41, 101, 138, 154, 166, 193, 199; and the Museum of Natural History, 9, 19, 124–125, 127–130, 134, 194, 199
Nature protection, 9, 92, 106, 109, 113–114, 119, 125, 135, 138, 191, 198–199
Netherlands, 114, 119, 121–125, 195
Nièvre (department), 48, 62, 71
Nostalgia, 7, 22, 30; and acclimatization, 148; definition of, 6–7; and ecocriticism, 7; and environment, 6, 7, 14; and landscape, 95, 105, 156, 162; and rural life, 95, 102, 105
Nussac, Louis de, 116, 119

Oak trees, 33, 95, 96, 98, 100, 102–103, 187; preservation of, 105–106
Onslow, Lord, 123–124
Oran (department), 131, 139–140, 148, 154, 160
Orléans, 70–71, 73

Parade, Adolphe, 56
Parc du Pelvoux, 127–128
Paris, 4, 9–12, 14, 154, 164, 166, 168; campaign for *espaces libres* in, 173, 175, 178–179; Conseil Municipal, 73, 179; and flooding, 70–71, 91; flood of 1910, 12, 87–90; Haussmannization of, 14, 168–171. *See also* Gardens; Parks
Parks, 14, 116, 119, 127–128, 164, 169, 187, 198; American conception of, 126; in France's overseas colonies, 120–121, 128, 131–132, 134–136; French conception of, 126; national, 115, 119–121, 123–125, 127, 128, 130–137, 161, 192; zoological, 126. *See also* Reserves
Parmentier, Antoine, 21–22
Patrimoine, 7, 13, 28, 48, 60, 92, 93, 94, 108, 112, 125, 172. *See also* Heritage
Perrier de la Bâthie, Henri, 134
Petit, Georges, 122, 126, 134
Physiocracy, 17, 22, 41–42, 47, 162
Picard, Alfred, 89
Pine trees, 25, 46, 64, 95–96, 102–106, 154; and Aleppo pine, 142
Poëte, Marcel, 173, 186
Poivre, Pierre, 11, 12, 43
Ponts et Chaussées, 6, 9, 13, 22, 30, 40, 47, 59, 64–65, 72, 74–76, 78, 80–82, 89–90, 92, 107, 109, 111; Ecole des Ponts et Chaussées, 12, 18, 28, 90

Preservationism, 3, 7, 13–15, 106, 127–128, 172, 197–198; and preservationist societies, 94, 115
Pyrénées-Orientales (department), 18, 19, 49

Rauch, François-Antoine, 12, 16–44, 47–49, 53–54, 62, 65, 76, 92, 189, 197
Reclus, Elisée, 107, 151
Reclus, Onésime, 107, 151
Reforestation, 12, 25–26, 29, 32, 41, 55, 62–63, 82, 96, 127, 133, 138–139, 146–149, 151–152, 155–157, 160, 198; and its effect on rainfall, 146, 156; of mountainous areas, 57, 60, 63, 80–81; and pastoral populations, 65; to prevent coastline erosion, 63; to prevent flooding, 79–80. *See also* Deforestation; *Restauration des Terrains en Montagne* (RTM)
Regeneration, 18, 19, 20–22, 24–25, 29–33, 36, 38, 40, 58
Regionalism, 108–109
Rémard, Charles, 97
Réserve naturelle intégrale, 126, 132, 134–135, 194, 199. *See also* Reserves
Reserves, 115–116, 120, 124, 126, 128, 130–137; artistic, 13, 99, 105, 119, 127, 137, 197; botanical, 128; forest, 116, 126, 134–136, 157; game, 115–116, 132, 135, 194, 198; natural, 14, 124–128, 130, 132–136, 198; scientific, 132, 135; zoological, 121. *See also* Parks
Restauration des Terrains en Montagne (RTM), 63, 81. *See also* French forest law
Revolution of 1848, 66, 86, 170
Rey, Augustin, 183–184
Reynaud, Paul, 123, 136
Rhine (river), 54, 56 113
Rhône (department), 73
Rhône (river), 12, 67, 70, 71, 73, 86, 90 195
Rhône (valley), 66, 71, 73, 84, 85
Ribbe, Charles de, 62
Risler, Georges, 180
Roanne, 70–71
Romanticism, 7, 17, 22, 41–42, 100–102
Roosevelt, Theodore, 113, 117
Rothschild Foundation, 184–185. *See also* Fondation Rothschild
Rougier de la Bergerie, Jean-Baptiste, 1, 44, 47–52, 54, 57, 65, 197
Rousseau, Théodore, 13, 100–105
Roussillon, 18–19
Russia, 72, 89, 119; and northern pines, 104, 105–106

Sahara, 139, 146, 150, 152, 154–156, 161
Saint-Hilaire, Geoffroy, 33, 129
Saint Hubert Club de France, 116
Sand, Georges, 100, 107
Saône (river), 71, 95
Sarasin, Paul, 118
Sarraut, Albert, 198
Second Empire, 45, 73, 75, 84, 152, 168, 171, 196–197
Second International Congress for the Protection of Nature (1931), 121–125, 128, 190
Seine (department), 10–11, 59, 82, 89, 168, 185–186, 196
Seine (river), 12, 67, 70, 79, 87, 89, 154, 170–171, 175, 177, 187
Seine (valley), 95
Sellier, Henri, 185–187
Settler colonialism, 139, 147, 160; and settlers, 8–9, 14, 133, 136, 138, 146, 151–152, 154–158, 160–163, 198; settlers' mortality, 147
Siegfried, Jules, 172, 178–180, 182–183
Société de fructification générale de la terre et des eaux de la France, 16
Société française des amis des arbres, 107, 179. *See also* Society of the Friends of Trees
Société nationale d'acclimatation de France, 119–122, 127, 135, 190, 198–199
Société pour la protection des paysages de France (SPPF), 106–111, 113, 115–116, 119, 122, 127, 136, 172, 178, 188, 197–198. *See also* Society for the Protection of the Landscapes of France
Société zoologique d'acclimatation, 33, 129–130
Society for the General Enrichment of the Land and Waters of France, 16
Society for the Preservation of the Wild Fauna of the Empire, 122–123
Society for the Protection of Animals, 196
Society for the Protection of the Landscapes of France, 13, 92, 106, 108, 115, 172. *See also* Société pour la protection des paysages de France (SPPF)
Society of the Friends of Trees, 13, 107. *See also* Société française des amis des arbres
Spary, E. C., 19, 41, 192
Sully Prudhomme, René, 109
Surell, Alexandre, 59, 76–78, 80, 107
Switzerland, 69, 114, 118–119, 121–122

Tarascon, 72, 83, 84
Third Republic, 63–64, 152, 165, 171, 197
Thomas, Albert, 178–179, 188
Thouin, André, 19–21
Toulouse, 72, 122
Touring Club of France, 13, 93, 106–107, 109–113, 115–116, 127–128, 133, 137, 178, 188
Tourism, 13, 96, 101, 107, 117, 122, 126, 131, 133–134, 161; and guidebooks, 97–99; and Office national du tourisme, 112
Tours, 71, 73, 81
Trolard, Paulin, 148–151, 156–158, 160
Tunisia, 132, 135–136, 139–140, 145

United States, 8, 89, 106, 118–119, 121, 124, 129, 165
Urbanization, 6, 9–11, 50, 96

Vallès, François, 78–80
Valois, Charles, 119, 122
Vandalism, 27, 48, 93, 102; and nature, 48
Var (department), 76–77
Versailles, 97, 118, 165
Vosges (department), 50, 80

War of the Demoiselles, 61, 105, 142
Wilderness, 7, 193–194
Woolsey, Theodore, 145, 159
World War I, 65, 89, 112, 116, 118, 120, 127–128, 130, 132, 137, 142, 145, 152, 161, 179, 180–181, 186, 193; and environmental impact, 118
World War II, 2, 12–13, 15, 93, 115, 121, 127, 137–139, 180, 191, 193

Yellowstone Park, 108, 126, 129
Yonne (department), 1, 48, 50